SPURRIER

SPURRIER

How the Ball Coach Taught the South to Play Football

RAN HENRY

LYONS PRESS
Guilford, Connecticut
Helena, Montana
An imprint of Rowman & Littlefield

To Mom and Dad, and Robby and John

CONTENTS

It may be the most serious kind of game there is, but if you don't see it as a game you're missing an important point.

—James Dickey, *Deliverance*

Prologue
Gainesville, Florida

STEVE SPURRIER COCKS HIS ARM AND LOOKS DOWNFIELD, TRYING TO show the other guys how you play quarterback. He's back in that stance that owned the yard, back when you had some friends, a ball, and a maple tree for a goalpost. Back when you could pick your teams, make up rules, and run like no one was scouting you, with your whole life shining down through the leaves, you already knew who'd be calling the plays and making the throws.

Dew is steaming off the grass he played on as a freshman at the University of Florida, on an August morning in 1997 when the Gators he now coaches are taking the practice field as defending national champs. Fans fill the bleachers bordering the field, shadowed by loblollies, sabal palms, and live oaks draped in Spanish moss, wondering what the Ball Coach will do next. Florida played football for 83 years without winning a trophy worth bragging about, until the school's top passer came back to campus wearing his coaching visor.

It's marking the spot on the grass where he threw it.

Sunlight glistens on his unlined face, cleft chin, and unmussable hair as he grips the tight white laces, eyeing the receivers running where he told them to. The veins in his arm and neck look swollen. His eyes have that look you don't want to get from your dad.

He sees the open man and fires a pass, arcing dark and far, across a world of grass. In the bleachers we have to wonder how it feels to make that football *fly*.

A smile crosses his face. Aim keeps flowing from his fingertips. The ball spirals into freshman Brian Haugabrook's outstretched hands in the end zone.

Take that, Gator Haters! That's pigskin poetry, that cocksure throw and catch. Better than sex for Florida football fans, a university researcher actually proved by hooking their brains to electrodes. In the bleachers strangers smack palms. One of those bombs from Spurrier, we all know, can subdue a stadium full of enemies with bourbon breath.

He claps his hands twice, picks up the visor with a fluid swoop, and rubs at the grass stain. Then he waves it at his receivers, motioning them to run back quick. These quarterbacks need the practice.

Is Spurrier too demanding? Too hard on his quarterbacks? That's easy to ask, from an armchair. Try following in the footsteps of a preacher's son who won the 1966 Heisman Trophy for passing, kicking, and willing his team to victory—and 30 years later coached a preacher's son named Danny Wuerffel to win the Heisman Trophy, and a first-ever national championship.

What is the measure of a man who succeeds where no one else can? What's not to love about a coach who does what he asks his players to do?

Enemies of the Gators, as Spurrier calls his adversaries, fixate on that visor. TV crews covering Florida games are ordered to keep a camera on it at all times.

Maybe, the announcers speculate, he wears the visor to shield the sandlot where his brain draws up "ball plays." Maybe he's reminding the coaches in shirts and ties on the other sideline that he'd also take their money on the golf course. Maybe the creator of the Fun 'n' Gun offense, which changed Southeastern Conference football from 3 yards and a cloud of dust to three-play drives, wears that visor to outwit the sun.

If you see it that way, he's gotten inside your head, too.

Those of us watching from the bleachers, shirking work on a weekday, believe Spurrier can get us back to that promised land God lets football fans glimpse every August. Thank the Lord and praise the Ball Coach, "Wait until next year" is Florida's motto no more. Spurrier took out the Goliaths of the SEC with a slingshot. And the gratitude of the Gator Nation knows no bounds.

Watching him hit that post pattern are alumni called Bull Gators, stepping out of motor coaches, your average fans in orange and blue everything, and the fry cook at the McDonald's in Ocala, who wears Gator gear under the golden arches. We're all for Spurrier, for a hundred miles around, without really knowing what the glory he brings us costs *him*.

Few of us can see what he sees.

How empty that practice field must look without number 7 on it. Danny Wuerffel, the top-rated college quarterback of all time when he graduated, has gone to New Orleans to be a Saint. The sophomore with the best arm and the best chance to take Wuerffel's place spent the summer in Princeton, West Virginia, drinking beer and playing baseball.

Spurrier saw it coming back in March, when Doug Johnson signed a minor-league baseball contract with Tampa Bay and went to Miami to get a boat on the first day of spring ball. Whatever his football coach demanded, it wasn't enough.

Spurrier watches Johnson fade back and fire one to a receiver streaking down the sideline. The ball is thrown to the man's inside shoulder—where a defensive back could pick it off in a few short weeks. Spurrier lifts his visor, eyes Johnson for one Mississippi, and drops the visor at the exact same spot.

What we're all thinking that August morning, watching those quarterbacks struggle, is *learn to do it his way, boys.* The people yelling at you will shut right up when you throw that scoring strike. But these quarterbacks Spurrier's turning to, so young and lanky, haunted by crew cuts, just can't do it yet.

Jessie Palmer, a recruit from Canada, gets behind center and says "hoot, hoot" instead of "hut, hut." Noah Brindise and Tim Olmstead get their chance, too. They're passers Spurrier fell in love with on film, visited in their parents' living rooms, and promised to "coach up." They have biceps bigger than Spurrier's ever were, muscles that made them high school stars, blue-chip college recruits, candidates to pilot the Fun 'n' Gun. Standing tall in their mesh shirts and spiky black cleats. Hands on their hips. Trying to see what their coach sees.

Johnson and Palmer could play quarterback in the NFL, in Spurrier's view, if they heed one of his sayings: "The enemy of great is good."

The Ball Coach has *eyes* under that visor. The effort he's seeing will be good for a 10–2 season, a spot on the couch for the SEC Championship Game, and a bus ride down the turnpike to the Citrus Bowl in Orlando. The premier league in college football, which Spurrier has dominated for seven years, will hand its trophy to another up-and-coming coach. He squints, shakes his head, and draws up more pass patterns in his palm.

The receivers run deep crossing routes. Johnson throws a tight spiral. The ball bounces off the grass.

"I can't throw it for you!" Spurrier yells, shaking a finger in his quarterbacks' faces.

They nod, look down, and scuff at the turf. Maybe watching their boyhood dreams evaporate. We still wish one of them could hit that corner route Spurrier probably completes in his sleep.

They watch him backpedal and launch a pass a small, speedy freshman can maybe run under. Ian Skinner reaches up and the ball is *there*. Spurrier lifts his visor and rakes his fingers through his hair.

We all have our hands on our hips, seeing our top recruits outdone by their 52-year-old coach. Feeling that failure no trophy from last year can excuse.

Maybe these young quarterbacks just need to throw some slant routes, or little look-ins, some of us are thinking in the bleachers. Probably our inner loser talking. Can anyone watching from the stands, or sitting in front of a screen, know what it *really* takes to be a Ball Coach?

Only Wuerffel, dodging 300-pound Tigers, Bulldogs, and Seminoles, almost always knew what Spurrier would do.

The coach whistles practice to an end and walks off the field ahead of his team. Trailed by quarterbacks leaving cleat marks in the Bermuda grass, and his namesake son, the receivers coach, keeping a respectful distance from a father who expects excellence.

Of course, we all believe in the Gospel of Sports: Glory to the one who brings the rage. When will these quarterbacks kicking at the grass get mad enough to do something great?

Striding toward the sideline, adjusting his visor, Spurrier eyes a bunch of reporters like he can see their questions in the air.

How can you go up against Peyton Manning of Tennessee, and the other SEC teams looking for payback, with these inexperienced quarterbacks?

Does winning make you want to keep winning, no matter what? Or do you just hate to lose?

Facing the cameras and microphones, Spurrier breaks into a smile. Knowing those opposing coaches scout the *News at 11*.

He looks into the lens and says he just wants his guys to play their best ball.

Part One

A Game of Catch

All my toys were balls.
—Steve Spurrier

CHAPTER ONE

The Home Team

THAT SAME SUMMER IN JOHNSON CITY, TENNESSEE, A RAILROAD TOWN in the hills flanked by Carolina's mountaintops, they remembered too well the day "Stevie" Spurrier showed up at Henry Johnson Elementary School, at the start of sixth grade.

Son of the new pastor over at Calvary Presbyterian. Had the eye and the arm, the kids said on the playground. Pick any sport with a ball.

They couldn't forget the pastor, Reverend John Graham Spurrier, either. Crazy about sports, and his youngest son. Recited the longest prayers you ever heard. Must've prayed for that boy to do great deeds, that first day of school.

Marjorie Spurrier, the preacher's wife who printed up the bulletins, taught Sunday school, directed the choir, and played piano at the services, walked her son out the door of the little red brick house directly across Wilson Street from Reverend Spurrier's red brick church. The family's manse, as Presbyterians called the minister's house, had a backyard for playing ball, like Dad promised, with an elm tree for a goalpost.

Stevie had to smile. Across the yard was a little brick gym called Scout Hall that had a basketball court. He had a key to the court, and a shot to beat his big brother.

Walking down the hill to the square red Coca-Cola stand at Kiwanis Park, he stepped onto a football field where big boys played, with real goalposts. And a baseball diamond, with bases and bleachers.

Crossing Market Street, climbing the concrete steps up to the big red brick elementary school that had a football and a basketball team, Stevie

Spurrier could see a place to make his mark—where people would cheer, and his family wouldn't have to leave.

He told his mom good-bye and walked into the classroom of Miss Grubb, a kindly, heavy-set lady, quick with a joke. He'd escaped the other sixth-grade teacher, Miss Boring.

From the get-go the other kids called him "Orr," hearing his brother, Graham, a ninth grader, call him that. Most every kid on the playground had a nickname. Orr had buzzed hair, a dimpled chin, ears he'd have to grow into, some serious blue eyes, and this quirky hand gesture they still talked about in Johnson City 40 years later.

He'd extend his index finger, bend his thumb into a gun sight, and ponder the alignment. Then he'd aim that finger at you, sighting through his upraised thumb. Or he'd aim past you at some spot on the horizon. He aimed at kids, adults, people all over town, with no explanation anyone could remember.

Walking across the street to church on Sundays and Wednesdays, playing ball in Kiwanis Park and Scout Hall, Orr grew up in a yard that had the best games on the block. When he got up to Science Hill High School and started targeting opponents of the Hilltoppers, what counted to people around town was the scoreboard.

On Fridays in the fall they packed the brick football stadium by city hall where number 11 kicked off, punted, kicked field goals, played safety, and quarterbacked the 'Toppers against the toughest teams in Tennessee—games that Coach Kermit Tipton scheduled after seeing how Spurrier could throw. In the brick bleachers they teased his folks about their son never leaving the field, saying, "You mean he isn't leading the band at halftime?"

In the winter they hollered "Gunner" in the Science Hill gym when his buzzer-beaters took down the big city schools, asking where he'd learned to dribble behind his back. In the spring they cheered when he hit and pitched the Hilltoppers to two state championships for Johnson City.

Sitting by the radio for the away games, they prayed his aim was true.

There was one story they told back then, about Reverend Spurrier and his son, that in the summer of '97 seemed to explain the town's downfall.

In the story word of the new kid with the arm and the aiming gesture had gotten around. Boys on the playground said he could zip the ball around the horn and hit anyone's pitch. J. Ross Edgemon, Johnson City's baseball sage, had a radio in his motel with a big red dial that could tune in major-league games, and a Babe Ruth League team sponsored by the big new Steinway plant on Walnut Street. Mr. Edgemon realized he could get that new kid on his team without going through the Little League draft—if he named the boy's father the manager of the Steinway Bears.

The first day of practice, so the story went, Reverend Spurrier knelt with his new team in the grass by the right field line, wearing his shirt with MANAGER written large.

"Fellas," he asked, "how many of you believe in the saying, 'It's not whether you win or lose, it's how you play the game?'"

The boys saw the big man kneeling, looking pastor serious, and raised their hands. Some held their hands high. Some had their hands at "half-mast, looking around to see who's going to vote for it," the preacher noticed.

"If you believe that, you might as well stay at home," he told his team.

"Why, if you don't keep score, there's no use in coming," Reverend Spurrier said.

He pointed upwards.

"There's a reason they have that scoreboard up there."

In the story Stevie never raised his hand. He already knew the Lord kept score.

"Those of you who are good, you're going to play," he'd remember his father telling the team. "If you're not as good, you're not going to play as much. We're going to try to win, square and fair, within the rules. We're going to score and win as much as we can."

In 1997, Tennessee Volunteer fans still held that preacher responsible for the deeds of his son.

"The owner of that little league team made a fast move right there," was how the son saw it. "We went nineteen and one."

The Steinway Bears' star player was ultimately honored by the national Little League office in Houston, Texas, and Johnson City commissioners voted to rename the baseball diamond in Kiwanis Park Steve Spurrier Field. Making Mr. Edgemon look like a genius for giving Reverend Spurrier that manager's shirt.

His son's autobiography, *It's Always Too Soon to Quit*, which wasn't on the shelves in Johnson City in the summer of '97, not even at Books-A-Million, revealed that the Bears' only loss came on a day Reverend Spurrier couldn't be at the game—and the boys neglected to pray before they played.

The team learned who was really in charge. Reverend Spurrier got a Babe Ruth League Championship trophy bigger than the mantle in the manse. And everyone knew the name of the pastor at Calvary Presbyterian.

They heard he got the job because Sidney Smallwood, athletic director of Johnson City Schools, saw Stevie and his brother playing ball at a Presbyterian retreat in Montreat, North Carolina.

"Who's your daddy?" Smallwood supposedly asked the kid zinging the ball through the mountain air. Within a week, they said, the steely-eyed athletic director who supervised ball fields and church elders had Reverend Spurrier moving his family into the manse above the park, making the town a winner.

And almost as quickly members of his church started walking the other way when they saw their pastor on the street—rather than hear another recitation of his son's stats. Washed-in-the-blood Presbyterians would turn the corner rather than stop and talk to their pastor. "I already read the sports page," they'd say.

Smallwood would answer Reverend Spurrier's calls and then put down the phone, picking it up every few minutes to say "Uh-huh," like he was listening. Not missing any of the fatherly pride between the lines.

People wished the most talked-about boy in town could've heard some of that praise from his dad. They lamented that long after he graduated to being called Steve.

What they wanted to call him in the spring of '63 was a Volunteer, seeing him weekly at the Peerless Restaurant, eating ribeyes with his family and another football coach from another college trying to sign him. Of course, he grew up rooting for the University of Tennessee, along with everyone else in town who wore orange and sang "Rocky Top."

UT offered him a scholarship in both football and basketball. He was set on becoming a Southeastern Conference quarterback. And the Vols still ran the old single-wing offense, calling for the quarterback to run instead of pass.

"Time Spurrier with a calendar," his teammates liked to say.

He took a recruiting trip to Knoxville anyway. Recruited by the governor to be a Volunteer. Served milk and cookies at the president's house.

"We'll change the offense for you," the UT president promised. Did a president really have that kind of power? Spurrier put off the other football coaches until baseball season filled the steak house with promises.

When Bud Kelsey announced on radio station WETB, "Steve Spurrier's going to Notre Dame because the Catholic Church has promised to make his daddy a cardinal," the spoof didn't sound that far-fetched to people around town. Sounded like he got his father another job.

They believed it when they heard the University of Florida signed Spurrier by promising he could play on the school's new golf course, and flying him home from Gainesville on a plane full of concerned coaches when he got the flu during his recruiting trip. Even some Vols had to admit it was a natural fit—Florida coach Ray Graves was a preacher's son who ran a pro-style passing offense.

Others saw it differently: Florida was as far as Steve could get from his father and still play football in the SEC.

Shouldn't they have expected a move like that, down the road, from a boy who always aimed at the horizon? Doesn't every hero eventually change uniforms?

He left town in August of 1963 to start fall football practice at Florida, and after a year on the freshman squad, he was on TV. Walking onto the field for his first play as a college quarterback, he pretended to "quiet" the crowd with a big wave that was for the gang watching back home on Channel 3. Then he faded back and threw his first college pass, a 56-yarder to Jack Harper.

In three seasons at UF he broke all the school's passing records and never had to play against the Volunteers. Spurrier signs plastered Johnson City when he won the 1966 Heisman Trophy and was picked third in the NFL draft by the San Francisco 49ers. State legislators proclaimed January 12, 1967, "Steve Spurrier Day" in Tennessee, and his hometown cheered his promise to be "that same old boy from Johnson City" when he became an NFL quarterback.

The population doubled in the years after Spurrier put the town on the sports page. The red brick heart of town, and the neighborhoods built of bricks from the General Shale plant on North Roan Street, sprawled into housing developments with vinyl siding on four-lane roads fronting strip malls. Country singers still sang about Johnson City, but the title of "Hardwood Floor Capital of the World" was lost. Steve Spurrier Sporting Goods, run by his brother, Graham, opened and closed on Route 11. Calvary Presbyterian went Baptist after Reverend Spurrier stood at the pulpit and said, "God has called me to Florida," and the congregation members exchanged knowing looks.

The drive-ins and hot spots Orr and his buddies cruised in the Spurrier family's "Blue Bomb," which they pushed more than drove, were bulldozed under. Memories of all those jokes, songs, pranks, fights, underarm farts, Coke floats, and stolen kisses haunted self-serve gas stations and a Target store. What was once considered the "edge of civilization" had been paved. What remained of Spurrier's junior high school and the huge old Science Hill building downtown was busted bricks and yearbooks.

People walked slowly on Main Street, on cobbled streets crisscrossed by train tracks, past pool halls and vacant storefronts. The gang that once took buckets of red, orange, yellow, green, and blue golf balls from John Broyles's driving range and bounced them all down Main Street was mourned by the time freight clanking through the crossing. The largest professional building downtown was the Volunteer Building—offices of a group of mental health counselors. Coincidence, perhaps, during the years top-ranked Tennessee kept losing to Spurrier's Gators.

Games went on at Kiwanis Park and Carver Park, where black and white kids played ball together. Not a big deal like in the times when Orr and his gang played basketball at the "black park" in the segregated days. The parks no longer had to be guarded by Science Hill's coaches to keep their star player from getting hurt in pickup games.

Spurrier would play "anywhere they'd drop a ball," Coach Tipton still liked to say.

His old gang, dubbed "the disturbers," had children of their own—who were sick of those Spurrier stories. They cruised their own hot spots, trying to outdo their parents' pranks. Somehow, though, in all the years since that lanky, crew-cut quarterback commanded the huddle, hit game-winners from half court, batted .400, and pitched nothing but wins for Science Hill, the Hilltoppers hadn't won much.

Sportswriters in the beige brick Johnson City Press building downtown no longer needed that thick brown thesaurus they had in the newsroom back when the paper was called the *Press-Chronicle*, touted the slogan, "What the people don't know will hurt them," and employed adjectives and superlatives to glorify Spurrier and the 'Toppers in big type. By the summer of '97, when Spurrier was coaching the Gators, the publisher of the press had a policy of not wasting ink on the coach down in Florida.

"I don't hate Steve Spurrier like some of you think I do," said the publisher, who had no local championships to cover. Science Hill's basketball team made a playoff run in the early '90s. But most of the trophies in the glass case at the school gym were won by the guy whose name people in town wouldn't say.

Johnson City was suffering through the most miserable summer imaginable because Steve Spurrier wouldn't go away.

They were still shaking their heads across the state—over a pass on fourth down only one coach would call. That bomb from Spurrier in September wrecked the season of the No. 2 team in the nation, on the·Vols' home field. Followed by a broadside worse than any lopsided loss.

How could Johnson City commissioners invite him back to town, for a ceremony renaming the football stadium downtown in his honor?

For some reason his picture hung above the beer taps at the Cottage, the tavern across Kiwanis Park from Spurrier's old house, flickering with TVs that had seen many a Tennessee game. Men sat at the bar clutching sweaty beers, wearing T-shirts that read, "Will Rogers Never Met Steve Spurrier." They had to believe even the homespun humorist who "never met a man I didn't like" would hate the Gator coach. The shirts came in every color, but the orange Florida and Tennessee shared.

The men at the bar said this was the year Tennessee quarterback Peyton Manning would clean Spurrier's clock. Then maybe they could stand to look at his picture hanging over the beer taps. That man shouldn't be claiming any kinship with the Volunteer State.

The official explanation for the stadium ceremony was that they wanted to honor Arthur Lady, who'd coached Little League baseball in Johnson City for 50 years. So they took Spurrier's name off the baseball field at Kiwanis Park and renamed it Arthur Lady Little League Field. The red brick football stadium downtown would be the town's new Steve Spurrier Field. And there'd be a "rededication ceremony."

Were they really honoring the man who won a national championship at *Tennessee's expense?* What the hell were they thinking down at city hall?

They had madness in their method. Chosen by the commissioners to be the keynote speaker at the ceremony was City Manager John Campbell—a known Volunteer fan, who hadn't missed a home game since Tennessee ran the single-wing. All of Orr's friends, and his brother, Graham, knew this would be a different kind of Steve Spurrier Day. But the old gang was past fighting city hall.

The Ball Coach stood in the sun shining down on his field, smiling gamely through Campbell's speech, which for half an hour extolled the history, philosophy, and virtues of . . . John Campbell.

"Now, I don't really hate Steve Spurrier like some of you think I do," Campbell finally said.

"This is out of order!" yelled a man in the crowd.

"I don't care," said the city manager. It was his microphone—his moment to commandeer the stadium, to look down at Spurrier and somehow countermand that pass from Danny Wuerffel to Reidel Anthony that sent the Gators to the national championship game, and Manning and the Vols to the Citrus Bowl.

On fourth-and-long, near midfield, with Florida's opening drive stalled and 106,000 fans in orange screaming, Spurrier didn't even call time-out. He called for a post pattern, lifted his visor, and ran his fingers through his hair. When the Gators scored the CBS announcers blistered listeners' ears. The largest crowd in the history of college football got quiet. Spurrier took a 35–0 lead, calling plays like he was back in Kiwanis Park, keeping Peyton Manning on the bench. Campbell's response was, *Tennessee wouldn't forget Steve Spurrier.*

Just as well his dad wasn't invited, his old gang said, walking out of the stadium.

The next day Spurrier drove down Route 23, into the mountains on the horizon, to talk to the Gator Club down in Hickory, North Carolina. Still smiling. Telling those high-fiving Florida fans that Johnson City had just renamed its football stadium for him. His coaches at Science Hill High School had taught him the meaning of leadership, he said. And Tennessee had the loudest crowd he had ever heard back in September.

Pause. Big smile.

"During warm-ups."

The Hickory Gator Club roared, then stood and applauded the coach who had finally made them champions. Not hearing any real concerns about sophomore Doug Johnson, who was expected to replace Wuerffel. Johnson could do it, Spurrier said, even though Johnson hadn't done it yet.

Of course the Hickory Gator Club expected more digs at the Volunteers next year. Like Spurrier saying that Manning came back to Tennessee for his senior season, even though he'd be picked first in the NFL draft, so he could be three-time Citrus Bowl MVP. As Spurrier pointed out last year, "You can't spell Citrus without UT."

Back across the hazy peaks overlooking Johnson City, the city manager had to hurry past the brick ticket office at Steve Spurrier Field to get to work, gasping for air-conditioning. Beyond the Police Canine Training Center, there was no missing the cinderblock enclave of Lonnie Lowe, head of parks and rec.

In Lowe's cavernous office Spurrier looked down from every wall, framed in photographs, posters, newspaper pages, and an enormous oil painting, numbered and signed—an artist's rendering of the field goal Spurrier the Gator quarterback kicked to beat Auburn and win the Heisman. The portrait showed his foot meeting the ball, defensive linemen trying to stop him, and Gator fans open-mouthed in the stands. The kicker had the calmest eyes, his teeth grit just right. Any Spurrier fan would want to walk into that painting.

Lowe couldn't count the hours his friend had spent practicing that game-winning kick every kid imagines booting through the maple limbs.

And still Lowe wondered, looking up from his paperwork, what unseen force was in play on that field.

"It was simple," he remembered Florida's backup quarterback, Harmon Wages, saying after the winning kick. "God loves Steve Spurrier."

Who wouldn't look up to a buddy like that? The painting and the friendship inspired Lowe to keep going in his game.

"I'm a better parks and rec guy," he said, "for knowing Steve Spurrier."

Once, they posed together, crouched and flash-lit, in a *Press-Chronicle* photo of the all-regional basketball team Lowe had on his desk. Spurrier squatted, with his 21 points and eight assists a game, a player apart from Lowe, Adam's apple ready for action but blue eyes looking bored. Like, get this 60th of a second over with—it's baseball season.

Hard now for Lowe to imagine how they beat all the guys playing high school baseball across Tennessee—and the joy in Johnson City when they gassed up that double-decker bus with the top taken off *again*, for yet another state championship victory parade, after Spurrier pitched the win instead of Lowe.

In that basketball picture Lowe looks wide-eyed behind chunky black glasses patched together with medical tape. Like he knew this was the highlight and he'd be gathering flab and newspaper clippings from there on in. Lonnie Lowe's life story was that he saw talent and befriended it. Fated to work where another generation of hotshots played hoops, in the shadow of the old brick football stadium with the new name.

From a couch deep inside his office, you could see the trouble coming.

"All the Tennessee fans we got in this town," Lowe said, stroking his walrus mustache, "they're not always happy when they come in here."

They walked in wearing their Will Rogers T-shirts, clutching manila folders full of volleyball net orders, and told Lowe, "Those pictures don't belong in an office of city business."

They called Lowe a "Spurrier groupie." He shrugged that right off. Lowe knew the people in the Will Rogers shirts from the playground. They were the kids who never could do what Spurrier did.

Lowe looked his age. Thick mustache going gray. Slouching and joking about it, dragging his feet on the way to the grave. Even though he was about the same age as Spurrier, a man who looked like he could still suit up and play. Which really set off the people who didn't like Spurrier. He'd made a deal with the devil and Peter Pan.

Success hadn't changed him, Lowe said. Same guy who'd always talked about being competitive, playing fair, remembering where you came from.

"I'm a friend with nothing to offer except friendship," Lowe said. Yet at every game Spurrier ever coached, he had a sideline pass for his brother, Graham, and Lonnie. Those Vols fans mad at Spurrier could stay mad, Lowe said.

They'd just have to stew about him winning the national championship at Florida and then handing reporters in Tennessee *his* version of the Volunteer's goals for the '96 season, without cracking a smile.

Spurrier's list of UT's goals had "National Championship" Xed out. "SEC Championship" was scratched out. "State Championship" was crossed off because the 10–2 Vols also lost to Memphis. "Knox County Champions" was circled.

In the UT trophy case in Knox County, more than one crystal football would be gleaming alongside the old gold ones, the Volunteer faithful believed—if only the people of Johnson City hadn't helped Steve Spurrier make it big. They complained about it endlessly in Lowe's office.

After Spurrier won that year's Game of the Century in Knoxville, and *Sports Illustrated* stopped the presses to switch the cover from Manning to Wuerffel, keeping it orange, did they just cancel their subscriptions? They couldn't miss the commemorative national championship issue of *Sports Illustrated* on Lowe's desk, opened to the story of how a championship mentality developed in the manse overlooking Kiwanis Park.

Back in that red brick house on the hill, a father could kneel for bedtime prayers with his children while crickets chirped in the park. Giving thanks for what we all give thanks for, a place to call home.

But there was no joy in Johnson City in the summer of '97 for believers in the Gospel of Sports.

What is it that Spurrier's trying to prove? they kept asking Lonnie Lowe down at parks and rec.

Even the regular Spurrier haters at the Cottage had to admit, the guy in the picture above the beer taps had learned to stand there and take some criticism.

CHAPTER TWO

Out of the Blue

A SON WHO PUT POETRY IN MOTION, A BOY WHO COULD REALLY PLAY ball, was conceived in the summer of 1944 by a preacher at a crossroads. He sat under the gas lamps in his study behind the altar of the First Presbyterian Church in St. Albans, West Virginia, pondering his letter of resignation as rain poured on the roof, cascading down the stained glass in the sanctuary, ushering in a cold front.

They had a fireplace with iron scrollwork in the bedroom of the white, three-story manse a block down Kanawha Terrace, with a porch over-looking the railroad and the river, that he'd give up to obey the law of the Lord. He believed that two men chosen to be his deacons, Earl Crum and John Taylor, didn't properly keep the Sabbath and couldn't in good faith be ordained—even though they were duly elected in May, and answered all the questions in the Book of Church Order. He offered to install them as elders the Sunday he halted their ordinations, but the congregation still wanted those men ordained.

The Lord knows, feeling small can cause a man to act bigger. He took up his pencil to write "with heartfelt regret" that rather than be a "church-splitter" he would resign.

It is my sincere prayer that these events which have been so unpleasant to all may fall out rather to the advancing of the Gospel of our Lord and Savior, Jesus Christ.

He typed out "J. Graham Spurrier, minister," sealing the deal.

Rain fell on St. Albans the February day in 1943 when he rode in, on the Chesapeake and Ohio tracks hugging the river and the hills. Crossings clanged as those massive new "Kanawha" locomotives steamed through, hauling miles of coal cars, Dupont chemical tankers, and coaches taking troops to the war. Leaving Reverend Spurrier at the depot, looking up at the rock church on the hill where he'd preach at 4 p.m. Praying for the Pulpit Committee to like his sermon and hire him away from the First Presbyterian Church in Eudora, Catfish Capital of Arkansas, that was seven hundred miles from his mother.

He sure knew the way out of town, in his '41 Chevrolet, past the chemical factories smoldering on the banks of the Kanawha, down through the Appalachians and across the piedmont to his mom's house in Charlotte, North Carolina. He'd take his growing family back to the red brick duplex at Amherst Place where he had grown up, near downtown— in a neighborhood split by God's law of segregation.

His brothers were fighting evil overseas. Reverend John Graham Spurrier would make sacrifices on the home front.

Through the doorway into the sanctuary, he could see his wife's piano and choir loft, and the oak font where he'd baptized their daughter Sara in the spring, before the big eyes of his namesake son. In the circle of oak pews, he'd met many eyes, preaching the Gospel under stained-glass palm trees on a tropical ocean shore.

He'd done his best in St. Albans. Upped the church's contributions to the Defense Service Council and the War Relief Fund, visited his mom twice, and got a raise in March to $2,400 a year he'd do without. He'd present the letter of resignation that evening to the church elders sloshing out into the strangely cold summer rain.

They sure wouldn't forget Reverend Spurrier. A strapping young man with wiry hair, a broad forehead, intent eyes, and a dazzling smile, hearty in his enthusiasms, outspoken in his beliefs, he defied them, they'd remember, the week God gave him the son of his dreams.

They never had a pastor at the First Presbyterian Church in St. Albans who hustled harder on the tennis court or coached more boys to play ball.

Stephen Orr Spurrier was born on a tropical peninsula, opening his eyes to a world of Florida blue. Biscayne Bay lapped at the palms ringing the rocks around St. Frances Hospital in Miami Beach, under sparkling skies. The wounded soldiers and weary doctors and nurses could see victory on the horizon, on Adolf Hitler's last birthday, April 20, 1945, as an expectant father peered into his newborn's blue eyes.

He had his father's face, everyone would say, and the chance every boy has to outdo Dad. Born in the Year of the Rooster, astrologers from the Orient would note.

They'd name him Stephen, his mother told the nurses, in honor of the first Christian martyr. That Stephen, she said, was "full of faith and power, doing great wonders and miracles among the people."

The nurses nicknamed him "Little Mutt," which prodded him right off to stand up for the little guy. At 8 pounds, 14 ounces, he was born free. Dr. J. Randolph Perdue, husband of renowned Miami cardiologist Dr. Jean Perdue, delivered the baby at no charge for his pastor at the First Presbyterian Church of Miami Beach.

Optimism filled the air as the Spurriers brought their newborn into the sunshine. Reverend Spurrier drove that bundle of potential across the sliver of land between St. Frances and the beach, past the ornate fountain at Normandy Isles, and the Art Deco bistros and homes, to the door of a small stucco house the church had rented for the new minister at 1768 Everglades Concourse.

The littlest Spurrier could see they had a football field, a baseball diamond, and a basketball court at the park across the street.

The Lord hadn't forgotten His servant Graham, living in limbo with his mother and brother and pregnant wife and children. Driving away from the duplex at Amherst Place in the family Chevrolet, he had friends Jerry and Mary Smith, formerly of Caldwell Memorial Presbyterian Church in Charlotte, North Carolina, to thank. When the Smiths' new church in Florida lost its founding pastor in the fall of 1944, the Smiths recommended Reverend Spurrier, because he "preached salvation."

Driving through the midlands of South Carolina, across veins of Winnsboro blue granite his forefathers had unearthed, he couldn't help but think of the Spurriers who went before him, leaving settled lives to blaze new trails.

Past the military bases and monuments of the capital at Columbia, he drove his family south through the palmettos into Georgia, across the St. Marys River, and into the Sunshine State. The Dixie Highway took them down the Florida coast to a city in the tropics, where a bridge across the bay led to a guarded island. The Spurriers had to pass through checkpoints keeping out German spies and black people without permits.

No amount of wandering could have prepared Reverend Spurrier for the sight of his new brick church under the coconut palms, on the banks of a canal—with cleats for worshippers to tie up their yachts. Everyone back home who thought he was crazy for leaving the church in West Virginia should look upon the Lord's dwelling place in paradise.

He was expecting to see soldiers covering the sand. Half a million troops trained on Miami Beach during World War II, including actor Clark Gable, billeted in the hundreds of resort hotels along the shore. Every night they scanned the waves for German U-boats behind blacked-out windows, with posters warning, "Loose lips sink ships."

Through the winter that was like summer up north, the ambitious minister did the Lord's work in a new world—conducting Sunday services, officiating candlelight weddings, running Bible study groups, moderating session meetings, spearheading the collecting of books, papers, magazines, and clothing for the men overseas, with Bible verses attached. While overseeing the church's mission in China, Reverend Spurrier joined two other area ministers directing the Presbyterian Historical Society and led a young adult group that met in the church kitchen.

Marjorie taught Sunday school, played piano, led the choir, and grew ready to bring a child into a world that would not be ruled by a German tyrant. Nothing beat seeing her husband in his sporty new clothes, heading off to his golf lessons. The Normandy Shores Country Club, built on land dredged up from the bay, was a 1-iron shot from the manse, giving Reverend Spurrier a chance to rub shoulders with the members of the church who golfed there.

But he couldn't get on the links across the inlet, at La Gorce—where church members teed it up with boxing legends Jack Dempsey and Gene

Tunney, aviator Eddie Rickenbacker, and captains of industry and commerce. In the clubhouse overlooking the ocean they toasted La Gorce member Will Rogers, who'd never met a nomad preacher he didn't like.

Reverend Spurrier had reason to fear that the well-to-do members of his church saw him as different.

Days before his wife's due date he passed his final exams on sacraments and church government (administered by Reverend J. C. Pilgrim), signed the ex animo obligation, and was officially installed as pastor, in time to represent the church at the spring meeting of the Presbytery, across the causeway in Miami. The hubbub of downtown, and the whistles of trains steaming north from the port, wafted over from the mainland on those quiet evenings when he could walk his family to the beach.

On April 20 the *Miami Herald* was calling for "scattered showers, little change in temperature" in South Florida, as Germany's Fuhrer celebrated his 56th birthday awarding Iron Crosses to distinguished Hitler Youth, his last glimpse of sunlight. Under the banner headline, ORGANIZED NAZI RESISTANCE VIRTUALLY ENDED, GERMAN MANPOWER SMASHED, the *Herald* reported that General George Patton, "taking advantage of the German weakness, crossed the Rhine without a shot being fired." Soldiers were being ordered back to boot camp on Miami Beach, to reunite with their wives in the resort hotels.

Bells rang, horns honked, and cheers filled the streets on the eighth day of May, when Germany surrendered to the Allies. Reverend Spurrier stood behind the pulpit, leading his congregation in prayers and praise, celebrating Victory in Europe. Preparing to baptize his youngest son in Florida's water.

Reverend Spurrier lifted his son above the azure waters and bobbing boats and dunked him in the font, baptizing Stephen Orr Spurrier in the name of the Father, Son, and Holy Spirit.

That boy would take the plunge and be ready for more, his dad had to believe.

Willie Spurrier waited back in Charlotte for her two youngest sons serving overseas to come home. Her elder son wrote glowingly about the baptism in Miami, on a victorious May day, assuring his mom she'd be proud of her newest grandson.

In the afterglow of the war, not everyone was rooting for the little guy.

With the soldiers going home and tourists returning, people around Miami couldn't help but notice the yachts tied up at Reverend Spurrier's church. His members mingled with civic leaders and socialites in the pages of the *Herald*, bolstering the belief that the First Presbyterian Church of Miami Beach was "for the rich," as the church's next pastor put it. The real challenge at that church was ministering to a diverse flock.

The high rollers came ashore to worship with professional people arriving by car, from the mainland. The congregation of around 120 full-time members included six doctors (other than the Perdues), attorneys, architects, pilots for Pan Am and Eastern Airlines, nurses at St. Frances, teachers wanting their children in Sunday school—joined on Sunday by soldiers seeking an hour of peace and sunburned tourists with the only dark faces in the sanctuary.

Reverend Spurrier took them all in, in the light streaming through the church's clear glass windows. No stained glass colored that sanctuary. What religious icon could outshine herons and pelicans gliding over the sea grapes and gumbo limbo, and the sleek hulls bobbing in the azure waters by the altar? A preacher wanting to get his message across had to focus on the people.

They could count on Reverend Spurrier to proclaim the kingship of Jesus, the power of the Holy Spirit, the authority of commandments etched in stone. Follow the narrow way, renounce your possessions, and you will find treasure in heaven, he would always declare—even to disciples with really big boats. He told the captains of the congregation they needed to come to Wednesday night prayer meeting, too.

In their view donning spiffy clothes and joining church members on the golf course didn't atone for his pointed sermons, damning those who met God only halfway. So said the preacher who succeeded Reverend Spurrier at the church under the coconut palms.

Dr. Willis Garrett served during World War II with the Army Air Corp in Algeria, maintaining planes and ministering to the airmen. Back in Palm City, Florida, reunited with his wife, Ruth, he was packing for a thirty-day leave when church elder Henry Schreiber called, saying the First Presbyterian Church of Miami Beach needed a new pastor.

Dr. Garrett had been guest speaker for a First Auxiliary meeting the church held before the war, when Reverend William C. Cumming was still the pastor, before he went back to mission work in China and Reverend Spurrier was hired. Dr. Garrett liked the people he'd met at the meeting and said yes. He showed up at the church at 7141 Indian Creek Drive in April, 1946, still in uniform.

"Graham Spurrier didn't work out," Schreiber told Dr. Garrett, because "he couldn't cope with the atmosphere here."

Whether Reverend Spurrier suddenly resigned or was asked to leave didn't matter to Dr. Garrett. He knew his predecessor tried to blend in with the members who filled the collection plate, working to dress and socialize with the best of them. But he had the mannerisms and accent of a simpler place, Schreiber told Dr. Garrett, and sometimes talked about running the money changers out of the temple.

Now he had to call his mother and tell her he was coming home. To his little brother Bob he lamented that he "loved that church with the windows on the water."

Concern must have clouded the face of his 4-year-old son, Graham, as the family packed up for yet another move, out of paradise, back to the crowded half of a duplex in Dad's old neighborhood back in Charlotte.

Why did they have to leave Miami Beach, little Graham wanted to know.

"The former pastor came back from the war and wanted his church back," Reverend Spurrier told his namesake son. Graham would pass down that story to his little brother.

On a bright blue April day on Miami Beach, the family stood in front of the empty manse, facing the park with the ball fields and the basketball court. Camera in hand.

"Pose for a picture," they told their toddler. "Hold up one finger and show everyone it's your first birthday." Giving him his first memory—standing under a palm tree with a finger in the air, celebrating being number one.

Reverend Spurrier drove back across the causeway in the loaded-down Chevrolet and turned north on Dixie Highway, through the swamps and orange groves to the bridge over the St. Marys River, looking in the rear-view mirror. Checking on the squirmer in the back seat they'd taken to calling Stevie.

A man of faith could take comfort in the thought that Florida hadn't seen the last of the Spurriers.

CHAPTER THREE

Walk to the Park

THE HOUSE WHERE A BOY GREW UP WAS A PLACE TO PONDER: WHAT don't we know about our fathers that made them who they were? Did we inherit the secret ways of *their* fathers, too?

What happened to John Graham Spurrier, Stevie's grandfather, in January 1934, after he hobbled into the house on crutches from one of his sales trips and told his youngest son he'd been in a car wreck but he'd be fine, shaded the talk around Grandma Willie's table in May of 1946. Once again, John Graham Jr. was the man of the house, sitting with his widowed mother. Flanked by his little brothers, the athletes and war heroes.

Bob, the youngest, took up his big brother's sport and became the top-ranked singles tennis player in the state. Then he served three years in Europe, saved by the atom bomb from having to invade Japan. Bob was home for the summer, looking forward to finishing his degree at Presbyterian College in the fall.

Middle brother Eddie, the baseball player, was back from fighting the Japanese in the Philippines, having left his job at Duke Power in April of 1941 to enlist. Beside him was his wife, Julia, making room for five more Spurriers at the table.

Surely the missing father hovered over the family gathering, as summer winds blew street sounds through the window screens.

The new man of the house couldn't forget that Uncle Fred, Uncle Hugh, and Uncle Rezin Spurrier all lived nearby and would be dropping in to ask, in their avuncular way, what the unemployed preacher would do for work—while Marjorie went back to her old job downtown at Metropolitan Life. In that house a man with a car and the gift of gab better bring home the bacon.

His uncles brought stories to the table about forefathers riding through the wilderness to forge new lives, paving the way for the Spurriers' success in Charlotte. Those stories had made their departed brother's sales skills the toast of the city.

"Mother said he sometimes had to come in off the road," Marjorie gushed about her father-in-law, "because he was selling too much, and they couldn't keep up with his orders."

Reverend Spurrier hadn't backed down from preaching the Gospel to the captains of industry in Miami. Was his father proud of his fortitude? Or was Dad looking down from a celestial showroom saying, "Son, can't you reach your customers?"

When his uncles showed up, he'd have to talk about the Chevrolet that Uncle Rezin sold him, many miles ago. Of course, a spiffier model could be financed at the Spurrier Auto Company on Magnolia Avenue, where his Uncle Rezin rang up sales. But Reverend Spurrier wasn't going to work on his golf game, or get a new car, to buff up his image. Though he'd really rather have a Buick. What mattered in the religion business was God's word. He'd find a way to show them all.

He surely prayed for his calling, and his family, on Sunday, driving them to Caldwell Memorial Presbyterian Church, where Willie had raised her sons in her family's faith. Now her oldest boy was taking his wife and children into the stately brick church. They took in the fancy outfits in the oak pews, worshipping with department store mogul Henry Belk and his brood of future world beaters.

Reverend Spurrier sat in his boyhood sanctuary as a guest. He would never officially rejoin the congregation, because that would mean giving up his search for a church to lead, resigning himself to life as a civilian.

After the service, mingling around the refreshment table on the lawn, people would say they could see Graham Spurrier in Stevie's face.

After Sunday dinner, and some sermonizing around the table, you know those little boys just wanted to go out and play. Big brother Graham was still a giant to Stevie. They'd head out the front door to an empty lot across the street, with rocks for bases and field pines for goalposts. Or hope that their father would take them across Fourth Street, to Independence Park, where he used to play as a boy.

Out the back door, half a block down Luther Street, they had a baseball field at Monroe Park with mowed grass and real bases, bordered by purple and pink crepe myrtles. But as far as Graham, Sara, and Stevie were concerned, the world ended in Grandma Willie's backyard. Their father wouldn't ever walk them half a block into the Cherry neighborhood, to the park where the children of the first black homeowners in Charlotte played. Living so close to them had given John Graham Jr. a different view of segregation than his dad had.

Indeed, everyone residing on Amherst Place in the summer of 1946 was white—and only black people lived a block over on Luther. The street behind the duplex was "the other way," where Dad never went, a sharp-eyed lad would notice. Mainly, Stevie stood in awe of the cherry tree blossoming beside his grandmother's house. Those wild cherries made the best pies.

The Cherry neighborhood got its name from the trees brimming with fruit anyone could pick, in the days when rows of houses sprang up from the soil of a thousand-acre cotton plantation. The Meyers family deeded over the land in 1898 to make a community for their former slaves—who mostly took jobs as servants in the mansions in Meyers Park.

The salesman's son had seen what happens when your hometown turns into a city. His uncles' stories assured him the Spurriers weren't afraid to walk out their back door.

They'd left their home in the South, after Sherman's army marched through, migrating north to find land to farm by the Catawba River, outside of Charlotte. Edwin Rezin Spurrier, Stevie's great-grandfather, helped his folks till the fields until he turned 20 and fell in love with a North Carolina girl, marrying Margaret Elizabeth Auten in 1875 as his parents and brothers looked on.

Two years later Ed and his twin, John, and brothers Charles and William found a forlorn place on the family farm to bury Rezin William Spurrier, paying tribute to the father who had led them out of the Yankees' ruination to land that grew to be worth over $1,200, land where they could all work. In two more years they'd bury their mother, Harriet Hoket Spurrier, beside the husband she followed to the end.

Ed Spurrier's descendants should know that he had the gumption to leave *his* father's land, taking his wife and little daughter Mayme from the farm to the town. Moving the family to Paw Creek, where the Rozelle's Ferry carried travelers across the Catabawa River and black tenant farmers worked on the land of former plantation owners, Ed Spurrier went to work at his cousin Sam Oglesby's grocery store.

After serving behind the counter Ed took over the store, becoming Paw Creek's postmaster in 1889, inspiring Elizabeth to bear 14 children. They lost three at birth and buried little Sam when he was 2. They raised Mayme, Harriet, Powell, Ernest, Catherine, Rezin, John Graham, joined by Lawrence, Hugh, and Fred, in a neighborhood some Southerners would shun.

Does God really point us to a better way, while Satan sticks forks in the path? What possessed Sam Oglesby to open a store in an African-American community in the first place? Did he foresee his cousin turning the place into Spurrier's Store, a gathering spot so popular people started calling the neighborhood Spurrier?

At Spurrier's Store people of any color could get groceries, an earful of news, maybe a checkers challenge—and on weekends old Sam sold a dipper full of liquor for a nickel.

Talk on the front porch turned to people who "shuffled" home after drinking Sam's nickel dippers, and the Spurrier neighborhood became known as "Shuffletown." Maybe proof to a preacher that a different spirit took hold when blacks and whites intermingled.

Reverend Spurrier would always commemorate the date of September 24, 1893, when Willie Austin was born to Ida Austin and her husband, John, a farmer from Sharon, North Carolina, who gave his daughter Willie no middle name. When she turned six her father died, leaving her and six siblings sheltered by Ida Austin's boardinghouse, in the shadow of downtown Charlotte. Willie would have to find her own guiding light.

In Paw Creek, Spurrier's Store grew to be the Spurrier Chandlery Company, branching out into the Spurrier Sadler Company at the turn of the century. Ed bought his own family farm on Rozelles Ferry Road, near his beloved store, and found hired hands to help with the six kids still at home. Giving young John Graham and his brothers a chance to work with Dad.

Willie turned 17 and went to work as a saleslady in a dry goods store downtown, finding a charming salesman to marry in 1912. Sitting in the elegant new sanctuary at Caldwell Memorial Presbyterian, Ed Spurrier could reflect on a boyhood blown apart by the Civil War, the risk his dad took moving the family north, and his own bold move, taking over a grocery store in a questionable part of Paw Creek. Fathers had to make tough calls, sons had to learn. He could see that young John Graham would do fine with a wife smiling at his side.

The newlyweds rented a room at Ida Austin's boardinghouse, at 902 East Fourth Street, where the neighbors put their cows and chickens to bed by the city's lights. After a year of marriage John Graham mourned the loss of his father in Paw Creek and saw signs of new life. John Graham Spurrier Jr. was born on June 16, 1914, opening his eyes in a rented room on a mooing, clucking, bustling street.

Three years later he got a brother to tussle with, Edward (Eddie) Rezin. The family stayed in the rented room while John Graham hit the road as a salesman for the Dawson Paper Company. He welcomed his widowed mother's move from the farm in Shuffletown to a place a few blocks away.

The family cheered his new job selling flour for the Interstate Milling Company, headquartered downtown, with mills churning out truckloads of flour up in Statesville, North Carolina. He'd need a trusty car, for calling on bakeries across the state. His brother Rezin, a produce broker, was thinking of getting into auto sales. But John Graham believed in saving money during good times that might not last. He and his wife and boys moved in with Willie's mother and sister, two doors down, where they all shared quarters with Louis McCall, a civil engineer; his wife, an artist; and their daughter, Elizabeth. Graham Jr., as he was called, tried to adjust to the new people in a new apartment and the different-looking people on the street.

Graham Jr. and Eddie made room for baby brother Bob, and then an infant sister—who died after being named Margaret Elizabeth.

As buildings rose on Fourth Street, shortening the days of cow barns and chicken coops, Graham, Eddie, and Bob could thank their forefathers for afternoons without farm chores—creating a time when city boys could play sports. They picked up balls, bats, and rackets and walked past their church, and the turrets of Central High, to the fields and courts at Independence Park, shaded by live oaks teeming with owls. Schooling each other in one playground rule: Put the ball where the other guy isn't.

Their father drove the roads of Carolina ahead of his competitors, knowing people would always buy bread. Willie helped her sister and mother keep the boardinghouse going, waiting for her husband to come home. She'd spend hours talking to her oldest son, expecting his good influence to guide the brothers he watched over.

"There are two things especially I hope you never do," she said in their mother-and-son talks. "Do not drink, and do not smoke." Dad had a code of the road, but mother's word was law.

⌁

When Graham Jr. was 15, halfway through high school, adults spun the world around. The stock market crashed, banks downtown shut their doors, and his father made a move. John Graham had spent his 30s making a name at the Interstate Milling Company, living with his mother-in-law, and socking away his earnings. With the Depression descending he paid $6,000 for rental property that would be Willie's dream house—a solid brick duplex at Amherst Place, not so many blocks away, on the border of the Cherry neighborhood. In desperate times his family had a place to rent out and their own place to live. And he bought them a radio, to listen to in his absence.

The boys' familiar haunts were still nearby. His namesake son would just have to shepherd his brothers down different streets and recognize a blessing when he saw it. What kind of freedom came with owning a place? At last they were free to disagree.

They had farther to go to visit Grandma Elizabeth downtown. Thankfully she was out of Paw Creek. People there said bootleggers ran moonshine through the streets of Shuffletown into Charlotte at all hours.

To preserve their good fortune they had a family portrait taken in their new home, showing how much alike John Graham Jr. and Sr.

looked. The father had on his round-collar shirt and short black tie, his dark hair slicked to the side and the wide-open smile he'd pass along. Willie beamed at the camera in her Sunday dress and sepia brooch, her hair parted to the other side, her boys on display.

John Graham wasn't a big man, size wise, so he took up the sport that rewarded a straight shot, steady putting, and a low score. After traveling all week he headed to the newly sodded Carolina Golf Club on Old Steele Road, a pastoral setting for games between men.

"Never met a stranger," his sons would sum him up, after hearing his tales from the road and the fairway.

But they picked up balls they could hit with rackets and bats. Graham Jr. was growing big, maybe not graceful but quicker than he looked. He hit the tennis court every day, wanting to be good, and played hard enough to reach the championship round of the winter tennis tournament at Independence Park. His little brother cheered when he won, giving him the feel of a trophy he could hold above everybody else.

At Colonial Park, on the court closer to Amherst Place, he played all the way to the finals of the Colonial Park Tennis Championship and lost. His little brother learned to watch for a flying racket.

"He wouldn't curse when he lost a point," Bob told the folks back at the duplex. "He'd just yell out 'dadgummit' or something and throw his racket into the net."

Marjorie Orr could sense his intensity in the hallways of Central High, as she carried her violin to rehearsals for the school orchestra. He seemed to be all over the place his junior year, even hanging out with that skinny Billy Graham boy from out in the country.

In late May of 1933, the Spurriers lost Grandmother Elizabeth, nearby no more, after her girlhood had taken her through the Civil War to the Spurrier's dominion in Paw Creek. Her son Graham knew a doctor on East Sixth Street, Dr. J. C. Ranson, who did all he could, another luxury in those tough times.

At the "reformed" Presbyterian Church where Willie took her sons, they preached strictures her eldest seemed to accept but didn't trumpet—until summer turned to fall and he realized he would be a credit short of graduating. What extra class should he take? Word around Central

High was, the Bible studies class taught by Mrs. W. L. Walker was a "crip" course everybody passed.

Graham Jr. said he "got in the class that first day and a lady got up, the widow of a Baptist minister, and said we always wanted to open class with a prayer." With that prayer "something happened to me on the inside, on that first day. Jesus Christ came into my heart and became real and personal."

No one at home doubted Graham Jr.'s desire to do right and beat everyone at tennis. But the change wrought by Mrs. Walker's Bible class stunned Bob, who thought he had his racket-slinging brother sized up. Graham Jr. joined the Interdenominational Youth Club, noticed Marjorie at the first meeting, and "began to sense" that God wanted him to be a minister.

In the spring of 1934, as graduation loomed, Mrs. Walker invited her star pupil to a two-week youth revival she was putting on with evangelist Katherine Dangerforth from Augusta, Georgia. After the final altar call, Graham Jr. came in the door of the duplex leaving no room for doubt—he was a new man in Christ.

"*Then* I was converted," he said, seeing the difference between hearing God's word and acting on it. "Not necessarily just in the one-credit Bible course." Now he would talk about the Lord to his friends, like that Graham kid from the country—and dare to witness to the woman who'd taken him to church all those years.

In the summer leading from Independence Park to the future, a boy's concern for his mother made him say, "I don't think she was saved. Don't think Christ was real to her at all." Seeing her home alone brought forth the fear that she "just went through the motions on Sunday."

He sat her down and used his best words to convince her salvation is an all-or-nothing proposition. The Lord's saving plan might take time. He returned serves at the park wondering if he'd gotten through to his mom.

He came home and again found her alone at the table. She looked up and said, "Son, I don't know whether I have been saved before or not, but I know it now."

A moment of triumph for a young man looking for his calling. If an aspiring preacher would keep track of souls saved, he had a big first score.

The duplex at Amherst Place lost thousands of dollars in value as the Depression wore on, but the rent money kept coming. The salesman closed the deal to send his namesake son to college. Leaving an empty place at the table in August of 1934, when Graham Jr. left for football practice in Due West, South Carolina. At 150 pounds he was going out for the freshman team at Erskine Bible College, hoping to play offensive guard for the Flying Fleets.

Eddie, overshadowed by his older brother, stepped up to the plate at Independence Park. Bob took Graham's place on the tennis court. Back at the duplex, the boys could only nod their heads at a surprisingly understandable phone call from Due West.

Through Dad's dismay, and Willie's soothing words, their elder son insisted Erskine Bible College was "too wild" for him. His roommates drank beer, he said, and the guys on the football team used curse words. He'd been raised to resist sin, and he'd had enough.

Bob and Eddie thought their upbringing in a reformed Presbyterian Church could conceivably make Erskine Bible College seem like Sodom.

"I can't stay down here," Graham Jr. told his dad over the phone.

The father, who'd already paid for tuition, told his son to come home.

Back around his parents' table, Graham Jr. floated the idea of transferring to Columbia Bible College in the spring—even though the school in the turrets of the old Colonial Hotel overlooked South Carolina's capital city.

His father said yes, reaffirming his faith in young Graham. They celebrated a family Christmas at Amherst Place, and in the new year Graham Jr. packed up and headed south to yet another divinity school under the crescent moon.

Columbia Bible College suited him, he called and said to his dad. He had reverent roommates, and Columbia seemed like a city worth saving.

A father raised on Civil War stories in Paw Creek could only marvel at the circular road of the Spurriers—then get back on the road with his order pad. Heading due east across the state, to a tobacco and cotton town on the Neuse River where he had business on January 25.

At the end of January, Willie called Columbia Bible College to tell her boy to come home. His father had been in a car accident and needed surgery. Graham Jr. raced through the door of the duplex, asking 11-year-old Bob what had happened.

Bob was eleven; he'd been home. Ed was 15, out playing ball when their father's car pulled up to the curb, a day early, the car door opening slowly. The familiar footsteps sounded different. Their dad struggled up the front steps and through the door on crutches.

"A guy pulled out of a side street and hit me," he told Bob. Out of the blue, on a balmy winter day near the Carolina coast. Bob looked out the window at his father's car by the curb. The car was just dented. He'd driven it home from Kinston.

Bob was too stunned to ask their dad if he went to a doctor in Kinston or drove all the way back to Charlotte to get the crutches from Dr. Ranson. They'd never seen their father need any kind of help.

"'Don't worry,' he kept saying, 'I'll be fine,'" Bob told his big brother.

But their father got worse. Both legs, his left arm, his chest, and his head hurt, despite all Dr. Ranson could do. At Presbyterian Hospital, three blocks from the duplex, the diagnosis was septicemia—blood poisoning from the wound inflicted by the choke knob. Doctors operated but couldn't stem the infection.

Cold rain lashed the hospital windows as John Graham Spurrier passed away at 1:15 a.m. on Friday, February, 1, 1934, with his wife, brothers, and sons at his side, in the neighborhood he called home. Twenty-six degrees and rain kept falling as the Spurriers grieved.

Headlines in the *Kinston Free Press* on January 25 announced outlaw John Dillinger's capture in Tucson, Arizona. Apparently no police report was filed in Kinston about a Charlotte man in a car wreck. No autopsy was performed. John Graham Spurrier was just gone.

Willie knew the shock, the numbness, the undertaker's cloying words and cologne, from losing her dad when she was six. Nothing prepared her for this loss. She couldn't stop crying. Couldn't ever see having another husband. Still had his children to raise, his namesake son to get through college.

Her sons wondered if she would ever quit crying. "She really loved that man," Bob said.

"He was just 43, he was just 43," she kept saying to the people at the door bringing more food to the table.

Graham Jr. said he had to go right back to school and take the opportunity his father had provided. Looking down on the corner of Hampton and Pickens Streets from the turrets of the Bible College, a freshman divinity student began to understand how you could root for someone you couldn't see.

Blessings flowed back in Charlotte on a November night at the Tabernacle, at a revival led by Dr. Mordecai Ham. The radio evangelist known for railing against alcohol had leveled accusations in the *Charlotte Observer* about debauchery at Central High School, and posters advertising the revival urged, "Hear Ham." After a fiery sermon he called to the altar those who wanted to commit their lives to Christ. Marjorie Orr and Billy Graham came forward.

She could see that country boy was his father's son.

"Frank Graham, we knew that family," Marjorie said. "He was a dairy farmer, and his family was pretty rich."

Marjorie's father, a railroad man, took in Dr. Ham's sermon and grew concerned his outspokenness would taint his message, maybe shorten his career. Harry Orr knew the Graham family well enough to spend an evening in their pasture, praying with his daughter.

"We sat out in the pasture praying for God to raise up an evangelist, to raise up a boy to take Dr. Ham's place," Marjorie marveled. "Nobody thought it'd be that skinny little boy in the farmhouse."

The divinity student away at school could only pray for his bereaved mother and brothers to find their way.

On the baseball diamond Eddie Spurrier played catcher for local youth league teams like a man possessed. Small, wiry, quick with a throw to second, he left high school after a year to play ball every day. Willing the ball into his glove when scouts wanted him to play for the Charlotte Hornets—the city's Boston Red Sox farm club, named for the "hornet's nest of rebellion" British general Charles Cornwallis said he stirred up trying to occupy the city. The Hornets' manager in 1935, former Major League player Frances O'Rourke, knew talent when he saw it. His team of working-class heroes would play next season in the American Legion Stadium being built by WPA workers in the lot by Central High.

A contract with the Hornets could take Eddie all the way to Fenway Park in Boston—where the Red Sox worked to dispel what their fans swore was a curse.

He staggered back through the door of the duplex clutching his shoulder, telling Bob he'd slid into second and hit the ground hard. The shoulder felt "out of joint," he said. Bob worried another brother might not ever be the same.

On a sweltering day in May, no hint of rain or a breeze, Willie, Eddie, and Bob went to see Graham Jr. graduate from Columbia Bible College. The man they all missed would have been proud of his son's acceptance to Union Theological Seminary, the storied stone divinity school in Decatur, Georgia, where he'd start work on his doctoral degree in the fall.

A group of ministers who put on a summer tent crusade in Charlotte asked young Graham Jr. to be a guest preacher. They had a pianist who'd played the worship music for several years named Marjorie Orr.

Her mother was glad to see John Graham Spurrier's son when he came courting at 88 High Street, down Providence Road, near the Meyers Park Country Club. "His home's just 2 miles away," Marjorie pointed out to her mom, adding that she and Graham Jr. "felt right at home together." Marjorie played the piano when he preached at youth crusades and Vacation Bible School classes, before he left for divinity school in the fall. In Decatur Miss Orr was not forgotten.

Graham Jr. graduated from Union Theological Seminary with a doctor of divinity degree in May 1940 and came home to brothers heading in different directions.

Bob was graduating from Central High School and bringing home championship trophies from Independence Park like the one his brother had won. He'd be on the University of North Carolina tennis team in the fall, and on the football field, drumming in the Tar Heels' marching band.

Eddie couldn't play ball like he could before hurting his shoulder. At age 22 he worked for a candy company, hoping to get work outdoors on a Duke Power construction crew.

Marjorie still lived with her folks on High Street, working as a clerk at the Metropolitan Life Insurance Company downtown. She believed her love of the Lord, and her talent as a pianist, caused Graham Spurrier to pop the question, on a day made for making a play.

Mr. and Mrs. Spurrier joined hands at the altar of Caldwell Memorial Presbyterian Church on September 16, 1940. The newlyweds came to live with Willie at Amherst Place while Bob studied at UNC, Eddie labored for Duke Power, and Graham Jr. waited for a phone call from a church in need.

He was ordained the next year, in the Pine Bluff, Arkansas, Presbytery, 700 miles away from his mother. His ordination would have been back in Charlotte, but the First Presbyterian Church in Eudora, Arkansas, needed a pastor right away.

On the eighth anniversary of her husband's death, as Willie sat alone in the duplex, Graham Jr. called from a hospital in Lake Village, Arkansas, to tell her that Graham Spurrier III had been born that very day, healthy as could be.

Little Graham grew bigger without his grandmother seeing him, putting Reverend Spurrier on the train to St. Albans, West Virginia, where a church in need of a pastor would bring him closer to his mother. Then he went to the end of the earth, to further his ministry in Miami Beach.

Desperation reunited mother and son at 1700 Amherst Place. Her faith in him wouldn't waver when no church called him that first year back in Charlotte, filling him with despair.

Graham, Sara, and Stevie stayed with Willie while Reverend Spurrier drove around town, knocking on strangers' doors, selling Metropolitan Life Insurance policies with his wife. His father might appreciate his sales pitch, evoking a time when the man of the house would be gone and the product would be sorely needed.

"If we'd just had penicillin," Dr. Ranson told Bob, Ed, and Graham on a house call to see Willie, lamenting the loss of a lifetime. A new family portrait showed the three brothers standing tall by the white columns out front, with Willie behind them on the porch, looking wistful.

You don't go to a doctor unless you're about to die, Stevie would think. The secrets a boy wants to know, that will make him a man, can sometimes be grasped by a toddler in a high chair.

At the start of another sweatbox summer in Charlotte, walking down the streets shaded by walnuts and white oaks to Independence Park, Stevie's dad said their hope for the fall was a running back for North Carolina named "Choo Choo."

CHAPTER FOUR

Stevie's Ball

On a fall Saturday in Athens, Tennessee, after the war, when talk turned to football, people on North Jackson Street could hear the radio in the preacher's house crackling with excitement about "Choo Choo."

They knew that little boy who stood on the front porch tossing a ball to himself, waiting for someone to play, was in there listening to a North Carolina game. When Charlie "Choo Choo" Justice scored, that boy would run out the door with his football, making like number 22 in Tar Heel blue. Making a move, running where the other guy wasn't.

He'd throw in the stutter-step of a running back at Tennessee Wesleyan, across College Street, where the local heroes played ball.

Must've seemed normal to the minister at Mars Hill Presbyterian. They'd see him playing at all hours on the campus tennis court, volleying with Dean J. Van Coe. Reverend Spurrier was known for ministering in his tennis clothes, a towel over his shoulder, always ready for a game. But on North Jackson Street, they still had reason to wonder: What made the preacher's little boy want so badly to play with the big boys?

Because he could, his father would say. Scouting him in a game of catch back in the church lot, under the mimosa tree.

For Stevie Spurrier the college town in Tennessee was a field of dreams, with real goalposts. Coaches and choo choo trains whistled and steamed. The Lord and Dad had come through.

They'd packed up the Chevrolet and pulled away from Grandma Willie's house in September of 1947, heading west on Route 74. Crossing Carolina, curving around the Great Smoky Mountains, they saw sugar maples reddening the peaks and swayed down the road like pioneers. In the foothills of Tennessee they passed through Indian lands, jounced across the L&N Railroad tracks, and rode up North Jackson Street to a quaint brick church under a giant oak, beside an old white wooden house.

They had to stretch to take in the bustling street. The *Daily Post-Athenian* office across the alley clattered with news. The Southern Soda Shop across the street was hopping with college kids calling the place the "Slop Shop." A few doors down, the red call letters of radio station WLAR stood for "We Love All Republicans," people on North Jackson Street would say. The floor above Duggan's Cleaners held a roller skating rink. The grocer, the barber, and more serious brick businesses led to the McMinn County Courthouse on the square.

Reverend Spurrier looked up at the bell in the white wooden steeple, ringing people into church for more than a hundred years. He could be forgiven for thinking that his mother and brothers should see the Lord's place in the Volunteer State.

Graham and Sara had to be looking at the big brick grammar school on the hill. Stevie could see he'd be sharing another room with Graham.

People welcoming the new minister to Mars Hill saw him as a god-send. They'd been without a full-time pastor since April of 1946—when the former pastor of the First Presbyterian Church of Miami Beach had become available. The courting of pastors by Presbyterian churches could get complicated. Rarely was a minister out of work for a year and a half. Driving to Athens and delivering his "trial sermon" at Mars Hill in June, Reverend Spurrier had demonstrated his fervor.

The family moving into the manse looked like Christian reinforcements in a town cleaning up from a war.

The Bridges Hotel across from the courthouse was the first footfall on the Trail of Tears, when Cherokee Indians living around Athens were marched west in 1838. After Fort Sumter was fired on, Athens voted to stay in the Union and sent more men to fight for the North than the South. General Sherman took the Bridges Hotel for a headquarters on his march to torch Atlanta and Columbia. Leaving a town opposed to slavery, that welcomed black businessmen setting up shop on Free Hill during Reconstruction.

Many young men from Athens fought in World War II and didn't like the place they came home to—governed by Democrats who harassed soldiers returning to the town's bars. Outraged veterans ran for sheriff and mayor. On Election Day the ballot boxes were hustled over to the county jail, to be counted by the incumbents. That wasn't the democratic process the vets had fought for. They gathered on the hill and fired on the jail, demanding the ballot boxes. When no ballot boxes were forthcoming, they dynamited the jailhouse door. Then National Guardsmen marched in and ended what was called "the Battle of Athens" on the cover of *Time* magazine and the front page of the *Charlotte Observer*. The ballots were finally counted, and the veterans took office in the fall of 1946.

Christian soldiers needed leaders. Mars Hill had lost pastor H. L. Love to the army on the same day faulty organ wires caught the altar on fire. Still making up the insurance shortfall, the church had done without a minister for nearly a year when the elders met in April of 1947 to square their annual budget with what little they could offer a pastor.

The first Sunday in September, Reverend John Graham Spurrier gave his first sermon as pastor of Mars Hill, pleasing the crowd and the elders. They knew he couldn't be pleased with the state of the manse. The elders met yet again to discuss giving the old house they'd used for Sunday school rooms a fresh coat of paint, maybe buffing the ancient wood floors. They voted instead to raise money for a new Sunday school building.

The next month Marjorie Spurrier ceremonially joined the congregation at Mars Hill. They sure were happy to have her playing the piano, directing the choir, and putting out the bulletins. Her children helped fold those bulletins on Sunday morning, taking to the rites of autumn in Tennessee.

Stevie took in his mother's Sunday school lesson, and his father's sermon, and vowed to be in church every Sunday and Wednesday. After a year of perfect attendance, his dad would see he needed a football to play with.

The moment he had the big leather ball in his hands, he wanted to play catch. His dad wanted to play, too. First pass went for a short gain. Stevie called a longer play. Game on.

The completions added up. After a season passing the ball in the church-yard, oblivious to the workers sawing and hammering on the new Sunday school building, the 4½-year-old boy had two college teams to root for.

On North Jackson Street they wore Volunteer orange in the fall, but Reverend Spurrier kept talking about a war hero who wore North Carolina blue. Charlie Justice played high school ball across the Smoky Mountains in Asheville, averaging 25 yards a carry, outscoring opponents 400–6, until Uncle Sam called. At Bainbridge Naval Center he caught the eye of the football coach by booming punts better than the team's punter. And his commanding officer said he ran the football like "a runaway train."

After the war North and South Carolina wanted "Choo Choo" to play for their schools. He believed athletes ought to represent their home state. As he lit up the scoreboard at Chapel Hill his senior season and WLAR played "All the Way Choo Choo" by Johnny Long and His Orchestra, Reverend Spurrier maintained that Charlie Justice could punt as well as he could run and throw.

That fall, when the hammering quit and the new Sunday school building was dedicated, Stevie was allowed to walk with Graham across College Street, through "the Arch" welcoming them to Tennessee Wesleyan, and up the hill overlooking the field where the Bulldogs practiced, coached by a man quick with a whistle. The team had to run up the hill double-time if they messed up a play.

That little boy could only imagine how it felt to make those blocks, tackles, and runs and make that football *fly*. He would learn that imitation gets you places.

At the Mars Hill Christmas service in 1949, he stood up on the altar and sang, "I Love to Tell the Story." That song introduced the guest minister program on WLAR that had his father's voice booming out of the radio. Stevie warbled the tune in the manse before performing for the congregation. Then the Spurriers drove around the Smokies and through Carolina to Grandma Willie's house, home for Christmas.

Under the tree Stevie found his first Bible, a gift from Grandma Orr to guide him through the new decade dawning. Around the table Reverend Spurrier asked what college athlete could possibly take the place of number 22 in blue. Choo Choo was graduating from North Carolina as the Heisman Trophy runner-up, two years running, beaten out in 1949 by Doak Walker from SMU.

Christian athletes should outscore everyone else, Stevie heard his dad say, for the glory of the Lord. Maybe he was too humble, that Choo Choo.

Back in Athens Reverend Spurrier walked the walk, greeting everyone on North Jackson Street with a plug for Jesus and Mars Hill. In 127 years the church had never had 85 children enrolled in Sunday school, or fuller coffers. Reverend Spurrier had raised almost the entire cost of the new Sunday school wing, which was $29,160.72 that didn't go to manse improvements.

From his ordeal in Miami he'd learned how to promote his church, proclaim His truth, and keep patrons like the Hubers in the fold. Deacon Huber worked tirelessly for the church. His wife preferred to remain anonymous. Her gyrations to ignore the collection basket passed through the pews at the end of a long wooden pole had the congregation chuckling.

In the spring of 1950, the elders raised their minister's salary to $2,708 a year but still wouldn't fix up the man's house. It just seemed like the preacher with the tennis racket would be striding down North Jackson Street forever.

Stevie sat on his bench, framed by the columns holding up the porch, waiting for friends to play. He could sit only so long. Bunny Duggan, son of the dry cleaner, saw something different about a kid who could pass to himself, and kept his distance.

Older boys came to play ball in the yard when the press at the *Daily Post-Athenian* broke down and they had to wait for the afternoon edition to run their paper routes. Hearing bored boys cutting up by the curb, Stevie jumped off the porch with his football, his big brother close behind.

Rusty Shultz, who went to the school up on the hill, saw Stevie walking up with the ball and told the little guy to throw it. The pass wobbled across the patch of grass between the manse and the alley.

Throwing the ball around morphed into a game the boys called "Touchdown." Fall off the curb or get stuck in the hedge and you were out of bounds. Get the ball past everyone else and you scored.

Boys bigger than Stevie ran with the ball, went out for passes, and tackled whoever they wanted. He wanted in on every play. Seeing how friends only threw to friends. He leapt to pick off passes, but he was too small. Only Graham seemed to see his little brother was open.

Finally, he had a chance to grab the ball and show the other boys what he had.

"That's my ball," he told them.

Took him eight steps to get to the house. Rusty counted. Stevie bounded up to the porch and ran inside, slamming the door. Graham went in there to try to get the ball back.

Long wait for the press to roll, with the linotype machine clattering and the time freight rumbling through town. One day the boys laughing in the alley would see that Stevie could play.

In the summer Bunny Duggan got a paper route. He'd sit on the curb folding his papers into squares, so he could "sail 'em," and see Stevie out back working on pass routes with the minister in the shade of the mimosa tree.

"Every moment Stevie can catch his dad at home, he has him out there throwing passes," Bunny told his father at the dry cleaners. Didn't do any good. Mr. Duggan was always dry-cleaning and never had time to play catch.

But Bunny wouldn't join the other paperboys playing Touchdown with Graham and Stevie. That was a pressure-packed game. The littlest player out there was the one Bunny didn't want to cross.

Couldn't miss hearing Mrs. Spurrier hollering at them when the game got too loud.

"Break it up," she told the boys arguing a call.

"Calm down," she said to her youngest son.

Bunny went back to the cleaners and told his dad he'd told him so. That Stevie Spurrier would do anything to win.

Graham played Little League baseball that summer for the Athens Giants. Stevie had to be a Giant, too, even though his uniform had to be pinned, his sleeves rolled way up, and his belt doubled. Their dad got gloves and a ball and worked with them both in the lot out back.

Before a big game they posed by the curb in their uniforms. Graham looked ready to knock one out of the city park. Stevie's ball cap hit his brother at the shoulder, as he turned to see how far he had to grow. Both Giants, in their father's view, boys of July.

The Mars Hill Congregation heard a replacement preacher in August while Reverend Spurrier drove to Carolina to see his mother and brothers. Then he took everyone except Uncle Eddie, who had to work, to Cherry Grove, South Carolina, where a friend from church loaned the pastor a beach house for a week.

Stevie thought they were going to the end of the earth, with Dad cheerfully driving and Mom looking grim. Twenty-some Spurriers and Orrs would be staying at the three-room house, which Marjorie didn't like because it was near the beach. Where would all those people sleep?

The littlest Spurrier felt fortunate to find a spot on the floor, indoors, or swaying in the swing on the screened-in porch. He'd been inland since he turned one, and the skeeters at the beach liked fresh meat.

He woke Graham at sunrise to go see the two guys in two little boats who rowed through the night and hauled ashore a net full of fish at dawn. When they emptied the big net, a heap of fish and every sea creature you could name flapped around on the sand. Graham and Stevie didn't miss a morning seeing that catch hauled in. Then they went back and played ball in the sandlot by the beach house until the family hit the surf where all those fish swam.

Marjorie stayed in the house, out of the sun, salt, and sand. Graham, Sara, and Stevie watched their dad dive into the waves and float out in the ocean for hours, out beyond the breakers, finally riding in on a wave and walking out of the water with a grin.

When Stevie's big brother tried to do that, he got stung by a jellyfish. Running behind him back to the house was Grandmother Willie. She led him to the medicine cabinet, took care of the wound, and stayed with John Graham Spurrier III until the stinging went away. Graham got ribbed about all that hollering when the men gathered around the radio for the ball game at night.

On August 11 football was in the air. The Spurriers huddled around the radio at the beach house to hear Charlie Justice play in the 1950 College

All-Star Game against the NFL champion Philadelphia Eagles. The radio announcers blamed the "small crowd" of 90,000 at Soldier Field on those newfangled TV stations televising the game and talked up running back Doak Walker, the Heisman winner. Stevie beamed when the announcers named Choo Choo the MVP, showing up Doak and the pro players.

Back at the manse Reverend Spurrier tuned in WLAR for the pennant race, rooting for whoever played the New York Yankees. Those spoiled, arrogant New Yorkers deserved to lose, Reverend Spurrier responded to the radio.

———

On fall afternoons in 1950 when the school bell rang on the hill, Stevie had his spiel ready.

"We're going to watch the big boys practice football. Don't worry, Mother. Graham will watch after me."

Marjorie trusted Graham to take Stevie around "the Friendly City," where people took vacations without locking their doors and kids said everyone downtown was "your daddy and momma." Of course, the Spurrier boys wanted to watch the Bulldogs practice. Coach Rankin Hudson had come back to his alma mater and put Tennessee Wesleyan football on the map in his second season.

He looked huge from up on the hill, calling plays, calling out players, glowering and whistling until they ran the play right. At last he whistled the Bulldogs into the locker room in the big brick gym, and the neighborhood boys had the run of the football field.

None of them could run 100 yards, so they played near the end zone that had an actual goalpost, though they couldn't kick the ball over it. They needed official rules and captains to choose up sides. They'd play three against three until other guys stopped to watch and wanted to play, too. Stevie said teams should be able to trade picks, so he could be on Graham's side.

In the huddle he had the first play. Why run that play? the other boys asked. Stevie explained how the play worked against the defense, down, and distance the Bulldog offense just faced in practice. It was easier not to argue with him. Graham always took up for his kid brother, anyway.

The boys lined up in the T formation, like the Bulldogs, with the quarterback able to pitch to the halfback on either side. If Stevie had his way, that quarterback would be him. If the ball wasn't pitched, the halfbacks could go out for a pass. He had the patterns all worked out. Some plays called for a lateral downfield.

"If you're getting tackled, lateral it back," he always said.

The main rule was kill the guy with the ball. Maybe girls played touch; the boys on the Bulldogs' field played tackle. Other rules could be debated. Stevie always seemed to know how Coach Hudson would whistle it. When he got tackled behind the line on a running play, the tackler had to be offside.

When Graham took over at quarterback, Stevie had to okay the play. Or he'd draw up his own pattern and say, "Toss it to me, Graham, toss it to me."

He was the smallest and the slowest. Couldn't outrun his sister. Bunny saw them race. But Graham always managed to get the ball to his brother, with a handoff or a pass. No one would run harder or squirm more going down.

"All you have to do is get past the guys in the backfield," Graham advised.

He got loose down the sideline and hauled in a long bomb. Bunny went after him, dove at those little legs, and got kicked under the chin. He could smell his teeth smoking, like at the dentist. Stevie jogged back to the huddle like it was no big deal.

"Good catch," guys said to him. "Way to go."

Stevie shrugged them off. He'd expected to score. But when they got the ball back and Graham threw it to someone else, Stevie let Graham know he'd been open.

Bunny skinning his teeth was about the worst injury out there. The grass was thick, and the boys didn't have far to fall.

Losing hit Stevie the hardest. He couldn't stand falling behind. When the other team scored and a comeback didn't look likely, he started crying. Then he grabbed the ball and ran off the field.

"I'm going home," he yelled over his shoulder.

"Leave the football!" Graham hollered. Everyone else yelled, too.

"Why are we always using Stevie's ball?" Bunny had to ask.

Why does he take the game so seriously? they all wanted to know. He played like a crowd was watching, cheering or booing. The kid was five. No one could remember him ever playing Cowboys and Indians, or Blind Man's Bluff. He only played ball. He only played to win.

Grumbling about the game ending, walking back to North Jackson Street, they knew he'd be out on the porch flipping the ball in the air, waving them over. His mom would ask if they wanted lemonade and home-baked cookies.

The manse always seemed dark, even with the windows open, letting in the clattering across the alley. The wooden walls were darkly stained, with dark brown trim. But the old oak floors held a golden vision. Mrs. Spurrier was taking harp lessons at the college and had a heavenly harp in the living room.

While the boys downed drinks and cookies and rehashed the game, Reverend Spurrier dashed through the living room like he was off to save someone.

"The minister's wife is a great housekeeper," Bunny told his folks back at the cleaners. Keeping up that dark old house had to be hard.

Rusty Shultz's mother didn't allow her son inside other people's homes. He'd go as far as the front porch if he and Stevie had played on the same side. But Mrs. Shultz approved of Rusty attending the youth rally held every Saturday at a different church in town. The night the youth gathered under the solemn oak rafters at Mars Hill, Reverend Spurrier called new believers to the altar and Rusty came forward.

"That's where I became a Christian," he'd always say.

Reverend Spurrier's sermon had sealed the deal. He was out to win souls. He'd saved Rusty from entering that den of iniquity across the street, the Slop Shop.

The minister forbade his children to go in there. College guys drank Cherry Cokes and twirled girls around to the doo-wop on the jukebox. Pinball machines clanged at all hours and took nickels out of young people's pockets to play.

It looked like the picture of a small-town Southern drugstore, from the porch across the street. Stevie's friends said it used to be a stagecoach stop. It sure sounded like fun in there.

Also off limits to the Spurrier children was the Strand Theater, where Saturday matinees cost 15 cents, soft drinks were a dime, and popcorn took 5 cents. Graham, Sara, and Stevie never went in there, either. But no ball playing on Sunday was a hard rule for the boys to follow. Sneaking off to play, they watched for lightning bolts. Of course, they believed people shouldn't *work* on the Lord's Day, when all the stores were closed—except the Slop Shop, which had clearly signed away its soul to bop nonstop.

On a crisp fall afternoon, with the jukebox playing the Platters, Burkette Witte served up a burger to a new guy sitting in the booth by the window. Everybody on North Jackson Street knew Burkette, the jovial black cook at the Slop Shop; one day he'd be elected mayor of Athens. Lee Willett was just another guy getting into college on the GI Bill. He looked out the window and saw a man in tennis clothes running out of a "parsonage," leaving a boy standing on the porch, flipping a football in the air.

The new guy on campus turned to see that he was the talk of the Slop Shop and told them all to call him Doak. He'd be playing for the Bulldogs, wearing No. 22. Nicknamed for Doak Walker, he said fans mistook him for Choo Choo.

He'd made it to college after the war because a 300-pound lineman for the Bulldogs named Big Ed heard Doak was organizing an all-star game for veterans in Lenior City, and he loaned Doak Tennessee Wesleyan's uniforms. After Doak returned a punt 95 yards for the game's only score and Big Ed returned the uniforms, he told Coach Hudson about the army vet who could play ball. But the only "scholarship" Coach Hudson had was a cheese sandwich before every game, and a pint of milk from Mayfield Dairy if the team won.

"He offered me that and I grabbed it up," Doak told the crowd in the Slop Shop. "Got my GI Bill paying for classes."

They were ready to root for number 22.

Getting the hang of college life, Doak passed by the clay tennis court above the football field and saw that minister from Mars Hill was out to win. If he lost a point, he'd sling his racket into the net and yell "Dadgummit," or something. Not shy about trying to beat Dr. J. Van Coe, dean of students, professor, and Tennessee Wesleyan's tennis coach.

Then Doak saw the minister running down the serves of local bigwigs Brody Ellis and Jones Beeme, two of the "suits" who ran the town. The man of the cloth had connections. Doak saw him shooting baskets in the gym. Pretty athletic, to be built so big.

On North Jackson Street Doak saw the minister make a smooth move in the barbershop, where he brought his boys in for a haircut, nodded at the barber sweeping hair off the floor, and walked out without paying. Mr. Duggan let the minister walk out without paying for the family dry cleaning. And in Harrod's Grocery Doak watched the minister give the cashier a nod and walk out with a full sack of groceries, saying, "A preacher's salary is not too much, especially in a small town."

The cashier there was a cute blonde named Johnnye, whom Doak couldn't forget. He would marry that girl someday.

Feeling more hopeful, curious about the minister, Doak went to Mars Hill on Sunday and found out Reverend Graham Spurrier preached to a packed house in a three-piece suit. His flock said they could count on a good sermon every week—and a visit from the pastor right around suppertime. They knew he'd been raised up in the land of Billy Graham, the evangelist who was converting huge crowds to Christ at "Crusades" around the country. Reverend Spurrier would talk about Billy over a good home-cooked meal.

Late in the fall, when Stevie and Graham took turns jumping off the garage roof into the mimosa leaves, Doak finally saw Reverend Spurrier at a Tennessee Wesleyan game. Didn't take long for the minister to start talking about his youngest son.

Stevie still rooted for Choo Choo, Reverend Spurrier said, even though Charlie Justice hadn't lit up the scoreboard for the Washington Redskins.

Doak told Reverend Spurrier he'd worn No. 22 in high school, and when he was warming up for a game in Asheville, "the colored kids in the stands started yelling, 'Choo Choo!'"

Reverend Spurrier said he looked forward to seeing how number 22 for the Bulldogs would do.

As the fireplace warmed the manse and Mrs. Spurrier played her harp, a big snow blanketed a park near town with a hill. Reverend Spurrier took a cardboard box from Harrod's and made a sled for Stevie and Graham to slide through the snow. Not for anything would they have slid down the hill at the college, onto the football field.

The schoolhouse doors would open for Stevie in the fall. Around Eastertime Stevie wanted his big brother to walk him up to the schoolhouse and show him the ball fields. Not shrinking from passing the big Victorian house on the corner, Quisenberry's Funeral Home. The Quisenberrys lived there and had a swimming pool and a barn out back.

The big barn doors lurched open. Stacked up in the gloom were the shiniest, most frightening boxes Stevie ever saw.

"What's a funeral?" he asked his dad, back at the manse. He'd never been allowed to go to one at Mars Hill.

Reverend Spurrier explained that when your soul goes to heaven, your body stays in that box. You don't get out, once they put you in, was what Stevie remembered.

People sat with dead bodies all night at Quisenberry's, burning candles and chanting, his friends said. Bunny told Stevie they stacked bodies in the boxes in the barn, trying to shake him up like he shook up people on the field. Even though he was a Giant again that summer, the funeral home was one place he didn't have to be told not to go. Had to be a reason he never saw the Quisenberrys in their swimming pool.

On the family trip in August to see Grandma Willie, and the fish haul at dawn at Cherry Grove, his uncles would see how much he had grown. And in September he'd walk right past that barn, looking down on the big trains steaming through.

⚊⌒⚊

When summer vacation ended and two-a-day football practices started, Doak dropped into his booth at the Slop Shop wondering why a cloud of bats circled the parsonage in the daytime.

Those bats flew around North Jackson Street every August, said Burkette Witte. The cook wanted to know how that little boy could pace around that porch all day flipping a football up to the ceiling without ever hitting it. Weren't preachers' sons more . . . prayerful?

Doak had to agree about the boy with the ball. If he took it to the yard, the bats were gonna get beamed.

Back on the field for afternoon practice, the players ran up and down the hill until some keeled over. At the final whistle Doak limped off the field with "Socks" Alexander, the other running back in the T formation, griping about the wind sprints after the hill runs. They looked up to see the minister's son throwing the ball to some other boys. Running onto the field when the last Bulldog stepped off.

From the sideline Doak and Socks watched the boy huddle his team, take the snap, throw a completion, and huddle 'em again, drawing pass patterns on his palm.

"Littlest guy out there," Doak said to Socks. Kid looked like he'd been coached. He just needed to play. He saw Doak watching and stared back at the halfback wearing No. 22.

After the game Stevie went home like always and told his dad what he'd seen and done on the Bulldogs' field. Saying that running back with Choo Choo's number ran like the field was downhill.

On the first day of school, he got a talk from his dad and a hand from his mom. Bunny directed them past the barn full of coffins, wearing the belt and badge of the Safety Patrol. At the big wooden doorway, Stevie had his picture taken. In his short pants, short socks, and short-sleeve button-down white shirt, he stared at the camera, arms open wide, fists clenched. His neatly buzzed hair made him look all ears.

At morning recess he got to the baseball field and found out they played softball there, and kickball. Stevie wasn't going to kick a big rubber ball. He couldn't take on the giants on the basketball court, with the hoop 10 feet high. Behind the building where his brother and sister had class, he saw a rocky field with room to play a real game.

No other first grader wanted to get tackled on those rocks. A boy tried to get up a game of tag football and got shouted down. Stevie wasn't gonna just pass the ball around and not keep score.

He played softball at afternoon recess, he came home and told his folks, sadder but wiser. Soft was how they played at Forest Hill Grammar School. He'd work on his game after the last bell rang. Knowing now that no other adult cared about toughening a boy up like Coach Hudson did, and Dad.

On a Christmas without snow, Santa somehow made it to Grandma Willie's house with a big surprise. Both boys got football uniforms, with helmets, shoulder pads, and jerseys with numbers sewn on by Santa's helper. Stevie suited up and became number 22. Graham wore No. 57, like Peanut Parker, the big lineman blocking for Choo Choo his dad liked.

Ready for the gridiron, they agreed to be photographed. Graham was the big brother, so he had to play center. He got down in his stance, ready to snap the ball. Crouching behind his brother, barking signals as the camera clicked, Stevie realized the boys he played with hiked the ball by passing it, and for the first time ever he was "under center." Any team that ran the single wing lost him right there in front of the duplex on Amherst Place.

He could barely sit still for Christmas dinner, wearing his uniform at the table, making his uncles think he'd gotten even bigger.

He could imagine the surprise of the Bulldogs' halfback looking out the window of the Slop Shop, seeing number 22 in blue, white, and gold on the porch across the street.

At spring practice the TWC players saw him up on the hill in his uniform, looking with longing at the sidelines. Where the players stood and strategized was where he wanted to be.

In the Mars Hill sanctuary a Brazilian missionary seeking help educating Brazilian boys asked the lad in the front row, "Son, you're in school now, aren't you?"

"No, sir, I'm not," Stevie said. "I'm right here in church with you."

All through another Giants season, the manse and the family Chevrolet moldered in the heat. Taking a page out of his father's playbook, Reverend Spurrier had saved every penny that could be saved. He could do something about the car.

The people on Jackson Street did a double take, seeing the Spurriers cross the train tracks and pull up to the curb by the manse in a tan 1950 Buick LeSabre. Didn't come from Uncle Rezin's dealership in Charlotte. A church member owned a car lot in Athens and took care of his pastor at dealer cost. Stevie couldn't miss his dad's smile behind the wheel. When they needed a fill-up, Mars Hill member Miller Blackburn down at the Gulf station would say, "This one's on me."

When the bats overflew Mars Hill at the end of August, Stevie walked with Graham past the barn of death, up to the little brick schoolhouse by the softball field where Miss Sharp taught second grade. Fidgeting until the school bell rang and the work began.

The field at the college got stretched that fall by an older boy named Bill Heater with a major-league arm. He'd quarterback both sides, putting post and flag patterns in Stevie's palms. Bill could throw those long crossing patterns that were like pick plays, getting a little guy open way downfield. Adding to the stories of scores Stevie brought home even though he couldn't outrun anyone.

On a day made for football, he ran down the hill after Coach Hudson ran his team ragged and saw a man with a camera approaching Doak and Socks. It was the photographer from the *Daily Post-Athenian*, wanting a picture of the Tennessee Wesleyan running backs. As they lined up for the photograph, Doak hollered at the other number 22 to come down and get in the picture. The two halfbacks needed a quarterback in the middle.

Looking out at the town from the front page of the paper, the littlest player in uniform wore a goofy grin instead of his game face, with a big hand on his shoulder pads.

Doak dusted defenders that season, earning his cartons of Mayfield milk. No one could stop the "Willett Special" play he drew up for Stevie, and Coach Hudson, where the tackles shifted outside like tight ends. The photographer found two number 22s working on pass patterns after practice.

"To the post," Doak said to Stevie, motioning him long.

"Willett, turn around and pose," the photographer said.

Doak turned and posed. Stevie ran almost a hundred yards while the photographer snapped away.

"Then I turned around and threw it," Doak said, going for the bomb. "I mean, he usually caught it," he told his audience at the Slop Shop.

He lived over in the "Vet's Dorm," an ancient Quonset hut at the edge of campus where old soldiers could find quiet time. Doak's room had a cot, a pile of sweat socks his friends marked with humorous signs, and a curved ceiling plastered with pinup pictures. One afternoon before practice Doak came by for his socks and saw Stevie lying on his cot, arms behind his head, gazing dreamily at the unclad women on the ceiling. For the first time in Doak's memory, the lad look relaxed.

Doak held back a laugh and went to practice in dirty socks, hoping Stevie hadn't seen him. He had to show that boy the life of a football player was not all pinup girls and Mayfield milk. First thing he needed was bigger shoulder pads. Doak had Big Ed procure the smallest pair the Bulldogs had, big enough to make Stevie brazen.

The boy with big shoulders walked down the hill to the Bulldog sidelines, helmet on, ears alert, edging near the huddle. Coach Hudson looked over at him for a heartbeat and let him stay with the team. Giving him the biggest story to take home. Doak had introduced him to all the players as the Bulldogs' "mascot."

That got him in to see the wrestling matches Doak put on at halftime of the Tennessee Wesleyan basketball games, when the season started in November. Stevie had a pass to see "Kid Slop Shop," wearing a towel from the locker room for a cape, taking on the "Boston Strong Boy" at center floor of the sweaty brick gym by the ball field.

"I'm the good guy, Kid Slop Shop, pride of Tennessee Wesleyan," Doak explained to the *Daily Post-Athenian* reporter sent to cover the match. Doak knew a winning formula when he saw it on one of those newfangled TVs. When his opponent, Fred Fenston, made his entrance, his manager held his robe in center ring while the Boston Strong Boy sprayed his armpits with a tobacco sprayer.

"'Kid Slop Shop' put on a valiant fight," the *Daily Post-Athenian* reported, "'till Big Fred unmercifully lifted little Willett over his head and threw him to the canvas, as a moan went up from crowd."

When Big Fred walked out of the gym into the night, Stevie's friends threw rocks at the dastardly Bostonian. No rocks were thrown at heroic Doak. One of Stevie's football buddies took a shot at the Boston Strong Boy with a BB gun. But that wasn't what ended the wrestling matches.

"The action was fake, but it hurt worse than real," Doak told Stevie. "Just like on TV."

Stevie said he didn't throw rocks at the Boston Strong Boy and hadn't seen any wrestling on TV. Refusing to believe Big Fred could get the best of a player Coach Hudson had toughened up.

Stevie would take more lessons away from that field of dreams.

His mom did her work with fading hopes Mars Hill would fix up her house. A harp in the living room didn't atone for the way her family had to live. On a dark day at the manse, Reverend Spurrier heard about a church on the far side of the Smokies that needed a pastor—a downtown church with a nice manse in the neighborhood. With his wife's blessing he wrote the Pulpit Supply and Nominating Committee about replacing the pastor who'd resigned in September from the Newport Presbyterian Church.

People on North Jackson Street would tell Reverend Spurrier about Newport, in Cocke County, where Tennessee's rivers carved up the Appalachians. People came from dry counties all around to drink the moonshine bubbling in the hills, bet on roosters filleting each other with razors, proposition perfumed ladies, and fight like a bunch of drunk strangers. Making headlines around the country for mixing moonshine, cockfighting, prostitution, and murder.

Well, Reverend Spurrier had to figure, they needed a *really* good preacher at the Lord's stronghold in Newport. He drove into town for a trial sermon as a full moon lit up the railroad tracks and the river. No other pastor would outpreach *him* in that sanctuary.

At the next meeting of the Pulpit Supply Committee, Elder Reid Bailey stood up and said, "We've got to have this guy." The 42 committee members voted unanimously to offer Reverend Spurrier $3,600 a year, plus moving expenses, updates for the manse, and the monthlong vacation he needed in August. The Sunday before Christmas they read his letter at the altar, accepting their call, as a crescent moon rose over the Pigeon River.

With prayers and pep talks, Reverend Spurrier prepared his family to leave the college town they loved. Graham and Sara "understood it more," Stevie would remember. People on North Jackson Street tried to understand why the preacher would take his family to Cocke County.

Bunny saw the moving van pull up to the curb, looked at the empty lot in back of the church, and wondered if his dad would buy him a football. Realizing that no matter how aggravating it was to play with Stevie's ball, no one had been more satisfying to tackle.

The night before the Spurriers left Athens, people on North Jackson Street celebrated New Year's Eve. But they didn't carry on at the Slop Shop so loud and late; Doak Willett was a married man. Reverend Spurrier drove across the train tracks to the house Doak built to tell him and his new wife, Johnnye, good-bye.

"You showed up at just the right time," Doak said, inviting Reverend Spurrier to stay for supper. Telling Stevie's father his boy would be missed.

"He has something inside of him none of the rest of us have," Bunny told his dad at the cleaners, as the moving van rumbled away from Mars Hill.

"What does he have, son?" Mr. Duggan asked.

Bunny thought for a minute, remembering how Stevie said his dad would "reprimand" him about a bad route, a poor throw, a dropped pass, in their game of catch.

"He lives and breathes football, works at it with his whole soul. He wants so bad to be on top," Bunny said.

Mr. Duggan nodded and went back to the dry cleaning. Bunny would see how hard it was to run that business someday.

People on North Jackson Street watched Stevie leave his front porch and get into the backseat of the Buick with the football. No way did he trust the guys in the moving van with *his* ball.

CHAPTER FIVE

Backyard Rules

THE BROWN LEGHORN ROOSTER WOULD CROW IN THE NEW YEAR, sharpening his spurs to catch the smallest, slowest boy on the field. Stevie and his dad had to puff up, too, riding through a warm, drizzly hillside neighborhood in Newport, Tennessee, to a white, two-story frame house with a wide front porch and a pecan tree out back for a goalpost.

Stevie jumped out of the car with his ball. The pecans didn't stand a chance.

They had a manse with two parlors and two fireplaces, an airy kitchen, and shiny maple floors. Of course, Stevie had to take his stuff upstairs to the corner room he'd share with Graham. Their windows looked out over the mountains beyond the river running through town. Those mountains were where Stevie's friends back in Athens said that "bad stuff" happened.

Volunteer fans filled the hills they'd driven through, flying orange banners and red, white, and blue rebel flags, raising legions of roosters in hutches called "cock houses" out back. His dad probably saw that Newport wasn't a tennis-playing place.

They seemed ready for him on Sunday at the big brick church downtown with windows shaped like boats, shamrocks on the bell tower, and a buckeye tree out front. A hundred members and their curious countrymen filled the hard oak pews for Reverend Spurrier's first official sermon, about Aaron and Hur.

Standing in the lofty sanctuary with a big choir in the choir box, he put his listeners in the ranks of the Israelites, facing an army of Amalekites. Winning the battle as long as Moses held up his arms to bless the troops. As the day darkened, Aaron and Hur had to help hold up Moses's arms, biceps burning, so that his hands stayed steady until sunset.

"And Joshua smote the Amalekites with the sword," thundered the big, plainspoken man in the pulpit.

Stevie could see his dad's strategy, asking *his* troops for a helping hand to prevail over the foe. Could Moses himself lead a church to victory in Cocke County? Preachers and coaches showed you the promised land and made you face your fears.

After church the boys kicked through the buckeyes and walked around town, checking out the train station, Newport Dry Goods, the Cafe Coffee Shop and House of Country Ham in the big stone hotel, and a ball court by the river with a 10-foot basket, behind the Brown Funeral Home. That wasn't going to scare Stevie in this town. He'd learned in church you smite your enemies with assists. He'd learn to cut past Graham and spin the ball in.

Passing Cocke County High on the steep street to a new school, Graham, Sara, and Stevie saw an odd car speeding by. Why would someone jack up the back of an old Ford way off the ground? For a town half the size of Athens, Newport moved fast. Time freights and coal trains rattled the classroom windows, whooshing through downtown, with two passenger trains a day clanging into the station.

After school Stevie went home and went to work in the backyard, propping up his football with a rock and kicking at the pecan tree. He kicked it low and wide, taking out pecans left and right. When his toe hit the spot, the ball split the upright limbs.

He moved it back, propped it up, and kicked it again. Doak and Coach Hudson always wanted more scores. He kicked a muddy brown bare spot in the backyard and got no reprimand when his father got home. Just more coaching.

"Mom and Dad think I'm more important than grass," Stevie would console himself, and keep kicking. The rough part of moving to a mountain town in the wintertime whipped through his leg and sent the ball flying over the pecan tree, making him raise his arms like a ref.

"Calm down, son," he could hear his dad say. "Work, work, work at gaining excellence."

On Sunday Reverend Spurrier preached about the need to help the Holston Presbytery Negro Work Campaign and talked up Volunteer Day in March. No one in Newport wanted to play tennis or have the preacher in for supper. The only kids at Wednesday night prayer meeting were Graham, Sara, and Stevie.

The mountains seemed homier when the snow melted, the river rose, and the cherry trees bloomed like the trees around Grandma Willie's house. Stevie felt like taking a kitchen knife and carving "Stevie" in the bookcase in his room.

When the mountains greened up all the way, the boys' thoughts turned to baseball.

At the city park they found a field for all seasons, with bleachers, bases, and goalposts, by a pavilion that held square dances and a tennis court used mainly for cakewalks. People paid to walk past mounds of homemade cakes and cookies on the clay court until the music stopped, and they could claim the cake or cookies they stood beside. Most everyone in town went to the park, to see who was there. But they didn't play tennis or Little League baseball at Newport City Park, the boys told their dad.

He said he'd go to bat for them, and he wouldn't have to go far. The town dentist, Dr. Hobart Ford, known to give horse hide instead of toothbrushes to ball-playing patients, would be the baseball man to see.

Dr. Ford had been part owner of the Charlotte Hornets when the team scouted Eddie Spurrier. The Knoxville Smokies and the late Newport Canners, who'd played their last season in 1950 at the city park, were likewise partly owned by the dentist, a buckeye throw across East Broadway.

Pictured in his waiting room was the team he named for the Stokely–Van Camp workers at the plant on the river, which canned the vegetables growing on the bluffs around Newport—except for a slice of the corn crop that went to the distillers. Dr. Ford liked to hire ballplayers from Cuba who could help with the local harvest and train there all year. In the glory days of the Canners, he'd looked into bringing over a college star from Havana. But that left-handed pitcher named Fidel Castro turned out to be too mean even for Newport.

Reverend Spurrier came home and told his boys they'd be playing in the new Little League he and Dr. Ford had started. And they were invited to the dentist's house by the river to play ball with his son, Toby, and meet the meanest rooster in town.

Everybody in Newport probably said their rooster was the meanest, but a ball game was a ball game.

They showed up at the Fords' house on a Saturday when the ConAgra trucks rumbling by on the Asheville Highway, and a time freight crossing the trestle over the river, couldn't drown out the football game in Toby's front yard, the basketball game in his driveway, or the boys playing baseball out back, cheered on by girls on the sidelines and a pent-up rooster screeching.

The Fords had a sloped front yard, with good grass, brambles, yuccas, and a big white bush with snowball flowers that could factor into pass patterns. To get in the game, the brothers from Athens had to play on different sides.

"What are the rules?" Stevie asked in the huddle.

"Rules?" said the kid playing quarterback. "This is Newport."

No counting "Mississippis" before rushing in. Just kill the quarterback. They didn't even count first downs. Score in four plays or die. Bleeding players kept playing. They all towered over Stevie. So he knew he could score on them, with their ball. He wouldn't run home from this game unless someone got killed.

Under the tall white columns of a plantation house, windows gleaming with mahogany furniture and a grand piano, Toby's folks watched 20-some kids play ball in their yard. Mrs. Ford set out lemonade and hot dogs on the porch and made a store run when the hot dogs ran out. Girls came around front to cheer on the football players. Graham's team had him guarding his little brother.

Stevie ran straight to the snowball bush, got Graham going the other way, button-hooked back for the ball and got it in the end zone. Not hooting or throwing his arms up. Showing he'd been in the end zone before, on a real field.

After always playing on Graham's side, scoring on him was a whole new ball game.

At halftime Stevie heard crowing from the baseball field.

They played on some good grass out back, a field of dreams between the garden, the tobacco crop, and the rooster pen, with a ball made from a paper bag wrapped in "tar tape." A spiked tobacco-picking stick was the bat. A hit into the rooster pen was an out. The two smallest players on the field had to "choose up" on the bat to see who went in there after the ball. At least that was the rule when Stevie showed up.

That big rooster with the giant red comb didn't have a name, Toby said, it was just fast. His dad went in the henhouse for eggs on Sunday, hoping the Saturday ball game had tired that rooster out.

After a hit into the rooster pen, Stevie lost the "choose-up."

"Grab the ball and run for your life," said the boy whose fist topped the bat.

Stevie wasn't that fast. The rooster spurred him, drawing more blood and jokes from the football players. They all said he wasn't getting picked on because he was the littlest. Friends fought all the time. The rooster just hated everybody.

"That rooster picked you out special," Toby said, knowing a rival when he saw one.

Back at the manse his dad asked if he got beat up at the Fords' house.

Just met the rooster, Stevie said. Didn't have a name you could say in church.

A rooster wouldn't quit fighting until it was dead, people in Newport said. Stevie believed that if you could hit a wadded-up bag with a tobacco stick, you could hit a baseball.

———

Reverend Spurrier thanked Dr. Ford for keeping his boys off the streets on Saturday, when people from the hills came to town. The salesmen with the microphone and the umbrella sold an elixir that would eat though leather and cure any ill. And at the Winston Theater, wayward youths handed over 14 cents to see what happened to Hopalong Cassidy, Lash LaRue, Gene Autry, and Roy Rogers that week. But Graham and Stevie didn't care if Kryptonite killed Superman. They had ball games to play.

When school let out up on the hill, Reverend Spurrier's children spent the first two weeks of summer at Vacation Bible School in the church basement, where their father, the "superintendent," huddled the young people for talks about the Lord. Then the games began at the city park, in the new Newport Smoky Mountain Little League.

Stevie was finally on "a real team," he said, playing for the Cardinals, not a Giant like Graham.

The Giant played. The Cardinal sat on the bench, sweating in his wool uniform until the last out of the season.

Reverend Spurrier stood in the bleachers at every game, hollering, "Give us a pitcha'! Give us a pitcha'!" Wanting whoever was pitching replaced by one of his sons.

Only one fan in a hundred yelled that loud, Graham and Stevie heard other parents say—the preacher who "despised getting beat." Little Leaguers had to go up against all the Spurriers, people in Newport said, claiming the Spurrier family would "storm out of the park" if the Giants or Cardinals got beat. Some parents went to games only on Wednesday, the Spurriers' prayer meeting night.

On hot summer days when the river lazed through town, Graham got Stevie to play basketball behind Tip Brown's father's funeral home and schooled his little brother in front of their friends. In Newport Stevie had Graham guarding him in a whole new way.

He played baseball better, in the lot between Brown Funeral Home and city hall—where you had to get a good hit. Foul balls dropped into coal cars rolling down the line, or landed on top of the police station, where Stevie's gang went to jail for 15 minutes for climbing on the roof to get their ball back.

The boys took him over to the Gateway Garage and showed him a Ford getting a set of "special shocks." Those cars looked jacked up when they were empty, but any kid could see they rode normally with a ton of liquor in the trunk.

"Can't figure out why people make such negative comments about my home," Stevie heard Junior Clark, a Sunday school teacher, say to Reverend Spurrier after church. Junior taught the adults in the Pioneer class.

"Those bootleggers, after all, they're making a living."

The preacher just nodded.

Can't argue with Mr. Clark, Stevie's dad said. He stormed the beach at Normandy on D-Day and couldn't talk about the war without crying. He lived out in Jaybird, where they had a colored church and lots of blue jays.

The guys who played ball at Toby's house on weekends played football during the week in the Shepards' yard by Lauren Alley, a vacant lot near Paradise Alley, or the Johnsons' backyard, on patchy grass bristling with shrubs and pecan trees that worked into play calls. Stevie took the ball and ran until he scored or got nailed. No amount of blood would make him quit.

Afternoon pickup games broke up in time for Stevie and Graham to get in a swim at the pool in the park, dash home for dinner, and show back up at the park in baseball uniforms.

Graham was "intimidating" on the mound, Tip Brown said after Graham struck him out three times in one game. When Tip went home from school the next day, Reverend Spurrier stood on the church steps, waiting to say, "You couldn't do anything with Graham last night, could you?"

Tip said the minister trying to break his spirit had that killer instinct Stevie was going to get.

In the last game of the season, with the Cardinals way ahead in the final inning, they finally sent him in, to play right field. A rope strung on poles marked the fence line, and it was pretty dark out there. Twice the batter swung and missed. Then he hit a high fly ball across the night sky, "getting closer and closer" as Stevie backpedaled into the rope.

"Did you catch it?" The umpire had to walk out into the dark to ask.

"No, I dropped it," Stevie, the preacher's kid, had to say.

He'd never forget having to say that.

———

In August they followed the Southern Railway tracks across Carolina to Grandma Willie's house, where the road didn't end. Graham Spurrier drove his children 8 or 10 miles out Sardis Road to their Uncle Bob and Aunt Blandina's new house in the country. Passing a windmill that caught Stevie's eye, whirling over a miniature golf course. He had a quarter in his pocket from his mom, betting that when they got to Uncle Bob's house his brother would have coins jingling—and they could get golf clubs in their hands.

The Spurrier brothers shook hands, and the Buick drove away. Mom and Dad would stay with Grandma Willie. Graham, Sara, and Stevie took in the empty lot across the street, marked by hickory, magnolia, and maple trees with roots jutting up but not too many rocks.

The kids in the neighborhood played hide-and-seek and kick the can in the vacant lot until the boys from Tennessee showed up; then they only played ball games. A tomboy named Mary Boyd Abernathy, who lived in the dark red brick house next door to Uncle Bob, didn't mind playing tackle football with whatever rules they had in Newport.

Stevie threw a touchdown pass over his big brother's outstretched hands, in the Carolina sun. He could see Uncle Bob watching the game from his window across the street. When their dad drove out to check on the children, Uncle Bob had his big brother watch from the window instead of coming out on the field.

At night, Stevie had visions of out-dueling that windmill. Uncle Bob agreed to take the boys to the miniature golf course and stake their game.

"Give Stevie a quarter, he'll come back with a dollar," he told his new wife.

"Why's that?" Blandina wanted to know. He was just a little boy.

"He has to be the best at everything," said Uncle Bob, waiting for the day he could beat his nephew at tennis.

Stevie didn't have an answer, walking back in the door, for why he still had a quarter from his mom, the quarter from Uncle Bob, and three of Graham's quarters. Their father drove out to the country to get his children and found Bob at the window, watching Stevie draw up a play in the dirt and make it work.

~

Back in Newport, time to hit third grade and then bike down to the high school to see what the Fighting Cocks could do. They had a hill for watching practice, but their field couldn't be stepped on. It was brick-hard clay.

"Eat salt tablets," the coach told the players. "Don't drink water." That team would be ready to play a game on grass, with a water bucket on the sidelines, Coach Hudson would say.

Seeing how the Cocks' kicker kicked the ball off the clay, Stevie biked down the alley and propped up his ball with a Stokley–Van Camp can. Kicking it over the cross-limb, he pumped his fist, settled down, and kicked the next one through, like the kicker for the Cocks could do.

When autumn leaves blazed up English Mountain, a church member gave Reverend Spurrier three tickets to a University of Tennessee football game, in Knoxville, just a little more than an hour down the road along the river. The Spurriers walked through the game day throng, admiring the sparkling SEC school on the Tennessee River. In their seats high in the stadium, by the huge Volunteers sign, they watched the orange team score and felt the stands rock. Tennessee's new coach had been the team's quarterback, and he celebrated with his players like he still was one. Turning Stevie and his father and brother into Volunteer fans on that Big Orange day in Knoxville. That would be news to people on North Jackson Street in Athens.

With the zeal of a convert, Stevie drove to Montreat with his dad for a church synod meeting, on a weirdly warm, crystal-blue Florida kind of October Saturday in the Carolina mountains when Tennessee was playing bitter rival Alabama at Legion Field in Birmingham—and the *Newport Plain Talk* reported the game would be "televised." Reverend Spurrier knew people from his old church in Miami Beach who had a house in Montreat, and a television.

Those church members were hosting their pastor, Dr. Willis Garrett, who'd driven up from South Florida to attend the synod meeting. They were all surprised to see the former pastor at the door, asking if he and his son could watch a football game on their television set.

"We've got to see this game," Reverend Spurrier said.

His former church members tuned the TV to NBC, saying that boy they baptized when the war ended sure had grown.

He watched every play, talking strategy with his dad, "fascinated" by the play calls and coaching moves, Dr. Garrett noted, watching Stevie watch the game.

Talk around the First Presbyterian Church of Miami Beach was that Reverend Spurrier got "very discouraged" after they let him go and had to sell insurance in Charlotte. Making Dr. Garrett believe his predecessor paid the price to preach the gospel to yacht captains trying to look like Christians.

The Volunteers and the Crimson Tide played to a zero-zero tie on the TV screen. Stevie bounced up and went outside to play like the Tennessee players played. Reverend Spurrier turned to Dr. Garrett and said, "No hard feelings for what happened in Miami."

Dr. Garrett just smiled. In some games a tie was a win.

—◦—

The devil hit Newport on Halloween, soaping windows, egging cars, toilet-papering yards, reminding believers he could be anywhere. The last Sunday in November, Stevie sat in church watching his dad ordain Reid Bailey—elected deacon by a grateful congregation. Thanks to Bailey's endorsement of Reverend Spurrier, they had a pastor who filled the pews, the coffers, and the youth room at Newport Presbyterian Church, defying the guy with the pitchfork.

"Didn't matter how old you were, you could understand his message," said Jimmy Lindsey, the young buck the preacher kept after to get more involved in the church. Lindsey played semipro baseball—and coached the basketball team at Newport Grammar that no middle school in the county could beat.

Lindsey admired Reverend Spurrier's winning formula: "He'd tell you a story out of the Bible in his words, so you'd get it."

Coach Lindsey told the preacher his son Graham had game. Filling Stevie with pride, and longing, on the front row in the big gym downstairs, where the Warriors got playmaking from his brother. He could sit only so long. Stevie wanted to blow past Graham to the hoop and asked his dad to put one up at the manse.

While Graham practiced at school, Stevie would dribble in the gravel and shoot at the hoop above the garage and kick the ball off the can, clearing the cross-limb higher and higher, until his brother got home to play one-on-one. Knowing their father had his belt handy if the boys couldn't just play ball.

When the Buick made it through the mountains to Charlotte to celebrate Christmas, 1953, Santa Claus and number 22 in blue were officially history. Stevie opened a package his mom had wrapped and got the best gift imaginable—a real plastic kicking tee. That tee cost her 49 cents, she said, after her grateful son was out the door. The maple tree down the block was in Yuletide trouble.

"I think I surprised him with that tee," Marjorie said. "He didn't know he was gonna get it."

Was he surprised to get that gift from Mom instead of Santa, the family wanted to know. Uncle Bob thought his nephew "smelled a rat" and "knew Santa was really Dad."

"I think Steve just sorta eased into not believing in Santa," Marjorie said. Back in Newport, he reveled in the truth.

"I now had one of the few kicking tees owned by any boy in town."

Almost perfect, kicking the ball off the tee and through the pecan tree, he burned to hit those field goals on a basketball court.

That summer Reverend Spurrier hollered, "Give us a pitcher," and Stevie walked out to the mound for the Cardinals. Graham went to bat for the Giants. Giving his best imitation of his big brother, Stevie struck Graham out. God and everyone saw that umpire send his brother back to the dugout. Stevie heard batters say they didn't know if his pitches would cross the plate or hit them in the head. But he knew he didn't intimidate batters like Graham did, not yet.

Reverend Spurrier took his boys on an August pilgrimage to three baseball shrines in New York City. At Ebbets Field in Brooklyn they saw the Dodgers play. At the Polo Grounds they saw Giant Willie Mays star in a win over the Philadelphia Phillies, catching the last out in center field and throwing the ball into the stands. Stevie wouldn't forget that someday, when he ran into Mays.

Lastly they went to Yankees Stadium, home of the hated New York team, for "Old Timer's Day." On the field in front of Stevie were Connie Mack, Cy Young, and former president Herbert Hoover. Showing that good people could be found in the enemy camp.

On a warm, clear November Saturday, Stevie told his team in Toby's front yard that he and his brother and father had tickets to see the Florida Gators play the Vols that night in Knoxville, thanks to Dr. Ford.

"I'm sorta thinking of rooting for Florida," he told the guys. "Because, you know, I'm from there. I was born there."

"You can't root for Florida," they scoffed. "This is Tennessee. We're all for Tennessee here."

He stood up in the stands, cheering for the team all in orange, looking down on the orange end zone Tennessee couldn't get into. The Gators pushed back the Vols, scored two touchdowns, and beat the home team 14–0 as the temperature plunged into the 30s. A chill couldn't keep Stevie from being a Volunteer.

Reverend Spurrier organized a year-end cleanup at the Presbyterian Cemetery, where tombstones from frontier days crumbled across the hilltop. His sons and their friends camped out in the woods in back of that graveyard, toasting marshmallows and telling tales, daring dead people to come out from behind the trees. Traffic and trains screeching through downtown sounded like screams from the hills in the stories Stevie's friends told around the fire.

He wasn't scared of flames and dirt, growing to believe if you played all out, every day, when they put you in that box you'd be ready to rest.

That Christmas Reverend Spurrier got a raise, along with annuity payments, money for manse upkeep, and all expenses approved for the youth services he wanted to conduct at Montreat. That was a holy place, high in North Carolina, where a preacher could breathe pure mountain air and get his boys out of Newport.

Marjorie Spurrier continued to receive $100 a year for playing the piano, directing the choir, and working up the bulletins her children folded for delivery on Sunday morning. No combat pay for living with the swats and yells overhead, back and forth across Graham and Stevie's room. Over the Ping-Pong table their dad brought home they fought like tennis pros.

When the last bell of fourth grade rang, the boys filled the yards with passes and the park with pitches. Stevie had worked up a curveball batters didn't see coming, and they struck out or got beamed. Toby watched the parade of strikeouts until the Yankees were one run down in the ninth, with a man on base.

"Get in the box and don't step out," said Coach Lindsey, seeing how Stevie's curveball could be hit. Toby blasted a game-winning home run off his rival's pitch. For once, Spurrier could be figured out.

"You have to fight Reverend Spurrier and Stevie both," marveled Junior the Sunday school teacher, watching father and son stomp out of the park like both of them gave up the winning hit.

Vacation Bible School took up the last week in June, and summer Christianity got competitive. Stevie outdid all the other believers in the youth room, memorizing 100 Bible verses and winning a free week at Children's Bible Mission Camp. The word of the Lord that his father handed down went from a piece of paper to his heart.

More reason to score all the points that could be scored at the Fords' house, on the Saturday a black kid calling himself Big Jim showed up to play football.

"We'll play with whoever," Stevie said, taking Big Jim on his team, acting like he didn't hear comments the other team made. Why should a kid who had to go to the black school have to stay at Tanner School? Big Jim saw a game going on at Toby's house and wanted to play. And Big Jim could play, Stevie saw.

He stood with members of his youth group, professing his faith in Jesus Christ in July 1955, before the deacons, the elders, and his father, who noted that, "Following an examination as to his faith, it was voted to receive him into membership of this church, on profession of faith."

"Made my personal decision during Vacation Bible School," he told the men of the church, getting in a plug for the VBS superintendent.

He got to go to Florida, spending the last two weeks of the summer in Orlando, where guys could play ball under the palm trees all year. The family stayed at the house of a preacher his dad knew from South Florida.

But they didn't talk much about Miami Beach, Stevie noticed. Trying to square the story his father told his brother, about the pastor returning from the war who "wanted his church back," with whisperings from his mom, that maybe the eager young preacher had "come on too strong" in his sermons by the water.

That didn't surprise Stevie. He'd seen that "Dad was an aggressive minister. There's no halfway being a Christian. He wanted everybody to be totally committed."

Maybe, Stevie thought crossing the bridge back to Georgia, he could show the people down South what a team of believers could do.

His fifth-grade teacher, Miss Reba Williams, demanded excellence and took no sass, he found out the first day in her class. She had a big oak paddle with a hand-carved handle she wasn't going to use on him. Some kids hated her—until she got them doing work no one else thought they could do. Stevie would have to work hard to please her. Maybe all great teachers had great expectations.

"Whoever makes it big," she told Stevie's class, "send something back to your teacher."

Stevie saw how big a man could make it when his father brought an actual television set through the door. Set up in the back parlor by the fireplace, with rabbit ears that brought the signal down from the mountains, that TV showed games Stevie never thought he could see, sitting with his dad by the fire.

The big people downtown couldn't thank their pastor enough for his "strong evangelistic effort" that added over 100 new church members, evening the odds against the moonshiners and murderers. Did Reverend Spurrier feel like a big hitter in the minor leagues? Some of his competitors shouldered rattlesnakes during sermons.

It took a hard-liner to face the devil in Cocke County. Some members of Reverend Spurrier's church would suffer a misfortune and then get a call from their pastor, asking, "What great sin have you committed, that this has befallen your family?"

Sometime they would have to answer.

Since the days he spurred church boys in West Virginia to play ball, Reverend Spurrier had organized ball games that made his youth group a force on the street. Miraculously, 30 or 40 young believers in Newport fit into a tiny lot by that big rock hotel on East Broadway for a baseball game, and no cars got hit.

The pastor who was a coach knew not to telegraph a squeeze play.

On another golden day in October, he drove across Carolina's mountaintops to evangelize young people at Montreat. That same youth retreat brought a believer named Sidney Smallwood across the mountains from Johnson City, Tennessee—where Smallwood was the athletic director of the school system and member of a committee placing pastors at satellite churches founded by the First Presbyterian Church downtown.

Smallwood had a big frame, a steely look behind his black glasses, and no children. He lived to guide young people to the Lord and the ball field, and he took on the role of guidance counselor at Montreat. At a vesper service in the mountain twilight, he heard a pastor from Newport, of all places, speak stirringly about God's plan for young souls.

When stars rose over the firelight at the final evening service, Smallwood said the kids he'd been counseling all week liked the way Reverend Spurrier told Bible stories.

"They said you talked their language."

Reverend Spurrier began talking about his family back in Newport, and how his boys played ball. Smallwood could see that pastor in a rawboned mountain town wanted out. He'd done his homework and "had heard about Science Hill High School in Johnson City, and the excellence of the academics and athletics."

Reverend Spurrier took Smallwood's hand and said, "If ever there's an opening at a church in Johnson City that needs a pastor . . ."

Smallwood promised to keep the pastor in mind. Reverend Spurrier prayed the men would meet again.

Did the Lord bless battlers on a ball field if only a leader would raise his hand? When he got back to Newport, Reverend Spurrier realized a veteran at his church needed medical attention at the Mountain Home Veterans Hospital in Johnson City, and volunteered to drive the veteran there to get care.

Stevie just wanted to outscore Graham. He hit the hoop every hour he wasn't in school, biking home to practice at lunchtime. Dribbling between his legs and laying the ball in, trying not to land in the garage.

There had to be a game. He wasn't going to just shoot and not keep score.

He'd remember that "Dad put that game together with a preacher from Morristown, whose son was a fifth grader. We had seven or eight kids come to our place for a game and we went up to their place. That was my first basketball team."

The reverend whistled the boys together in the school's tiny upstairs gym, put the ball in his son's hands, and saw what he could do.

In the first elementary school basketball game at Newport Grammar, lack of official uniforms had the team from Morristown agreeing to be "skins." Before tip-off Reverend Spurrier squeezed into the huddle and addressed the four boys who'd play with his son.

"If you start," the coach said, "you finish."

Stevie could see his big post-up guy, Mike Proffitt, working to stay out of the way. No one on either team could stop Stevie. When the last whistle blew and the shirts and skins shook hands, he'd dropped in 42 of his team's 44 points, to Morristown's 30. Hearing cheers that were his own.

Back at the manse his coach went over the missed shots, bad passes, and lost scoring chances. His dad summed up the game, in his mind's ear, by saying, "You could have done a little bit better."

Expect a different defense in the rematch at Morristown, his coach warned. And sure enough, his dad fumed, "They threw a box-and-one at him and slowed him down." Fighting through double coverage, Stevie hit 27 points to beat Morristown again, knowing a player with his ability should've scored more.

He told his dad the box-and-one defense didn't bother him. He'd never played on 8-foot baskets before. But that would be his last excuse.

"He had two men on him, the whole team on him," his mom told people after the game.

"Their two biggest men," her husband said.

"I'd get the ball, dribble up and shoot every time," he admitted to the guys at Toby's, finally stepping onto the driveway for a game.

Did that cocky scouting report get in their heads? Or could they just not stop him? Refs didn't call a charge in those days when a defender got in the way, he'd learned from playing in a real game. Suddenly, he wasn't the littlest kid playing ball at the Fords' house.

Stevie had "shot up," Toby explained to his dad, defending his defense.

The church elders gifted their minister with another raise in the New Year, to $4,200. He was fighting the good fight in Newport, but the devil could still win.

On St. Valentine's Day Stevie brought a box of chocolate-covered cherries to that new blonde in his class, Beauanne, whose dad had been hired to coach the Fighting Cocks. The old coach didn't know football players needed water. She seemed to see something in Stevie, too, her other admirer, Toby, couldn't help but notice. Toby joked that Stevie sampled the chocolate-covered cherries to make sure they were good before handing them over.

Starring in two games against Morristown got a fifth grader on the middle school's third consecutive Cocke County championship team, which went undefeated in the spring of '56. Sara cheered with the cheerleaders in their blue and gold outfits Marjorie had sewn. Reverend Spurrier stood up at every game and yelled at both teams, fitting right in with the Warriors' fans.

Parents of eighth graders who didn't make Coach's Lindsey's team were outraged his backup shooting guard was still in elementary school.

Stevie had "ball intelligence," saw the whole floor, and passed and shot as good as Graham, Coach Lindsey told the reverend. The younger Spurrier had some point to prove, diving for loose balls, contesting every shot.

Why didn't my kid make your team?" asked someone's father, busting into the conversation.

"I only keep the best," Coach Lindsey said.

"Your backup shooting guard's just a kid," said one pissed-off father.

"That kid can dunk," his coach said.

Reverend Spurrier had to be feeling like a coach whose star player had outgrown him.

They still loved him downtown. Businessmen in Newport gave him that preacher discount, too. The word *moonshine* never thundered down from his pulpit. He did what it took to win. When snow melted down the mountainside, churches and business establishments helped Reverend Spurrier promote his "March to Church in March" campaign.

In his sanctuary Graham sat on one side of Coach Lindsey and Stevie sat on the other side of the coach about to get voted out of the county by the other coaches, for winning too much. Graham told his coach he was still sore from losing a Ping-Pong game, jumping on his brother and destroying the table.

"That's hard to take, when your younger brother starts beating you."

Miss Reba Williams dismissed her fifth-grade class for the year just knowing, she said, she'd hear from Stevie Spurrier one day.

The doors opened and closed at Vacation Bible School and the summer games began. Reverend Spurrier faithfully continued driving the veteran from Newport to Johnson City every month, the church elders couldn't help but notice, in the mountain heat. Driving to Knoxville was one thing, they said. Johnson City was "a faraway place."

That was the summer Stevie would learn to sink or swim.

"Hard to learn to swim in the ocean," he said to his dad's offer of swim lessons in the surf at Cherry Grove. Hard to learn to swim at the Newport City Park with the big boys doing laps in the pool. And Stevie was still too young to attend the church camp at Montreat at the end of July.

"But they said to bring him anyway," Marjorie recalled, happy her son could get in the pool with Christian young people and learn his strokes.

Of course, her boys took their baseball and football to church camp, where they'd study the Bible in the morning, take swim lessons and play ball in the afternoon. Only the good Lord and their father could imagine how a game of catch at Montreat could change their lives.

Plenty of people would stop and watch those boys play ball. In Toby Ford's yard full of cheering girls, even beautiful Beauanne didn't get a glance from Stevie when the game was on. The Spurrier boys paid no attention to any onlookers on a summer afternoon at Montreat. Believing God always blessed their battles, they kept their eyes on the ball.

Sidney Smallwood was back in his office in Johnson City, sitting behind a desk strewn with books and magazine articles about helping young people play better ball. Where he sat when Reverend Spurrier made his monthly appearance to talk about the games his sons played in Newport and ask yet again if a church in Johnson City needed a pastor.

On a real fateful day in July of 1956, Smallwood saw "Brother Spurrier" in the doorway and greeted him with good news. An athletic booster and church official named Raymond Huff needed a pastor at Calvary Presbyterian, one of First Presbyterian's four "mission churches" in a hard-working neighborhood above Kiwanis Park.

Reverend Spurrier wanted that job. Smallwood picked up the phone and made his pitch.

"Raymond, I got someone in mind I know you're going to like. He's a minister I worked with who'd like to come to Johnson City. He gets along with the young folks and the old folks."

Huff said he wanted to hear a trial sermon. Smallwood said he wanted to know "how the youngsters like him."

God had opened the door. Reverend Spurrier would go into that sanctuary and preach until the devil ran out. After being called back for a second trial sermon at Calvary Presbyterian, missing yet another Sunday service at Newport Presbyterian, Reverend Spurrier got the job offer he'd prayed for, day after day, mile after mile, for almost a year.

Johnson City didn't make headlines like Newport, Smallwood told the preacher, but people in the neighborhood around Calvary Presbyterian were "mean as snakes." They needed strong sermons, the men agreed.

As far as the story Reverend Spurrier would take back to Newport, and bring to Johnson City, why not say Smallwood saw Stevie play ball at Montreat and then got his father the preaching job?

Only two people could know any different. Reverend Spurrier made Smallwood swear he'd tell no one in the preacher's lifetime, not even Mrs. Spurrier or Mrs. Smallwood, that he'd "recruited the reverend" and "Steve was a bonus."

Of course people would believe the athletic director of Johnson City Schools brought an 11-year-old to town to light up the scoreboard, Reverend Spurrier said, professing his faith in his son's stardom. After Reverend Spurrier had finally gotten his family out of Newport, his first impulse was to make Stevie the hero of the story.

The good father gave his son the glory, Smallwood had to agree. The impressive one at Montreat had been the preacher.

Their story didn't fool the elders of the church in Newport. Since April 22 someone else had signed the session minutes in Reverend Spurrier's name, initialed by clerk L. W. Morrow. Did a tipster reveal their pastor's intentions, or were they just street-smart? They'd undercut Reverend Spurrier's authority and paid him only $370 all summer, session minutes showed.

But no church elder would contradict the tale of an athletic director seeing Stevie Spurrier play ball and hustling his family to Johnson City. No Christian father would question how that kid could be so good a Presbyterian church would hire his dad within a week.

To his mom Stevie was simply "something special." He had the biggest fifth graders in Morristown guarding him, and still scored.

What story would her husband have to tell two boys getting back from church camp to find their lives uprooted?

Their dad promised them a football field out front with real goalposts, a "Scout Hall" next door with a basketball court, and a baseball diamond with bleachers. School would be a walk across the park.

When Stevie's father stood before the congregation of Newport Presbyterian and announced he was leaving for Johnson City, no one looked surprised. After they voted to accept his resignation and thanked him for his service, he prayed for their church, signed the session minutes himself, and walked off through the buckeyes.

"Stevie's going to be a great baseball player," Toby told his dad. Never threw down his glove, or kicked the dirt when he made an error, even though he wanted to win worse than anyone.

"I'm like that, too," Toby assured his father, "on the inside." He'd get an opportunity to play pro baseball one day—if he could battle through the injuries from the ball games in his yard.

Dr. Ford remembered Stevie always wanting to play quarterback—drawing up plays where a receiver took the ball and hit the quarterback for a score. Playing every game like he *had* to win.

"We thought we were UT in the front yard," Toby agreed, knowing the rooster out back would miss Stevie the most.

When, out of the blue, Marjorie gushed about her boys meeting the athletic director of Johnson City schools, then a moving van rumbled up to the manse, Stevie just had to realize trickery was part of the game.

In Newport they said he cried and cried when he left town, crossing the Pigeon River in the backseat with his football, watching the phone poles blur into the cock houses on the hillside. Going down the road his dad drove monthly. Still not understanding why people raised roosters to do their fighting for them.

Think how big even the littlest boy looked to a rooster.

CHAPTER SIX

Keeping Score

Who was the lone guy on the football field in Kiwanis Park, punting the ball back and forth to himself? Johnson City would find out. They'd been talking about the new kid in sixth grade, and his finger aiming, he knew.

Who could believe he and his brother had been playing ball across the mountains at Montreat in August when Sid Smallwood, athletic director of Johnson City schools, supposedly asked, "Who's your daddy?"

"He told my husband, 'We ought to have those boys in Johnson City,'" his mom liked to remember Smallwood saying. Then he got the Spurriers moved into the manse above Kiwanis Park before there was even a chance to meet him.

That was a story from a simpler time, almost another world, in the fall of 1956 in Johnson City—the first hometown in Tennessee Stevie could call a "city," boasting 25,000 people, even though he lived in a lunch pail neighborhood and shared a tiny back room with his brother. The houses on Wilson Street, the manse, the church, and Scout Hall were built from the same batch of home-baked bricks. Families ran in and out of the hillside houses without locking their doors. While just down Market Street the lights shone on brick buildings that took up the block, a big brick football stadium, and streets teeming with taxis from two cab companies, wide enough to hold a parade.

The clank and blare of downtown trains echoed through Kiwanis Park like old friends. Kids at school joked about the Tweetsie Railroad, the tourist train in Boone, North Carolina, that had steamed through Johnson

City during the Depression and the war, when people around town called the ET&WNC the "Eat Taters and Wear No Clothes Railroad."

Guarding Wilson Street from the west was Mountain Home National Cemetery, where war heroes slept under blade-perfect grass behind black iron gates. Yet the rows of tombstones didn't haunt a boy living a block away. Old soldiers saluted, limping proudly through the graveyard to the big brick Veterans Hospital—like the veteran from Newport Reverend Spurrier still brought to the hospital every month. He'd drive over to Cocke County, transport the veteran to Johnson City, drive him back to Newport, then drive home, showing great gratitude for that man's service.

Happy to have the field to himself, thankful for another "neat" place to live, Stevie put his foot through the ball, into the sky. Aiming to show how a boy from Johnson City played ball. Wondering who could *really* coach him here—and make his dad sit down.

—✦—

From the get-go Kiwanis Park was his turf. The football field below his little red brick house was part of his yard. The sixth-grade football team at Henry Johnson Elementary School played on that field, with helmets, shoulder pads, and real rivals.

Of course, he heard the snickers in the game against Stratton Elementary, playing fullback, going up against big Jerry Harkleroad on defense.

"How'd that slow kid get by you?" teammates razzed Harkleroad.

"I went to hit him and he wasn't there yet."

Who or what was "Orr," the boys from across town wanted to know.

"Dunno," Harkleroad said. "That's what *his* team called him."

Mostly, they listened to his play calls, even though he wasn't the quarterback. Seeing how badly he wanted the ball with the game on the line. Eleven was turning out to be a good year—thanks to the athletic director his dad called to talk over every game his son played. Orr had big ears poking out. He heard things.

On Saturdays he heard radios on the hillside squawking about the Volunteers. On Sundays, after folding bulletins and listening to the Sunday school lesson and the sermon across the street, he, his brother, and their father could watch the Washington Redskins play in the living room. The Lord permitted watching sports on Sunday on TV. The rabbit ears pulled in Channel 3 from Charlotte, where they broadcasted the games of "Dixie's Team."

Funny how a team your father watched became yours. The big guy in the recliner would have to sit up and take notice if his son became a Redskin. But rushing out the door with the ball to imitate the players in burgundy and gold wasn't allowed that day.

When a beer commercial came on, his father got up and stood in front of the screen. When the boys went out the door, maybe to sneak in some ball playing on the Sabbath, he watched the yard, the park, and Scout Hall.

That fall the Hilltoppers of Science Hill High School played in the red brick stadium downtown, and the Spurriers walked right past the Doughboy statue and the red brick ticket booth. Church members made sure their pastor had tickets for the Oak Ridge game, even though no one gave the home team much of a chance against the defending state champs.

Somehow, the 'Toppers beat the Wildcats 26–13 that night, with the band gyrating and the crowd screaming loud enough to hear in Kingsport. Orr went home talking over the winning plays with his dad, saying someday he could play on that field.

Reverend Spurrier wouldn't tell his son he had no doubt. Lot of work ahead to make that happen, he insisted.

The boy looked out the window at Market Street speeding by, maybe aiming his finger at just the right spot.

Driving from Johnson City to Willie's house in Charlotte for Christmas, the Spurriers headed south through the hills on Route 23 and drove up a winding, gut-churning two-lane road across Sam's Gap, where the brakes started squealing. From 3,800 feet Dixie looked like Switzerland.

Wasn't Stevie getting tall? his uncles asked. When would he graduate to being called Steve?

When would Uncle Eddie get over his woes, the boys wondered, and put down that drink? He got all wound up, hollering at his brothers and his mother, until they had to put him to bed. Giving them all reason to fear his wife, Julia, was leaving him.

Maybe losing the chance to play ball was something a man couldn't get over.

When winter swirled around the manse, the boys dribbled across the yard to Scout Hall. Who'd school who, one-on-one, in that little gym? Orr never forgot a beating. Graham was still taller. When he got going, he didn't miss. But he'd have to shoot the ball with a flatter arc, under that low ceiling, which helped Orr block Graham's shot. Graham wasn't gonna just shoot and shoot, like before. The little brick gym was Orr's court. After a few chest-smashing blocks, the kind of fight that had destroyed the Ping-Pong table back in Newport got going in Scout Hall.

The whistling sound they heard was their father's belt, whirling in his hand across the yard. Graham got the whipping for fighting with his little brother.

When their father went away, they realized they could practice batting in Scout Hall on winter days, if someone would climb up to the ceiling and dig out the baseballs.

***

Graham was burning up the net downtown at the junior high, leading his ninth grade team in scoring. Maybe opponents misjudged him, seeing that lump on his knee from getting tackled in Toby Ford's yard. After football season ended at Henry Johnson Elementary, Orr asked his mom for a ride downtown to Parks and Rec. His beefy football coach, Cot Presnell, would coach the sixth-grade hoops team, too.

Coach Presnell would be stunned by the ballhandling of his fullback, who had a deadly jump shot. If you wanted to get better, play someone bigger.

Henry Johnson won the Elementary Schools Conference Championship, with Orr hitting the shots, taking the team to the Midget Gold Medal Basketball Tournament. The lights blazed on the hardwood and a huge crowd cheered, a long way from Newport. Orr scored 29 points to beat Columbus Powell School. Up against St. Mary's School for the title, some bug kept him in bed.

"He wants to play, but he looks pretty weak," he heard his mom tell his coach on the phone. From his brick bedroom in back he hollered that he *had* to play.

"It will kill him if he doesn't get to play," Marjorie told Coach Presnell, "so let him die happy."

Feebly, he put up 25 points to help Henry Johnson beat St. Mary's, 43–5, for the trophy. Dragging himself back to the floor to accept awards for high scorer, best offensive player, most outstanding player, and best sport, he stood at center court with his dad, soaking up the applause.

The man walking up to them was all business, introducing himself as Ross Edgemon and immediately offering the job of managing his Babe Ruth League baseball team to Reverend Spurrier. Giving the Steinway Bears the rights to his son for 500 points instead of a draft pick, Mr. Edgemon said, making both men smile.

"Awful anxious for me to be his assistant," his dad said at home, knowing his son "would come automatically."

That man made a good bet, the Spurriers agreed. Making spring a fresh reminder that Sid Smallwood knew talent when he saw it, making Reverend Spurrier a local legend.

On a breezy April afternoon in the ballpark below the manse, the reverend put on his shirt with MANAGER in big letters and had his team kneel by the right field line. Speaking out against the sporting belief that "It's not whether you win or lose, it's how you play the game," he told his boys they would play to win, and win big.

He told them to bow their heads, picked a player to pray for the team, and put his son on the mound and at shortstop. Made them practice their guts out. Especially the pitcher and shortstop.

The other players would never forget it, they told Orr after practice. No coach ever talked like that in Little League, much less a preacher.

Jimmy Sanders was real shook up, saying, "It's an article of faith to me that Grantland Rice was right." Of course it matters how you play the game, Jimmy argued. He'd be a great lawyer someday.

He might be able to quote some sportswriter from Nashville, Orr said, but Jimmy didn't know his manager.

That manager got the Bears off to a fast start. The team kept winning until the day the manager had to be at church and the Bears suffered their lone loss.

"Say," one of Orr's teammates pointed out, "we forgot to pray before this game started."

Reverend Spurrier picked another player to pray for the team. With the Lord's blessing restored, the Bears played team ball, without anyone grousing that the manager favored his son. Orr would be the star of any team in town.

The boys who played for Young's Supply Company, the Dr. Pepper bottling plant, the Coca-Cola plant, the VFW Hall, Morton Brothers, and Seaver's Bakery battled for the American League title, while teams representing the Dairy Queen, the Pepsi-Cola bottlers, UCT, Paty Lumber Company, and the *Press-Chronicle* all went down to the Bears. Reverend J. Graham Spurrier, manager, coached the boy he picked to pray before the title-clinching game not to ask God for a win: "Just ask the Almighty to help you play your best ball." That prayer guided the Bears to a National League Championship.

In the first game of the championship series, Orr took the mound and beat the American League champs 7–5. The Bears won the title game 11–6. Felt like that huge trophy was won in his backyard, when his dad held it overhead.

Johnson City saw moral lessons in Little League. After Reverend Spurrier brought the trophy home to the manse, Orr heard people say Ross Edgemon was the real heavy hitter, making his father a manager and the Bears champions. People who weren't regulars around the radio at Mr. Edgemon's inn, people who didn't even follow baseball, talked about how the boys who played for Reverend Spurrier got some kind of religion on the first day of practice.

The pastor at Calvary Presbyterian believed in smiting foes, and everyone in town seemed to know.

On summer days when kids could play ball until lightning bugs blinked in the dusk, Orr could tell which familes on the block had television sets.

"They should film the show *Leave It to Beaver* right here in this neighborhood," said the kids with TVs. Some guys wore coonskin caps on the street. Orr knew Daniel Boone had hidden from the Indians under a waterfall two miles away. And he remembered passing the place where Davy Crockett was born, driving into town. But he only watched ball-players on TV.

He did catch the eyes of the girls in the neighborhood looking his way. Even guys looked longingly at the ball games in the Spurriers' yard. Orr would only play tag football with girls who were cute. They were more annoying when they played basketball at Scout Hall. He liked girls who could hit shots and wouldn't ever play against them.

His father had the power to make Bible stories come alive, making church fun, bringing the neighborhood kids to Calvary Presbyterian "any time the doors were open," they liked to say. Even though Reverend Spurrier "prayed for everybody in the world," which took time. No one said they needed to be out the door by noon. Nor did any young people disrupt the sermon, Mrs. Spurrier made sure, shushing whisperers from the choir box. Graham, Sara, and Stevie served as examples of children who believed in "the old book, the new birth, the precious blood, and the blessed hope."

Their father always wore a suit when he preached, and a shirt and tie around town, picking up kids every morning in the Buick to go to Marjorie's kindergarten. And he always answered the phone at Calvary Presbyterian. The church line rang right into the manse, carrying word of another church youth event.

Summer nights meant hayrides, bonfires, games in the park, horse-shoes, and dinners in the church basement, twice a month. No one had to bring a covered dish. The Calvary Ladies Circle cooked it all, working from morning until evening in the kitchen of Fellowship Hall.

Mrs D. R. Beason, wife of the founder, architect, and benefactor of the church, made the lightest yeast rolls—that Orr could eat more of than anyone, though he was far from the biggest boy in the contest.

The girls eyeing him wore their best dresses; their moms wouldn't let them wear slacks to church. The menfolk talked sports in the hallway.

"Winner," Orr heard them say. "His daddy just expects him to be the best."

They hadn't heard anything yet.

His friends at church sang his father's praises. In other churches, they said, the sermons went over their heads and the "Amens" were deafening.

"Your dad's not a shouter," they told Orr. He just nodded.

A cute girl named Phyllis Owens, who lived a few doors down from the manse, had worshipped with the Free Will Baptists and the "frozen chosen" Episcopalians. She was thankful, she said, that "nobody in our church says amen very loud. If they do, they're on the back row and they're a deacon." Phyllis was "scared to death" of the deacons, and of his father, Orr could surely tell. And she had a big crush on him.

She'd never forget how he urged her on in his yard, sending her long when both teams were tired, saying, "It's always too soon to quit."

The yard was empty in August, when the Spurrier children went for a history lesson at the Jamestown Festival in Virginia. Their father wanted to show them where America got started. Dwelling on the country's history, but not his own.

"Not too much did Dad talk about losing his dad," his youngest son noticed. "He'd move onto the next thing; he didn't harp on the past."

Passing back through Charlotte, they all got hugs from Willie, tearfully proud of John Graham Spurrier Jr.'s family. Her tenant, "Aunt Josie," loved hugging Stevie, too. He heard the adults discussing the baptism of Uncle Bob's son Robert, presided over by Graham Jr., who "managed to sneak in a blessing for Stevie," Uncle Bob wouldn't forget.

Uncle Eddie would still be surly when he got home from driving a truck around the state, without a wife to fix his dinner. His big brother would put him to bed and pray for a miracle.

———

Johnson City seemed bigger in the fall of 1957, with Orr going downtown to Johnson City Junior High, in the shadow of the brick fortress that was Science Hill High School. Becoming a "Baby Hilltopper" made him friends with guys he'd run into at sixth-grade football games, full blast, and guys he'd played against in the Babe Ruth League. He remembered who the "hot dogs" and cheaters were, picking teams on the playground. He could see some guys who went after him in grade school wanted to be on his side all along.

Tough little Cotty Jones (son of the *Press-Chronicle* publisher), Carroll "Mo" Vance, "Big Boy" Ken Lyon, witty Joe Biddle, "Corsica" Joe Cowell, stand-up guy Ralph Cross, Larry "Choo" Tipton, Gary "Fish" Fisher, Tommy "Little Scab" Hager, wily Jimmy Sanders, and loyal Lonnie Lowe, all friends of Orr, ready to take on junior high. With all the fights at school, they'd best stick together.

Playing ball in the gym one day, they looked up to see the athletic director of Johnson City schools standing on the overhead running track, looking down at Stevie Spurrier like he'd never seen him before. He hadn't. Orr looked up and got back to the game. Smallwood was his dad's friend. Orr was just one of the guys, puzzled why his friends kept saying he didn't have a best friend.

"Do you have to pick just one?" Orr would ask. Winning took a team. Those guys were his linemen, his receivers, his backs, his center, his point guard, his power forward, his outfielders, fellow pitchers, and shooting guards. Enough friends for an afternoon game, with a lifetime of possibilities shining down through the leaves.

"What's with that finger-aiming thing?" they all asked Orr on the ball field. No one could seem to remember his answer.

They all wanted to play football with the high school guys in Kiwanis Park. The big guys played rough, and they'd let only Orr play. He could punt for both sides. Real boomers. Cotty paced around like he'd do anything to get on the field. He lifted weights every spare moment, trying to bulk up. Couldn't get Orr to pick up anything heavier than a basketball.

"The Lord made us different," his father preached to the white people on Wilson Street, "and we are supposed to live apart."

His youngest son was never seen in the Slop Shop in Athens, or at the Saturday matinee, but he dribbled down Market Street in broad daylight to the "black kids' Boys Club" that opened in Johnson City in the summer of 1958. Carver Park "probably wasn't part of the real Boys Club," Orr realized, but the park had the best pickup basketball games in town. So that's where he and his friends went to play ball. Shirts and skins, gotta win by two, winners kept the court.

"Game over, we go back to our side of town and they go back to their side," he explained to people wondering what he was doing playing ball over there. Knowing people would talk.

Back in the pews, thinking on his sins, he listened to his mother play the piano and sing "How Great Thou Art" and "Peace Like a River," sounding like an angel, making his dad smile. Those old hymns would resound inside him whenever critics got loud.

He took up the trombone and, when drafted, sang in his mother's choir. Still hadn't missed a Sunday at Sunday school. Holding the rank of "Tenderfoot" in Scout Troop Thirty-Seven, no matter how many times he went over to Scout Hall without his basketball. He told people he went to the movies once a year, whether he needed to or not.

He could see Phyllis, down the street, and her friend Regina watching him throw a football in his yard, where his dad still wanted to play. Of course, he heard the question asked around church.

"Does the minister push Stevie more than his other two children?"

"Reverend Spurrier just expects more of all the young people of Calvary," Phyllis said, calling her pastor "a mentor, somebody to look up to." She'd see Orr passing the football in the yard every day with his dad, or with Graham, but not the three of them together.

When eighth grade started, Orr borrowed a tennis racket, entered the citywide tennis tournament, and brought home a trophy, to show his father how equality worked.

—◆—

On the football field he was stuck at fullback. Coach Clarence Mabe had him banging into the line, toughening him into a blocker, battered by teammates trotting out the line that he should be timed with a calendar. Coach Mabe, who had a bad leg, kept challenging him to a footrace.

Had to be another way to get the ball into the end zone.

Looking everywhere for an edge, a way to shake up the pile, he trooped into the stadium at East Tennessee State College, at the foot of Buffalo Mountain, on a golden fall Saturday when the ETSC Buccaneers faced the Wasps from Emory and Henry College. The Spurrier men sat in a church member's seats, ready to root for the local college team.

A crew-cut coach with a skinny tie named Conley Snidow commanded the Wasps' sideline, calling plays that looked like that "Willett Special" shift play Doak showed Stevie. Coach Snidow lined up his team in that spread formation every play. Sending both tackles way wide, flanked by the tight ends and receivers, making the defensive backs cover the sidelines, fearing the pass—while the fullback ran down the middle of the field, where the other guys weren't.

The Wasps weren't bigger or faster than the Bucs, his father and brother surely saw. But the only thing stopping the Emory and Henry offense was the goal line. No wonder that little school went to a bowl game in Orlando.

When defenders scrambled to the middle of the field to stuff the run, the quarterback hit easy completions, Orr wouldn't forget back in Kiwanis Park.

The cramped junior high gym had the crowd on top of the players, standing shoulder to shoulder on the running track circling the rafters. The rim looked bigger every game to the shooting guard for the Junior 'Toppers. He hit shots at the buzzer like no one was hollering overhead, taking one-point wins over the junior highs in Bristol and Kingsport.

People in Johnson City hated those big schools. Kingsport got great players by offering jobs to their daddies at the Eastman Kodak plant, people in Johnson City believed. When an eighth grader's clutch shooting toppled those uppity rivals, sportswriters at Cotty's dad's newspaper thumbed through the big brown thesaurus, tossing around nicknames.

Coach Jack McCorkle's "Gunner" led the Junior 'Toppers to 27 straight wins, a 33–1 season, and the Washington County championship, the *Press-Chronicle* reported. Getting his father, carrying the paper around, wondering which way his church members went.

"Already read the sports page," Orr heard people at church say, after sidestepping the pastor they listened to raptly on Sunday.

One man never seemed too busy to talk about Stevie's latest game. The administrator of sports programs at dozens of city schools had the heart of a coach, sitting behind his desk, seeing Reverend Spurrier at the door. Smallwood knew Brother Spurrier would be "good for an hour, easy," going over the finer points of his son's performance.

He could have spent that time on the tennis court, playing his own game. The reverend could still sling a racket, Smallwood had seen. He fooled opponents, seemingly moving slowly, then smacking the ball right back. His youngest son had his imposing build and moved a little faster. Maybe the coordination between eye and arm came from his mother's piano playing. That boy would win more trophies for his father and the town, Smallwood was sure.

How many men did the athletic director know who used to be great athletes? Dwelling on old scores, making history they couldn't outrun, players from another time told their stories in that office, knowing what Smallwood knew. The pastor of Calvary Presbyterian could be found playing ball with his boy in the yard any afternoon the sun shone. Pouring his aspirations into Stevie. Working to make the athletic director look like a real sharp talent scout.

He hadn't even told his wife how Stevie Spurrier really got to town. He knew Reverend Spurrier came by their apartment one day and grilled her. Of course she had no idea what "secret" the minister was talking about.

Keep the faith with your teammates, Smallwood's football coach in Jonesboro had drilled into him. The team's secrets stayed in the locker room. And Brother Spurrier fought for the Lord's team.

When the reverend spoke at youth events around town, Smallwood heard a man trying to be the best preacher there ever was.

Kids from up the street and down the block hung together at Calvary Presbyterian, and Phyllis's friend Regina was missed when her folks moved away. She said the day she came back to visit "was hard," Orr heard.

She toured the old neighborhood on a pair of skates, rolling down Wilson Street to the church, looking up to see her old minister in the doorway.

"Where have you been?" Reverend Spurrier asked. "I haven't seen you."

"Well, my parents go to another church now," she replied.

"We haven't seen *you* in church," the pastor said.

"We moved away, and I started going to another church."

"After I saved you, what a fine appreciation you've given me," he said, shaking up a former member in good graces.

She skated away but couldn't forget what Reverend Spurrier said. Other kids in the neighborhood groaned at Regina's story. Orr understood his father had that power.

———

All the guys going out for Junior 'Toppers football in the fall of '59 knew Jimmy Sanders was the quarterback. He'd quarterbacked guys on the team since grade school and was ready to make all the handoffs in the coach's playbook. When the Junior 'Toppers played some scrappy boys from over the mountain in Erwin, Sanders eyed the slowest back in the huddle, thinking no one would cover him long.

"Twenty-three Pass Fake," Sanders called. He'd run left, Orr would hit the line like a blocker, Sanders would roll right, and Orr would be open down the sideline, grabbing the ball in stride for the score. Trotting back like he'd been in the end zone before.

That play took the air out of Erwin, and the Junior 'Toppers won 27–0. Call it a flag pattern, Orr told Coach Mabe.

Coach Mabe sent him running back into the line. In a tight game against Lyn View, he carried the ball off tackle for the extra point and made the paper for a football play.

He admitted he felt "awkward" as a fullback, "clumsy" as a linebacker, trying to live up to his own expectations. Thinking of hanging up the cleats and hitting jump shots and home runs.

Home is where you talk and people listen. His father said no, he could not give up football. It wasn't a sin, he assured his son, to jump rope on Sunday while watching the Redskins game. He could still wear the burgundy and gold if he could get quicker.

"We're taught in my family that you don't quit things," Orr told his friends, back on the field. However many times Coach Mabe sent him into the line, they wouldn't call him a quitter.

"You stick your head in there," they all assured him.

"You're always ready to play," said Sanders, predicting a big future for Orr in baseball or basketball.

He needed the football in his hand to make the plays that deflated opponents in Kiwanis Park.

⌐—⌐

"Spread out wide," he'd say in the huddle, on his field. He might get clobbered without blockers, but the defense could get stung up the middle.

He'd send one guy long, to the post, while the other receivers baited defenders with shorter routes. He'd throw a lateral that looked like a pass and watch the receiver launch it to a man who didn't need a snowball bush to run around to score.

To really mess with the other team, he'd flip the ball to a receiver running a reverse, who'd flip it to another receiver running the other way, who'd throw it back to Orr, who'd be open. Sending guys home vowing to cover him next time, like Bunny Duggan had to learn the hard way.

To get a few tough yards Orr called "Biddle over the middle," sending Joe on a square-in route and hitting the receiver seemingly too slow to cover.

Back in the huddle he always asked his receivers, "What you got?" Wanting to know whose man was playing too loose, or too tight. Telling his guys to stay short when defenders gave 'em cushion and run right past aggressive coverage. Everyone on the field knew he'd target the slowest, smallest guy on the other team, again and again, putting the ball where that kid wasn't.

Of course, Orr got in the faces of teammates who didn't run the right route. His saving grace was making the play that sent the other team home mad. Did those crazy plays stay in Kiwanis Park? Was anyone, besides those poor drunk veterans staggering between bars, watching the game from the pine trees?

He had no reason to look out for wiry, buzz-haired Emory Hale, hero of that legendary 1957 Oak Ridge win with three picks for Science Hill, now the Hilltopper coach keeping tabs on the junior high football prospects—until the day Stevie Spurrier got called out of class. Summoned over to the high school. Sent down to the head football coach's office in the dank brick locker room, where Kermit Tipton waited for him.

Coach Tipton was Sid Smallwood's choice to be Science Hill's football coach, the athletic director told the school board, because "he handles kids well." Coach Tipton would lead the Hilltoppers into a new era the following January, when the brand-new high school opened on the hill overlooking Kiwanis Park.

Orr sat across the desk from the small, dark-haired man with a high forehead like his father, piercing eyes, and a whistle on his chest, knowing he'd be a great coach because he had played quarterback for Science Hill. Tipton led the 'Toppers to 20 wins, no losses, and a tie he couldn't stand, calling his own plays, throwing scoring strikes and ferocious blocks. He was a leader who looked into his players' eyes. The junior high fullback fielded the coach's questions with a winning smile.

Of course, Coach Tipton knew Graham Spurrier, a basketball and baseball player at Science Hill who never met a stranger. Was his younger brother more of an introvert than he let on? There wasn't a less bashful soul in Johnson City than their father.

"Who's your daddy?" Coach Tipton kept hearing that Sid Smallwood had asked the young man sitting on the other side of the desk. Coach Tipton believed he could see why Smallwood got the boy's father a job preaching at Calvary Presbyterian—and why something smoldered behind that young man's smile.

Tipton had the heart of a player and some hard-nosed beliefs. He believed Reverend Spurrier was "smart enough not to try to overcoach that young man." And Tipton believed the young man would be "smart enough to know what to turn his back on." Coach Tipton believed he'd call the young man "Steve," shaking his hand.

Steve Spurrier walked back to the junior high school knowing the football coach at Science Hill would give him a chance.

A sign came from on high. Stunning the Junior 'Toppers football team, in the last game of the season, Coach Mabe sent Spurrier in at quarterback.

"Pissed us all off," Lyon said, seeing the anger in the huddle.

The new quarterback hit Jimmy Sanders for the score that sent the Junior 'Toppers home winners.

Coach McCorkle's shooting guard had the Junior Toppers back in the county championship game in the spring of 1960, but he was "loafing" on defense, the coach yelled, as the team won another championship.

Holding up another trophy for the *Press-Chronicle* photographer, Orr blinked. He'd "seriously displeased my coach," he said, realizing there's a right way and a wrong way to win.

At Kiwanis Park, picking teams for a football game, Orr didn't always pick the best players. He took guys he wanted to win with, who knew his plays. Throwing scoring passes into an April wind, sending the other team home losers, Orr could see a moral lesson in baseball season.

"We don't pull for the Yankees at our house," he told his friends, wiping off the blood from another football win. "We pull for the underdog." No one could argue with that. "That's the American way," Orr assured them, squinting into the gusts making the trees and the goalposts dance. When he grew up, he said, he'd be playing for a team that didn't get respected, a team nobody thought could win big.

"That's what I look forward to doing, more than playing for the favorite," he concluded, looking up at his little brick house on the hill, where maybe someone watched him play in the park.

That was the only time his friends could remember him saying anything at all about his father.

All the junior high guys going out for high school football in the fall, hoping to start practice up on the hill even though the campus wouldn't open until January, had to spend summer days picking rocks out of the new field, Coach Tipton said. He didn't want to see anyone tear up a knee.

Orr bent down and filled up the rock bucket with Cotty, hearing again how he better hit the weight room to play high school ball.

All summer he threw the football with Graham in the park. Their dad knew where to find them, if he wanted to play.

CHAPTER SEVEN

The Mission

THE BIRTHDAY BOY LACED UP HIS CLEATS, EYEING THE MUDDY PATCHES on the field where he'd picked up rocks and the coaches he'd have to bowl over. Spring practice would mean more work at fullback—without a word from the man in the Bears cap who had Coach Tipton's ear.

Could Spurrier still be the quarterback Tipton saw in his old office downtown, or was that hope gone along with the building, busted into bricks in a vacant lot?

Back in August, walking up the stone steps to the grand old high school where he'd go in the fall, Orr already knew he had Science Hill's new basketball coach in his corner. Elvin Little had played shooting guard for the University of Tennessee, served his country in Germany, and coached little Lenoir City High School to a state championship in 1958. When Sid Smallwood hired Coach Little in the summer of 1960, he met with the basketball prospects at Science Hill and singled out Spurrier.

"Heard about him soon as I got to town, the kid that was awful good," people heard Coach Little say. He took a look at the "young, gangly kid" starting high school and told him he'd be the focal point of the offense.

A great player doesn't need that praise, his father taught him. But it cheered him up and kept him going on the "dark, dismal day" the Science Hill football coaches said he was too slow to play quarterback. The 145-pound sophomore would be a fullback, said Cot Presnell, his sixth-grade coach who'd coached his way up to the high school, still not smiling. Probably stay at fullback, said the muscle-bound coach.

"Yes, sir," a Spurrier boy had been taught to say.

Coach Tipton looked him in the eyes and told the team Tommy Grogg would be the quarterback. Then he whistled them to warm-ups for a two-hour scrimmage with Rogersville in the August heat.

"Shattered what little confidence I did have," Orr would later admit.

His dad knew a quarterback when he saw one. "You're quick," he assured his son, watching him jump rope while the Redskins played.

Alone on the field at Kiwanis Park after a rocky practice, Orr punted into the sunset. Then he teed up his ball and hit field goals. Thinking he could earn a maroon and gold uniform as a kicker.

When the Hilltoppers beat Boone Creek 80–0 in the season opener, Spurrier made the paper by kicking the 80th point. Then Senator John F. Kennedy's campaign visit to Johnson City grabbed the headlines.

After another bruising day on the practice field, walking down the hill as the time freight moaned downtown, he was happy to find star senior Roland Henderson at the manse, seeing his sister, Sara. Up for throwing the football in the yard with her younger brother, while their dad glared through the kitchen window.

Had to hit passes with people glaring at you to be a quarterback.

⌁

Wilson Street flickered with jack-o'-lanterns on Friday night after the game against the Greeneville Greene Devils, when Phyllis Owens had her slumber party. The girls were still sleeping when dawn reddened the neighborhood.

"You won't believe what somebody's done to the Spurriers' yard," Mrs. Owens said, rousing her daughter and her friends. "Girls, you have got to get up and see what Preacher Spurrier's yard looks like!"

The girls dragged themselves to the window to take in the maroon and gold "roll job" covering the manse, the porch, the yard, and the elm tree, glorifying Science Hill with maroon crepe paper and yellow toilet tissue, the closest color to gold they could find.

"That could get someone banned from church," Phyllis told her mom.

⌁

A nod from the head coach got Spurrier on the field as quarterback, for one drive. A "53-yard punt by Spurrier" in the Chattanooga Central game also made the sports page. Hilltopper fans cheered the 17 extra points he kicked, as the 1960 Hilltoppers pounded out a 6–4 season. They needed a pitcher, his father hollered.

Coach Tipton didn't let Reverend Spurrier say anything at the practice field on the hill. No one was being picked on, the football coach said. He didn't let any player's father holler. His son kept his mouth shut and did what the coaches said.

Time for the preacher to relent and let his sons play ball on Sunday. Not even the wrath of God could keep Graham and Stevie out of Kiwanis Park, no matter how many uniforms they wore during the week. Every boy in town played ball on Sunday. Better not to be seen sneaking around, in the eyes of the Lord.

A quarterback needed the practice.

"Time for Stevie to be called Steve," his father said when it was time for Santa to show up.

"And you," Reverend Spurrier told the hardest-working guy in the Science Hill weight room, "ought to go from being called Cotty to being called Cot."

The publisher's son said he'd stick with the name he had.

—•—

"When they introduce you, tell them you're going to win a state championship," Reverend Spurrier advised Science Hill's new basketball coach at a PTA meeting in the old high school's brick cafeteria.

Coach Little just smiled and talked about Science Hill's new gym opening up on the hill, with those new glass backboards Sid Smallwood had ordered—waiting for loyal 'Toppers to fill the new bleachers and Preacher Spurrier's son to hit the court after football season ended.

"Your dad believes in saying things to increase confidence in yourself," Little told Orr.

His shot ripped through the net, his first day at practice in the new gym, making Coach Little gape and draw up pick plays for a kid who'd clearly spent his life on the playground.

Down 2 in that howling cylinder of Hilltopper fans wanting to beat Tennessee High from Bristol, Orr hit a long one-hander at the buzzer to tie the Vikings at 37. Standing at the line with four seconds left in overtime and the crowd screaming, he saw his father's face as he calmly swished two free throws. Making "Mr. Ice Water Veins" feel like a new player, seeing his father carrying around the sports page again.

In the District Two playoffs in March, the Science Hill sophomore was named All-Tournament Player in a losing effort. Clearing out his basketball stuff, the first day he could play baseball, he heard Coach Little call him "the best player I've ever seen under pressure."

Orr wouldn't disagree with his coach, but a one-handed buzzer beater wasn't real pressure.

\—

John "Satch" Broyles, broad-faced, bespectacled Sunday school teacher, owner of Broyles' Batting Cages and Driving Range, Science Hill history teacher and baseball coach, had a team of rivals from the Babe Ruth League who played to each other's strengths. Making Orr happy to finally get on the field with those guys, hoping to contribute. He knew a star among scrubs could rise to be a scrub among stars.

When he hit the dirt practice field downtown, his father stood at the chain-link fence by home plate, because Coach Broyles didn't say he couldn't stand there and holler at players. Fans cringed when his dad stood up at games and yelled at players who'd better be doing better. Only one father could yell that loud, people said—the preacher who wanted to be the coach.

Smallwood fielded complaints from the parents of the players, saying Reverend Spurrier kept yelling at their children. The athletic director would have to call the reverend into his office and lay down the law.

"Reverend Spurrier, these are 15- and 16-year-old kids you're yelling at," Smallwood told him. "If you don't back off yelling at Steve and these other kids, you've seen your last baseball game at Science Hill."

The reverend seemed to see the virtue of humility. "Should I apologize?"

Smallwood had to smile. "Just don't do it again and it'll be alright."

The reverend got the benefit of the doubt, for insisting that the town would thank Smallwood for getting that Spurrier boy to Johnson City.

"Me and the preacher get along," Smallwood said to people who couldn't understand why he let Reverend Spurrier talk and talk about his son without hanging up the phone.

———

The week the Bay of Pigs invasion in Cuba made headlines, the big news at the Spurrier house was the Appalachian Preaching Mission, bringing around 80,000 worshippers to four Tennessee towns, with nearly 40,000 gathering in Johnson City, the *Press-Chronicle* reported. Providentially, the Mission was moved to the third week of April in 1961. For years the churches and auditoriums of eastern Tennessee had filled with evangelistic fervor in the depths of February, when no one would be playing football except crazy kids in the park.

The day Orr turned 16 was sunny and breezy, almost seventy, chilling as the sun set in the hills. Plunging to 30 that night, the paper predicted, for "Laymen's Night" at the Preaching Mission, featuring professional football star Bill Wade.

Wade starred at quarterback for the Vanderbilt Commodores, Orr knew, after that Vandy graduate Grantland Rice got Wade on the cover of *Look* magazine. Wade quarterbacked the lowly Commodores to some wins, became the SEC's most valuable player his senior year, and was drafted by the L.A. Rams—who had traded him that week to the Chicago Bears, for Zeke Bratkowski. The paper said Bears coach George Halas would let Wade call his own plays. He put on his new Bears cap and came to dinner at the manse on Wilson Street.

Sitting around the table in the small brick dining room, Mrs. Spurrier said dessert would be served but didn't mention birthday cake. Sid Smallwood had invited the young people of the church over for ice cream and a pep talk from a pro quarterback.

"Bill Wade, when he says something, that's what he means," Smallwood promised the young people who sure didn't get to eat ice cream every day.

Wade noticed at the dinner table that when the talk turned to Jesus, the Spurriers' youngest son was all ears. Maybe the ice cream made the spring night seem colder, crossing the hill to East Tennessee State College's jam-packed gym. Accompanying Cincinnati management consultant Fred Smith, Maryland governor Theodore McKeldin, and the East Tennessee State College (ETSC) choir, Steve Spurrier stood up and prayed for the young people, with the eyes of Bill Wade on him. Then Jimmy Sanders testified about his faith.

"The basic facts of football are the same as the basic facts of life," Wade told the crowd. Just as modern football players are filmed when they play, he said, the Lord is "filming the actions of people as they play the game of life." Review your life, Wade urged, and be "sorry and humble" when mistakes show up in the "divine film" of your actions.

"More and more athletes across the nation over are endorsing Jesus Christ," Wade noted, "instead of lending their names to certain commercial products." Backing a father's move to block any beer commercials his sons might see. Reverend Spurrier couldn't help but notice Science Hill's football coach in the audience, hearing the good word. Hard to catch him out without his whistle.

"Kermit Tipton, he talked to Bill Wade and said, 'Come watch us practice. I'd like for you to come out, and if you have any suggestions we would appreciate it,'" Reverend Spurrier exulted, celebrating with the birthday boy back at the manse.

Hearing his prayer at the preaching mission, Wade saw that "Steve was a good person." What seemed to work wonders was his last name. After sharing the spotlight with that intense young man, Wade realized, "Spurrier's a name for a person who could spur you on. And I looked at him in that light."

A warm spring rain misted the practice field on the hilltop. Coach Tipton stood on the sideline, enjoying how Bill Wade "didn't put on airs" walking through the mud in cleats and sweatpants. When Wade "said a few words, not many," and started throwing the ball around, Tipton was ready to listen.

Wade tossed the ball to Spurrier, who sent Sanders long, knowing he could make cuts in the mud.

"He's good," Wade said after Spurrier hit Sanders down the seam. "Maybe Steve should play a little more quarterback."

Did he hear that, standing there poker-faced like he'd scored at the park?

"Probably," Tipton concluded, watching Steve's finger etch out another post pattern.

"If I had a quarterback who could throw the ball like that," Wade told Tipton, "I'd go to a pro-type offense with a split end and a wide receiver."

At the end of practice Wade huddled with Tipton and Spurrier while Smallwood looked on, glasses gleaming. He'd have to report to the school board that Science Hill's football coach wanted to "toughen up the schedule some."

"We have a good chance against anybody," Tipton told Smallwood, "with Steve behind center."

Didn't feel like Johnson City would be so cold that night. For those who'd kept the faith, salvation was at hand.

———

After Bill Wade left for Chicago, Coach Tipton sat his coaches in front of the blackboard and started chalking up new pass plays.

The Hilltoppers' play caller was a burly American Indian named "Snake" Evans, who had a glass eye. As a boy, he'd played with a window shade rod with coiled springs that shot up and left him looking defiant. He got his nickname playing offensive tackle for the Buccaneers at ETSC, talking about the water moccasins that supposedly slithered through his front yard in Cajun Country. Coach Evans brought the Rajin' Cajuns' offense to Science Hill, where he put in two tight ends, called runs up the gut, and questioned how much the offense should change for a former fullback.

"Change it enough to suit him more, suit his talents more," Tipton said. Asking Coach Evans to consider some option plays even though Steve was slow. He knew Snake wasn't going to just start chucking the ball down the field.

Coach Hale remembered seeing a little square-in play that couldn't be stopped in Kiwanis Park. Coach Evans didn't want to hear about plays boys called in pickup games.

"Just send Sanders straight down the field," Coach Tipton said, putting down the chalk.

Something smoldering in his friend inspired Lonnie Lowe to take the mound and pitch a two-hitter against Tennessee High, hurling Science Hill into first place in the Big Seven Conference. To win the title, they'd have to beat Kingsport at Cardinal Park, next door to the brick football stadium on Market Street. With Lowe "hurling the distance," the 'Toppers took an 8–7 comeback victory over Dobyns-Bennett, winning the Big Seven Championship in baseball. Cheers erupted across the street at city hall when Kingsport got its comeuppance.

Playing center field for the team that finished third in the state, Orr found the keys to the "Blue Bomb" in his hand. Oh yeah, he could drive a straight shift on the column. His father had bought an old blue Buick for his teenagers to drive—when the car could be coaxed to go anywhere.

True to his word, he bit his tongue when other players made errors. But Smallwood couldn't make him quit coaching his son.

The Doughboy statue was mobbed and the ticket line stretched down Market Street, Orr heard in the stifling hot locker room. Could a season that started with him hurt end up with a win over Dobyns-Bennett, making Kingsport share the Big Seven football title with Johnson City?

The quarterback loved being a two-touchdown underdog. When the team stood at the top of the hill and the band struck up the 'Topper fight song, he could see his family standing in the record crowd, and Sara cheering. Running down the hill through the maroon and gold–draped goalposts to the field, like the Hilltoppers made their entrance when he was a kid in the stands, all he could see was Kingsport. Maroon and gray players with arrowheads on their helmets, warming up on his field under a crescent moon. As always, he zeroed in on the defenders he wanted to dodge and the defensive backs he wanted to burn.

Bring on the Indians. He'd gained milk shake weight, driving and pushing the Blue Bomb between the Dixie Drive-In, "the Pride of Tennessee"; the Dutch Maid Drive-In, "East Tennessee's Finest"; and the hangout that boasted, "You Are Always Welcome at . . . The Spot."

He told his dad he'd been called into Coach's office. "Mr. Tipton sat me down and said, 'You have a chance to become one of the greatest athletes ever.' He gave me the opportunity to play and run the offense."

"Don't let it go to your head," his father said.

—⁓—

"1961 'Toppers Open Slate Friday Minus 7 Starters," the *Press-Chronicle* front page had proclaimed on August 21. "I think we have one of the best punters in the state in Spurrier," said his coach, who'd given his new quarterback the new number he asked for, number 11.

What about protection for that 162-pound quarterback, Cotty's father's sportswriter wanted to know.

Coach Tipton wouldn't tell reporters, opponents, or his quarterback about his 150-pound center, who was all hustle. When the son of the publisher of the paper was 9, he had polio. Johnson City had no stores with barbells for sale. Cotty Jones got inspired watching the Ringling Bros. strongman Saturday morning on TV and sent away for barbells from Dan Lurie, which he lifted night and day to get to play. Cotty never talked about having polio; he just lifted himself red-faced and blocked the biggest high school defensive linemen in Tennessee, never seeing one pass Orr threw in a game.

"Don't let him get hit," was all Coach Tipton said about protecting his quarterback.

The first time he stood behind his center and called an audible in the August heat, Snake Evans stopped the play.

"Who's the coach, Spurrier?" Evans asked. He didn't yell; he just talked loud—and got a respectful answer. "Then you stay out here. If that's not the way it is, go get you a shower."

"Yes, sir," the quarterback said, and ran Coach Evans's play. Throwing completions on 8 of the 12 pass plays Evans called in a scrimmage against some big country boys from Church Hill. Turning it up the week of the opener against Jonesboro, he got slung down hard at practice—by a "third-stringer," Tipton growled.

The team doctor wouldn't let him play with a dislocated left elbow. He'd miss starting the first game at home and stay on the bench for three games.

Down 19–0 at Bristol, with those city people screaming, Coach Tipton called on his hurt quarterback to make something happen. It happened in the huddle, when Coach Evans sent in a short-yardage play.

"What you got?" Orr asked Sanders.

Bristol had their defensive back playing Sanders tight. Orr drew up a post pattern on the turf, faded back, and threw a pass Sanders grabbed at the 10 and ran in. The 56-yard scoring strike was the first touchdown the Viking defense gave up all season. The stadium got quiet enough for Snake Evans to question that audible when Orr got to the sideline.

Only thing the old offensive tackle could say was, "Good call."

Orr's elbow still couldn't take a hit. He sat out a loss to Oak Ridge at home, leaving his team 1–5 going into an open week. They practiced banging the ball into the line while Buffalo Mountain turned red and gold. Couldn't wait for the elbow to heal. Coach Tipton had the cure.

Elizabethton, the rival school Tipton had targeted when he played quarterback, wouldn't know what hit 'em. Coach Tipton huddled up his team and said, "Just let Steve call the plays."

Finally starting a game in his stadium, running the offense, throwing the ball like he'd been out there all season, number 11 finally played a complete game to go over with his father, play by play.

Roland Henderson wanted to come see Sara and talk football. Everybody who fit in the Blue Bomb wanted to talk football with everybody at the drive-ins. Kingsport guys "slumming" in Johnson City would want to talk football. The Blue Bomb crew stayed on the lookout.

Orr's extra point kick put the 'Toppers up 7–6 and took the fun out of a Friday night in Greeneville for the Greene Devils. His passing had Hilltopper fans riding over the mountain to Erwin, where he ran for a score to lock up a 12–0 win. Coach Tipton missed talking football with his quarterback after the game, outside the locker room, seeing "his buddies all thick as flies."

Some guys talking over the game asked, "Man, didn't we see that play in Kiwanis Park?"

Orr had to know. He brought out people's inner quarterback. Got everyone talking about the way he went after the smallest, slowest guy on defense.

When his father, his brother, and his sister wanted to talk football, he made them run patterns in the yard, ran them ragged and "gave myself my own little lessons on keeping cool." When time came for his Friday afternoon nap before the big game, his brother turned into a parent.

"You won't be alert," Graham warned when Orr lay down in their little brick room in back.

"Don't eat so much supper," Graham said at the table.

Orr just ate. Eighty degrees on the first Friday in November. Too hot to argue.

His dad showed him the front page of the paper. Cotty's father's banner headline read STOP THIS INDIAN BACK, 'TOPPERS, atop a huge picture of Kingsport running back Sam Bartholomew. Orr thought it was a fine idea, talking to the team through the press.

The maroon and gray guys with arrowhead helmets came after him, but he took the team 86 yards for a score, hitting Vernon Humphries in the end zone to draw first blood. The hits were brutal, the locker room still stifling at the half. Walking back to the top of the hill, the team saw fellow students lined up to cheer them back onto the field, talking to number 11 as he passed by.

The Indians' front-page running back couldn't run against Science Hill. Trying to cross midfield in the second half, Kingsport went to the air and got picked off by Spurrier the defensive back. Standing behind his center with a 6-point lead, he saw big Ron Pelfrey open for 22 yards, hit Jim Martin for 22 more, and had Humphreys open again in the end zone for a door-slammer score.

Together they knelt in the locker room built from the same bricks as the town and thanked God for helping them win "the big one." Beating Kingsport in football for the first time since '53. Winning a share of the Big Seven football title after an awful start.

"Biggest comeback in Johnson City history," Orr heard, driving around town in the Blue Bomb, hoisting milk shakes, watching out for the Kingsport people.

His father had the men of the church around him after the Sunday sermon, praising the gridiron warriors. Orr slipped down the stairs and out the back door, crossing over to basketball season.

In the Dobyns-Bennett gym they jeered the Hilltoppers for three over-times, with the Kingsport paper celebrating a 32–30 "whipping" of "Mr. Cool" from Johnson City.

Back in his school's gym, "Mr. Clutch" downed Hampton High 62–60 with a shot from downtown they talked about in two towns. Averaging over 20 points and 10 assists a game, Spurrier outscored some of Science Hill's opponents single-handedly, sending the sportswriters downtown to the thesaurus and Orr back to Scout Hall, to take on the real rival.

Science Hill won the Big Seven basketball title and took the regional title from Elizabethton, finishing No. 5 in the state in the AP Poll. The Hilltoppers Sports Club named Spurrier the team's MVP. His teammates named him captain for next year. His father went over the plays on the hardwood that season. Orr listened to the words that would help him.

"You could have done a little bit better."

In the halls of the church he heard the basketball talk and went out the basement door to the baseball field, where getting named all-state quarterback didn't mean anything.

CHAPTER EIGHT

Preordained

LOOKING DOWN FROM A SUNLINER BUS WITH THE TOP OPEN TO PARADE the state champions through town, Orr waved at his big brother holding a Welcome Home Champs sign and watched 'Toppers young and old clap Sid Smallwood on the back. Maybe for making Orr's father calm down, when his boy's errors got to be too much to take. Everyone caught up in a spring a ballplayer lives for.

From the time five of them played together for the Bears and his dad, they'd honed their game, throwing, hitting, and forging a 19–2 season at Science Hill in the spring of '62. Winning the right to wear those wool Hilltopper baseball uniforms in Nashville in June, at noon.

That kind of heat Coach Broyles wouldn't let his players take. They got to play in T-shirts, writing their numbers on the back with a black magic marker and taking on Messick High from the Memphis suburbs, a school privileged to play all their games at night. Taken by the 'Toppers 4–1 that broiling afternoon.

The next day rain slicked the field for the double-elimination championship game. With Lowe striking out six Messick High Panthers, giving up just two hits, Tommy Hager got a walk, then got to second on a bunt; Choo Tipton walked; and "Spurrier rifled a single to left field," the papers said, knocking in the only run Science Hill needed to be the best baseball team in Tennessee. Winning the trophy 200 schools wanted, with the guys he wanted to win with, felt like winning a national championship.

Named with his school and his town in headlines across the state, how did a young man driven by an obsessed father keep his feet on the ground? Wasn't a question he'd have to field. Only the guys standing with him on the bus, seeing people look up with joy, hearing cheers building since the Babe Ruth League days, could know how much he had to prove.

Tommy, running home when Orr's bat cracked, and Lonnie, standing taller on the mound than on the bus, had to hold his father back, until he quit trying to make his son play perfectly. The gusty spring day Sid Smallwood had to get between Reverend Spurrier and Steve, nothing changed. His father was back at practice the next day, hollering about the plays a Spurrier better make.

So maybe it was his father putting the fear of God in him that won them the state championship trophy. Maybe his dad's coaching got those five Steinway Bears and their teammates to Kingsport, to face Dobyns-Bennett on their field, with a trip to Nashville on the line.

Orr pitched a 5–4 win over the Indians that day, still undefeated as a high school pitcher when Lonnie got the start in Nashville. Orr hit that single with a vengeance to get Hager home. Coaches had ways of making players play harder. Maybe Coach Broyles had made a smooth move, letting Orr's father get on him at the practice field, in front of his team.

Holding the trophy overhead as the Sunliner bus rumbled through the people celebrating "Hilltopper Day" in Johnson City, he'd say it was worth the fight.

What else would his father coach him to say?

———

On summer days without a game to suit up for, waiting for payback time on the football field, Orr and Graham and Joe Biddle put on masks and umpired the Little League games at Kiwanis Park. Running up the hill between games for homegrown-tomato sandwiches and cold glasses of milk in Marjorie's cool brick kitchen. Talking around the table about plays made by the boys they had been.

At night, picking up friends in the Blue Bomb, Orr could hear crickets chirping the play-by-play. No such thing as a friendly game at the pool hall downtown. He liked to score mental points. Looking down on an opponent's shot and saying, "Just can't get that ball past the eight ball, can you?" He didn't mind a reputation for keeping people in the pool hall until he won.

Back on the road gears would growl and the Blue Bomb had to be pushed and parked. Orr, Cotty, Carroll, Tommy, Jimmy, Ralph, Joe, and Lonnie had air in their lungs, and Ken had his guitar. They went to the closest friend's house and harmonized with the lineman's chords. Making up songs, riffing on the hits of the day, singing folk songs, filling the air with sounds of young love and the way the world ought to be.

Orr sat in a circle of all-American guys who ran his plays, grabbed his throws, and protected his backside. Guys who'd go out and change the world, not just sing about it, he had reason to believe.

Parents listening around the corner had to smile, hearing in the harmonizing a cadence changing the town. Rustling up something from the kitchen so their sons would say, "Mom thought the world of that boy, and fed him many times."

One hot Saturday night, singing about a better world wasn't enough. What influence did athletes really have? They'd won bragging rights for the mayor and the commissioners, the Jaycees, the Optimists and the Lions Club, bookies and bootleggers, the adults in charge of the young president's "New Frontier." All inspired by the New Testament sayings and Old Testament dustups of the preacher and the Sunday school teacher.

What really got the gang going was this: What did a championship team have to do to practice with a real baseball?

"Coach Broyles," Hager said, shaking his head. "Really big on keeping those baseballs."

The Hilltoppers always had to practice with rubber balls from the "bat bat" at Broyles' Driving Range. Rubber-covered balls thrown by the pitching machine at kids in batting cages all weekend got moved to the dirt field downtown where Science Hill practiced during the week, helping Broyles safeguard the "real balls."

Did winning a championship really change things, any more than singing protest songs? A plan to make the grown-ups play fair turned into a ride over the hill to those green acres weekend golfers aimed for, dark as midnight, dark as the batting cages, the pro shop and a shed where the golf balls weren't locked up that tight. The mysterious gang took buckets upon buckets of colored balls and spirited them downtown in one squirrelly car, pulling up to the headquarters of WJHL, News Channel 11, "In Your Corner," at the top of Main Street.

Letting loose all those red, yellow, green, blue, and orange golf balls in front of the TV station, watching the bouncing balls cascade down the parade route, smashing into the Belks Building, Hamilton National Bank, and the John Sevier Hotel, coloring streets, alleys, train tracks, and parking lots where Sunday schoolers would gawk, the gang made history for sure. Officials inquired all around town about "the disturbers." No one had a clue how they got those balls from Broyles' Driving Range to Main Street, turning the cobblestones into a fairway.

Science Hill's football coach would hear from one livid baseball coach about hoodlums creating a traffic hazard and mocking authority.

"Coach Tipton has ways of knowing what's going on," Sanders warned Orr. The coach would look thoughtfully at his quarterback at that first practice in August, always a killer, and see the hope for the season hiding behind a smile.

"They accused me of rolling golf balls down Main Street," was all Spurrier would officially admit.

"Good chance he was one of the pranksters," the head football coach said when he got off the hill, leaving Coach Broyles and Coach Evans to pursue the investigation.

⁓

Maybe Orr owed the game of golf. He became a caddy at the Johnson City Country Club and picked up a 3-iron, needing only one ball to get on the course for "Caddy Day." Sid Smallwood made a point of watching that boy tee off for his first 18 holes. Sure he'd be a star.

Encouraged by a man who knew talent, Orr jumped the fence and hit shots down the fairway until the real golfers chased him away. Another Spurrier trying to get on a course that wouldn't have the likes of him on the links.

"He taught me how to hit a 3-iron," Biddle told the gang. "Only club he had. We climbed over a little fence in a neighbor's yard that butted up against the country club."

Orr would hit a shot to the pin and "act like it was old hat, with a touch of his cap," Biddle said. Until the day a ranger or whoever patrolled the course in a uniform hollered, "What are you boys doing out here?"

Orr gave Biddle the signal for "Don't answer, just run."

───◆───

Spurrier would do the quarterbacking, kick off, kick field goals, kick extra points, and punt for the '63 'Toppers, Coach Tipton told the *Press-Chronicle* in August, adding that number 11 wouldn't get off the field when the defense ran out.

At 170 pounds he was king of the hill in the August heat. Smiling about whoever let loose those golf balls on Main Street. Letting Coach Tipton worry about being favored to win the Big Seven football championship because of Spurrier. At age 17 he wasn't supposed to see how empty that field would look to his coach next August. The future was Friday.

He threw three touchdown passes at Jonesboro, side-stepping blitzers and bringing home a 25–0 win that had the town fired up for the home opener.

Standing at the top of his stadium, running down the hill to the field with the band playing the fight song, Orr faced Chattanooga Central believing he could win. On the second play Sanders went for the ball and got hit in the head by a purple and gold defensive back, who was a top University of Georgia recruit. Spurrier's team was unnerved. The football thudded off the shoulder pads of his other receivers—all 15 of his passes they couldn't catch. When Spurrier lost confidence everyone lost it, losing 12–0 to Chattanooga. He could see the frustration in his coach's eyes, and a chalk talk coming at home.

Press-Chronicle oddsmaker Dr. E. E. Litkenhous judged the Hilltoppers were a three-touchdown underdog at Morristown, where the head coach said the game plan was simple: "Stop Spurrier." He aimed to beat the Hurricanes with coffin-corner punts, keeping those grade-school basketball bullies pinned deep on the football field. They still hated that hotshot when his kicks went out of bounds at their 2-yard line. He kicked a field goal that looked like the game winner, shushing a crowd of 8,000 in Morristown—until a returner ran right by him on the ensuing kickoff. His dad told Coach Tipton the boy could do better.

Getting a shot at Knoxville Central in his stadium, the quarterback of the underdogs hit eight passes for 148 yards and ran for 66, his jersey torn to shreds by Bobcats. Those missed tackles made Spurrier the AP Back of the Week in a 14–0 upset of Knoxville.

Bobcats came to the Hilltopper dressing room to pray with one tough quarterback. When they left he had the team chant, "Beat Bristol!" Bobcat coach Frank Boring said he didn't usually "go on like this" about one player, but "Spurrier is terrific."

Edwin Graves, the postmaster in Knoxville, drove back from that game in Johnson City thinking he'd better call his brother in Gainesville, the football coach at the University of Florida, who hadn't heard of Spurrier.

"The kid does everything," said one son of a Methodist minister to another.

The next Friday Bristol came to Johnson City as big city favorites. They had quarterback John Boring and a 20–0 advantage at the half. Orr ran back down the hill through a "cheering corridor" of students hooting and hollering, keeping the faith, putting the fear of God into the Hilltopper band. He went after Bristol's slowest cornerback, throwing two touchdown passes, then running the ball in from the 3 to make the score 20–19. His extra-point kick for the tie got blocked by Tennessee High's fullback. No time for the after-game party at Parks and Rec, with his father waiting at home.

Going all the way to "the Atomic City" the following week and allowing Oak Ridge to score with one second on the clock hurt worse.

Should the town applaud a great effort, after another loss to another big school? Coach Tipton marveled at the crowd greeting his beaten team back at the high school, in the middle of the night. He'd never seen support this strong. Never had such a leader galvanized the team and the town.

"Steve convinces people they can do it," Smallwood said to Tipton. "And he doesn't panic."

Tipton had to agree.

"Steve and his dad have one thing in common," Smallwood insisted. "The word *lose* isn't in their vocabulary."

Tipton just nodded. Reverend Spurrier still wasn't allowed near his sideline.

The men could see the preacher had no problem finding rides with Hilltopper fans who'd drive across the state to watch Steve play ball. Couldn't miss Reverend Spurrier coaching from the stands at every game. "I'm Steve Spurrier's father," Orr could hear him say.

No one should brag about anything after a loss.

———

With an open date before Orr could take out his frustations on Elizabethton, Tipton sent his assistant coaches to guard the parks. Watch 'em after practice, and all day Sunday, Tipton ordered. Pick a park. Pick a sport. Spurrier better not get hurt playing in a pickup game.

Keeping him from playing ball was a losing battle, his father would testify. Only Coach Tipton thought he better have Carver Park guarded, too. Knowing his quarterback went where the best ballers played and "made friends based on the person, not their color."

Most every boy in Johnson City went somewhere to play ball on Sunday. Orr knew a field no coach from Science Hill would think to guard—a vacant lot on North Roan Street where some black guys from Langston High played tackle.

"Toughest game I ever played in my life," Ken Lyon told Orr after they played three hours without scoring. Barely got off a pass. On the second play a Langston guy ran for a touchdown, and that was it. Orr's side couldn't move the ball.

Sid Smallwood talked about the athletes across town deserving a chance to show what they could do. Maybe Smallwood really could spot talent a long way away.

Man, Science Hill could use those guys. Tennessee fans waving rebel flags around Knoxville kept out some big-time players from Langston High, the boys agreed on the long walk home.

———

With the mountains turning red and gold, the team boarded the bus for the 10-mile trip over Sabine Hill to Elizabethton, where Orr struggled to find receivers downfield in an orange and black swarm. After one long drive led to a score, maddened blitzers left Sanders open for a 32-yard scoring strike.

The second half turned into a slugfest, with Orr making and taking hits on defense as the crowd roared. The head coach saw some Cyclones taking cheap shots at the defensive back who was also a threat on offense—unless they took him out. Which Coach Tipton decided to do.

Not getting run off the field, Spurrier told his coach. Hard hits were the best part of the game.

Coach Tipton reminded his star player "who was running the show," making him watch from the sideline. When the quarterback got back in, he started calling those option plays Coach Tipton had chalked up to placate Coach Evans. Keeping the ball and banging into the line, showing those fullback moves, Orr kept the ball away from the Cyclones to seal a 14–6 deal.

Russian nuclear missiles were clearly in Cuba when Orr ran Greeneville out of Johnson City, passing and grabbing a pick to beat the Greene Devils 20–0. As America's navy blockaded Castro, Orr crashed into Erwin's line and threw for two scores to take a 33–12 win. Fans braved arctic winds to see what the Blue Devil's coach saw: "too much Spurrier." When Castro sent the missiles back to Russia, Orr's friends "gigged" him about working on that aiming gesture, in case his country needed him to shoot straight.

～～

Could the devil finally nail him on Halloween night? He was in the dark, hoping not to be in the headlines on the eve of the Kingsport game. The gang had been egging houses and cars, and police were in pursuit. Reportedly the perpetrators crashed a slumber party and hid in the girls' sleeping bags—everyone except Orr, Biddle realized.

"No boys here," he heard the daughter of the town dentist tell the men in uniform.

That blanket denial sent the dragnet back through the neighborhood, where a quarterback needed room to run. Crouching in the undergrowth with flashlights trained on him, Orr gave up, he told his friends. When officers asked him his name, he told them.

"Got us a hotshot quarterback here," his friends heard one officer say.

Would they throw him in the slammer? Depended on whether they rooted for 'Toppers or Indians. Orr took one for the team, saying "Yes, sir," and "No, sir," working out a deal with the police, agreeing to clean off all the egg yolks and egg whites and eggshells smearing the windows of the houses and the cars he hadn't hit.

Admitting to being "with a guy who threw eggs one Halloween night," his lesson learned was, "I didn't throw one but I was running around with 'em, so I was guilty as they were." God knew how many windows he had to clean, but Reverend Spurrier did not know.

"Hate to see that one, if he got arrested and his father had to go bail him out," Joe said, to agreement from the gang. "He thinks Steve wears a halo."

Reverend Spurrier's son didn't drink, didn't smoke, and didn't cuss. Didn't hang around anyone who did. He did like to throw things, the tempter knew.

He mixed runs and passes on drives that kept Kingsport's offense off the field, and their fans quiet. When the Indians lost patience and blitzed, he made them pay. When the ref raised his hands for the score, Coach Tipton heard Reverend Spurrier talking about "using some of that Kiwanis Park football."

Tipton turned and gave Steve's father a smile. Coach Hale hadn't been the only one watching the games at the park from behind the pines.

Orr threw for a final touchdown to claim a 27–7 win for the underdogs across Route 11. In the visitor's locker room, he called for silence. Seeing Indians in the doorway offering congratulations, and his father.

The winning quarterback said a prayer for everyone on the field of battle. His father choked up with pride, shaking his hand.

❧

The 'Toppers ended the season in the AP top 10, invited back to Kingsport to play in a postseason game called the Exchange Bowl—against Church Hill High School from over in Hawkins County.

Cotty thought the team ought to celebrate one big win before playing in Kingsport again and invited everyone to his father's lake house outside of town. Ken Lyon celebrated by sneaking in some beer. His quarterback "moseyed over" to the record player and started sniffing.

"You've been drinking beer," he said, getting in the big guard's face. Ken couldn't deny it.

"There's no beer drinking here," Orr said. "We're football players."

"That ended the beer drinking for the night," Cotty observed.

"Never seen a worse practice in my life," Coach Tipton told the team on Tuesday. "What's going on?"

Orr and his gang said they didn't know. The biggest guy on the team, a 200-pound tackle, looked down at Coach Tipton and said, "We're tired of getting bitched at."

"They're tired of getting bitched at," Coach Tipton explained to Coach Evans.

"Tell you what we'll do, boys," Coach Tipton said. "Come out tomorrow if you want to. Wear pads, or shorts, whatever you want to wear. Want to walk your girl home after school, that's fine, too. I promise you I won't bitch. And you'll get the living hell beat out of you Friday night."

After an icy rainstorm they were down 7–0 in the mud in Kingsport's stadium when Church Hill forced another three-and-out.

"Big bunch of tough country boys we took for granted," Cotty told Orr, shaking his head. Orr went back to punt and watched Cotty's snap sail over his head, into the hands of a Church Hill player who ran it in for a score. When Cotty got to the sideline, his quarterback patted him on the shoulder pads.

"Don't worry," Orr said. "We'll get it back."

Church Hill scored again, to take a 21–0 lead. Getting the ball back just before the half, Orr started rolling out, dodging Church Hill boys smelling blood, looking for the receiver who could make cuts in the mud. Jimmy Sanders's leaping catch got the 'Toppers on the board. Trailing 21–7 in the visitor's locker room, Tipton played devil's advocate.

"You get that much ahead, you ought to be home free," he said.

The quarterback told his coach not to worry; they had this one won. No question in his mind or his eyes.

Getting the ball at midfield in the second half, he hit two passes to Ron Pelfrey and found Sanders in the end zone again. Orr's kick made it 21–14. Two more touchdown passes and some banging on defense gave his coach an improbable 28–21 win. Impressing the scout who drove up from South Carolina, hoping to see Spurrier in Gamecock colors.

Mud-splattered 'Toppers shook hands with stunned Church Hill players, and the team captain thanked the Lord for coming through, inspiring a trophy-raising song. At an assembly honoring the football team in the Science Hill auditorium, Lyon got out his guitar and Orr led the "Five Fellows" in singing, "We're the champs of the Exchange Bowl, and number nine, praise God, in the AP poll."

Spurrier could sing for a living, people said. Only Tennessean to be a 1962 *Scholastic* magazine all-American. Did he have a girlfriend, they asked his football coach.

"He has a lot of girls interested in dating him," Coach Tipton said. "All good-looking, of course. He wouldn't date anybody that wasn't good-looking," the coach growled, living through his quarterback.

———

Monday night after the comeback in Kingsport, the Jaycees held their annual Hilltopper Football Banquet. Invited to address the Outstanding Hilltopper award winner, his team, his fans, and his father was the triple-threat tailback and two-time Heisman Trophy runner-up from North Carolina, Charlie "Choo Choo" Justice.

Standing at attention in a dapper suit, eyeing the high school athletes beneath a shock of dark hair, number 22 needed no name tag, preaching about the importance of sports. While President Kennedy advocated developing the mind, Choo Choo said, "Forty-seven men had to be drafted to find five fit for military service."

Did he prefer the offense he ran out of in college, the single wing? T formation? Pro-style?

"In any system you've got to have the horses," Choo Choo told the Vols fans in the crowd.

"Triple-Threat Spurrier" took the trophy from Jaycee president Bob Good like it was a surprise and held onto it while Choo Choo admired it,

Reverend Spurrier beamed over Choo Choo's shoulder, and Coach Tipton and Miss Johnson City looked on as the *Press-Chronicle* photographer snapped away. The hero of the Tar Heels could punt as well as he could run and throw, Reverend Spurrier would always say.

Downtown was a winter wonderland, and the tree still twinkled in the den as the Spurriers tuned in to the Gator Bowl in Jacksonville, Florida, where underdog Florida faced Penn State. Duke University had declined an invitation to the game, giving the Gators a chance to play the Nittany Lions, because at the end of the season, Duke players told their coach they were tired of getting bitched at. "And Duke coach Bill Murray called the Gator Bowl and said, 'We ain't coming,'" said the Spurriers' college prospect.

His father harrumphed. The only coach tough enough for his son was Bear Bryant.

Orr thought the Gators looked "all fired up," playing the Nittany Lions on New Year's Day under the palm trees. Watching Florida hit passes downfield, he said, "Maybe that would be a good place to go to school."

His father laughed. But the man who answered the phone at the manse would have to take messages from Florida's coaches. Not every recruiting call for Steve was accepted by Reverend Spurrier. They'd better be reverent coaches, from pious schools, calling the church line.

The underdogs beat Penn State 17–7, and Gator coach Ray Graves rode off the field on orange and blue shoulder pads. The son of a minister could win, people better believe.

Studying for the ministry, to cleanse souls instead of clothes, Bunny Duggan came to Johnson City for a ministers meeting led by Layton Ford, one of Billy Graham's pastors, and heard Reverend Spurrier's booming voice. Calling Bunny by name, after all those years. Still calling his son Stevie.

"Would you remember Stevie in your prayers?" Reverend Spurrier asked Bunny. "Because he's got 25 different offers from 25 different colleges."

"He is very proud but concerned that his son goes to the right place," Bunny told his father back in Athens. Adding that everybody in Johnson City seemed to think Steve Spurrier was going to the University of Tennessee.

That was the winter the mountains flanking the town seemed smaller. Orr visited Vanderbilt, the Universities of Tennessee, Kentucky, Mississippi, Alabama—and Clemson, Georgia Tech, Duke, and North Carolina on weekends he could watch ACC basketball games. Telling all the coaches he met with to recruit Jimmy Sanders.

Hitting the court for basketball practice, beefed up to 180 pounds after football season, Orr greeted Tommy Hager, his point guard since they were Junior 'Toppers, and some players who hadn't played much, standing where last year's veterans stood. Coach Little sat down with a chalkboard and worked out a four-corners offense that a noted North Carolina coach could claim, chalking up the only X authorized to shoot from outside. Pitting Spurrier against the world.

"With Steve we'll get ahead, and they'll be playing zone," Coach Little explained his new, slow-it-down scheme to the team. "Then we'll get the ball and spread out, make 'em come out of it and play man-to-man. If they pick him up, he'll dish. If not, he'll shoot."

That was the pick-and-roll play they'd run all season for Orr. He looked at his teammates with downcast eyes. He could see the floor and make the good pass, and he didn't really want to take every shot. But he had to respect what his coach chalked up.

A teammate got him ready for the pounding he'd take by busting his nose in practice. The X-man would wear a mask. The masked man got tossed out of the game at Morristown when his nose got smacked by one of those big boys Orr wasn't afraid to smack back.

He was embarrassed, he told friends, scoring 48 of the 'Topper's 52 points in the next two halves he played.

"Not really proud of that," Orr said. "Only one shooting."

Reporters whipped through the thesaurus to describe Spurrier scoring all those points with only two missed shots. Averaging 20 points a game, while the teams he played against got around 30, said the sports page in his father's hand.

"If they don't switch, he hits the jumper. If they do switch, he throws a perfect pass for the man rolling for a crip shot," Coach Little tutored reporters. "If they counted three-pointers, he'd be unreal."

His fifth-grade basketball coach didn't disagree. While Coach Little barked orders at practice, Reverend Spurrier stayed mighty quiet in the bleachers.

The boy's biggest fault? Constantly changing the way he shot free throws, imitating Bob Cousy of the Celtics or whoever else played on TV that week.

Players he outplayed wore masks of frustration. They hated that "Gunner," people in the bleachers could see.

"Don't think it bothers him any," Coach Little said. "He welcomes it."

<hr />

In first period they handed over the recruiting letters mailed to Spurrier's high school from as far away as Hawaii, and he'd make plans to visit the colleges in the SEC. Praying with his father before visiting the University of Alabama, where Paul "Bear" Bryant offered a scholarship.

In Tuscaloosa, Alabama, it was still cold. Even in the South, Florida seemed like a distant dream. Spurrier walked into Coach Bryant's office and sat across the big desk from the Bear, who took a look at the tall kid from Tennessee and said, "You're a good enough athlete to play safety here if it doesn't work out at quarterback."

Orr nodded, knowing Joe Namath was the only quarterback ever invited up to Bryant's famous practice field tower. Steve Sloan took snaps for the Tide, too, since his home state university ran that old single wing. Orr told Coach Bryant to talk to a receiver named Sanders at Science Hill and walked out so the next recruit could walk in.

Competition at quarterback wasn't what would keep him out of Tuscaloosa.

"They've won the SEC," he said to the gang. "I want to go to a school that hasn't done much. That's what appeals to me."

Not everyone who watched Joe Namath play ball for the Bear on the TV in the den felt the same way.

Reverend Spurrier's namesake son was looking at another fine season on the baseball diamond at ETSC. A father couldn't preach and coach everywhere. Graham was a good player, and a great brother, everyone said. He dismissed his father's ways with a wave of his hand.

"Steve and I know that's just Dad."

It was his brother who'd have to hear from friends, neighbors, church members, teachers, coaches, reporters, and the guys in the gang that his father "chewed my ear off," about *him*.

"That would bother me," Cotty said to Orr, in case he wanted to talk about it.

Orr just nodded. The town was the town.

In the depths of February, Reverend Spurrier joined area ministers welcoming back the Appalachian Preaching Mission. Held in April the one year Bill Wade appeared. Orr stood up with Jimmy Sanders in the ETSC gym and told a packed house what the Lord had done for him, on the field and in his life.

He'd talk if it'd make a difference.

Kingsport had four seniors who'd signed college basketball scholarships. But Orr torched the Tribe in the fourth quarter to give the 'Toppers the win, and the inside track to the Big Seven title, which went through Erwin. With the game knotted at 46, Orr "heavily guarded" and the clock dying, "he made a long one as the gun went off. Knocked the bottom out of it," Coach Little exulted.

"Talk about a heave from half-court that won the game," moaned Danny Jenkins, Orr's old neighbor from Wilson Street who'd become a Blue Devil. Stuck over in Unicoi County, telling that story.

Four nights later a win over Bristol made the 'Toppers Big Seven basketball champions as the home gym howled. Orr had played his way into a 165-pound skeleton that could hit jumpers. His coach had him bulk up to number 22.

University of Mississippi football coach John Vaught sat on the front row in the Science Hill gym as Orr sank two free throws in the final seconds to beat Elizabethton, 39–37. The coach of last season's unbeaten Sugar Bowl champions said he knew that boy would sink those free throws. Vaught posed with Reverend Spurrier for the paper and the men walked out into the night to talk football. Orr had breakfast in the kitchen with the coach of the Rebels, said he had more colleges to visit and went off to school.

More than thirty colleges offering scholarships . . . pick a sport . . . Spurrier still unsigned . . . were words the *Press-Chronicle* kept on the linotype until the total hit 40. A reporter realized the kid who kept asking for Spurrier's autograph was selling his signature to other kids. A braggart swore that Spurrier was dating his sister.

At University High the Junior Bucs didn't play football, and basketball mattered in March. The Junior Bucs scored 32 points and Orr scored 36, his father let the losers know as Science Hill took the district finals tournament trophy. The Big Seven champs ended the season ranked ninth in the state, losing in the state semifinals to Kingsport. Orr felt terrible. At the hospital they diagnosed mononucleosis and asked who he'd been kissing.

Coach Little got all he could out of "Gunner," a reporter suggested.

"Let me tell you, nobody takes credit for Steve Spurrier except Steve Spurrier," Coach Little said. Whatever coaching he did, a father would have done.

———

The snow evaporated and the hills budded up. Time to finally pick a college. Sanders told Orr he could "hardly walk anywhere" without a reporter asking, "Where's Steve going?" They smacked palms when Sanders got a scholarship offer from Vanderbilt, from coaches hoping he'd bring along his quarterback.

He asked if he could sign on the dotted line while Orr was still seeing coaches over steaks at the Peerless Restaurant, and signed.

Local radio stations, including WJHL, headquartered with the TV station at the top of Main Street, aired daily Spurrier college rumors, boosting ratings from antsy Volunteers. WETB general manager Bud Kelsey decided no one would outrumor radio station 790 on the AM dial.

"Steve Spurrier's going to Notre Dame," Kelsey announced, "because the Catholic Church has promised to make his daddy a cardinal." Kelsey's spoof just added another school to Orr's list.

Reverend Spurrier was hailed on the street by people who really wanted to talk about making his son a Volunteer. He said he'd be happy to drive Steve to Knoxville in the LeSabre, with Tommy Hager in the backseat.

Orr and Hager went to eat at the "jock cafeteria" on the campus in Knoxville, then had prime seats to watch Tennessee beat Adolph Rupp's Kentucky Wildcats in basketball, 63–55. They were welcomed to Tennessee by the governor and whisked to the president's house.

"You need to come to school here," said University of Tennessee president Andy Holt, offering the boys a plate of home-baked cookies, cold glasses of milk, and four free years at UT.

President Holt loved football and knew that the state's top quarterbacks didn't like the single-wing offense football coach Bowden Wyatt swore by.

"We'll change the offense for you," President Holt promised, as the Orange faithful held their breath. Maybe the president really could drag Coach Wyatt into the future, the boys said on the way home.

Wyatt had been a captain of the 1938 Tennessee team that went undefeated, a legendary Vol. But he hadn't taken his team to a bowl game in five seasons and was single-minded about the single wing, despite all the Vols clamoring for the T formation the coach at Alabama ran. Bryant had finally won in Knoxville that fall, with Namath passing for 148 yards.

Reverend Spurrier knew the local score and told his son that he'd open the door of the manse to the coach of the Vols.

On a day a young man dreamed of, Tennessee's football coach parked on Wilson Street and walked up the sidewalk, smiling at a future star. Ready to talk about the Big Orange crowd that would watch Spurrier run the single wing—at the stadium just expanded and renamed for legendary UT coach "General" Robert Neyland.

Orr revered the General and the Vols but hated the spirits he smelled on Coach Wyatt's breath, his parents would never forget. No coach who drank alcohol was gonna coach Steve Spurrier, no matter how spirited his spiel. Wouldn't matter what offense he ran. That coach just wasted his breath, the prospect told his parents when Wyatt was gone.

"They tried their best," his father said, knowing he'd be talking to some unhappy Volunteers.

Coach Wyatt was friends with Science Hill's basketball coach and called about his star shooting guard.

"Elvin, what's going on with Spurrier?" Coach Wyatt demanded.

"Coach, it's nothing to do with you or the university; he just doesn't feel like he can play single-wing football and be a tailback," Coach Little had to say.

"Hell, football is football," Coach Wyatt said. "Blocking and tackling! Tell him if he wants to he can come down here and kick for us."

Alabama really was the best, Orr told his friends, because the Bear expected to be the best. At the other SEC schools, a coach who didn't tell a prized recruit he would beat the Bear was "already done," Orr said. That coach was "just trying not to upset the natural pecking order." Orr planned to be a "disturber" in college.

"You ever going to sign with anybody?" friends kept gigging him.

"Those free steaks are pretty good," he had to admit.

He dragged himself to the Johnson City Lions Club Hilltoppers Basketball Banquet to get his MVP trophy and be honored with the Big Seven champs, thinking of the dirt field downtown where the defending state baseball champions warmed up.

Coach Little stood at the podium and summed up his Spurrier strategy that season: "Put the ball in his hands at the end and he'll win it for you."

His baseball coach knew Spurrier felt better when word got out he was playing matches with the Science Hill golf team. The baseball coach charged onto the links and took his player back.

"Told you 'Satch' Broyles wouldn't let him stray too far," star golfer Jerry Harkleroad told golf coach Cot Presnell.

Townspeople who had lived and died with number 11 for seven years, in all seasons, kept asking if he'd play in Knoxville.

"I'd go there in a heartbeat if they ran a different offense," Orr told people. He would never mention Coach Wyatt's drinking, no matter how much the town got on him.

Single wing, so what, they scoffed. Why, he could take up the Vols on that basketball scholarship offer. Orr just smiled, still thinking about playing baseball in college.

Florida Gator football coach Ray Graves drove from Gainesville, Florida, to Greeneville, Tennessee, to see Steve Spurrier pitch a baseball game, and believed he had the arm and the eye. Told him he could play football *and* baseball at the University of Florida.

Graves was back home in the hills, raised near Knoxville to play center for General Neyland. His snaps and blocks helped the Vols go 28–4. After playing in the NFL for the Eagles, Graves coached UT's offensive line, then spent 13 years at Georgia Tech under Bobby Dodd, legendary Volunteer and Kingsport player, until the Gators called in 1960. Graves had seen enough running plays to know he needed a good passer. The way Orr threw a baseball made Graves drive back to Florida, get his wife, Opal, and pay a visit to the Spurriers at the manse.

"There's this steak house in town," Orr said.

The Graveses had Peerless owner Jim Kalogeros put out shrimp cocktails and serve "the works." Reverend Spurrier sat at the head of the table, threatening to send the Methodist minister's son back to Florida for not thanking the Lord before digging into the shrimp. He patched that one up.

"Come down for the Spring Game," Coach Graves told the Spurriers' son, loud enough for the man who monitored his phone calls to hear.

———

At the Orange and Blue Game at Florida Field, an excited crowd enjoyed a perfect Florida day as the quarterbacks and receivers zipped the ball down the field. After the game Graves showed the young man from Tennessee the practice field under the sabal palms and the baseball stadium. Then he played the golf card.

"We just bought a golf course here at the university," Coach Graves told Orr, and took him to see the rolling green fairways. "You can play out here."

Graves got him some clubs and a bucket of balls and let him hit a few, as sunshine sparkled on the gator ponds by the greens.

Orr started feeling something else hit him. Stricken by the flu. Taken to the school infirmary, where Graves sat with him until the doctors had him feeling better.

Then he got that look, from a leader expecting greatness. Graves said a player at Florida had to earn everything, especially a starting spot. However, since Spurrier wasn't feeling up to par, he would be flown home on Bull Gator Jim Wellman's private plane, accompanied by two assistant coaches.

On the ride home from the airport, he told his dad the coach of the Gators was "an East Tennessee guy, like me," who'd "played at Tennessee for General Neyland," but "wasn't satisfied just to let places like Alabama and Tennessee do their thing while everyone else laid down because they're supposed to."

Coach Graves wouldn't just "run the ball and play defense. He wants to do something different. I like the sound of that," an excited quarterback prospect told his father, who had to agree.

Three days after turning 18, the quarterback greeted his new coach at the door of the manse, surrounded by people who'd helped him get to this day. Marjorie's dad drove up from Charlotte to see his grandson sign with the University of Florida, still talking about praying Billy Graham into the ministry. That sure intrigued Raymond Huff, who had hired Reverend Spurrier to preach at Calvary Presbyterian, taught Steve in Sunday school, gave him punting pointers, and wasn't missing this moment.

You bet Coach Graves had Reverend Spurrier say a prayer before his son signed, reminding them all of the brief time we have on this earth to grab glory.

Leading the broadcast on Channel 11's *News at 11* was the signing of Steve Spurrier by Florida Gators coach Ray Graves in the family den on Wilson Street, "as newspaper and television cameras clicked." The new Gator told reporters he'd major in business administration at Florida, although he "might switch to coaching later."

"He was born in Florida," Smallwood tried to explain to Volunteers on the street. "I think he has an attachment to the state."

"Florida's sort of an underdog," Orr said to his friends. "They've never won anything."

For once, they said, he was bragging.

The Tennessee people told him he was crazy to go to a school without any real trophies in the case. Then an Alabama assistant coach called the church line.

"We know you didn't sign with Alabama," the coach said to Reverend Spurrier, "but you won't amount to anything in Florida. You can't throw when you're flat on your back."

That didn't faze Orr either. He was focused on the biggest game of any season, against Kingsport, when a devil on his shoulder got him eyeing Jim Edgemon's pickle in the Science Hill cafeteria.

In a second the son of the man who made Reverend Spurrier the manager of the Bears had his pickle snatched. Orr fired it across the cafeteria, nailing teammate Richard Johnson—who hurled his mashed potatoes in retaliation.

"Thought he'd get by with it, but he got caught," Coach Tipton said when he heard Spurrier was "trying to play football in the cafeteria."

"Big game, Kingsport," the football coach added, heading to the principal's office with the baseball coach.

Principal Greenwell allowed the coaches to argue that, biblically speaking, Spurrier's punishment should begin Monday, so David could go up against the Goliaths that night. Leniency was granted for the boy Coach Broyles claimed had perfect Sunday school attendance.

Snowflakes floated onto the field at Kingsport as Orr pitched the win. Then he served his three-day suspension at Kiwanis Park, him and his ball. He couldn't understand how that was punishment. Did a lot of thinking in the park, though. No more hot-headed moves.

"Coolness," he realized, was "a must for success."

His mother went in place of his father to Principal Greenwell's office to reinstate their son.

———

On the hill above Kiwanis Park, the gang gathered in graduation robes in the roasting heat, talking about life after high school, hearing that a chilly night would roll down from the mountains on the horizon.

Cotty offered his quarterback a page in his annual. "Orr," he wrote at the top, where Cotty would expect to see his own name:

Don't forget the ol' football games and practicing. I hope you get that long snap down pat. Remember that snap against Church Hill,

"Whew," that was a "killer." Be good at Wofford and don't raise too much good night.

Turning to the page "reserved for Coach Tipton," Orr handed his yearbook to the coach who wouldn't let his father holler. Tipton wrote that his quarterback would be remembered, and missed, his whistle dangling across the page.

"Terrific doesn't take care of it," Coach Tipton said, telling number 11 his jersey would be retired and displayed in the trophy case.

As parents, friends, and girlfriends gathered, Ken and Cotty vied for the praise they claimed their quarterback never gave.

"He never has acknowledged I'm the reason he's not a cripple," Ken said.

"I'm the reason he's still alive," Cotty countered.

His parents said they never saw anyone ignore more camera flashes. Then they got in the Buick and drove 500 miles to Memphis, where their son had a ball game to play.

The 'Toppers took the field at the Fairgrounds in Memphis and whipped Chattanooga East Ridge High School 18–9, making Chattanooga people swear they'd root for Memphis Christian Brothers High School to pound little Science Hill.

The schools split the first two games. The 1963 title game got underway in freakish heat, with Science Hill breaking out T-shirts and magic markers to face the Christian Brothers a third time. Orr took the mound knowing his dad was praying in the bleachers, not hearing him.

Must've prayed for that boy to do great deeds, his last time on the mound. Hurling a six-hitter, allowing one earned run, batting two-for-three, and scoring. Hitting .500 in Memphis, finishing his time in Science Hill wool with a .400 batting average and no losses pitching, the papers would say. When the scoreboard read 7–5 'Toppers and he pitched the last out, his guys carried him off the mound and came back for Coach Broyles.

"Champions of their faith," Broyles said, seeing Orr lead the team in a winning prayer. The giant killer had a long bus ride home. Even if he won a national championship at Florida, there wouldn't be a celebration like the one in his hometown. The team would ride into town in style, after Orr insisted at a Western Wear store they all buy cowboy hats.

At the city limits on the Jonesboro Highway by the National Guard Armory, a big sight when the Spurriers' Buick first drove into town, the team was officially greeted by the mayor, the superintendent of schools, local dignitaries, and hundreds of Hilltoppers cheering the champions riding in from the west. The Sunliner bus awaited. The city fathers decreed that the men who raised those boys up right should ride beside their sons in the parade, the *Press-Chronicle* proudly reported.

Reverend Spurrier took his place beside his son in the 10-gallon hat, at high noon.

Looking down from the Sunliner bus with the top off, a father could see the end of the road. All he'd worked and prayed for, helping his boy at 7:30 p.m. to go play ball far away. The promise of a game of catch in the churchyard had been fulfilled. Stevie never missed a Sunday school class or a worship service in his father's church. Front and center Sunday evening. Prayer meeting every Wednesday, for a decade and a half.

And every time he played under a scoreboard, his dad was there too, one way or another.

He waved at his brother, tipped his cowboy hat to the crowd, and pulled out one of Coach Broyles's rubber practice balls. Bouncing it off the pavement, all along the parade route. Watching 'Toppers young and old clap Sid Smallwood on the back.

PART TWO

GREENER FIELDS

Thirty-five first-half points and Steve's unhappy.
Let's go back to New York.
— CBS ANNOUNCER VERNE LUNDQUIST

CHAPTER NINE

Florida Starr

FORGET THE PAST AND THE FUTURE, PLAY IN THE PRESENT, THE LESSON learned in Kiwanis Park, got Florida's quarterback playing like a Heisman Trophy winner. Standing at that podium in New York City feeling grateful, he held out the bronze statue of a player stiff-arming a tackler that weighed 25 pounds.

Saying, "This isn't my trophy, this belongs to the University of Florida," he called up UF president Dr. J. Wayne Reitz in front of all the cameras.

"I want to give this back to the University of Florida, and to the people of Florida for what they have done for me," said Steve Spurrier, handing the Heisman to President Reitz.

"Here, let the school have it."

Team award, really. Distant second to an SEC Championship.

The real prize smiled up at him from the front row.

Let the historians count the passing records and the defensive backs he'd torched since the first day of freshman football in August 1963, stepping onto the practice field under the sabal palms with players bigger than the guys from Church Hill.

Jim Ritch, his mom's brother in Starke, Florida, had smiled at the tall, skinny boy being driven to Gainesville in the family Buick.

"Steve, those boys at Florida are pretty big," Uncle Jim said. "They have some mighty good boys on that squad."

Big boys, he had to agree. What would they call the twangy, some said bow-legged, freshman from Tennessee?

"Confident," he kept hearing.

"Orr," he told the guys in the huddle, with no explanation. Leaving his finger-pointing back in the hills. He'd gotten where he aimed to be.

Not wearing No. 11 at Florida, though. Stuck with No. 16.

He called home on the pay phone in the dorm, hearing his dad pick up the phone in the manse. Telling him another quarterback from Tennessee had *his* number.

"The guy got here in the summer and already picked out No. 11," he explained, so his dad would know who to root for when he drove down for that first freshman game.

Win that number back, his father told him, then called Coach Graves anyway. The other quarterback from Tennessee agreed that whoever started the first game for the "Baby Gators" freshman team would wear No. 11.

That would be Orr, the guys said. They'd watched him do pushups with one hand, the other hand clutching the football. That number 11 drove the offense down the field against the freshmen in burnt orange and dark blue uniforms at the stadium in Auburn, Alabama. After the second touchdown pass, he looked up to see his father in the stands. The miles between Auburn and Johnson City couldn't keep him away, but the crowd swallowed his words. Or maybe the pitcher did okay.

The coach seemed to appreciate his quarterback leading a prayer in the visitor's locker room after beating the freshmen calling themselves War Eagles 21–7.

Back in Gainesville the quarterback from Tennessee who gave up his No. 11 jersey decided to transfer.

"Couldn't make it at Florida," Reverend Spurrier said, when he heard. God doesn't bless everyone on the battlefield.

That number 11 can play, said Pepper Rodgers, the play caller for Florida's varsity. Orr wondered if "Coach Pepper" said that to all the freshmen. Gator publicist Norm Carlson, who had met the prospect from Tennessee back in the spring and caught his confidence, wanted to be Spurrier's publicist. Carlson said he could make number 11 a star. Two number ones together were promotable.

Big books, history, biology, business, subjects of lectures in huge halls full of sleepy freshmen, had him studying the ways of ladies clearly not from Johnson City. They had beer on University Avenue, where looking like a football player got you a funky-smelling glass of cheer. Cotty and Ken saw a different Orr when they came to visit. Hard to imagine him sitting in a booth in the Purple Porpoise with a beer in his hand, his father would surely say.

Needing a gang to hang out with, Orr went to a frat party with Graham McKeel, his fullback and roommate, and joined the fraternity McKeel joined, becoming a brother of Alpha Tau Omega. The ATOs had a huge brick house with wide white columns holding up the front porch, across 34th Street from the president's office. The brothers could walk straight down Campus Road to Florida Field. They had that Gator attitude.

If a senior track star went out with a girl Orr was seeing, he had bigger brothers on the offensive line who'd pay the track guy a visit.

Freshman, the girls would say. Quarterback.

"What you got?" he asked his freshman receivers like they were huddling in Kiwanis Park. What slow Dawg can we go after?

Getting plays signaled in and drawing patterns on his palm, he threw scoring drives to beat the Georgia freshmen 44–12. His father cheered in the stands at Florida Field with Marjorie and the other parents and fans. If Baby Gator games didn't matter, they wouldn't keep score.

On a Sunday phone call to the manse, they went through the plays and highlights of another hard-hitting sermon at Calvary after a late-night ride.

"He gets in the backseat and goes to sleep when I drive," Marjorie said, "but I don't sleep when he drives."

His father got his mother to copilot the Buick from Johnson City to Miami, to see their son go up against the freshman team of the hated Hurricanes. No need to venture over the causeway, where the Presbyterian Church had become a synagogue. The pastor and his wife were expected at the Orange Bowl.

Hitting 10 of 15 passes, 2 for touchdowns, and nailing some coffin-corner punts wasn't enough for a win in Miami.

"You know, Steve had a good night," Reverend Spurrier said to Coach Graves, walking with the team into the visitor's locker room.

"He did have a good night," said the coach, wanting to agree with one dedicated father.

The reverend coming all those miles to brag about a loss just made his son mad. When the Baby Gators scrimmaged the varsity back in Gainesville, the freshman quarterback had the poise and the most points.

Junior Tommy Shannon quarterbacked Florida to a 10–6 upset of Joe Namath and The Bear, with number 11 watching from the sidelines. Only home loss at Alabama for decades. Watching Coach Graves carried off 'Bama's field on orange and blue shoulder pads, the Bear said he looked forward to seeing Florida in Tuscaloosa next year. His team didn't have to go to Gainesville to play the Gators. They were Alabama.

With Thanksgiving closing down the athletes' dorm, Orr and a teammate walked out to Waldo Road and stuck out their thumbs, hitchhiking to Tennessee to save some dough and see the hills through a Florida boy's eyes. A blizzard hit the North Carolina mountains, a white welcome home. Climbing into the cab of an 18-wheeler, full of freshman football stories, they heard from the truck driver that President Kennedy had been shot in Dallas.

Seemed like Castro paid someone to pull the trigger, like someone would do in Newport.

"You didn't have to hitchhike. We had enough money to pay your way," his mother said, shaking her head, mighty happy to see him. His dad hugged him. The Florida boy went out and rolled in the snow.

At Christmastime the college man returned, 205 pounds of SEC muscle that basketball wouldn't burn off. Feeling like he should be playing something instead of taking in the decorations downtown, he went to see Coach Little, Coach Tipton, and Coach Broyles. He listened to Ken and Cotty tell the gang about the parties at the ATO house. With the tree lights twinkling, he sat down with his dad to watch Bill Wade quarterback the Bears in the NFL Championship Game.

Wrigley Field looked frozen on TV. Chicago's "Monsters of the Midway" defense kept New York quarterback Y. A. Tittle and flanker Frank Gifford from running away with the game. Wade threw to tight end Mike Ditka only when the Giants crowded the line, and ran the ball himself for two scores.

Not the offense he showed Coach Tipton, Orr said.

Those were Coach Evans's plays, his dad agreed.

Kicking off Florida's spring semester with a party, the ATO brothers opened the doors of the frat house and transfer student Jerri Starr walked in. She'd left the University of North Carolina Women's College in Greensboro at the end of the fall semester to be closer to her boyfriend. He was at Florida Southern College in Lakeland that Saturday night.

Growing up in Fort Lauderdale with her sisters, she mourned their father's sudden death in 1952 and loved football, proud to be the niece of Penn State football coach Rip Engle. She wrote about football for her high school paper and viewed quarterbacks as a breed apart. All different. Not one of them boring, she told her friends in Fort Lauderdale.

"I'm happiest around men," she told her new sorority sisters at UF. "Just because I haven't been around any of them."

Plenty of people hung around the tall freshman standing by the fireplace in the ATO chapter room. How could a freshman have so many friends?

"That's Steve Spurrier," people said. Ah, he's a quarterback.

Did he notice her, with her swirling blond hair and soulful blue eyes, across the crowded room? He'd command big bucks for a date later in the week from a girl at a fundraiser called "Dollars for Scholars."

When he showed up in Jerri's biology class, or she showed up in his, she walked right up and said, "The girl who won dinner with you at the Dollars for Scholars fundraiser lives in my dorm."

He seemed to like it that she came up to him. Cool, like he stood by the fireplace, smiling that smile.

"You know, that cocky, out-of-the-side-of-his-face smile only quarterbacks have," she'd tell her sisters back at the dorm.

"You can call me Orr," he told her. She said she would.

Clearly he needed watching. She signed up to be his "little sister," along with the three ATO brothers she already looked after, "to keep 'em out of trouble." Especially the quarterback and the golfer. Maybe the fate of Florida football depended on her.

She had no illusions. A quarterback "dated a million people," she told her sorority sisters. She'd just dumped the guy who went to college in Lakeland and "certainly wasn't looking."

"We're going to a movie," Orr told her. She spent most of her money for the semester on a green Villager dress. He meant the drive-in. He'd borrowed a car. She rustled around for coins to help with gas. No need to open her closet and get out the green dress next time he asked her out.

"You don't just date him and he doesn't date anyone else," she acknowledged, strategizing with her sisters. "It's always a game, a competition."

In the spring, when Orr felt like warming up on the mound, he put on pads and worked with Florida's first-team offense while Tommy Shannon, the presumed starter, played baseball for the Gators. The rising sophomore knew Coach Pepper's playbook and ran the team like a veteran until he stepped back on the grass for a kicking drill. "Steamboat" Scales rushed the kicker and fell on his leg, tearing ligaments that would take all summer to heal.

Once more Orr rode around Johnson City with the old gang, spending time with his coaches and with Sara and her husband Roland Henderson's baby. Hearing Graham talk about his job at Channel 11. Hearing that their great-uncle Hugh Spurrier died in Charlotte, and that Grandma Willie and Uncle Eddie took it hard. Founders of the family gone. Mother and son living at the duplex like in the Depression.

Worshipping at his old church, taking in the power of his father's words, Orr heard his old neighbors making bets on how much longer their pastor would last.

"I want to be with Steve," they'd heard his father say.

He got back to Gainesville with a spring in his step, fired up to be practicing with the first-team offense at Florida, and found out his father would be preaching and coaching there, too.

At Calvary Presbyterian Church they wouldn't forget the day Reverend Spurrier left his place behind the pulpit, walked down to the pews, raised his arms, and said, "God has called me to Florida."

No one in the sanctuary looked surprised. No one could bring the Bible to life like Reverend Spurrier, they said. Filling Fellowship Hall to thank the Spurriers for nine years of service, they congratulated the new pastor of the First Presbyterian Church of High Springs, just 22 miles from Gainesville—where God and the Gators smiled on a pastor looking for work, his son heard people say.

The pastor of High Springs Presbyterian stood under the sabal palms and live oaks ringing the practice field, waiting to see how Coach Graves handled his quarterbacks.

Trimmed down to 195 pounds by September, Orr was ready to share snaps with senior Tom Shannon. Teammates said the guy no one could beat at Ping-Pong or pool would win the starting job. Nicknames are for stars. Coach Graves prepared his offense to "platoon" the quarterbacks. The senior would start the Gators' first game against Southern Methodist University, televised on ABC. Spurrier said that was a good way to do it.

He got on the field against SMU in the second quarter. As his dad and 33,000 Gators held their breath, the new quarterback flapped his arms, seemingly motioning for quiet. He'd told Graham and the gang he'd wave at them on TV before his first play, which was a handoff to the running back. Another run got stuffed. On third-and-9 at his own 37, he called time-out, jogged to the sidelines, and asked Coach Graves what to call.

"Son, you've got a four-year scholarship. I've only got a two-year contract. You call the play," Coach Graves told his quarterback for the first time in his coaching career.

Armed with his coach's faith, Spurrier threw a screen pass to Jack Harper, who took the ball 56 yards. Glancing at the stands after his first completion at Florida, Orr knew his dad had pointers for him. In the fourth quarter he threw his first varsity touchdown pass, to Charley Casey, to put his team up 24–8. Orr acted like he'd gotten the ball in the end zone before, in case anyone in Cocke County was watching on TV.

Next week in Jackson, Mississippi, playing in front of 50,000 Gator haters, Spurrier jogged onto the field in the fourth quarter of a tied game, huddling up the team 73 yards from pay dirt. Seeing guys who looked panicked, he got in their face.

"Do what I tell you to do and we'll win this ball game," they wouldn't forget him saying. With a minute to go, he hit five passes and Bob Lyle kicked the game winner, sending the Bulldogs home 16–13 losers.

The SEC Back of the Week was Florida sophomore Spurrier, his father had to picture people on Wilson Street reading in the paper.

Seemed like Reverend Spurrier had always preached in the maple sanctuary in High Springs and walked down Main Street with the *Gainesville Sun* sports section in his hand.

"I'm Steve Spurrier's father," he'd say, a sure conversation starter in Gator Country.

They knew him at the door of the Florida locker room, after a big win in October against Coach Vaught's Mississippi Rebels. Reverend Spurrier wasn't celebrating in the shower steam. He told Coach Graves to put in better plays for his son and get him on the field sooner.

Coach Graves banned players' fathers from the Gators' locker room. Reverend Spurrier had been the only one allowed in there.

Florida took on the South Carolina Gamecocks for Homecoming and won 37–0, showing why some people said that school was cursed.

Shannon took on the role of teacher, seeing what Orr could do, ensuring the guys on the team stayed tight. The upstart Gators were undefeated, ranked ninth in the nation. But quarterbacks have egos, reporters told Graves. He said the only people who could mess up his dual quarterback system was them. Then he started Spurrier in Tuscaloosa.

In his first start as a college quarterback, Orr staked his team to a 14–7 lead, "Roll, Tide" ringing in his ears. He kept 'Bama pinned deep with his punts. Then Namath twisted his knee. Backup quarterback Steve Sloan brought Alabama back, leading 17–14 with three minutes on the clock.

Spurrier drove the Gators 12 yards from glory with a minute to go. He scrambled for 5 yards, and a Crimson Tide helmet took out two of his teeth. Reeling from the hit, spitting Gator teeth on 'Bama's field, he thought the 7-yard line was the 2 and called a fullback dive instead of spiking the ball. With the clock dying Jimmy Hall's kick went wide.

"Just plain lost track of things in the confusion," he apologized to his coaches, his team, and his dad after losing by the skin of his teeth. That Alabama team would win the national title.

"Best offensive team I've seen," said the Bear, after watching that other quarterback from Tennessee play ball.

After beating Auburn 14–10 at Florida Field, he heard his father talk about his 1 completion out of 6 pass attempts. Told his dad he lost to

Georgia because the Dawg's field goal kicker grabbed the ball and scored on a broken play. But the reverend saw redemption in a downpour, with his son going long to get the Gators into the muddy end zone for a 12–10 win over the hated Hurricanes.

After beating the seventh-ranked Bayou Bengals in wintry Baton Rouge, the 7–3 Gators got no bowl game invitation. Time to go over every play of the season over Christmas 1964 with his dad and mom in High Springs.

——

Watching Spurrier's every move from the Baby Gator squad was number 16, Harmon Wages, a quarterback from Robert E. Lee High School in Jacksonville, where long-haired guys in a rock band got sent to the principal's office by crew-cut gym teacher Leonard Skinner. The school had just retired jersey No. 16 and hung it in the trophy case.

Wages topped the list of quarterbacks who couldn't beat out Spurrier in the spring. Signal callers better be cold-blooded, Jerri Starr said. When Coach Graves whistled for wind sprints, number 11 talked number 16 into hanging back so they'd both look a little slow.

Coach Pepper left Florida for UCLA, to coach Heisman hopeful Gary Beban. Spurrier took the practice field in August like always, hearing his coach say, "You call the plays." The signal caller huddled up the offense and looked into everyone's eyes.

"Play the best you can on each play and the score will take care of itself," Orr said. "When the game's over you can look up and see how we did." Gators, he told his teammates, fixate on *now*.

Florida's starting quarterback had to stay away from the newsstands, where *Look* magazine had him pegged as a star like Bill Wade, instead of an "undergator."

Beating Northwestern University 24–14 at Evanston, Illinois, then losing to Mississippi State 18–13 in Gainesville, had Coach Graves talking with UF research scientist Robert Cade, developer of a "sports drink" he wanted to test out on Gator players.

When Graham felt left behind in Johnson City, he picked up the gang after work on Friday and drove south, telling 'em they had a place to stay in High Springs. Everyone wanting to see what Orr could do in Gainesville on game day.

Toasting the gang in the stands with Gatorade, he took them all the length of the field to beat LSU. Coach Graves blamed a massive traffic jam squarely on Orr, since "No one can leave early." He was Back of the Week across the nation, giving Sid Smallwood and his Hilltopper coaches a good headline to read along with news of former players fighting in Vietnam.

His dad and mom drove across Georgia and Alabama to see their son "knocked cuckoo" at Auburn, as his publicist Norm Carlson put it—scoring 10 points he couldn't remember scoring. Losing to Auburn 28–17 had his dad grumbling in the Buick crossing the Suwanee River to preach the Sunday morning sermon back in High Springs.

They opened the thesaurus at the *Florida Times-Union* when Spurrier beat Georgia in Jacksonville on a last-ditch drive and he became "Goldflinger," bonding with "Golden Orr" on the *Gainesville Sun* sports page. The *Alligator*, UF's student newspaper, said SOS always saved his school's team. "Super Steve," his father called him in interviews, making him mad enough to score more.

The Seminoles arrived in Gainesville Thanksgiving weekend to face vengeful Gators, after a first-ever win over Florida the previous season in Tallahassee. At Florida Field the 'Noles led 17–16 with 2:10 to play. Orr told his coach not to worry and got the Gators 25 yards from the goal line in four plays. Seeing Charley Casey covered, Spurrier sprinted out, motioned Casey downfield, and hit him in the end zone for the win.

On University Avenue, where they celebrated beating FSU with a fervor that made Gainesville police grease the phone poles, keeping fans on the sidewalks, they saw their hero squiring around Jerri Starr.

He finished ninth in the 1965 Heisman Trophy voting, just behind Purdue quarterback Bob Griese and just ahead of Alabama's Steve Sloan. Happy to help his school get its first major bowl bid, an invitation to the Sugar Bowl that made Coach Graves beam.

On the bumpy ride across the Gulf Coast to face the Missouri Tigers, Albert the mascot got his snout banged up. Mizzou's pass rush bruised the Gators in the wilting heat. The Tigers led 20–0 as the fourth quarter began, held to a field goal on their last drive. Seventy-seven thousand looked down from the stands, with a nation of doubters behind the TV cameras.

Spurrier started rolling out, buying time to throw his first touchdown pass. Graves had the team go for 2 to make the score look more respectable, but the conversion try failed. Getting the ball back, Orr threw to tight end Barry Brown underneath the coverage, then went deep to Casey for another score. Again a 2-point play failed. After the third touchdown pass in eight minutes, a 2-point try fell short and Florida lost to Missouri 20–18. Hitting 27 of 45 passes for 352 yards, Spurrier took home the only Sugar Bowl MVP trophy ever awarded to a player from the losing team.

For Christmas he brought his roommate, center Bill Carr, to High Springs to help his mom's choir sing the Christmas cantata. Standing with the believers in the maple choir box, celebrating the birth of Christ, Orr could see the spirit of Christmas past in the pews. Maybe giving thanks for those who love to tell the story.

The big Gator center told the Spurriers his dad was a Baptist minister, and he was proud to hike the ball to the son of a Presbyterian minister coached by the son of a Methodist minister.

Could a preacher's kid have any more names? On his father's TV Orr heard Auburn football coach Shug Jordan talk about next season's opponents, with a Southern drawl that had him wanting to beat "Steve Superior."

———

What prospects awaited Jerri Starr in 1966? Her mother in Fort Lauderdale planned to take her far from Florida. She'd spend six weeks at a "language school" in Switzerland over the summer.

"Mom's making me go," Jerri explained to the quarterback she'd leave behind. "She said she paid the money and we're going."

Among the workers installing 10,000 extra seats at Florida Field that summer was the quarterback who made Gator fans buy more tickets. Thinking, as he pounded tenpenny nails into aluminum slats, that if he ever took charge of a football program he'd make sure hammers hammered, new facilities rose on campus, and school colors splashed progress for the recruits to see.

Riding around Gainesville in a convertible with his Florida gang, remembering how it felt to cruise hometown streets, he sat on top of the seat and fell out. Tried to hold onto the car and the road. His hands hurt. Left hand sprained. Thumb on his throwing hand sprained. Backup quarterback Wages warming up.

A *Gainesville Sun* reporter dug up the fact that senior quarterbacks at Florida hadn't prospered. Remember, a sophomore took the starting job from senior Tom Shannon. Senior Spurrier tucked that story into his billfold, then took it out and read it before jogging onto the practice field in August.

Seeing his dad in the distance. Rubbing his hands. Missing his girl.

"I want you to be my date at the ATO house after all the football games this fall," he wrote to Jerri, a sentence that would leap off the page at her in Switzerland. Speaking a whole new language.

She was greeted back in Gainesville with a little box and a disclaimer.

"He gave me a little ruby ring and he said, 'Now, this is not an engagement ring, this is not an engagement ring,'" she reported back at the sorority house, showing off the ring from Orr.

"When you date a quarterback," she told her younger sisters, "nothing is written in stone."

He probably thought twice, "or five times," she guessed, before mailing that letter to Switzerland claiming he'd built bleachers at Florida Field and earned an A in summer school in Human Growth and Development.

A great quarterback knows when to pull the trigger.

The Wednesday before the home opener, Spurrier made the call of his life. Going against his father's coaching, making a date for all seasons.

—❦—

Coach Graves looked up from studying Northwestern University's defensive personnel to see his quarterback in the doorway.

"Coach, can I get off Wednesday morning? I'm going to get married."

"Yeah, I guess so," his coach said, telling him to be back at practice that afternoon in case he wasn't kidding.

He had a car, and teammate Fred Goldsmith and Jerri's roommate Louise Warren for witnesses, hitting the road to Folkston, Georgia,

Wedding Capital of the South. Speeding through Yulee, Florida, like a man on a mission.

Spotlit by the law, the "hotshot quarterback" had to take a ticket, despite his delivery of that gotta-get-married-before-afternoon-practice line. Probably a Bulldog on patrol near the Georgia border.

Across the St. Marys River, the back roads through the red clay cow fields all look alike. When the wedding party looked up, they were entering the city limits of Kingsland, Georgia, not Folkston.

Orr called an audible. They drove downtown, to the "Royal District," passing art deco buildings like on Miami Beach and a mural of a steam train chugging through history. Walking with fishermen through the coastal streets, Jerri found a gold ring for $10 in a tackle shop and vowed never to take it off.

The Kingsland Clinical Lab on Lee Street pronounced the couple fit to be man and wife. A few doors down, they bought flowers.

At the First United Methodist Church on the corner, Reverend W. E. Dennis took one look at the intent in their eyes and married them at a candlelit altar, in a "beautiful ceremony," Jerri gushed, bestowing the blessing of the Father, the Son, and the Holy Spirit on Mr. and Mrs. Stephen Orr Spurrier.

Whooping back across the river to Florida, they found a Holiday Inn in Jacksonville serving Southern fried chicken and BLTs, and the groom fired up a 50-cent cigar. Confident that in his father's eyes that would be the least of his transgressions.

Would this be where he'd get his comeuppance? What blessing would he receive in High Springs? Was this the confrontation he'd aimed for all those years, booting the ball through the backyard, shooting at the hoop above the garage? Working out his own moves. Making the choice to start his own family, without permission from the man who'd want to help him say his vows right.

Maybe telling his father he was a married man would be like jogging back onto the practice field and getting word that a reporter and photographer from *Life* magazine had waited around for him all morning and left without pictures or a story. Maybe eyes had not seen, and ears had not heard, but he had a ring on his finger. Details after the game.

Orr got his new receivers running good routes at practice and dropped off his new wife at the sorority house, where she had a story for Rush Night.

"We just didn't want to have a lot of people there, so we didn't," Jerri said, basking in sisterly congratulations, showing off her gold ring.

"Plus, it's football season."

—◆—

The First Couple of Florida football moved into a brick apartment building on Seventeenth Street behind the post office, across University Avenue from campus. They had a porch for grilling out, in apartment 11, even though quarterbacks don't grill. Jerri said she'd withdraw from school and be a wife.

Bill Carr handed her a notepad and a pencil, for all the messages Orr's roomies previously had to take. Orr was a man of the people, had his number in the phone book. His line rang into his room, and rang and rang.

Reporters called to ask who he'd throw to, since receivers Jack Harper and Charley Casey had walked across the stage at graduation.

"Adjustments are continually being made on any football team," Orr said, in case the reporters got their own team.

Wednesday's groom kicked off the season Saturday against Northwestern and saw two Wildcats on the kicking team get up slowly. They were the safeties Orr targeted with a throw to Richard Trapp for a 53-yard score. After pushing the lead to 26–7, the groom kicked two field goals, making him UPI's National Back of the Week.

Jerri cheered in the stands beside golfer Steve Melnyk, the other star Gator she little-sistered, saying, "I've got something to show you after the game."

"After the game they showed me the ring," Melnyk reported back at the ATO house.

"Couldn't have had a big wedding with all our friends anyway," the bride explained to her big brothers. "Steve's father would have had a fit if anyone drank beer."

Sunday was the day to visit the father wanting to go over all the plays, with word of an adjustment in the game plan. The parents met the newlyweds with disappointment in their eyes and on their lips.

"There should have been a nice church wedding in August, when a preacher usually has time off," said Reverend Spurrier.

"Why did you elope?" he asked.

"We were ready," Jerri said.

"I guess," said her new father-in-law, "but you should never have run off like that."

Steve and Jerri just smiled at one another. No one could make them stop.

❧

On Saturday a quarterback let his playing do the talking. Throwing strikes to beat Mississippi State 28–7. Then he played in Tennessee for the first time as a Gator, beating Vandy 13–0 on a freezing day in Nashville as the gang from Johnson City cheered the offenses led by Spurrier and Sanders.

"Spurrier was throwing those passes under his leg, sidearm, and behind his back," he read in the local paper, remembering how sports-writers from Vanderbilt exaggerate.

After riding with undefeated Florida into Tallahassee to face the Seminoles, napping on the way, he lofted a 41-yard scoring strike and a 2-point pass to Trapp to take a 22–19 lead in the fourth quarter. A sideline-slicing punt with three minutes to go stifled the Seminoles, who swore they scored, and had riot police on University Avenue putting out fires of celebration, another rescue by SOS.

In Raleigh, NC State's field had a high grass crown, aiding water drainage, discombobulating a visiting quarterback. Behind in the fourth quarter, Spurrier lashed together two scoring drives, throwing 31 yards to Trapp to take a 17–10 victory over the Wolfpack and the clock. Inspiring John Logue at the *Atlanta Journal* to write, "Blindfolded, with his back to the wall, with his hands tied behind him, Steve Spurrier would still be a two-point favorite at his own execution."

The SEC Back of the Week in a 28–0 win over LSU had Coach Graves "running out of adjectives to describe him." Wanton wordsmiths could take over.

"Here comes Batman, holy touchdowns," Trapp shouted at his quarterback at practice, so a reporter could hear. That writer would go with "Splendid Steve."

At "Gator Growl," UF's Homecoming celebration, a packed stadium swayed to the sounds of the Pride of the Sunshine marching band, cheered with the Florida Dazzlers, and hooted at student comedians joking about Steve Spurrier expecting a visit from the stork.

He heard the talk on Campus Road. Sixty thousand people headed to the Homecoming game to fill those new bleachers. Facing Auburn.

At breakfast on game day, he told a teammate he'd dreamed about kicking the winning field goal that afternoon, Coach Graves heard. Orr would say he was always saying that.

Defensive coach Gene Ellenson always gave the Gators uplifting words in the locker room. Saying fate favors men who want to win.

After Auburn matched Florida's first score with an 89-yard kickoff return and Auburn linebacker "Gusty" Yearout grabbed a fumble in midair and ran 91 yards for a 14-7 Auburn lead, Ellenson called the game "the closest runaway I've ever seen." Yearout grabbed another loose ball to forge a 27–27 tie with 4:32 left in the game.

When Wages ran out to receive the kickoff, number 11 was the picture of frustration, knowing his team should be winning. He looked to the Florida blue sky for calm, huddled up his guys, and went to work, hitting clock-stopping passes. Facing fourth-and-13 at the Auburn 24 with 2:12 on the clock, Orr jogged to the sideline.

There was talk of a kick among the jawing Gators, with Coach Graves thinking Wayne "Shade Tree" Barfield would do the kicking, though he hadn't made many over 30 yards. The quarterback zipped on his kicking shoe and jogged back onto the field, convinced his coach had faith in him. No need to look back to the sidelines to see his coach in shock.

Looking at a kick he'd practiced every day as a boy, aiming at upright limbs, Orr prayed for strength and courage, not for God to get the ball over the goalposts. That was the kicker's job.

"Watch for the fake!" players and coaches screamed from the Auburn sidelines.

"We better hope it's a fake," Coach Shug Jordan told his team. "If Superior kicks it, he'll make it."

Orr knew the threat of a pass would slow down the rushers, make the defensive backs hang back, let him kick the ball lower and longer.

Stevie Spurrier's football hero, Doak Willett, posing on the practice field at Tennessee Wesleyan College. PHOTO COURTESY OF LEE "DOAK" WILLETT

Spurrier looks downfield against the hated Bulldogs in the annual Florida-Georgia game at the Gator Bowl in Jacksonville, Florida. UF LIBRARIES

Florida coach Ray Graves entrusted his team and livelihood to Spurrier's play calling, quarterbacking, kicking, and punting. UF LIBRARIES

Spurrier, No. 11, played SEC teams like the game was in his backyard.
UF LIBRARIES

Shannon sees a special talent at quarterback at Florida in the fall of '64 and willingly shares the field with Spurrier.

Sophomore Steve Spurrier, No. 11, and rising senior and experienced SEC quarterback Tom Shannon, No. 12, prepare to split time behind center at Florida in the 1964 college football season. UF LIBRARIES

The Ball Coach has a fist bump ready for Alshon Jeffery after the Gamecock freshman catches his first touchdown pass in 2009. PHOTO BY THE AUTHOR

In a crowd of 85,000, Spurrier talks to his son Steve Jr., an assistant coach sitting in the press box upstairs. PHOTO BY THE AUTHOR

Spurrier sings "Health, Carolina" with his "hero of the game," Spencer Lanning, after USC's first win in history over a top-five team: the 2009 defeat of Ole Miss, 16–10. PHOTO BY THE AUTHOR

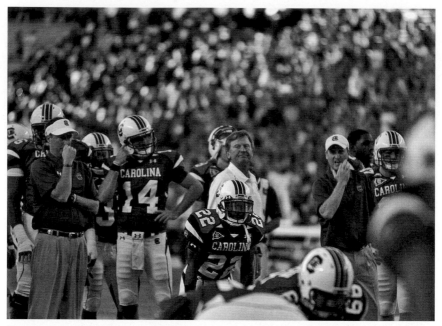

Warming up the Gamecocks for a home game, Spurrier gives his offense the play call. PHOTO BY THE AUTHOR

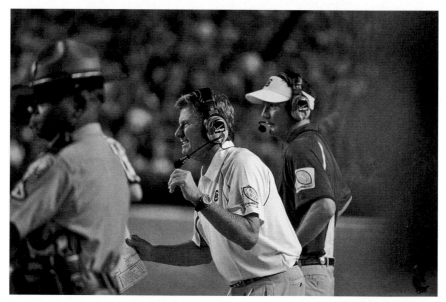

Spurrier sees what his quarterback better see if the Gamecocks are going to soar.
PHOTO BY THE AUTHOR

The snap, the hold, the hush had him kicking into the laces in a moment frozen like a painting.

"Straight down the middle the whole way," Graves burst out. Graham couldn't breathe with Jerri clutching him as the ball tumbled over the crossbar and into the end zone seats. Luck, fate, or God smiling on the Gators?

"God loves Steve Spurrier," said number 16, diving on number 11 with the rest of the team as 60,000 Gators roared.

After the fans ran onto the field and the players ran into the stands, Spurrier got the locker room quiet, got down on his knees, and thanked God for the victory.

A legion of reporters, including the first *New York Times* writer ever sent to cover a football game in Gainesville, wanted to talk about Spurrier's 259 yards passing, his 7 punts for around 47 yards a pop, and the pressure he faced lining up for a kick his coach didn't look like he'd okayed.

Worst thing that can happen, Spurrier said, is a tie ball game.

Florida was undefeated, with a chance to beat Georgia and win the school's first-ever SEC Championship. Was that due to Spurrier's marriage, which to Coach Graves meant "maturity"? Or that newfangled Gatorade, quaffed now at every game?

"Our team drinks it regularly and faithfully," the quarterback told the press.

That hero behind the face mask was "Bat Gator," the *Gainesville Sun* declared. The *Alligator* called the winning kicker the "Wizard of Odds."

———

Historians would say Florida sports information director Norm Carlson, publicist for Steve Spurrier, invented the modern Heisman Trophy campaign that season, sending film clips of number 11's exploits to TV stations across the land. Gators bearing grudges say Georgia coach Vince Dooley unleashed red and black ops.

"It will take 13 men at the very least to stop Spurrier," Dooley said, buttering up the Gator. The Dawgs' best defender lay in the hospital with a wrenched neck, Dooley claimed. Then he lined up extra defensive backs in three-deep coverage, with a safety sticking to Jack Coons, the tight end, no matter what. That safety had played against Spurrier in high school, got targeted on the Gators' winning touchdown the previous year, and didn't want number 11 to forget the name Lynn Hughes.

Dooley's defensive ends would cover Florida's receivers laterally, his tackles would loop in, and his linebackers would stunt. Defensive tackle Bill Stanfill would get a shot of cortisone in the neck and rise out of his gurney.

Dooley had a monster game plan but feared the Gatorade, that secret concoction Florida drank for endurance. What if a couple of cars forced a Florida pickup truck off Waldo Road Friday night, pulled out the 26 gallons of Gatorade, and stomped on every carton of that lizard elixir? They wouldn't get a new batch to the Gator Bowl in time—and Spurrier would take a beating a generation of Bulldogs might wish he'd forget.

"Late hit! Late hit!" he hollered at the refs, according to the guy who got a shot in the neck and smashed the quarterback to the ground.

"What's the matter, Stevie, did I step on your skirt?" Big Bill Stanfill said he asked Florida's star, at the winner's press conference, noting that the Gators got one first down in the second half and Lynn Hughes got two picks, returning one for Georgia's go-ahead score, and the quarterback with all the nicknames threw no touchdown passes.

On the field Spurrier went down on one knee as the Bulldogs cheered his worst defeat on any scoreboard. In Florida's locker room he asked for quiet.

"I'm sorry," he told his teammates. "I lost the game for us."

He looked his coach in the eyes and apologized for blowing the chance to get Florida an SEC Championship.

"Coach, I'm going to try to get even for what they did to you," his quarterback said, knowing that was the worst defeat of Coach Graves's career.

"I'm gonna hate Georgia as long as I live," he vowed to all the Gators.

Walking out into the November wind to face the press, he had fans with pads and pens hemming him in.

"Don't they realize how bad he feels?" Jerri asked.

Orr had to smile through the hurt, like he'd practiced. His wife would realize how badly Florida still needed a hero.

Facing the cameras and microphones, he wouldn't mention the play Dooley and the Dawgs ran for a touchdown with six seconds left to make the score 27–10, maybe setting back Florida football for decades. He'd just . . . remember.

Lucky Big Bill Stanfill was ill, Coach Graves told reporters. "If he had been well, he would have killed Steve and they'd have to put him in jail."

After a spunky Tulane team went down 24–10 in a hailstorm on Florida Field, the third anniversary of JFK's assassination was observed with a Heisman Trophy announcement. Thirty big city reporters wanted interviews with Orr. Visited that Saturday by the "Mad Stork," Miami's ungainly defender Ted Hendricks, number 11 glared at "Visitors 21, Gators 3" on the scoreboard and brought his team back against the hated Hurricanes.

Down 21–16, with the ball at Miami's thirty, he couldn't get his guys lined up in time for one more play at Florida Field.

"Florida Fizzled," a father would say, "an awful lot."

He slammed the ball to the ground at the gun and cried.

Cheers cascading down from the stands made him look up. The announcement that jersey No. 11 would be retired at Florida, and displayed in the trophy case, led to an uproarious ovation.

They had an empty spot in that trophy case, he knew. Nothing to celebrate after a loss.

They'd remember better days in High Springs savoring the breathless announcement on WJAX, "the Big Ape," that Bob Griese of Purdue was voted a distant second to 1966 Heisman Trophy winner Steve Spurrier, the third player from the South to win the Heisman, the first from Florida.

Hard to interview, with that Southern accent, reporters noted.

Interview more Southerners, Spurrier said.

He got his folks seats on Bull Gator Jim Wellman's private plane, the same one that flew home a Hilltopper with the flu. Of course, they stopped in Johnson City to pick up Graham. His folks gazed down at the world winging past, at the peak of their parenting.

"I declare, this little five-seater, we drove right up to the door up there in New York City," Reverend Spurrier would tell people who asked about his first plane ride. "That plane was so small we could drive right up to the door."

"We went to see Broadway shows and the Radio City Music Hall Christmas Special with the Rockettes," Marjorie gushed about what she saw because someone saw her son play ball.

"Would you like to go to the New York Giants?" reporters asked her son, the NFL's top quarterback prospect.

"Worth a million dollars," his father said, slamming the limo door.

Just the same, after their boy gave that big trophy to his school and smiled down from the podium at his wife in the pink dress, the Spurriers happily rode home in Florida governor Haydon Burn's plane, which was "kind of like a big living room," Marjorie Spurrier said.

Orr was pretty much hoarse from saying no matter what team drafted him, he only worried about what he could control. Missing too many classes that fall to keep his grades up, he vowed to return to Gainesville to get his degree.

On the *Ed Sullivan Show*, Sullivan introduced all-American quarterback Steve Spurrier, and Syracuse running back Floyd Little looked into the camera lens. Sullivan introduced Spurrier again, as the quarterback for the Miami Hurricanes. Finally Sullivan got it right, to thunderous applause.

The Downtown Athletic Club announced before Christmas that two Heisman Trophies would be awarded in 1966, one to the winning player and one to his school, starting a new tradition. Spurrier said he'd trade both trophies for another shot at Georgia. He'd settle for taking Florida to its first Orange Bowl, against Georgia Tech, with Bobby Dodd coaching his final game for the Yellow Jackets.

Speaking before kickoff at the First Presbyterian Church in Fort Lauderdale, the Gator quarterback told the youth group he didn't pray for touchdowns, just "the strength to do his best," pleasing church member Nellie Starr, his mother-in-law.

Feeling uplifted on the field, number 11 torched the passing records at Florida and across the SEC, playing his last game as a Gator in the

Orange Bowl, helping Coach Graves beat his coaching mentor 27–12. Dodd told reporters the difference in the game was, Florida had Gatorade.

Florida had Spurrier, Coach Graves countered. The practice field under the sabal palms would look empty in August.

Already in the past, for a man looking at a new life.

CHAPTER TEN

Sitting Out Sunday

DID GOD WANT NUMBER 11 IN A 49ERS UNIFORM ON THE SIDELINE, watching another quarterback run the plays, take the hits, make the headlines and the money? Testing the faith of his father, a continent away. Playing with a bigger ball, harder to grip, and even bigger boys. Wearing the jersey of a city, not a school.

Why was he there, columnists in the *San Francisco Chronicle* kept asking, "with veteran quarterbacks George Mira and John Brodie already available under center?" Just who is Steve Spurrier, the pro football player on the Topps bubble gum card, he had to ask himself.

Away from his father at last, thinking maybe his coaches needed to yell at him more.

The guy he looked up to out west wasn't his coach. Number 12, John Brodie, the tanned Stanford man, had a decade of experience as the Niners' signal caller, the biggest contract in the NFL, a pot full of the team's card-playing money, and a better golf game than number 11. Their quarterback coach, Y. A. Tittle, said the plan for playing three quarterbacks was "turn Spurrier loose in the third quarter to satisfy the teenagers."

San Francisco head coach Jack Christensen "gave me the punting job," Orr could go home and tell his wife.

The courting of players by professional football coaches could get complicated. New York Giants head coach Allie Sherman went to Gator games and spent days in the film room at Florida, bedazzled by Spurrier. Then Coach Sherman traded the top pick in the 1967 NFL draft to Minnesota, throwing in some players, to get quarterback Fran Tarkenton, the scrambler from Athens, Georgia. Tarkenton could take on the role

Spurrier wanted to play on the Great White Way—the Fellowship of Christian Athletes' counterpart to the Jets' Broadway Joe.

Reverend Spurrier had bemoaned the NFL-AFL merger that gave college stars less leverage, and tried to create a bidding war between the NFL and the Canadian Football League, issuing statements generating headlines like Six Canadian Clubs Can't Afford Spurrier. His son wouldn't speculate about his worth with reporters. Salary negotiations were the private business of a man with a wife and a child on the way.

He'd have banked a $1 million signing bonus if the leagues hadn't merged, the pundits declared.

"I never had it," Spurrier said, "so how can I miss it?"

He delivered the ball every way except over the top, and his release was a tad slow, said pro scouts who couldn't throw.

"Can't teach a man to play quarterback anyway," the Heisman winner believed. "It's inside."

At least the third pick in the 1967 NFL draft bested Bob Griese, who was picked fourth by the Miami Dolphins. He beat Griese again in the July '67 Coaches All-America Game, quarterbacking the East to a win over Griese's West team. Still in the world of college awards and all-star games. That meant teaming up with black players for the first time, and horsing around on the practice field with Floyd Little.

"Spurrier, you're more fun to hang out with than other white guys," said his double on the *Ed Sullivan Show*.

Had to laugh in that whirlwind, going from all-everything college quarterback to third-string NFL rookie. Remembering how it felt to do a town proud.

On Thursday, January 12, 1967, they'd celebrated "Steve Spurrier Day" in Johnson City and across Tennessee. He brought his wife up from Florida to see his hometown. The day was clear and cold, the sun whitening the mountaintops, Kiwanis Park dusted with snow.

At a luncheon at Calvary Presbyterian Church honoring the women who'd helped Spurrier win the Heisman, Reverend Spurrier proudly escorted his mother, Willie, into Fellowship Hall. Sitting by the upright woman who'd passed along some sharp eyes and dark hair, and had always believed in the Independence Park tennis champion, the preacher happily ate with the ladies. Marjorie Spurrier wore her Sunday best, seated by her daughter-in-law Jerri; her daughter, Sara Henderson; and Graham's wife, Mrs. J. Graham Spurrier III, who was expecting J. Graham Spurrier IV.

Six hundred Spurrier fans crowded into the Majestic Theater downtown to see Steve and his trophy, flown in for the day, and his Florida football highlights, shown on the silver screen. The national Little League headquarters in Houston, Texas, honored him for his "worldwide" contributions to Little League baseball, starting with batting .758 and going 9–0 as a pitcher for the Steinway Bears.

The governor made Spurrier a Tennessee Colonel. Col. Spurrier thanked the young fans on hand, probably there "to get out of school." The Magnavox Corporation gave Steve and Jerri a color TV. He thanked the promoter of Steve Spurrier Day, J. Ross Edgemon, boss of the Bears.

At a press conference at the country club where Orr had jumped the fence to play golf, Tennessee reporters still hounded him for not playing for the Vols.

"Coach Graves is a former Tennessean," Col. Spurrier diplomatically pointed out. "And he said he'd take care of me down in Florida."

A thousand Hilltoppers met him at the high school, holding Hooray for Steve and Batman Is Back Home signs. The band played the fight song as he walked across his basketball court. He got called to Coach Tipton's office, to talk about his future.

At a dinner for 500 in the ETSC gym, Coach Graves thanked God that Spurrier called all the plays, starting with that screen pass against Southern Methodist that picked up 56 yards and got the head coach a contract extension. Greatness was thrust on Spurrier at Florida, Graves said, when the team got behind and the clock wound down.

New York Giants running back and receiver and CBS sportscaster Frank Gifford came to Johnson City and took the podium to personally invite Spurrier to play for the Giants, saying, "They could use you."

In his mind he'd been a Giant since Athens.

"No matter how many awards I get, or where I go, you will always know me as that same old boy from Johnson City," concluded the hero in the tuxedo. He would fight tooth and claw for the underdog, they'd have to remember after presenting the Gator with a gavel cut from a tree Daniel Boone had carved his name into.

Reverend Spurrier rose from his seat beside his mother to say he had some son, and clapped Sid Smallwood on the back.

Steve pleased his mom by driving back to Florida and singing "Chug-a-Lug," "Cindy," and "You Are My Sunshine" with Minnie Pearl at her concert in Tampa. Picturing another kind of homecoming. Playing against Joe Namath on the links at the Citrus Open.

At the Nob Hill Hotel in April, he signed a contract to play for San Francisco, with John Brodie looking on under the chandeliers. The newest 49er rented a tan and pastel apartment in Palo Alto for the fall. Then he went back to Gainesville and bought a home in the Duck Pond neighborhood, where he could hear trains rolling through late at night and owls hooting in the live oaks.

In Gainesville he received the key to the city and then a baby daughter, Lisa Starr Spurrier, both delivered by Dr. Walter Muphree, obstetrician, mayor, and Gator.

In the steaming heat the three Spurriers drove to High Springs to say good-bye until winter in Florida.

"I'll go see you play anytime except Sunday," Reverend Spurrier said.

His son gathered up his wife and baby, locked up the trophies and the pool table, and flew across the country to St. Mary's College in Moraga, California, for an NFL training camp.

———

Spurrier jogged off the practice field at St. Mary's College, a third-string quarterback who'd done his job, and sat in the chill of the mountains above San Francisco Bay, telling his roomie, rookie tight end Bob Windsor from Washington, DC, what plays the offense should've run that day. Windsor said he'd rather run Spurrier's plays.

When they played an exhibition game against the hated L.A. Rams, number 11 jogged onto the field in the second half and "the old calm came back." He hit tight end Monty Stickles for a 10-yard score and acted like he'd gotten the ball in an NFL end zone before.

The team decamped to 49ers headquarters in Redwood City, in a lunch pail neighborhood with championship dreams. The tiny weight room had a few benches and barbells. Spurrier would be out back throwing with his receivers, listening to the trains rumbling through Sequoia Station downtown.

The practice field stretched only 80 yards, with a green carpet to simulate artificial turf. Quarterbacks could warm up in the south corner and run seven-on-seven drills to the goalposts. Everywhere Spurrier turned, there was the tanned Stanford man.

"Brode" and "Spur," teammates called the pair. Both had that quarterback swagger. Called their own plays. Ran a "West Coast offense," throwing underneath the coverage, happy to dump the ball to a running back. Brode took the fewest sacks in the league; Brode saw all.

"Spur throws those duck passes," Brode said, quacking.

"He gets you in the end zone," other guys said. Spur *willed* those duck passes to be caught—or maybe it was God's will.

Hippies and sea gulls welcomed him to Kezar Stadium in Golden Gate Park on Sunday, when Jerri drove him down Haight Street to the game. The team bus the Niners promised would be along. They had no lot to park in, following fans down side streets to find a spot in front of some long-haired guy's crash pad.

"Characters you couldn't figure out with a slide rule," muttered Spurrier, taking in the Haight-Ashbury scene in the Fall of Love. Scarlet and gold Niner fans rolled out of bars and appeared in a puff of smoke, all bleary-eyed, to watch the game.

The home team would walk through the tunnel under the stands, "dusty as a rodeo." They'd stomp around, stirring up the dust for the visiting team to choke through. By Sunday the field oozed with mud, torn up by high school teams Friday, junior high teams Thursday, and Little League teams whenever they fit in.

In the stands 43,000 drunk football fans and hippies got along cosmically, seeming to share an understanding that 49ers games were theater. When there'd be a fight, in a crowd where it was rare to see a cop, the sea gulls broke it up. Fans watching on TV got eyeballed by gulls flying into the cameras. Fans sticking it out in the stadium got blitzed by "the birds," dive-bombing those hardy souls who weren't getting chased to no parking lot.

Kezar Stadium had high fences for a reason, veterans told Spurrier. "They'll throw beer on you if you lose, coming back through the tunnel."

Brode got the Niners off to a 5–1 start, then a beer wave hit. Standing on the sidelines watching blockers block, receivers run routes, and cover guys cover, Spur's mind worked overtime. After four straight losses Coach Christensen told Spur he'd start Sunday, against Johnny Unitas's Baltimore Colts.

He worked with his receivers through epic rainstorms at practice; settling for field goals in the mud at Kezar Stadium wouldn't win. The rookie quarterback would see his toss to the flat picked off and run back for a score in his sleep, after a 26–9 loss to Unitas and a beer shower.

Number 11 threw fifty passes in 1967, seven to the wrong team. Ready to get back to the place where they called him Orr, and Dad.

Jerri spent the fall turning football friends into family. Lisa would be raised to enjoy having two schools, and two sets of friends, when the locker in Redwood City got cleaned out for Christmas and the door to the house by the duck pond swung open.

On the patio under the Florida palms, the pro quarterback smoked a cigar, savoring the owls and the trains. A beer and an occasional smoke wouldn't hurt in the off-season. If there was nowhere to stay in shape in Gainesville, he'd open his own health club. And loft some balls over the gator ponds, so he could at least beat Brode at golf.

He needed to get back that Gator mentality. Really, what life lessons could a coach of professional athletes impart?

Coach Graves would be stunned by a Spurrier revelation from San Francisco: "You can learn as much sitting on the bench as you can on the field."

On the sideline, he told his coach, he could see how different blocking schemes, pass patterns, and defensive coverages played out—if he watched with a coach's mindset.

Trying to see the game at ground level wasn't easy, Graves agreed. Most play callers had to take the elevator to the press box. Few coaches could call a play in the quarterback's ear.

Orr said he'd serve as a recruiter, while he was home, helping Coach Graves bring more Gators to Gainesville. Meanwhile, his dad had a few plays to go over after watching his son play on TV in the den.

⸺ ⸺

Dick Nolan played for the New York Giants in the '50s with Tom Landry, joined Coach Landry's staff in Dallas, and helped draw up the "flex defense" that made a star out of the Cowboy coach in the fedora. Nolan could be a head coach and take the middling Niners to the top, they believed on Nob Hill. Could this coaching change be Spurrier's chance to take Brodie's place behind center?

After a season in San Francisco, even a preacher's son had longish hair and wore wide ties. Nolan was the kind of gruff authority figure the hippies protested. Brode was the establishment's quarterback. Primed to be the top passer in the NFL in 1968. Could be the season Spur wouldn't throw a pass in a game.

Coach Nolan was what people called paranoid, erecting a 10-foot chain-link fence with spy-proof covering around the practice field. Any stranger approaching the fence was to be challenged by security.

"Whoever it is," Coach Nolan ordered, "send 'em away."

Everyone saw him take a hard look at the two biggest cutups on the team.

Gamesmen make good quarterbacks, gamesmen say. John Brodie played in the World Dominoes Championship. The only cardsharp in back of the team plane who didn't fold at the sight of Brode's poker face was Spur. Same story at the bowling alley and over a Ping-Pong table. Backgammon to Brode was a contact sport. Then they'd talk about golf. Brode would be out on the PGA Tour after football season.

The most competitive man east of the Mississippi had seemingly met his match, and he couldn't stop challenging the Stanford man with a grip on the quarterback job.

They golfed together like sharks in a pond, every hour after practice that God lit the greens. Brode belonged to Sharon Heights Country Club, where he invited Spur to play a round with Willie Mays. Brode thought Mays should see the look Spur got on his face at the end of his swing.

"The day the Giants played the Philadelphia Phillies and Richie Ashburn fouled off 12 of 13 pitches, and you caught the last out in center field and threw the ball into the stands," he said to Willie Mays, "I was there."

"I remember that game," Mays said, leading Brode and Spur ten paces to the first tee.

Number 11 had one thing number 12 couldn't take: the punting job. That still came down to a foot and a ball. He could hold that ball in his hand, lay it out on his toe, and make it spiral way down the field. Pushing back the other team like he was 13 men. Kicking some crazy trick punts on the practice field.

"Bet you," he'd say, "I can stand on the sideline and punt the ball through the crossbar on the goalpost."

Teammates kept their hands in their pockets. They all knew how badly he needed someone to bet against him. He could almost always pull it off. A soccer kick from the corner, banging off the left goalpost, he'd call like a pool shot.

When no one would bet, he'd bounce the ball off the ground, walk forward so the ball went over his head, and catch it behind his back. When no one would play catch, he'd spiral the ball to himself. When Brode got pranked, with no one owning up, Spur covered his laughter with his hand.

Coach Nolan noticed.

Number eleven hit 141 punts his first two seasons, averaging nearly 39 yards a punt. Driving back to the tan and pastel apartment knowing he'd made himself valuable to his employer, filling two positions and one roster spot. The underdogs he championed were the Starrs.

Why couldn't he beat out that other quarterback, instead of gnashing his teeth? Was he really as good as he thought? A man hit what he aimed at. Coach Nolan looked at him like a backup, and so he was.

When would the quarterback kicking at the grass get mad enough to do something else great?

Few NFL punters and backup quarterbacks were published authors. His autobiography, *It's Always Too Soon to Quit*, was on the shelves in the fall of '68, with the author predicting, "In a few years in Florida they'll be saying, whatever happened to Steve Spurrier?"

Back home, Georgia stomped the snot out of Florida; Dooley wouldn't let up until someone made him. The first two black football players at Florida signed letters of intent, knowing they'd be playing in SEC stadiums where Confederate flags waved over cold Southern souls. Willie Jackson told Spurrier he'd take all that grief to give his children a chance to be Gators.

How many Volunteer fans watched Gator and Niner games on North Jackson Street in Athens? One fall day Doak and Johnnye Willett felt the need to drive their children south to see Reverend Spurrier in High Springs, Florida—where he was babysitting his son's biggest trophy. The Heisman stiff-armed a tackler on the coffee table at the manse while its owner played football in San Francisco.

"Doak, I suppose you were his first football hero," Reverend Spurrier said. "You gave him his start."

Made Doak's heart swell.

Little Skip Willett reached up his arms for that 25-pound bronze football player. They sat and looked at it awhile, holding that pose. Then the Willetts drove back to Tennessee.

———

Florida was always a dream, a state of mind, a place of birth, swirling through the thoughts of a boy in the mountains, drawing him south, followed by his mom and dad. Watching the Florida hero stand on the sidelines across the country on a snowy TV screen turned a preacher with a dream toward Carolina, following his forebears.

Reverend Spurrier took a job as pastor at Kentyre Presbyterian Church in Hamer, South Carolina, a hamlet near the stretch of I-95 where "South of the Border" billboards took over the cotton fields. Signs declaring, "Pedro says, You never sausage a place," directed tourists to a metal oasis under the slash pines. On Kentyre Road a country church blessed the borderlands.

Number 11 could imagine his father not owning up to having a backup in the family in South Carolina.

He could hold his head up in Johnson City in July, when the city celebrated the dedication of Steve Spurrier Field—the baseball diamond at Kiwanis Park renamed for the kid who'd claimed it from the start. The former manager of the Steinway Bears prayed for the astronauts rocketing to the moon and the players in the little and big leagues.

Maybe the quarterback from Johnson City would get a fairer shot in San Francisco after George Mira got traded to Philadelphia. Hired hands on defense limped off the practice field in Redwood City in August, and Brodie's arm got sore. The Niners started the '69 season with five straight losses.

Nolan told Spur he'd start against the Colts, the defending NFC champions, in Baltimore.

His third-quarter scoring strikes got the Niners a 24–21 lead that Unitas tried to trump. Near the Niners' goal line he talked to Coach Don Shula and waved off the field goal kicker, going for the win. Spur's fist shot up when the defense held. He'd matched Johnny U's completions with far fewer attempts, getting even with him on Maryland soil.

When Brodie's arm got better, Nolan sent the veteran back in.

The depth chart didn't matter the Friday before game day when Jerri gave birth to a daughter in Palo Alto. Baby Amy joined little Lisa in the modernistic duplex the Spurriers had bought in Redwood City. Back fenced in for the kids, front half rented out, a salesman's dream. Dad went to work down the street at the football field.

In December the Niners took on the Vikings in a Minnesota blizzard. The California quarterback couldn't play. Foot of snow on the field when Spurrier went in.

"We're in the huddle," said tight end Bob Windsor, "and all of the sudden this old Southern voice says, 'Boys, I don't know any of the plays, and I doubt they'd work anyway. Let's draw some plays in the snow. You'll run there, and you'll go there, and I'll get it to you."

Windsor swore by Spurrier's game plan. "Most fun we ever had," the tight end told the quarterback, even though Minnesota's "Purple People Eaters" won the snowball battle 10–7.

Spur got in six games that season, throwing for 926 yards, five touchdowns, and 11 interceptions; he wouldn't talk over any of it with his father in Florida. Not even the plays that beat Johnny Unitas.

The next season he'd have no plays to talk over. In the manse in Hamer, watching the Niners play on the TV the Spurriers got in Newport, Marjorie said their boy looked "disappointed" on the sideline.

"I think the coaching staff got hoodwinked by Brodie," Reverend Spurrier said. "Who did John Brodie ever really beat? Never won a thing with him at quarterback, did they?"

Brode lead the Niners to a 10–3–1 season in 1970, and the team's first-ever NFC West Championship, losing to Dallas 17–10 in the NFC Championship Game. Niner fans stormed the field anyway, looking for souvenirs of the last NFL game in Kezar Stadium. Nolan won Coach of the Year. His team would join the baseball Giants next season at Candlestick Park, a big-league oval overlooking San Francisco Bay.

Scene of the Beatles' final concert in 1966, Candlestick had been a baseball stadium until the Niners rolled out a 100-yard rug that the football players feared falling on. Wind shields went up to block the gale-force gusts, taking away the fans' view of the bay. The stadium looked beachy on TV shots from the Goodyear blimp. Spur looked to be a long shot on the sidelines at Candlestick; Brode was the man on the field.

Reverend Spurrier took what he hoped would be his final job as pastor at Central Presbyterian Church in St. Petersburg, Florida, back under the sabal palms. The idea of an NFL team playing on the shores of Tampa Bay was just talk, so far. The Spurriers watched Brodie take the Niners to another NFC West title, and another playoff loss to the Cowboys, on the TV in the den.

"Take out the old man! Put Spurrier in," the backup quarterback heard from the fans at Candlestick. Youthful Niner fans wanted a quarterback change, no matter how Brodie was playing. The backup knew to count his blessings.

On Sunday, September 26, 1971, he flew on the team plane to punt and stand on the sidelines in New Orleans while Jerri went to Stanford Medical Center to give birth to their third child.

"When I get back, I'll be the father of three girls or our first boy," Spur said on the plane ride home. Telling the fellows he wasn't betting on a boy or a girl, just a healthy new member of the team.

"They're waiting on you to have the baby," said big offensive tackle Cas Banaszek's wife, Diane, at the San Francisco airport, her car revved and ready. Jerri had been given a spinal injection to "put the baby on hold," without any danger, the doctor had said. The newest Spurrier waited for a signal from Dad.

"Did you win that game?" the doctor asked, rushing down the hospital corridor with the ball player.

"Brodie won it," he said. "I punted."

He had a noteworthy name in his family, at the birth of Steve Spurrier Jr. In his father's arms lay a healthy reminder that a quarterback needs a steadfast receiver, eyes in the press box, and a hand to high-five. The boy would start out as Stevie and work his way up.

His young eyes saw a world of football, with a locker room full of big guys. Dad had a receiver who was a real-life cartoon character, Gene Washington, the "Cookie Monster."

The Cookie Monster was a Stanford man, too. Loved to kid around with Stevie at the duplex while Jerri baked cookies. Sugar and dough made Washington a monster to cover on Sunday. Someone a budding receiver could look up to.

Looking up at the blimp watching over Candlestick Park, toddling around the green carpet, Stevie Jr. first said he wanted to be a quarterback.

His dad and granddad had a tough loss to talk over in Charlotte. Willie Spurrier died April 3, 1972, with two of her sons at her side, at the duplex where her husband's memory lived.

John Belk, one of Henry Belk's boys who'd worshipped with Graham, Sara, and Stevie in Grandma Willie's church, grew up to be mayor of Charlotte. At the funeral of the grand old lady of Caldwell Presbyterian, Mayor Belk heard her eulogized by the backup quarterback for San Francisco. A paragraph in the *Charlotte Observer* noted the passing of Willie Austin Spurrier, not mentioning she'd been the heartbeat of old Charlotte, and Shuffletown, and a football player's grandmother.

Knowing the Spurriers had come a long way, not sure from where, Steve told his grieving father he'd get a new contract and take his parents to the Holy Land, to see Jerusalem, at last.

Five games into the '72 season Brode limped off the field with a twisted ankle. Spur jogged in to quarterback the team to another NFC West title—nothing less would do.

Blitz the new quarterback and he'd flip the ball to running back Larry Schreiber in the flat. Give Spur time and he'd hit the Cookie Monster downfield for a score. Finding receivers all over the field in Dallas, Spur sent the Cowboys crowd home early on Thanksgiving. Griese stayed unbeaten in Miami. HAVOC IN THE WEST, *Sports Illustrated*'s Spurrier cover forecast.

SPURRIER BLOSSOMS AS PRO QUARTERBACK the *Los Angeles Times* heralded before his Monday Night Football appearance, setting him up for a 26–16 loss to the Rams. His receivers dropped three passes in the end zone. Spur made no excuses.

SPURRIER COMES OF AGE the *Chicago Tribune* blared after his five scoring strikes matched a record game by Brodie and took down the Bears. "Steve and the 49ers made a believer out of me," avowed a Chicago sports columnist, who asked, "If he keeps winning, would you put Brodie back in?"

Number 11's 18 touchdown passes and 5–2–1 record got the Niners a game away from the division title. Facing the Vikings' Purple People Eaters at Candlestick Park. In the fourth quarter of a tough ball game, Nolan sent in Brode. Spur's backup got the Niners a 20–17 win, the NFC West won by both men.

After a week of speculation, Nolan started Brode in the playoff game against Dallas. His two picks gave Roger Staubach the chance to score two touchdowns as the game wound down, and the Cowboys ended the Niners season for the third straight year.

"Amazing season, horrible end," said Schreiber, after Spur became the NFC's fourth-best passer and got handed the headset.

Brode limped through a final season and retired, along with his jersey, after 17 years as San Francisco's quarterback. Coach Nolan at last named Spurrier the starter and got a new contract written on Nob Hill. The backup quarterback and punter earning about $60,000 a year, if people must know, was worth twice that now. Able to take his parents to the place of Jesus's suffering and redemption.

At the grand opening of Steve Spurrier Sporting Goods in Johnson City, with 2,000 old neighbors at the ribbon cutting, he introduced Graham as the manager. They talked about the doings at his favorite hangout, the Cottage, facing Kiwanis Park, where a picture of Steve above the beer taps spurred football bets.

In Gainesville the local hero worked out at the Steve Spurrier Health Club, running a treadmill toward the promised land.

After eight years as a backup, Spur jogged onto the practice field in August as The Man, taking charge in the huddle. The week before the season opener, playing his last series in an exhibition game against the Rams, San Francisco's starting quarterback got thrown to the turf and heard his shoulder snap. Doctors operated on the shoulder and pronounced him out for the season. Schreiber told his friend his life had just changed, speaking from the experience of a professional football player.

Schreiber's new roommate, Norm Snead, had been an ace quarterback in Minnesota but "didn't have any idea how the Niners did things," Schreiber said, while Brode and Spur were "like coaches on the field." A guy with a hurt shoulder had to think like a coach on the sidelines, watching Snead take the Niners to seven straight losses.

Haunted by a shoulder hurt in 1935, mourning a pro baseball career that never was, Uncle Eddie died in May of congestive heart failure at age 58, alone in the duplex at Amherst Place. Reminding a pro quarterback who had just turned thirty to play hard.

Nolan named Snead the starter in '75, and Spur hated the Rams worse. When the rainy season washed through, the Niners were 2–5, facing the team from Los Angeles that had beaten them 10 straight games. Spur cornered the coach in his office and got the start against the Rams.

When rainstorms rattled the spy fence at practice, Spur told his teammates to forget their fears.

"Start playing for fun."

Fun to go into the Los Angeles Coliseum and call the plays, throw for almost 300 yards, and hit three scoring strikes. A 68-yarder to the Cookie Monster and a clutch drive for the winning field goal took down Roman Gabrielle and the Rams, 24–23. A day of vengeance couldn't keep Coach Nolan or Spur in San Francisco another year.

Fate or fluke, God's plan or a pitchfork wielder's curse, visited the Coliseum in L.A. that day, in the guise of University of Southern California coach John McKay. The cigar-chomping coach known for running power sweeps and sarcastic press conferences was preparing to lead an expansion NFL team called the Tampa Bay Buccaneers. Impressed with the Niner quarterback despite his fearless passing, McKay would be just the coach to put the clamps on a free-wheeling signal caller.

⁓

April was a cruel month in Tampa Bay, with the Buccaneers bringing home a Florida legend and signing some cast-off linemen to protect him. To get a marquee name in front of season ticket buyers, the NFL's newest franchise sent a receiver and a linebacker to San Francisco, along with a second-round draft pick sure to be high, to bring quarterback Steve Spurrier back to Gator Country.

No doubt he'd be The Man for the Bucs in the 1976 season. The question was whether Tampa Bay's football fans or his father expected more. Reverend Spurrier preached at Central Presbyterian Church in St. Petersburg, just across the Courtney Campbell Causeway from Tampa Stadium, awaiting a homecoming that would make his son a headliner in the *St. Petersburg Times*.

When Steve and his wife and three children pulled up to the house they'd rent in Tampa while Dad worked at One Buccaneer Place, a preacher had to revisit a wedding he didn't officiate, patching up an old wound at Easter.

"Jerri sure means a lot to Steve," his dad had to say. "She's been right in there with him."

Coach McKay heard John Brodie say way out in San Francisco that "Steve Spurrier throws one of three passes into the ground."

"That's okay," the Bucs coach responded. "We'll just get shorter receivers."

⁓

Shorthanded at every position, the Tampa Bay Buccaneers took the field for the first time at the end of July in the Los Angeles Coliseum, against the Rams, in an exhibition game the Bucs lost 26–3.

"Unaggressive, uninspiring, lethargic, and unacceptable," McKay branded his new team in his old pressroom. Really, the only player he had faith in was his son, John Jr., the Bucs' big, slow receiver.

Number 11 in orange jogged onto a familiar field for a preseason game against the Atlanta Falcons, on a steamy August night in Jacksonville. Expecting his folks to drive up from St. Pete and see him play in the Gator Bowl, on a Saturday. The father who never went to a ball game on the Sabbath would be his coach in the stands once more, after a decade of talking through the TV.

The odds-makers favored the Falcons. Spurrier took over the huddle, sending his guys where the other guys weren't. Dodging blitzers, throwing big gainers, and running for a score, he and the Bucs beat Atlanta 17–3. With cheers ringing through the Gator Bowl, he stood by the locker room door, happy not to hear a peanut gallery from Georgia. Seeing no sign of his father in the crowd.

"Didn't hang around after the game and hug me. Got back on the road, to get to church the next day," he figured, and went in to celebrate with the team.

The beginning of the end of Spurrier playing quarterback for the Bucs was the University of Southern California playbook McKay brought to Tampa, calling for runs and more runs—which worked when his running back was O. J. Simpson. McKay had no patience for a gunner at quarterback who was not throwing to the head coach's son, deemed the slowest guy on the team.

That was saying something. Spurrier threw for 244 yards and two touchdowns in the Bucs' first preseason game at home, hearing cheers from 71,718 fans in Tampa Stadium despite losing by a touchdown to Bob Griese's Dolphins. Number 11 started the regular season with two losses and no points, completing a total of 11 passes, wondering why the impossible always seemed doable. He had no lineman who could block an all-pro defender, and tried to take the vicious hits and boos in stride. After four games the Bucs finally got in the end zone, running back a fumble in a 42–17 loss to the Colts. In the pressroom reporters asked Coach McKay about his team's execution.

"I'm in favor of it," he said.

Across the bay Reverend Spurrier had to lower the volume on his TV. A son honored on the *Ed Sullivan Show* had become Johnny Carson's punch line. The winless Bucs got outscored 412 to 125 that season, and after every loss they gathered with the only sympathetic people in town, at Steve and Jerri's house. Still wearing the jersey of the city they played for.

He collected $125,000 for taking 14 beatings and got a call from his coach, saying he should find a better team to quarterback.

His father didn't have to drive across the country to see him play in Tampa, just across the Courtney Campbell Causeway. But Reverend Spurrier stayed away for a season of Sundays, and his son didn't win one game. Lot of mistakes to talk through Monday at the manse across the bay, black and blue.

Did God send him back to Florida to show him a player needs a coach who cares enough to yell?

The September day in 1977 Spurrier got waived by the Dolphins in Miami, after being waived that spring by the Broncos in Denver, he realized that Y. A. Tittle, his quarterback coach in San Francisco, never told him there's a right way and a wrong way to throw a pass.

"Just throw it how you throw it," Coach Tittle had said to Spur. "If you want to hold it somewhere down here while you're looking for a receiver, fine."

It took a decade of playing professional football to learn that nothing great happens without hollering.

Back in Gainesville, he cut out the three stories in three newspapers saying he'd been waived and tacked them up like trophies.

CHAPTER ELEVEN

Air Ball

Spurrier walked into the Gators' locker room, looked in the mirror, and saw a quarterback wearing a golf visor. He could show the other guys how to play quarterback. He'd take the chance head coach Doug Dickey gave him to work with the passers and call the plays at Florida for the '78 season.

"Thought the kids would like him," Dickey explained to his boss, UF president Robert Marston, who gave his football coach one more year to make the Gators winners.

"Spice up the offense," Coach Dickey told Coach Spurrier.

He could do what he'd always done, teach people to run his plays, and bring glory back to his school. He'd watched Dickey's team run that old wishbone offense from up in the stands, in his first season without a team to quarterback since he learned to throw. Any team running the wishbone would've been run out of Kiwanis Park. In those aluminum bleachers at Florida Field, he could see how an SEC defense should be attacked. Listening to Gators all around him rooting for the Boys of Old Florida as "Mr. Two Bits" led the cheer:

Two bits, four bits, six bits, a dollar!
All for the Gators, stand up and holler!

They stood up and hollered, a nation of Gators. People needed a team to fight for them, and a team needed ball plays. Just playing hard didn't do it. Spurrier had played his guts out in that stadium, and Florida was still an undergator.

A good ball coach could help his people hold their heads up.

And so he found himself on the practice field under the sabal palms, under a bright blue Florida sky, outthrowing the other Gator quarterbacks. Huddling 'em up, drawing plays in his palm Alabama hadn't seen. The Enemies of the Gators were out there.

At night, while the children slept and the trains rumbled through the sawgrass, he asked himself why the Bear and Lombardi beat most other coaches, with the same size guys and the same size playbooks. He went up to the press box on game day and saw what most offensive coordinators saw, the field laid out like a textbook. He watched his revamped Gator offense make plays to beat Mississippi State, Army, and Auburn, firing balls where Kentucky wasn't to notch a comeback win in the Bluegrass State.

Hosting his folks on Saturdays in Gainesville, hearing how his dad would've called the game, he had to admit other teams had the horses. The 'Noles and 'Canes overpowered the Gators at the end of the season. The president said Spurrier was too young to be head coach at Florida. Coach Dickey and Coach Spurrier had to leave the locker room to Charlie Pell, the ex-Clemson coach who wanted to bring his own people to Gainesville.

Seeing doors closing in the coaching fraternity, Spurrier looked at his sleeping children and thought he'd better call someone who knew what number 11 could do.

Pepper Rodgers, mentor to a freshman quarterback at Florida, traveling across the country coaching college football teams, leaping off a boat exploding in shark-infested waters, and surviving, so far, as head coach of the Yellow Jackets—Coach Pepper had an idea of what Coach Steve could do.

The president of Georgia Tech had given his football coach one more year to win big, or else.

"Atlanta, Georgia?" Orr asked Jerri.

"Let's just go," she said.

His wife painted a sign for the children, resilient as preacher's kids, to hang in a strange new place: Home Is Wherever You Are.

Crossing the bridge over the Suwanee River to Georgia's red clay, a man of faith could take comfort in the thought that Florida hadn't heard the last of the Spurriers.

As the calendar turned to July 1979, his father was honorably retired from the Presbyterian Church, after coaching congregations for nearly 40 years, leaving the city of St. Petersburg for cozy Green Cove Springs. In an old Florida town on the St. Johns River, a father could walk down Palmetto Avenue and talk sports with the mayor.

Tacking up a motivational headline from the *Gainesville Sun* in his den in Marietta, Georgia, Coach Pepper's protégé hit the field with the passers at Georgia Tech, showing those guys how to play quarterback. Fellow coach and quarterback legend Norm Van Brocklin said it should be done another way.

Spurrier won the argument with Van Brocklin when Mike Kelly became the first Yellow Jacket quarterback to throw for over 2,000 yards. Still, the situation looked dicey for Coach Pepper at Georgia Tech.

On a historic day in Atlanta, Spurrier stood in the head coach's doorway, asking if he could call the plays Saturday against Duke University.

"You know I wouldn't be doing this for anyone else but you," said Coach Pepper.

"I know," said Coach Steve.

"Are we ever going to run the ball?" the offensive line coach asked Saturday.

"Yes," Coach Spurrier said, "but not yet."

With all those passes riddling the Blue Devils defense, why shouldn't the quarterback keep throwing?

Coach Red Wilson of Duke couldn't get his mind off that 24–14 defeat. In all his days coaching college football, he had never seen an air attack like that. The field in Atlanta was like a sandlot, with the kid in the huddle sending everyone long.

Spurrier called the plays that beat Navy and Air Force. He drew up some ball plays to take on Georgia in the Thanksgiving rivalry game but didn't have the horses to beat the Dawgs. Coach Pepper's play-caller took over too late to save his job.

An old offensive guard for the Yellow Jackets, Bill Curry, would be Georgia Tech's new head coach. Spurrier appeared in his doorway, thinking he could coach Curry's quarterbacks and maybe call the plays.

"You're an applicant for the job," Curry said to Spurrier. "I'm interviewing some other people."

"That's all I need to know," Spurrier said, going back to his new house in Marietta to break the news to his family. They'd be taking the Home Is Wherever You Are sign someplace else.

As a For Sale sign got pounded into the clay, the head coach at Duke called, looking to hire the man who'd called the plays that beat the Blue Devils in Georgia. Did he want to coach football at a basketball school in Durham, North Carolina?

"Let's just go," Jerri said.

Spurrier wouldn't forget Bill Curry when his family left the house they loved in Marietta.

———

At Duke the head football coach and offensive coordinator impressed each other. Coach Wilson talked to his coaches and players about the differences between winners and losers, taking a game plan for life to the football field—where he'd been running the old single wing. He told Spurrier to call the plays he would run if he were the quarterback.

The man in the Duke visor said thank you as often as possible. He was a ball coach, working up guidelines to help others have a successful life. Some football has-beens were making TV commercials hawking pantyhose.

He cocked his arm and looked downfield, eyeing receivers running crossing patterns, showing freshman Ben Bennett there's a right way and a wrong way to throw a pass. With players that smart and that small, some plays from Kiwanis Park could even the odds. The Enemies of the Dukies were out there.

"Air Ball," he called the aerial attack that brought fans to Wallace Wade Stadium to cheer for a team starting out 0–5.

Play without fear and have fun, he told his team, sending Bennett into Death Valley with some plays the Clemson Tigers hadn't seen. The Dukies ran off the field at Clemson with a 34–17 win, ready to fly with Air Spurrier.

The morning of the Wake Forest game, the Ball Coach pulled up a chair as his quarterback ate his oats. Spurrier used the bowl as the field to show how the ball could get flipped to a flanker and back to the half-back, who'd hit a receiver sure to be uncovered for a 60-yard touchdown pass. Sure enough, the defensive backs got fooled, the receiver was open down the sideline, and basketball-crazed Dukies stayed excited about a 2–9 football team.

Spurrier's first call next season was moving from a perch in the press box to the sideline, where a ball coach could talk to his quarterbacks and receivers between plays. Turned out the old Niner backup quarterback could read most any defense at ground level and still ask his receivers, "What you got?" A 6–5 season filled Wallace Wade Stadium with cheers, with Bennett on pace to break the NCAA record for career passing yardage.

In the 1982 season opener, Spurrier sent Bennett onto the field in Knoxville armed with ball plays that would beat Tennessee. During the Big Orange exodus, Coach Spurrier looked up at the nosebleed seats he'd sat in as a boy, by the big Volunteers sign, remembering how Jimmy Lindsey explained his coaching strategy to his undefeated Newport Grammar School basketball team.

"Coaches coach the way they were coached," Coach Lindsey said.

A coach who'd gotten some coaching should know there's a right way and a wrong way to holler at players. In the "Guidelines for a Good Ball Coach" Spurrier was working up, he'd try to heed rule No. 28.

When things are going good, you must stay on their butt to improve every day. When things are going bad, you need to lighten up a little.

The words of General George Patton, Sun Tzu, and Attila the Hun helped Spurrier prepare for battle. He studied masters of motivation, like Coach Wilson, to get his players thinking like winners. They elevated an offense ranked 127th to the fourth-best offense in the nation.

Now and then, the quarterback brought the team to the line and Coach Wilson asked the play caller what play he'd called.

"Touchdown, Coach," Spurrier said.

"Dadgummit," Coach Wilson had to say, "it was!"

The namesake son of a local hero felt at home at Duke, where the players weren't so big. Stevie Jr. was getting bigger. He wondered who the big men were from Tampa, coming in the door with his dad after a steak dinner in Durham.

He was his father's son. Couldn't help but notice how much Mr. Bassett and the man called "Bugsy" enjoyed petting Stevie's black cocker spaniel, Bandit.

Back in Green Cove Springs, Reverend Spurrier could walk the streets with a smile. Missing helping his son with the play calling. Able to say he "first went into coaching at my suggestion," when the papers said Spurrier would be returning to Tampa to coach a team that would play in the spring, in the United States Football League.

That fired up the play caller going up against North Carolina's top-ranked defense. Giving Coach Wilson a 23–17 victory over the hated Tar Heels in Spurrier's final game as offensive coordinator of the Blue Devils.

With an ear rub for his son's cocker spaniel, he would get a chance to wear a head coach's visor.

⌐ ⌐

Redemption was right here on Earth, the newly anointed Head Ball Coach had to believe, wearing his white Tampa Bay Bandits visor, standing in the spring grass preaching to a team that was all his—with a chance to finally light up the scoreboard at Tampa Stadium and get back at the Bucs.

John Reeves, a Gator quarterback who'd been playing catch with his son after drinking himself out of the NFL, and Eric "ET" Truvillion, a receiver selling tires when Spurrier called, joined a bunch of other NFL washouts and never-weres who had to agree with their new coach.

That scoreboard was up there for a reason.

The youngest head coach in pro football, at age 37, listed himself as player/coach on the 1983 Bandits roster. *Tampa Tribune* sports editor Tom McEwen had told Canadian brewing magnate John Bassett, the Bandits' majority owner, he should talk to the offensive coordinator at Duke. Minority owner Burt Reynolds, enjoying a hit with his movie franchise *Smokey and the Bandit*, approved Spurrier's hiring. He'd been offered the job driving Bassett and Bugsy Engleburg back to Raleigh-Durham Airport, and got so excited at the prospect of coaching his own team in Tampa he forgot to ask what the job paid.

"Banditball," Spurrier called his offense, selling more season tickets than they sold for the NFL's Bucs in 1983. Coach McKay chewed on his cigar and said his team would play "Bucball." That didn't quite catch on like the no-huddle offense Spurrier debuted in Tampa Stadium on Sunday, March 6, 1983, against the Boston Breakers.

Stevie Jr. was on the sideline, working as a ball boy. The Raiders' and Redskins' logos from Super Bowl XVIII still colored the end zone grass. Jim Neighbors sang the national anthem, filling in for Reynolds, on location for *Smokey and the Bandit III*.

The Bandits took the ball right down the field, stunning the defense by not huddling, running what Cotty Jones and the gang watching back in Johnson City called "some of those fancy plays." After a touchdown on the Bandits' opening drive, Smokey and his masked rider shot out to celebrate. Spurrier tipped his visor as Jerry Reed's "Banditball" theme played and 42,437 fans cheered.

At halftime the PA announcer picked a random fan in the stands and the Bandits "burned" his mortgage. If a renter won at halftime next week, they'd pay up the rent for 10 years.

Leading Boston 21–17 with a minute to go, facing fourth down deep in Bandit territory, the head coach waved off the punter. Reeves got his coach a first down. Spurrier jogged off that field for the first time as a winner, with the Bandit's six-gun exploding.

Reverend Spurrier could see the fireworks in Tampa over in Green Cove Springs, on the old TV. Waiting for Saturday's game, against the Michigan Panthers, when he could personally oversee his son's team.

In three weeks Spurrier faced the Philadelphia Stars, and former NFL coach Jim Mora, notching a crucial win in his career. Showing everyone watching at home on ABC he could play with the big boys. Going 11–7 that first season, with the league's top offense bringing unbridled glory to a town dying for some touchdowns. Filling Tampa Stadium with more fans, points, and T-shirt buyers than the Buccaneers could muster up.

"All I ask is patience," said Hugh Culverhouse, owner of the Bucs, after McKay won two games in the fall and Tampa Stadium stayed half empty on Sundays.

In 1984 Bassett got his coach a fast, fluid halfback from Arkansas named Gary Anderson, who in Spurrier's scheme ran for over 1,000 yards, caught 66 passes, and scored 19 touchdowns. Revitalized John Reeves became the first pro quarterback to pass for over 4,000 yards, with a record-breaking 1,000-yard rusher and 1,000-yard receiver on the same team.

Twice that season Spurrier's Bandits faced Pepper Rodgers's Memphis Showboats, with a defense anchored by Reggie White, in a battle of coaching wits.

"Steve was at a point in life when he was young and didn't think anything bad could happen, because it hadn't happened yet," Coach Pepper said after beating his pupil with onside kicks. In the rematch the Bandits' ball boy boasted on the Showboats' sideline that more onside kicks were coming from his dad, who won anyway.

"All the Fun the Law Allows," Spurrier sloganized, again beating the local NFL team at the box office. He had no doubt his team could beat the Bucs on the field. The Stallions were a tougher opponent, beating the Bandits 36–17 in Birmingham in the 1984 USFL playoffs.

New Jersey Generals owner Donald Trump hired running back Herschel Walker from Georgia, skewing the league's pay scale, then challenged the NFL in court in an antitrust suit, forcing the USFL to play in the fall. Outraged, Bassett planned to start his own spring league, featuring the top team in Tampa, until his headache turned out not to be Trump but brain cancer.

Spurrier led the only USFL team with the same coach, owner, and home stadium for three seasons and was willing to talk with a writer for a local magazine about his love for the Bandits, the Gators, and his wife.

"I get a bigger kick out of coaching that I did out of playing," he told the surprised writer. Nodding under a ball cap that read, simply, "Head," Spurrier said, "I believe that in coaching you have a little bit more control."

His Bandits had twice as many plays in the playbook as the 49ers or the Bucs. He wanted the team to take the field again, somehow.

"The Bandit license tags, I see just as many as ever. Nobody's taken them off yet, I hope."

He loved living beside Coach Graves and Opal, "right there in the neighborhood," sharing with his daughter Amy's godfather the joy of a child he and Jerri adopted before birth. Not betting on a boy or a girl. Going to Tampa General Hospital and bringing home the brother Stevie Jr. always wanted.

"Tampa brought us Scotty," Jerri rejoiced, seeing a divine reason for the long wait between seasons.

The court awarded the USFL a dollar, trebled to $3 in Trump's antitrust case. The league folded. John Bassett passed away. The people of Tampa wouldn't ever take those Bandit tags and "All the Fun the Law Allows" stickers off their cars.

Seventeen Bandit players made the Buccaneers roster that fall. But Hugh Culverhouse, the team owner from Alabama, picked University of Alabama coach Ray Perkins to be the Bucs' new head coach, turning down the creator of Banditball, who really wanted the job.

Spurrier wanted to lead the Bucs out of the valley of 10 losses a season for a decade and a half. He'd wait for another Florida orange underdog to call.

＊

Saying good-bye to Tampa Bay and Coach Graves, leaving his father and mother across the peninsula, Spurrier was welcomed back to Durham as head coach of the Blue Devils. You can't win at *Duke*, old Florida friends tried to say, giving him the disbelief he needed to go after an ACC Football Championship.

Durham was still a place where fall Saturdays marked time until basketball started. No one blinked when Spurrier advertised for a wide receiver in the school paper. The improbable looked doable at Duke.

No worries about players flunking out here, Spurrier said. Happy to field a team without needing academic exemptions to keep underachieving student athletes eligible—unlike most of the teams Spurrier had to play. His starting quarterback, Steve Slayden, caught on quick: "His quarterback is him on the field."

Tipping his Duke coaching visor, he gathered his team on the field at Wallace Wade Stadium. Leading them up through the bleachers and across the beatific campus to the stones and spires of Duke Chapel, preaching to his small, smart team.

"If we can't block 'em, we'll let 'em run by us." Secret to the draw plays and screen passes that made Spurrier's undersize team a threat downfield to the Enemies of the Dukies. He asked his rising seniors to set the team's goals for the season. Duke had gone 13–30–1 without Spurrier on the sideline. His newspaper ad was answered by a would-be receiver named Clarkston Hines, who got on the field.

When Tommy Hager and Cotty Jones drove from Johnson City to Durham to see Orr before his first kickoff as a college head coach, they found him carrying around baby Scotty, promising his little boy the "most bizarre" first play in the history of Duke football.

After a halfback sweep, a reverse to the flanker, a pitch back to the quarterback, and a pass back to the halfback gained 3 yards, Slayden hooked up with Hines to get the underdog Blue Devils a 5–6 record in 1987. Fans filled Wallace Wade Stadium to cheer more "Air Ball." A lateral to Hines, and a pass back to Slayden, snookered the defense almost every time.

Spurrier's rising seniors set higher goals in 1988, believing the team could win seven games. Quarterback Anthony Dilweg broke the school's all-time passing record, throwing for 3,824 yards, and with seven wins at Duke, Spurrier was the ACC Football Coach of the Year.

He cautioned his rising seniors in the spring of '89—the goal of winning an ACC Football title would be tough to reach. That was before senior quarterback Billy Ray got hurt. The morning of the Wake Forest game, Spurrier sat down to breakfast with his new starter, sophomore Dave Brown, asking, "What do you want to run as your first play?"

For Brown's first collegiate start, he'd let his coach make the call.

Crumbling a piece of toast, Spurrier made the crumbs defensive players and used Brown's cereal to fake a cornflake into the line. The cornflake that was Hines streaked across the edge of the table.

"Think it could work," the coach said.

Brown jogged onto the field, faked a handoff to his halfback, and threw to Hines down the sideline for a 76-yard score. The team goal wasn't dead yet.

The season had opened with a loss to those accursed Gamecocks. Then the Vols claimed vengeance against Spurrier and the Dukies. Then the Virginia Cavaliers stomped Spurrier 49–14, starting off Duke's season 0–3, 0–1 in the ACC.

On a rainy Saturday in Durham Duke was a three-touchdown underdog to seventh-ranked Clemson. Lonnie Lowe had the flu but drove from Johnson City to Durham in the rain, against his wife's wishes, to cheer up Orr. The coach looked up from his desk in his office up in the press box, overlooking the field, to see a good old friend and teammate.

"Let me walk you downstairs," Orr said.

Looking out at the water mucking up the field, seeing the size of those corn-fed Clemson boys, Spurrier said, "Be a great day to gain national attention for Duke, wouldn't it?"

"Rush everybody," he told his defensive coaches in the locker room. "Every play. See what happens."

Stevie the ball boy stood on the Clemson sideline next to Danny Ford, watching a head coach panic when the other team kept blitzing. After a Clemson player grabbed a pick and fumbled the ball back to set up a Duke score, word flew around campus, putting more people in the stands for the second half than first came to the game.

When Clemson went down in the mud 21–17, the team shouldered Coach Spurrier and a stadium full of Dukies ran onto the field to tear down the goalposts. As a team, fans carried the goalposts up through the bleachers and half a mile across campus, to the magnificent doors of Duke Chapel, to be beatified.

They heard about that win down in Gainesville, where Charlie Pell's successor, Galen Hall, wasn't winning big. Up in Spurrier's office the phone rang with a Bull Gator's call from Gator Country, asking the Ball Coach if he could please coach Duke to "at least a break-even season" so he could be considered for the job of head coach at Florida.

Break-even season? Spurrier needed that disbelieving Gator's call. He beat every other ACC team on the schedule, whomping North Carolina 41–0 in Chapel Hill to clinch a share of the 1989 Atlantic Coast Conference Football Championship. Tar Heel coach Mack Brown was winless, glaring at Spurrier as he led his Dukies back onto Brown's field to take a team picture under the North Carolina scoreboard.

Why should that team picture upset Mac Brown? the Ball Coach wondered. "We've won more games on this field than he has." Spurrier was named ACC Coach of the Year again without Coach Brown's support.

The best field was the backyard, where the coach and his namesake son fired the ball around before breakfast. Back in Tampa, Stevie had gone out for quarterback in junior high, wearing No. 11. He'd been playing receiver in high school in Durham, wearing No. 88. Wanting to challenge the head coach's son for the starting quarterback spot. His dad went by the high school and scouted the opposition. The head coach's son could really zing the ball.

"If you want to play," Stevie's dad said, "you need to find another position. You won't play quarterback ahead of that kid."

A receiver should catch everything, no matter what's in the way. He sent his son long and started throwing the ball between the pine trees.

A man who could coach Duke to an ACC Football Championship could be the head coach of an NFL team in Atlanta or Phoenix. Until Florida called, asking him to come home and coach the Gators.

Dave Brown answered the New York Giants' call to be an NFL quarterback. Clarkston Hines graduated as Duke's all-time leading receiver, happy he'd answered Spurrier's ad. Fred Goldsmith, an upright wedding witness, could be Duke's head football coach, Spurrier recommended.

His namesake son stayed in Durham, *his* hometown, playing receiver for his high school. Believing he could walk on at Duke as a wide receiver, earn a scholarship, and become a receivers coach, called Stevie no more.

CHAPTER TWELVE

Delivery

Steve Spurrier saw greatness in a former fifth-string quarterback, looking through the tunnel to a field of dreams.

Shane Matthews, what do you want to run for your first play as starting quarterback at the University of Florida? Matthews thought a screen pass, or a draw play, might loosen up the team playing Oklahoma State in front of 75,428 Gators.

"Shoot no, they aren't paying me all this money to come down here and run the ball," Spurrier said.

"Heeeeeeeeeeeeeeeeeeeeeeere come the Gators!" the PA announcer bellowed.

Running out of the tunnel, waving to his father and mother beaming in the first row in the end zone, with his wife, children, and Florida teammates weeping for joy, Spurrier led the Gators onto Florida Field on September 8, 1990, as Florida's head coach—running across real grass, hoping to lay to rest the old school motto, "Wait until next year."

Scraps of that artificial turf Spurrier had ripped out and thrown to the curb got picked up and saved by disbelieving Gators, clinging to the past. He'd show them. Football is played on *grass*, under palm trees and tropical skies, with some guidelines he called "Gator Mentality."

"Trips left, X Short, Blue Slide, Z Cross," he told Matthews, clapping his quarterback on the shoulder pads and sending him out for his first play, a 35-yard completion.

A nation of Gators hollered. Eyes had not seen, ears had not heard, such a backpedaling of defensive backs across the SEC, fearing an offense that passed first and ran last.

"You know, I think we ran that play in the front yard," said Dr. Toby Ford, the town dentist in Newport, watching the game on TV with his wife, Beauanne.

Speaking in the pressroom after beating Oklahoma State 50–7, Spurrier wasn't happy about the 7 points the Cowboys scored.

What should sportswriters call the passing attack Matthews triggered? He allowed that "Fun 'n' Gun" might lighten up the sports section his father carried around Green Cove Springs.

That gave the Gators the mindset to go into Birmingham and withstand an early 10–0 Alabama lead, block a punt in the fourth quarter, and beat the Crimson Tide 17–13 at their stadium. Showing the disbelieving Gators back home Spurrier's team could play with the big boys.

He'd met the enemy, and it was Florida. Former coach Galen Hall's $360.40 "loan" to a player needing to pay child support in 1986 made UF ineligible for the 1990 Sugar Bowl—and therefore unable to compete for the 1990 SEC Championship, the NCAA ruled the week after the win over 'Bama.

Spurrier put on his go-to-meeting clothes and went to debate university officials over appealing that punishment. Looking the deciders in the eyes, he said no one on his team had done anything wrong. The doubts of Dr. Robert Lanzillotti, dean of UF's business school, could no longer be contained.

"We have never won the SEC! We're not going to win it this year! We've only won one conference game and we're talking about winning six more?"

"Wait until next year," the administrators had to say to the football coach, giving Spurrier what he really needed: someone to prove wrong.

Unfairness clouded his face when he huddled up his team and told them Florida would win that championship on the field—and he wouldn't let anyone forget who won it. Mississippi State and LSU got stomped at Florida Field, loud enough for the dean of the business school to hear.

In the stadium boasting the SEC's loudest crowd, Spurrier sent Matthews onto the field with plays the Vols anticipated. They'd watched lots of film of Florida. When his tight end dropped a touchdown pass that would've tied the game at 7, cameras caught the velocity of Spurrier's visor hitting the ground. Big Orange rolled over Florida, 45–3, with no one cheering Spurrier in the Cottage. The major networks told their TV crews to keep a camera on the visor at all times.

Disbelieving Gators resurfaced. Florida never could beat Auburn and Georgia back-to-back. Hearing that Auburn had lost its library in a fire, Spurrier sent his regrets: "Some of those books hadn't been colored in yet." No. 4 Auburn lost 48–7 to Spurrier.

Florida still had to play Georgia the next week in Jacksonville. Spurrier called up Gene Ellenson, former Georgia player, Florida defensive coordinator, and rabid Dawg hater, to give a pregame speech in the locker room.

Fate favors men who want to win. The Ball Coach added that the game the Gators annually feared was played in Florida, in a stadium called the Gator Bowl.

"We should beat them," he told his team. "We should beat them by a bunch."

With cheers ringing through the stadium, Spurrier stood by the locker room door, waiting for his mom and dad to celebrate a 38–7 win over UGA athletic director Vince Dooley's Dawgs.

Hearing about gatherings at cemeteries where cocktails were poured on the graves of Gators who'd lived and died without beating Auburn and Georgia back-to-back, Spurrier got ready to avenge the people who had to move out of a house they loved in Marietta, Georgia. His Gators clawed Bill Curry's Kentucky Wildcats, and stood alone atop the SEC at 9–1.

Scoring 35 points and gaining 450 yards a game, rewriting their coach's passing records, Spurrier's Gators ripped away 57 years of SEC futility and 84 years of mediocrity—fielding the best team in Florida football history.

A business school dean and a 45–30 loss to Bobby Bowden's Seminoles in Tallahassee couldn't deter the Ball Coach from painting "First in the SEC" on his stadium wall, to honor the 1990 team. What New Year's resolution should he make, watching another SEC team play in the Sugar Bowl on the TV in the den? What goals should his rising seniors set in the spring of '91?

With Matthews and speedy running backs and defenders returning, his team believed anything less than an official SEC title would be underachieving. Spurrier himself mentioned during a giddy round of off-season Gator gatherings he had a better team than Alabama, who'd finally have to play the Gators in Gainesville. Newspapers reporting that he'd predicted a 30-point win over the outraged Crimson Tide ended up off by 5. Beating 'Bama 35–0 as Florida Field jubilated, the Gators got back at the Volunteers, beat Auburn and Georgia back-to-back, and outlasted Bill Curry's Wildcats 35–28 to hold up the SEC Championship trophy generations of Gators had hoped to grasp.

Frenzied Florida fans drowned out Curry's audibles, reporters noted in the home-team pressroom.

"This is the Swamp," Spurrier said. "Only Gators get out alive."

The team's other preseason goal was to beat Florida State—a bruising battle won when Matthews threw a bomb on a busted play. Florida reclaimed bragging rights from the Team Out West, 14–9, sending the Gators to the Sugar Bowl full of themselves, Spurrier couldn't help but notice.

In the Superdome cameramen tracking the visor in the 1992 Sugar Bowl had a field day. Florida's players clearly spent too much time celebrating the SEC Championship and state "Chompionship" on Bourbon Street. Notre Dame coach Lou Holtz and running back Jerome Bettis gashed the Gators in the second half for a 39–28 upset.

"I think that just makes our coaches mad and want to work a little harder for next year," Spurrier told the *Orlando Sentinel*. Still not smiling in the spring. Could Matthews win a Heisman Trophy his senior season, making his coach the first Heisman winner ever to coach a Heisman winner? Commentators speculated. Football is a team sport, the Ball Coach would remind them all. Florida didn't have as much talent that year, he kept to himself.

In Knoxville in September the Vols avenged their avengement. Cowbells clanged for a 30–6 Florida loss at Mississippi State, hitting Matthews in the place where he was raised. Gator Mentality got the team past the favored Dawgs 26–24, with a Spurrier time-out wiping out a last-second Georgia score in a deluge in the Gator Bowl. Keeping the Gators alive to win an SEC Eastern Division Championship.

The league had expanded into two divisions of six teams each, with division winners meeting in a championship game—a format all other major college football conferences adopted. Arkansas joined the SEC West. A South Carolina team some called cursed became the sixth team in the SEC East.

On December 5, 1992, the underdog Gators played in the first SEC Championship Game in Birmingham, losing 28–21 to No. 1 Alabama. On the team plane home, Spurrier apologized to his new boss, athletic director Jeremy Foley, for underachieving.

Fog flooded the Gator Bowl on New Year's Day, sending the visor-cam man to the Gators' sideline for a 27–10 victory over NC State the players could barely see. Florida's first bowl win under Spurrier sent Matthews to the NFL. A new quarterback would have to run some ball plays.

When the Fort Walton Beach High School Vikings won their state championship game at the Swamp, Spurrier was in the stands, watching a quarterback who could be special—a preacher's son, Danny Wuerffel, who'd make a preacher in Green Cove Springs prouder to say, "I'm Steve Spurrier's father."

<hr />

Passing out the Gator Mentality guidelines in the locker room in August, Spurrier saw two quarterbacks who could be all-world. Two more reasons a congregation of Gators had expanded into the Gator Nation—a union that didn't exist until the Ball Coach made winning in Gainesville routine.

After all the miles and moves to get back to his alma mater and win, he spent the off-season protecting his family's privacy, praying for a peaceful meal at a restaurant, going home to a house behind a guard gate. Knowing the hopes and dreams of every autograph seeker depended on his next quarterback, or two.

Out on the Bermuda grass junior Terry Dean vied to be The Man, competing with Wuerffel, the redshirt freshman, whom Spurrier had to believe played better than he practiced. In the second week of the season, against Kentucky, Dean threw four picks and Wuerffel threw three. Curry's defense looked like they'd watched lots of footage of the Fun 'n'

Gun, giving the Wildcats a 20–17 lead with the clock running out. With eight seconds left Spurrier waved off the field goal kicker and called for a pass to receiver Jack Jackson. Wuerffel pump-faked to Jackson and looked for Chris Doering, the walk-on receiver from Gainesville who'd worked every day with Wuerffel after practice on goal-line plays.

"Doering's got a touchdown!" Gator radio announcer Mick Hubert hollered over and over to the Gator Nation, as Curry sagged in frustration.

Wuerffel's first start came against the No. 5 Volunteers and star quarterback Heath Shuler, who got the Vols a big lead in the Swamp—until a rain of touchdown passes from Wuerffel downed Tennessee 41–34. He credited God and his coach's game plan for a comeback booed in the Cottage by the regular Spurrier haters.

A hurt back couldn't stop Wuerffel from passing the Gators to a 58–3 win over LSU, making Florida 5–0. The Gators crashed back to earth on "the Plains of Auburn," losing 38–35.

Wuerffel threw those "duck passes," Dean told teammates.

In the Gator Bowl rain slicked the balls Wuerffel threw, and Spurrier sent Dean onto the sloppy field to beat Georgia. Dean quarterbacked the Gators to another SEC East title, and Spurrier's first home loss as head coach. FSU zipped past the Gators 33–21 and notched a national title with some fast footwork.

Spurrier started Dean in the '93 SEC Championship Game in Birmingham, and Dean made the plays that beat Alabama 28–13. The coach high-fived his MVP quarterback and held up another SEC Championship trophy, Florida's third by Spurrier's count.

In the Sugar Bowl Dean led Florida past West Virginia 41–7 for the school's first 11-win season. Spurrier's rising seniors set lofty goals in the spring of 1994.

After some Seminole players reportedly took shoes in an after-hours spree at a Foot Locker store, and Spurrier told the Polk County Gator Club that FSU stood for "Free Shoes University," word got around. To take on those maddened 'Noles in the fall, he would need a new graduate assistant. A receiver who'd earned a scholarship and a degree at Duke University and wanted to help coach the Gators was the man for the job.

For the first time Florida took the field in the fall as the No. 1 team in the nation, with Dean a Heisman Trophy candidate and Wuerffel on the bench. Dean looked like he could do it all.

"Obviously," Bill Curry answered to reporters after losing to Spurrier 73–7, "if I had known he was a genius ..."

Dean looked like the country's top quarterback in Knoxville, after a 31–0 manhandling that had Tennessee seething. After another big win over LSU, anger seeped into Florida's locker room. Dean's throwing motion needed correcting, despite his gaudy numbers, with undefeated Auburn coming into the Swamp to face a Ball Coach out for revenge. Dean threw four interceptions, the last one a real visor flinger. Spurrier sent in Wuerffel. He threw a pick leading to another Auburn score, and another devastating 3-point loss.

"What about all those interceptions?" ABC wanted to know as Auburn cavorted on Florida's field.

"Well, I made some bad calls on those, yeah," said Spurrier, turning away from the ABC guy to defend Dean in the home-team pressroom.

In the Gators' locker room, Dean told reporters Spurrier packed on the pressure that week, showing Dean his mistakes on film and saying, "If you don't get this Heisman talk out of your head, you're never going to play here again." Creating what Dean called "a self-fulfilling prophecy." Causing a nation of critics to pile on Spurrier for mistreating his quarterbacks. Making those critics enemies of the Gators.

At practice he reminded his quarterbacks there's a right way and a wrong way to throw a pass.

Wuerffel rose to the challenge, throwing for a slew of scores that took down Georgia 52–14, and lowly South Carolina 48–17. He torched the 'Noles defense through three quarters of the Free Shoes University game in Tallahassee. Somehow, the Seminoles scored four touchdowns in the fourth, salvaging a 31–31 tie Spurrier hated.

Waiting for him in the Georgia Dome in Atlanta, the site of the SEC Championship Game, Alabama took a 23–17 lead with the clock rolling in the fourth quarter.

Eighty yards from 7 points and a championship, Spurrier lined up both tackles wide, flanked by tight ends and receivers, sending discombobulated defensive backs to cover sideline routes—while Wuerffel and the running backs took the ball where 'Bama's guys weren't. Just the way Spurrier remembered Emory and Henry doing it in Johnson City in 1958.

Suddenly, Wuerffel limped off, apparently hurt. Backup quarterback Eric Kresser trotted in and fired the ball downfield, maybe catching 'Bama gloating about an injured quarterback. Wuerffel ran back in and lateraled to Doering, who threw to receiver Aubrey Hill for a first-and-goal at the 2. Wuerffel audibled out of a quarterback sneak and hit Doering for the winning score.

Glued to the TV in Newport, Stevie's fifth-grade sweetheart turned to Toby and said, "Those looked like plays from your yard, too."

Handing over another SEC Championship trophy to the Gator Nation, Spurrier hugged his quarterback.

"Coach, I love you," Wuerffel said.

Celebrating an SEC Championship in the Georgia Dome could never get old. Unless you were an early Heisman Trophy candidate who didn't see eye to eye with your coach or a Volunteer in the Cottage watching plays on TV you saw years ago in Kiwanis Park.

A Sugar Bowl rematch with FSU, which the T-shirt makers called "Fifth Quarter in the French Quarter," left Wuerffel rug burned after a 23–17 beating in the Super Dome. Giving Spurrier off-season dreams of an enemy with a spear on its helmet. Helping his young receivers coach get toughened up in the backyard.

◆◆

Spurrier's seniors set a goal in the spring only the brashest coach could uphold. Losing the Sugar Bowl to the star-studded Seminoles fueled a quest for an undefeated season—to redeem a coach vilified in the press for expecting too much.

On the practice field in August, running backs Fred Taylor and Elijah Williams both prepared for 1,000-yard seasons. Spurrier told reporters wanting predictions for the next Game of the Century that Tennessee coach Phil Fulmer scouted the *News at 11*.

An hour before the Game of Century kicked off, Lonnie Lowe visited his old teammate in the head coach's office behind the walls of the

Swamp—and found him working with 10-year-old Scotty on his golf swing.

"Show him your golf swing," Dad told Scotty.

"You should see it," Spurrier said to Lowe, "because it's the same as yours."

Coach Fulmer looked like a good scout when quarterback Peyton Manning passed the Vols to a 31–14 lead that had the regular Spurrier haters cheering in the Cottage. Who could have predicted Wuerffel would throw seven straight touchdown passes for 48 unanswered points? Florida 62, Tennessee 37 had *Sports Illustrated* scrambling to switch the cover photo from Manning to Wuerffel, with the same orange backdrop.

Taking the Gators into Athens, Georgia, that year because the Gator Bowl in Jacksonville was being renovated, Spurrier realized late in the game that no Bulldog opponent had ever scored more than fifty points "between the hedges." Backup quarterback Kresser got the ball back in his hands on a flea-flicker play and passed for a score stamped in the Georgia record book, 52–17.

The Bulldogs didn't seem mad, Spurrier told reporters in the visitor's pressroom, "since there weren't that many left in the stadium." Then he picked up the phone in the visitor's locker room.

"Coach," he said to Ray Graves, "I got you even."

Asked repeatedly why he kept passing when he was ahead, Spurrier responded. "Why is it that when Nebraska gets ahead nobody criticizes them for continuing to run the ball?" Nebraska had a running game that would prove Spurrier's point.

His seniors accomplished their goal of the first undefeated regular season in Florida history with a 35–24 win over the Seminoles in the Swamp, and a 34–3 triumph over Arkansas for another SEC Championship trophy presentation in Atlanta. The 12–0 Gators would play in the school's first national championship game in the Fiesta Bowl, against Nebraska.

In the Arizona desert the Gators got outcoached and outplayed 62–24 by a Nebraska team that kept blitzing and kept running. After the most lopsided game ever played between college football's top two teams, commentators questioning the Ball Coach had their volume turned down on Spurrier's TV. He got that long-awaited phone call—an offer to coach the Tampa Bay Buccaneers.

The *Gainesville Sun* reported that Florida's football coach had already resigned, to return to Tampa Bay.

Late at night, in the backyard of the Gator coach's manse, he listened to a train passing through the pines and palms, leaving that stillness they didn't have in a city by the bay.

"Maybe I'm just a college football coach," he mused, choosing to stay and lead his team where no Gator had gone before. Proud to coach running back Terry Jackson and receiver Willie Jackson Jr., who played for the Gators because their father, Willie Jackson Sr., had confronted the SEC fans waving Confederate flags and cursing Florida's first black football player.

If Spurrier was staying, he wanted the ball back quicker. So he called Bob Stoops, defensive coordinator at Kansas State University, and hired him away from the Wildcats. Stoops masterminded a defense that would take the ball away from the other team, reloading the offense the commentators were so quick to criticize after the Nebraska game.

For the most successful senior class ever at Florida, one team goal remained.

At September's Game of the Century in Knoxville, the Gators faced a fourth-and-11 on the opening drive. The hollering blistered ears in the upper deck. Here's where Tennessee takes over, they all said in the Cottage. Spurrier sent Reidel Anthony into the end zone, the announcers screamed into their mikes, and 107,608 fans in orange got quiet.

Was that first touchdown pass an audible? reporters asked Wuerffel.

"Yeah, right," Wuerffel said. "Like I'm going to have the nerve to call a post pattern on fourth-and-long."

Some Tennessee fans got so mad about that pass they grabbed renowned surgeon Mikel Reed, a guy wearing orange and blue, and threw him over an embankment on the UT campus, ending his career.

Spurrier and Wuerffel demolished LSU, Auburn, Georgia, and Curry's Kentucky team that season, causing the Ball Coach to say every week that his team just played its best game. LSU defensive coach Carl

Reese had to stop teaching a clinic on defending the Fun 'n' Gun—his expertise based on losing to Spurrier the year before by a score of only 28–10.

Gator hatred swirled around Tallahassee in late November, on a gusty day when Wuerffel's younger brother Ben cried in the stands. Florida's quarterback got hit nearly every play, knocked down 32 times by defensive linemen that Coach Bobby Bowden said played "to the echo of the whistle."

Bowden did his best to end Spurrier's national championship hopes with that 24–21 pounding, putting Florida State on track to play Nebraska in the Sugar Bowl for the national title.

Spurrier still had a trophy to win in Atlanta. At the team hotel the elevator doors opened for Wuerffel and his coach to wild cheers on the Gators' floor. Texas had beaten Nebraska on an improbable pass in their conference championship game. Making the Sugar Bowl another Florida rematch with the Seminoles.

Seeking redemption, Wuerffel threw six touchdown passes to take down Alabama 45–30 in the Georgia Dome and hand his coach another SEC Championship trophy. The following Saturday Wuerffel became the first Heisman Trophy winner to be coached by a Heisman winner. Walking onstage back in Gainesville to receive his diploma at the O'Connell Center, as his coach applauded.

On New Year's Day 1967, they watched Ohio State beat the new No. 1 team, Arizona State, on a last-ditch drive—that made the Sugar Bowl winner the undisputed national champion. But what chance did Wuerffel stand against the giant 'Noles?

Spurrier took on the media's glare, speaking out against Bowden's defensive tactics, while the Gators practiced plays out of the shotgun formation Spurrier had scoffed at for decades. Might give his quarterback an extra second against defenders playing to the whistle's echo.

"If I wasn't a good Christian man, I'd tell every one of you to go out and kick Steve Spurrier's ass," Bowden told his team.

"I let Coach Spurrier do all the talking," Wuerffel said.

In the Superdome the teams sparred for a half that ended 24–17, Florida. The preachers' halftime prayers uplifted Florida to a 52–20 win over the 'Noles for the 1996 national championship.

"God smiled on the Gators," Spurrier said, walking into the throng in the French Quarter and almost getting carried away. Telling reporters they were celebrating that "Knox County Championship" at Tennessee.

He asked the manager of the Sears store down in Ocala, "a real big Gator fan," to present the Sears Trophy, the crystal football given to the best college team in the land, at a ceremony in the Swamp.

Standing before a stadium full of ecstatic fans, with a nation of Gators watching on TV and his mother and father in the end zone, fresh out of coaching tips, Spurrier led a pent-up cheer:

"We're number 1! We're number 1!"

CHAPTER THIRTEEN

In His Father's House

Reverend Spurrier rooted for North Carolina, growing up in Charlotte, but seemed to search his whole life for an earthly home. Settling at last in a town on the St. Johns River in Gator Country, where everybody knew his name.

Live oaks draped in Spanish moss shaded a brick house like the Spurriers always had, flying an orange and blue national championship flag. No need for a bigger place, they told their son wanting to buy them a new house. All their pictures, clippings, awards, trophies, and framed portraits of the Last Supper and "the Kick" fit with the furniture they'd bought 50 years ago, in a living room ticking with antique clocks. Time and talent. Signs proclaiming Jesus Never Fails and Go Gators hung above three pairs of bronzed baby shoes, the littlest seeming like the shiniest.

On the August day in 1997 when the Gators took the practice field in Gainesville to start defending their national title, the Spurriers sat in their house down the road talking about their faith in Jesus and Steve. Reverend Spurrier's steely, enduring hair framed soulful eyes and a wide smile that turned into a gruff, portentous pucker. He wore a gold Gator watch. Mrs. Spurrier hovered around him wearing a floral print dress and a kindly but no-nonsense look as he chewed on his glasses, considering what made his youngest son such a winner.

"Desire to win, competitive spirit," Reverend Spurrier said.

Did he get that from his father?

"I'm afraid so," he said, smiling. "And it rubs off on the team."

"Steve is a lot like his dad; he says what he thinks," Mrs. Spurrier said, shaking her head.

"He jokes a lot," she said, "with the straightest face. And I'm afraid he got that from me."

The reverend put on his glasses like he was called to speak.

"I like to think I had a part in Steve's upbringing, getting him interested in sports," his father said. "So it's a little difficult when they have celebrations and don't mention you."

Still rankled that Johnson City officially changed the name of the brick football stadium downtown to Steve Spurrier Field and held a stadium rededication ceremony in March without inviting the reverend. In the picture behind him his son looked sympathetic, handing back the Heisman.

"It's probably true he wanted to outdo his older brother," his mom theorized. "But Steve took to it tough. Whatever he goes into, he wants to be the best."

His parents talked about the games he and Sara and Graham played, the movies they didn't see, and the theology of Gator domination. Remembering, near the end of the day, the pain and disappointment of hearing that Steve eloped with Jerri.

Then Reverend Spurrier showed a picture of Coach Ray Graves and all the Spurriers at Steve Jr.'s wedding, where they finally got to dress up and officiate and celebrate. Really just the start of the grandchildren and great-grandchildren whose baptisms and weddings would need officiating. Of course, the reverend could slip in a blessing for Steve, who'd won his dad a dynasty.

At the wedding Coach Graves had something to show off.

"That's the national championship ring Steve gave me," his coach said. "The players designed it. They wanted all these diamonds. And Steve said to me, 'We think nobody but players and coaches should have this ring.'

"Then Coach called me up for lunch one day, put something in my pocket, and said, 'Here's something I want to give you. I didn't win a championship while I was playing for you, but you got a ring now. I had to go to the players and ask their permission.'"

"I appreciate that, Orr," Coach Graves had said, looking down to see his name on the ring, engraved with "52–20."

"Showed you who came to play," said Coach Graves, celebrating Steve Jr.'s wedding with Orr.

Was it fate, or God's will, that some do mighty deeds and the rest of us are fans?

"I hesitate to say this," Reverend Spurrier said, straining against his cushy recliner, "but I'm pretty much of a frustrated athlete."

He looked out at the sunset orangeing the windowpane.

"I wanted to play," he said. "*Wanted* to be good. But I just couldn't do it."

Breathing louder than all the clocks.

"But you made suggestions to Steve," his wife said, craning her neck to look down at him. "You'd tell him, 'You should have done this or that.'"

"I remember saying a number of times, 'You did well, but you could have done better.'"

"No pressure, just suggestions," Mrs. Spurrier said.

"And he took me up on it," Reverend Spurrier said, nodding and nodding. Settling back in his chair. "Because he took to all sports like a duck takes to water. He's just one of the naturals."

With brisk sweetness Mrs. Spurrier started talking about her husband's time as a tennis player. The old story she worked at retelling, waving her arms and feet in volleys, showing how he ran down every serve. She loved a player with heart. Like any fan.

While she talked he sat silently, sunken in his massive chair. Fidgeting, adding nothing to the story. Seemingly lost in thought. She looked at her husband in his reverie, her head cocked.

"Steve," she said. Using their boy's name to get through to where her husband was. "You sort of lived your life through him."

The ticking surrounded us, echoing off the furniture. That dusty, deathly sound from childhood—the grandfatherly ticking that unnerved you in an old person's house. The aging, bent brass second hand moving, stopping, moving, stopping. Sounding like little ticking pleas, for Dad, Dad, Dad! You get one chance to ask the question of a lifetime.

"Why, why, why," the writer blurted out, "were you so hard on your son?"

"I declare, I don't think I was," Reverend Spurrier said. Not in a reverie anymore. Sitting up as straight as anyone could, in that chair.

"And Steve doesn't think I was, either."

He tugged on the lever at the side of the chair, pushed down on the footrest, sat up to his full fatherly height, and looked around at the pictures of Steve and Jesus hanging by the clocks.

"I must have done something right."

❧

The next morning Coach Spurrier threw more touchdown passes on the practice field under the sabal palms in Gainesville, trying to show his inexperienced quarterbacks the way to play. Watching Doug Johnson struggle on the practice field haunted by Danny Wuerffel.

"Doug and Danny are different," their coach said to the microphones and cameras thrust into his face. "Doug can throw the ball 70 or 80 yards. Sometimes he throws it too hard. Sometimes he throws it over people. But I think he'll be able to make all the calls, and all the audibles. He just hasn't done it yet."

Back in his office at the University of Florida, under the stands in The Swamp, he sat behind a massive desk surrounded by trophies, clippings, pictures, game balls, and a bulletin board sporting hard, encouraging words: "Practice the proper stance." For an office inside a stadium there was a lot of light. Tall windows oversaw one of college football's brightest programs. So the head coach kept his visor on, anticipating a question about how it was with him and his dad, growing up.

He shrugged, behind his desk, as if "growing up" was not quite right, and said, "We spent a lot of time playing catch."

Spreading his hands across all that wood, he said, "I was just the son of a father interested in sports."

The writer had a question all boys wrangle with: Do you feel like your dad showed you he loved you ... in his own way? The question came out as, "Did your ability to be so strategic, to read defenses and think up new stuff on the field, start when your father took you to see all those football games?"

His head shook like the visor was glued to his hair.

"It all evolved after I got into coaching," he said.

"Was it a help in developing your offense," the writer persisted, "when your dad took you to see Emory and Henry play?"

"That Emory and Henry formation was just something I recalled later when I got into coaching and was looking for something different to do," Spurrier said.

Glaring, arching his fingers, talking about the benefit of doing things differently. "Conley [Snidow] wants to send me a whole repertoire of plays you can run out of it [the Emory and Henry formation]," he nodded thoughtfully, a finger at his lips.

"Did your dad taking you to see that offense run get you realizing football could be . . . imaginative?" Wanting him to give his dad some kind of shout-out. But he wouldn't. Creating his unique offense, he said, "had to do with having teenagers in the house, and needing not to be just one more coach who lost his job."

What really helped him, he was saying, was being a dad. Asked if his dad ever helped him out, he stared upward.

"He's been . . . we've had a wonderful relationship, I think," he finally said. "He lives pretty close by. I doubt if you'd say we called each other all the time or anything like that. I think it's just a normal relationship."

"I think he's very, very proud of you," the writer said.

"Sometimes he can go overboard, I hear."

"He told me that he's a frustrated athlete, who has lived through you. Except for winning at tennis."

"Yeah, he loved that tennis, that was his sport. We're all products of our environment. Dad was competitive in sports. He believed in that and tried his best to win games."

Spurrier paused, pointedly. "You could say I learned that from him."

Maybe he was really saying, One more question about Dad and you're out of here. Maybe showing how we all communicate—by reading each others' defense.

If only talking about our fathers wasn't such a hard game to play.

The defending national champs were ranked No. 2 at the start of the season, rising to No. 1 after Johnson's three touchdown passes gave Florida a 33–20 win over the Vols, making Peyton Manning 0–4 against Spurrier. But in Baton Rouge the clinic was finally on, as LSU took down the Gators and the goalposts, 28–21. And in the Gator Bowl, Spurrier lost to Georgia for the first time as Florida's head coach, 37–17.

The No. 1 Seminoles pulled up to the gates of the Swamp, sure they'd give the Gators a beating and play for the Sears Trophy. A Seminole scout seemed to have stolen Spurrier's signals.

He stunning the team with the spears on the helmets, and the TV announcers and a nation of Gators, by alternating quarterbacks *every play*. Johnson and his backup, Noah Brindise, took turns getting "coached up" and racing out to the huddle with the play. The two quarterbacks combining for 336 yards and no interceptions.

After a goal-line stand held the 'Noles to a field goal, Johnson's fake audible set up a 67-yard bomb to Jacquez Green, and a Fred Taylor touchdown plunge. Denying the Team Out West a chance to play for the national title, 32–29.

Heading down the turnpike to Orlando for the Citrus Bowl, Spurrier had to wonder how a preacher kept inspiring a congregation with sky-high expectations, posing at midfield before the game with opposing coach Joe Paterno. Beating the Nittany Lions ended a seemingly lackluster 10–2 season in Gainesville.

In January opportunity called from Indiana, home of the Grossman family.

"We don't recruit Indiana," said chief recruiter Jim Collins.

The Grossmans kept after Collins until they got an appointment in Gainesville. When they showed up, Spurrier was back from a golf trip to Mexico to greet them. Showing highlights of the national championship season that had a young quarterback itching to run the Fun 'n' Gun. Then Rex's high school coach, his father, narrated highlights of his son's play, showing Spurrier a quicker release than any quarterback he'd ever coached.

Grossman sat out his first season at Florida, while vengeful opponents went after the Gators again. In the 1998 Game of the Century, Collins Cooper missed a 32-yard field goal in overtime and the goalposts came down in Knoxville. Tennessee capped off the celebration by winning an SEC title and the national championship. Who knew how many more crystal footballs the Vols could brag about if not for Spurrier? Gator fans settled for another 10–2 season, beating Syracuse in the Orange Bowl as quarterbacks Doug Johnson and Jessie Palmer took turns frustrating their coach.

In the spring of '99, Spurrier led his team onto the practice field without his son. Steve Jr. had been hired by Bob Stoops to coach the receivers at the University of Oklahoma. "He's right where he needs to be, in Oklahoma," his father said, looking around the Gators' practice field. "He doesn't need to be still hanging around Pop."

Spurrier moved the receivers around the field himself, demonstrating routes. Believing Johnson was finally ready to play quarterback, after he gave up baseball to please his coach.

Johnson led the Gators to a 23–21 win over the defending national champion Vols, making Spurrier less welcome than ever at the Cottage. He showed up anyway and had a beer with Graham and the regular Spurrier haters who liked him better for a day.

Alabama beat Florida in the Swamp, after a missed extra point in overtime, and the Spurriercam caught the friction between the quarterback and the coach. He owned Georgia again, 30–14, his hundredth victory at Florida. Making Spurrier the only coach in the twentieth century to win a hundred games in ten years.

Earning their first trip to Atlanta since Wuerffel led the Gators into the Georgia Dome, Florida got crushed by the Crimson Tide. Writers filled Reverend Spurrier's sports page with I-told-you-sos about his son mishandling his quarterbacks. A loss to Michigan State in the Citrus Bowl ended a 9–4 season full of bad routes and dropped passes, from a quarterback who never could pick apart a zone defense like Wuerffel could.

"Am I coaching as hard as I used to?" Spurrier asked his assistants.

"Harder," they all said.

Spurrier had to wonder if a professional coach would have more control over his players. Bucs head coach Tony Dungy had a championship-caliber defense in Tampa, now that the team was wearing Bandits colors. The team the Spurriers rooted for in the den on Sundays couldn't beat the Bucs in the playoffs.

In the spring Spurrier had a practice field without Doug Johnson on it. Grossman battled rising senior Palmer for the quarterback job, as March greened into April. The Gators basketball team made it to the Final Four. A son left behind in Johnson City called his father on Sunday, no matter what game was on TV.

"Dad, you're going to live forever," something made Graham say.

"I'm ready to go to heaven," a father told his namesake son.

Hours later Reverend John Graham Spurrier died in his sleep, on a moonless Florida night, lying beside his pianist, choir director, bulletin writer, and partner for life.

When his youngest son heard from his brother that their father was gone, he went off by himself to Crescent Beach, where he had a house, and his own burial plots.

Maybe he watched a little basketball, with the Gators playing Michigan State for the national championship on the TV in the den.

Out on the beach, ocean mists flowed past a Carolina crescent moon. Showing the way for a man to carry on.

PART THREE

MARCH TO ATLANTA

Everybody needs a home to come home to.
—STEVE SPURRIER

CHAPTER FOURTEEN

South of Leesburg

HE WAS THE LONE GUY ON THE FIELD AT TWILIGHT, SURVEYING THE stadium his team would fill the next day for the University of South Carolina Spring Game televised on ESPN. Stepping up to the stage where Hootie & the Blowfish would play, the coach met a writer excited about the back-to-back national championships the University of Florida had just won in basketball.

"How 'bout those Gators!" the writer greeted the coach, holding up a palm for a high five.

"Lord," Spurrier said, "I've got my own troubles right here at South Carolina."

He thought he knew the amount of trouble he'd stir up—walking up the stadium steps in the dusk, getting his wife and tie and heading downtown to speak out against a symbol of racial oppression in his state.

At the Columbia Metropolitan Convention Center on Lincoln Street, Spurrier walked on stage directly above the ballroom where a black presidential candidate from Illinois was delivering a speech. While accepting the Citizenship Award from a young adult advocacy group called City Year, Spurrier said, seemingly off-the-cuff, "The Confederate flag should be taken down from the State House grounds."

No one asked him about that flag, the Ball Coach said. But if they did, he'd say the people of South Carolina didn't need the Confederate flag waving over the State House, holding back the whole state.

Big speech at the convention center on the *News at 11*. Spurrier a hotter topic than Senator Barack Obama, across a state still fighting the Civil War. What kind of leader enrages his own people?

An army of rebels made a stand at the USC Spring Game on Saturday, April 14, 2007, disowning their coach. Giving roving TV crews comments about Spurrier that couldn't be broadcast.

"Send him on his way to hell if he wants to leave the South," one of the milder comments, led to a South Carolinian's ultimate put-down. "He's not even *from* here!"

Some USC fans recalled too well the day Spurrier first set foot in Columbia, as coach of the hated Gators—driven from the airport to the hotel to the stadium to humiliate the Gamecocks. That "Black Out Game" in Columbia, with Williams-Brice Stadium filled with USC fans dressed in black, "helped us see our receivers better," the Gator coach had said.

How did a "classic carpetbagger" who's "offended my whole family" and "played right into the hands of the racist NAACP" get to be South Carolina's football coach in the first place?

A city burned to the ground by General Sherman does not forget. Neither does Spurrier.

The Gamecocks had been "cursed," their coach knew, by a one-eyed South Carolina governor and senator named Ben "Pitchfork" Tillman— founder of Clemson University. Furious when the student body at USC wouldn't agree to march across the state and enlist in his "agricultural school" excluding black students, Tillman legendarily stuck his pitchfork into the ground at the USC Horseshoe, looked to the heavens, and hollered, "I curse the University of South Carolina."

A hundred and fifteen years later, fans of a school that lost more football games than it had won since the 1892 season still believed in that "Chicken Curse."

Steve Spurrier's father didn't raise him to let the guy with the pitchfork win.

The Ball Coach would defy the curse of a "citizens' militia" leader terrorizing former slaves after the Civil War, the prime advocate of South Carolina's 1895 segregation laws, a governor who approved of lynching his state's black citizens. Speaking on the floor of the US Senate in 1900, Pitchfork told his fellow senators, "We have scratched our heads to find out how we could eliminate the last one of them, and we would have done it if we could. We took the government away. We stuffed ballot boxes. We shot them. We are not ashamed of it."

On the South Carolina State House grounds, Ben Tillman's black marble statue kept a baleful eye on the Confederate flag in front of the capitol, from behind a palmetto tree. It was a sight Spurrier believed the Gamecock football team and a new generation of South Carolinians didn't want to see.

"He needs to be careful, very careful . . ." one rebel wrote.

The Ball Coach had to ask how he got to a place where some Gamecock fans hated their coach more than they hated Clemson, driving around town with bumper stickers urging, "Punt Spurrier, Keep the Flag."

ESPN, the *USC Daily Gamecock,* and a close family member reported that Spurrier received death threats for his comments about the flag. ESPN also reported death threats were received by "at least one member of his staff. The memories of the hate mail and the threatening phone calls won't soon be forgotten in the South Carolina Football offices at Williams-Brice Stadium," according to ESPN senior national columnist Gene Wojciechowski. Spurrier downplayed those threats, then denied receiving them. After an infamously hot summer in Columbia, Spurrier heard the flag wavers say, "If he's going to stick his nose where it does not belong, he'd better win."

That, Spurrier said, he understood. No one would listen to a football coach talking about taking down that Confederate flag until he won at South Carolina, and won big.

A grieving son could still hear his father's voice, in waves rolling out of the dark. Looking for his likeness under the crescent moon.

In April 2000 at Pinewood Presbyterian Church in Green Cove Springs, Florida, Reverend John Graham Spurrier Jr. got a tribute from his youngest son, letting mourners hear those endless echoes: Dad, Dad, Dad.

"Uncle Bob used to tell me that when Dad missed an easy shot, he'd have a tendency to sometimes fling that racquet into the net, or against the fence," Spurrier said at the pulpit. "So, when I throw things . . ."

When a golf-visor–flinging ball coach jokes about his dead father throwing tennis rackets, the living have to laugh.

Two days later, at Florida's Spring Game, Spurrier's voice broke, looking at an empty seat in the south end zone, telling his Gators at halftime, "This is the first home game my father has missed since I've been coach of the Gators."

Most of his linemen were hurt. He only had 18 players on the field all game. Nine-man football wasn't going to catch on, he told reporters in the home-team pressroom: "We need some people back."

A redshirt freshman quarterback took the practice field in August who could get his coach back to Atlanta, maybe farther. In the second game of the 2000 season, senior Jessie Palmer failed to see an open man Spurrier saw. On the sideline Grossman told his coach he saw that man open, and jogged onto the field to throw a touchdown pass.

Palmer and Grossman alternated at quarterback until Grossman rewarded his coach's faith by leading the Gators to a 28–6 triumph over Auburn for another SEC Championship trophy, at last, hoisted up by the Ball Coach as the Gatorade and confetti poured down.

A 37–20 loss in the Sugar Bowl, to the hated Hurricanes, stoked the fires of a coach with the quarterback to take Florida to another national title. Then Spurrier could jet off to an NFL deal, securing his family's future. Knowing that in Washington, the new boy billionaire owner of the Redskins, Dan Snyder, had hired Coach Pepper Rodgers as vice president of football operations to entice Spurrier to sign with the 'Skins.

Snyder flew to Florida in the jet he called "Redskins One" to get a preliminary deal with the Ball Coach, while Spurrier's rising seniors set a goal of a national championship in 2001.

Spurrier would have to win it without one of his oldest friends on the sideline.

"There wasn't a game I ever coached," he said, speaking behind another pulpit at yet another funeral, "that Lonnie Lowe didn't have a sideline pass."

The loss of Johnson City's head of Parks and Rec to cancer led like a bad dream to the death of Florida freshman Erasmus Austin, who succumbed to heat exhaustion in July after a voluntary workout, leaving Spurrier in tears again.

Scotty told his dad they should get out of Gainesville. Find an underdog team to lead. Top teams got targeted by unseen plotters.

On the practice field in August, Grossman put the ball where his coach would throw it. The Gators were the No. 1 team in the country terrorists attacked on September 11, 2001, postponing the Florida-Tennessee Game of the New Millennium until December. Spurrier's quest for another national title led to two season-ending showdowns: Win the annual battle with Florida State, and beat the Vols in the Swamp, and Florida would play for the national championship in the Rose Bowl.

As the Gators piled up points in a 37–13 rout, Seminole defensive lineman Darnell Dockett wouldn't go gently into the loser's locker room. From where Spurrier stood, it looked like Dockett tried to stomp on Grossman's throwing hand and twisted the knee of running back Earnest Graham in a pileup after a play.

Tennessee's running back Travis Stevens had been injured in September but could play in December. Spurrier would have to face Tennessee without do-it-all running back Graham, because of FSU's Dockett, the Ball Coach told reporters, showing film of the plays in question.

"That's the way they do bid'ness," Spurrier said about Florida State and Bowden—without the backing of his boss, Florida athletic director Jeremy Foley, who maintained the evidence didn't warrant Spurrier's accusations.

Without Graham gaining yards on the ground for the Gators, Spurrier's team withstood the Vols' 226 rushing yards and battled back in the fourth quarter, with Grossman hitting a touchdown pass to make the score 34–32. Hearing Spurrier call the same play again, the quarterback faded back to get a 2-point conversion that would send the game to overtime.

The Volunteers batted that ball down. Sending Spurrier walking across his field a loser and the Cottage into delirium. Florida bound for the Rose Bowl no more.

One last time, walking to the home-team locker room, Spurrier looked up at that empty place in the end zone where the last pass fell to earth.

Grossman barely missed winning the 2001 Heisman Trophy, lacking 62 votes to become the first sophomore ever to win—almost making Spurrier the only winner of the award to coach two Heisman winners. He spent Christmas with his mom and his family talking about the offer Dan Snyder in Washington had dangled in front of him for a year.

No one outside the houses of Spurrier and Snyder knew that a 56–23 takedown of Maryland in the Orange Bowl would be Spurrier's final game coaching the Gators. He walked off the field in Miami saluting the fans he'd fought for—who called the season disappointing when Florida ended up the third-best team in the country, with no trophy from Atlanta or Pasadena.

His alma mater would go on without him, he said, stunning the Gator Nation.

"I won't miss him," said Vols coach Phil Fulmer, celebrating the news with everyone in Tennessee.

Spurrier taught Florida fans too well not to celebrate being No. 2 or 3. He beat Georgia 11 out of his 12 seasons at Florida and would remind Robert Lanzillotti, dean of the UF School of Business, that counting the year Lanzalotti said Florida wouldn't win an SEC title, Spurrier's Gators won seven.

"It wears on you," he said, acknowledging the expectations he'd created in Gainesville at a news conference telling the Gators good-bye. "I'd kind of like to be the underdog again."

⎯ ⌣ ⎯

Could the coach with perfect Sunday school attendance mount a crusade with mercenaries instead of student athletes? Pro football called Spurrier, from Washington and Tampa, where the Buccaneers finally had a super team and wanted to hire the coach in the visor to call some ball plays.

Spurrier could still hear his father cheering for the Redskins in the den after church, where he preached that a believer in the Lord received everlasting life. He could still take notice if his son became head coach of the team in burgundy and gold.

Five million dollars a year from the tempter flying in on Redskins One made Spurrier the highest-paid coach in all of sports. He brought no agent to negotiate the biggest transaction in sports history, just pen and paper. Snyder brought his checkbook. The Bucs hired second choice Jon Gruden, a guy who wore a visor and idolized the Ball Coach, to call the ball plays in Tampa Bay. If only the Bucs knew Spurrier was a genius when he wanted to be their genius.

At the Washington news conference introducing the Redskins' new coach in January 2002, Spurrier adopted the Dallas Cowboys as his chief adversary, in a city in need of a hero.

"I realize there are no Vanderbilts in this league," he said, zinging a college team he always beat. His ability to coach a pro team doubted by reporters in the room, Spurrier rebutted questions about the hours he put in by saying, "Brad Scott had a cot at South Carolina." Spurrier's Gators played Scott's Gamecocks five times, winning by a combined score of 269–84. Spurrier, the Redskins coach, made only one promise at the press conference: When he beat Dallas, he'd give a game ball to "Mr. Snyder," the boy billionaire clearly pleased with his new acquisition.

"Make it easy for him," Spurrier's mentor, Coach Pepper, advised Snyder, who overspent for a mansion on a hill for his coach at Arthur Godfrey's old estate, overlooking a private golf course. Pumping another $200,000 into amenities. A man cave full of data ports for game planning adjoined a game room with an official Redskins pool table.

Snyder promised Spurrier the Redskins would re-hire general manager Bobby Beathard, drafter of the high-flying Redskin offenses that played behind "the Hogs." When the ink was dry on Spurrier's contract, his boss told him Beathard couldn't be lured back to Washington. Not hiring a general manager gave Snyder the personnel power usually wielded by a head coach and forced Spurrier to sit in meetings dickering over players and contracts with Vinny Cerrato, the director of player personnel that former Redskins coach Marty Schottenheimer had fired—and Snyder rehired after firing Schottenheimer to hire Spurrier.

His finest hour with the Redskins, said the owner adept at manipulating men in meetings, was giving a sales pitch that convinced Ravens defensive coordinator Marvin Lewis to ride down the Baltimore-Washington Parkway and coach Spurrier's defense.

"I'll leave you alone," Snyder said Spurrier assured the veteran coordinator, who'd give the new Redskins coach a grudging effort. Lewis believed he was better qualified than his boss to be an NFL head coach.

Few coaching families could work a room like the Spurriers, feted like royalty at Washington balls. Larry King hosted a gala where Dick Cheney, Orrin Hatch, Bob Dole, Alexander Haig, Dionne Warwick, and *Cosmopolitan* editor Helen Gurley Brown lined up to meet the Redskins' coach and his wife.

At Dickinson College in Pennsylvania, scene of Spurrier's first training camp with the 'Skins, thousands gathered around the practice field to watch a game of catch between the Ball Coach and new Redskins quarterback Shane Matthews. The pass patterns Spurrier chalked up from memory looked familiar to newly signed quarterback Danny Wuerffel. Washington's revamped receiving corps featured ex-Gators Doering, Anthony, Green, Willie Jackson Jr., and draft pick Taylor Jacobs—coached by Steve Spurrier Jr., hired away from Oklahoma.

The Ball Coach didn't draw up many plays for his big, fast running back from Auburn, Stephen Davis.

Jerri Spurrier hosted Family Night on Wednesdays at Redskins Park, where coaches, wives, and children gathered around the dinner table. Her husband warned the team there'd be fines of $20 for cursing, except on game day. At Loudon County High School, Scotty Spurrier's team had a special quarterbacks coach, with his dad showing up to work with the Raiders' quarterbacks and receivers after coaching Washington's NFL players.

Spurrier faced San Francisco in an exhibition game in Osaka, Japan, in his NFL coaching debut, with the NFL mandating that two local players get in the game for each side. Spurrier put in a call for Japanese defensive backs. Coach Pepper lobbied for two sumo wrestlers to play defensive tackle.

"All they'd have to do is push their guys backwards," Coach Pepper told his former pupil, who pushed his offense to overwhelm the Niners 38–16. The new NFL coach loved talking to his quarterback through the helmet radio the league allowed.

A media frenzy over his return to Florida followed the 'Skins to Tampa for a preseason game, where Spurrier stomped the Bucs under new coach Jon Gruden. The Ball Coach was booed by Bucs fans in Florida State jerseys, and cheered by Bucs fans in Gator jerseys.

At his regular-season debut in Washington, against Arizona, Spurrier wore black on the sidelines, not burgundy and gold, notching his first real NFL coaching victory, 31–23. Standing in the backyard of Snyder's mansion, looking out over his golf course, he could only wonder what criticisms his dad might have.

He led his team in the Lord's Prayer before the next game, and his Jewish boss joined in. When the wind picked up over the Potomac, Spurrier looked cold, and Snyder planned to build an indoor practice facility for his shivering coach but lost a fight with flood-plain regulators. When Spurrier wanted a fire pit in the backyard, Snyder commissioned an edifice that had neighbors worried about a second Stonehenge. And Snyder uncharacteristically said nothing, publicly, when his coach suffered some discouraging losses, alternating Matthews and Wuerffel at quarterback—leaving talented rookie Patrick Ramsey on the bench and running back Davis calling for more carries.

Florida sportswriters missing their favorite source of quips and quotations reported that Spurrier called Gainesville to encourage new Gator coach Ron Zook, who was proving to be no Steve Spurrier.

In late November Wuerffel started against St. Louis and hit 16 of 23 passes for 235 yards and no picks, bringing home a 20–17 win. That performance earned him the right to start in Dallas the following week, where he put up similar numbers and three touchdowns in a loss. Hurting his shoulder playing the Giants in December, Wuerffel was done for the year.

Media criticism for juggling quarterbacks all season added to the uproar over Spurrier's disregard of Davis's talents. Rookie running back Ladell Betts got more carries at the end of the season, further incensing commentators around the capital. With Ramsey starting at quarterback, Spurrier won his "bowl game," beating Dallas 20–14 at Fed Ex Field and giving his boss the game ball.

At the end of a 7–9 season, Lewis was named head coach of the Bengals in Cincinnati. Bone-chilling winds hit the house overlooking the golf course as Spurrier looked back at his first losing season since Duke went 5–6 his first year as a college head coach. On the TV in the den, the coach wearing the Buccaneer visor won Super Bowl XXXVII, holding up the trophy that would've lifted Spurrier's legacy into the stratosphere.

Hopefully his next season in Washington would go better, leading to a future for his family secured by Snyder's millions, endless days of golf, and the chance to finally live without battling Goliath.

When Washington's social events seemed less inviting, Spurrier hit buckets of balls off his hill and made birdies like always—by putting the last bogey out of his mind. There weren't many golf days in the winter of 2003 for an NFL coach needing to field a better team. The sight of Spurrier pouring through endless game films and 40-yard dash times had Vinny Cerrato telling reporters, "Coach feels very comfortable that he knows everything."

Wanting a burner wide receiver for his son to coach, Spurrier agreed to part with most of his guys from Florida, including Wuerffel, saying, "We've cleared the air about me bringing in my former players. A coach has to be careful about that."

FSU receiver Laveranues Coles, who landed in the NFL after yet another "Free Shoes University" shopping scandal, was wooed away from the Jets by Snyder. He offered to hire a big-name replacement for Lewis. Anyone Spurrier wanted, Snyder said he'd open his checkbook and get. Spurrier gave his loyal linebackers coach George Edwards a promotion to defensive coordinator. And in the dog days of August, Wuerffel's old coach brought him back to Redskins Park.

"Patrick is by far our best quarterback," Spurrier told the microphones and cameras, spotlighting Wuerffel's return on the *News at 11*. "Danny gives us insurance."

A move that made sense to the coaching staff slighted Cerrato. He'd just spent 2 million Dan dollars signing former Buccaneer quarterback Rob Johnson, who couldn't grasp the intricacies of Spurrier's offense and welcomed Wuerffel's savvy. In Jacksonville the Heisman winner took the field in a preseason game against the Jaguars and hit 13 of 19 passes. If

Cerrato had his way, it would be the last game of football Danny Wuerffel ever played. Waiving the $300,000 quarterback would make the 2 million dollar guy look like a better deal.

At the end of August, Cerrato told Wuerffel to clean out his locker. Silently, Snyder sided with his personnel director and racquetball partner. Spurrier spent the day knocking on every other door in Redskins Park, trying to save the job of the quarterback who best represented his coach on the field. Convincing the coach that Wuerffel had to go "took about 10 hours," Cerrato said.

Waiving Wuerffel was a "team decision," Spurrier told reporters asking about friction between him and Dan Snyder.

"Steve can never stay mad at Dan [Snyder]," Jerri said, missing Wuerffel terribly.

Washington opened the 2003 season at Fed Ex Field against the New York Jets, who faced four former Jets Snyder and Cerrato had plundered. Kicker John Hall beat his old teammates with eight seconds on the clock, after a gutsy scramble by Ramsey set up the field goal try for the 16–13 win.

"Thank goodness Mr. Snyder went out and got us a heck of a kicker," Spurrier said in the Fed Ex Field pressroom. Ramsey was developing chemistry with Coles, and the Redskins shot to 3–1 after beating New England, a team that would go on to win its next 21 games.

Better double-cover Coles, opponents said. Ramsey had to run for his life, behind a shaky offensive line. In Tampa Spurrier built a lead over the defending world champs—and the Redskins' defense gave up four fourth-quarter touchdowns. Ahead 23–10 in Miami, Spurrier lost. His loyalty to his offensive line coach from Florida, John Hunt, and defensive coordinator, Edwards, wasn't being rewarded.

Running back Trung Canidate couldn't replace Davis, who was churning out yards for the Carolina Panthers. Those guidelines Spurrier worked up to turn college players into winners didn't inspire millionaires. Veteran players like Bruce Smith called the head coach "Steve," walking past his office to see Snyder.

The man who called the plays must bear the blame, the DC media decreed. Making Spurrier decide to hand over his headphones to offensive assistant Hugh Jackson—who said it was tough sparking up the play calling with Steve Spurrier watching. After a few games they took turns calling plays. The offense Spurrier hoped would revolutionize professional football poked along without blocking all the blitzes his quarterbacks endured. His son was coaching Coles and receiver Rod Gardner to the best season of their careers, but it's a team sport.

Dad would've had him doing things differently, Spurrier had to believe, watching the sun set over the golf course out back that was losing members by the day. The Redskins ended the 2003 season losing 31–7 to the NFC East champs in Philadelphia. The coach told reporters at a news conference back in Washington that he "planned" to return.

Flying down the coast to Crescent Beach, looking back at all the losses, Spurrier concluded that 15 million more Dan dollars couldn't compensate for coaching in the "No Fun League."

Snyder and Cerrato were chomping popcorn in a movie theater when Spurrier's ringtone disrupted the show. They raced back to Redskins Park to learn his cell phone ran out of juice on a golf course in St. Augustine, as his resignation got faxed in.

When Snyder finally got Spurrier on the line, no amount of pleading could bring back the coach whose heart left Redskins Park when a bean counter cut his quarterback. A man didn't have to ordain deacons or coach a team he didn't believe in. Spurrier didn't want to leave Crescent Beach, but Scotty's senior year at Loudon County High School couldn't be missed.

Not living in my house, Snyder said. Spurrier spent his last days by the big stone fireplace banging balls off the hill onto an empty fairway. The course had been foreclosed on. Only a man who defied Dan Snyder could play on those brown fairways.

"Steve just wanted to be a ball coach," said Coach Pepper, leaving Snyder's employ, too. "He didn't want to go to meetings with people about money."

Snyder agreed that "Steve and Vinny didn't get along too much" and said the decision to cut Wuerffel at the start of Spurrier's second season wasn't made in the owner's office.

"I wasn't involved," Snyder said. "I'm usually told afterwards."

Losing defensive coach Marvin Lewis hurt Spurrier more than losing Wuerffel, Snyder believed. Surprised to hear the official Redskins pool table got carted out of the house on the golf course he provided for Spurrier.

"I'll buy him another one," Snyder said.

⁓

Living in a rented house west of Leesburg, Virginia, passing his old mansion on the way to golf games he couldn't really enjoy without a football team to forget about, Spurrier shivered and looked south. His curse was doing whatever he wanted all day, without a team to coach for the first fall since the USFL folded.

Golfing with the Redskins' team dentist, Spurrier played every course around Washington before Dr. Charles Nardiello finally said, "Steve, I have to go to work."

Spurrier drove back to his rented house and settled in front of the big screen to watch the Golf Channel, the Weather Channel, the country music channels, and Court TV. Waiting for his son's football practice to start.

Sitting on the top row of the bleachers at Loudon County High School on Friday with Jerri, cheering for Scotty and the Raiders, he had his dad's view of the game. Taking his son on trips to see colleges he might want to play for, sitting with Scotty in the Buccaneers' new stadium, watching the University of South Florida Bulls play ball. Spurrier could see the college kids still needed "coaching up."

"Go to school where you want to live," he told his youngest son, like his college coaches told him. Planning a trip to see Steve Jr. coaching the tight ends at the University of Arizona, Spurrier heard destiny calling, in the voice of University of South Carolina athletic director Mike McGee.

Gamecock coach Lou Holtz was retiring, McGee said, and believed Spurrier was the only man for the job.

Sitting in his rented, cherry-paneled office looking south, thinking about coaching the losingest team in the history of college football, Spurrier realized that a coach who could win at South Carolina would make history. Out in the kitchen Jerri said she saw "one door closing and another opening," like that Lee Ann Womack song, "I Hope You Dance" they loved to dance to.

Don't go *there*, their Gator friends all said. You'd have to coach the worst team in the SEC against Florida every year.

Fatefully, they were also looking for a ball coach in Gainesville, after Florida fired Ron Zook. The UF student government passed a resolution calling upon Bernie Machen to rehire Spurrier.

"When the job opened up I called Jeremy Foley," Spurrier recalled, "and he said, 'Wait awhile, let's see what direction we're going.'" Astoundingly, UF employee hiring procedures would have required Spurrier to submit his résumé. Giving rise to a story reported across the Sunshine State, and in the *Washington Post*, that Spurrier told UF President Machen, "My résumé is on your stadium wall, and in your trophy case."

"Somebody made that story up," Spurrier said. Probably because it sounded just like what the Ball Coach would say.

Machen told the *Orlando Sentinel* he "tried to call Coach Spurrier a couple of times," probably to appease a nation of Gators missing the Fun 'n' Gun days. Then the former president of the University of Utah decided to hire Urban Meyer, the Utes' former football coach.

Scotty Spurrier was named Loudon County Special Teams Player of the Year, bringing his dad to the table at the awards banquet with coaches of the local NFL team—that ended up 6–10 under Joe Gibbs and didn't beat Dallas. Maybe, Spurrier mused, he was a college coach at heart, and planned a trip to see a school he might want to go to.

Former Gamecock linebacker William "Hootie" Johnson opened the door for Spurrier at Augusta National Golf Club, home of the Masters. Driving back past the State House in Columbia in the southern sunshine, he saw the Confederate flag waving in front of Pitchfork's statue.

As the final seconds ticked off the scoreboard in Clemson, South Carolina, after a 29–7 beat-down and a fourth-quarter brawl marred Holtz's last game as Gamecock coach, a chant filled "Death Valley":

"We want Spurrier! We want Spurrier!!"

Look at the bright side, he told disbelieving Gators. The Ball Coach at South Carolina gets a shot at beating Georgia every year.

CHAPTER FIFTEEN

Proving Ground

INTRODUCED AS SOUTH CAROLINA'S 32ND HEAD FOOTBALL COACH ON November 23, 2004, before a throng of reporters and astounded Gamecocks, Spurrier borrowed a line from the Red Sox, the baseball team his Uncle Eddie wanted play for that Bostonians believed was cursed.

"Why not us?" he asked. "Why not the South Carolina Gamecocks?"

Amid the cheers in Columbia, some people asked, "Why us?" Trying to accept a coach who beat South Carolina by scores of 54–17, 52–25, and 63–7. "We were rarely even worthy of one of his patented one-liners," said one doubting Thomas.

Doubts ran rampant on the stage of the *College GameDay* show, with host Lee Corso opining, "I don't think Spurrier can win an SEC or national title at South Carolina. I don't care if he coaches there 400 years!"

Corso said he'd crawl across the field and salute the Gamecocks if South Carolina miraculously made it to Atlanta and won. To get there Spurrier would have to "coach up" Holtz's former quarterback Blake Mitchell, a roughneck from LaGrange, Georgia, who shared a name with a porn star. A quickly assembled recruiting class for USC wouldn't include quarterback Jimmy Clausen, Spurrier told his Gator friends, because the high school phenom had a "problem father."

Spurrier's first move in the locker room was taking down all the Beat Clemson and Hate Orange signs. Let Clemson worry about USC. Our goal is to win a Southeastern Conference Championship, Spurrier told his players.

His team better be spiritually straight, to send that curse back across the state.

Adrian Despres was hired as the USC team chaplain in 2000, by Lou Holtz. When Spurrier was hired as USC's head coach, Pastor Adrian asked people around campus, "Do you think he'd like a chaplain like me?"

He'd find out for himself, taking the elevator up to the coach's office overlooking the football field for an interview. Waiting in Spurrier's outer office, Pastor Adrian picked up the *USA Today* sports section and, "in God's providence," read the Stat of the Day question: Who is the sports personality you most love to hate?

The winner, right there on the page, was Steve Spurrier. His voice boomed into the room.

"How you doin', Reverend? Do you mind if I call you Preacher?"

Adrian said he didn't mind.

"Ah, you're a funny preacher," Spurrier said. "I like preachers with a sense of humor."

He pointed to his TV, where he'd been screening replays of the big fight on the field at Clemson in Holtz's last game as Gamecock coach. Spurrier had seven camera angles to view. The worst fighting was in the end zone, where players slung punches and helmets without an adult in sight.

Seven cameras caught the pastor as big as any player running into the end zone, wading into the brawl, pushing and pulling brawlers apart. A Clemson player smacked Pastor Adrian with a helmet in the back.

From seven vantage points Spurrier could see Pastor Adrian turn to the player who hit him and say something that sent his assailant running. The coach turned to the pastor and said, "Tell me what you said to that Clemson player."

"I'm the team chaplain. You better watch out for lightning," the pastor said he said. Making the Clemson player run "like he'd seen a ghost."

Spurrier exploded in laughter, repeating "preacher" and "lightning" until he gasped for breath.

"You better keep doing what you're doing," he said, telling the team chaplain he'd be staying on to shepherd Spurrier's team at USC.

Turned out, though, the men disagreed about when chapel should be held for players preparing for battle. Spurrier held chapel services for his players at Florida on Saturday morning, hours before the game. Pastor Adrian had been preaching to USC players on Friday nights.

"Why not Saturday morning chapel, Preacher?"

"Well, I think you should be talking about ripping the face off the other team on Saturday mornings. I rip their faces off spiritually, and get them thinking about repentance, on Friday nights."

"Brilliant," Coach Spurrier said. "Friday night chapel it is." He promised that he and Jerri would never miss worshipping with the team on Friday night. Then he warned the pastor that a powerful enemy confronted the Gamecocks—and a Ball Coach could not let his anger get the best of him in that spiritual fight.

Standing in his office overlooking the field, Spurrier vowed to Pastor Adrian never to throw his University of South Carolina visor onto the ground. No matter how many cameras the TV networks angled at him.

The march to Atlanta would start at the Proving Ground, across Bluff Road from Williams-Brice Stadium, where Spurrier would move heaven and earth to win—switching around the practice fields to face the same direction as the field in the stadium. Still a game played on grass, he said, despite the towering "Cockominiums" under construction around the stadium. Speculators around Columbia were betting Spurrier could beat the curse and fill their coffers.

While Jerri cheered Scotty at track meets back in Leesburg, Coach Spurrier lived in the Whitney Hotel, seeing fans and autograph seekers in the lobby, the halls, and the elevators. He greeted every fan and signed all the garnet and black footballs, helmets, and posters they put in his hand. "Everybody around here got real relieved," the limo driver at the Whitney said. "They love this guy. They think whoever talked bad about him before had it all wrong."

He had met the Enemies of the Gators, and they were on his side. Spring was now a season of hope in Columbia. Spurrier taught his team to run the "Cock 'n' Fire" offense in front of record crowds at the Proving Ground and the Spring Game.

After Scotty's graduation from Loudon County High School, Spurrier brought his family back to South Carolina at last, to a home on a golf course outside of Columbia, where his receivers coach, Steve Jr., had a house, too.

Everyone working to dispel a curse had to earn their way. Spurrier took away two scholarships awarded by Holtz and gave them to walk-ons who'd proved to be better players, getting a letter of protest from 90 high school coaches—though it wasn't unusual for a new coach to reconsider scholarships. Demanding excellence at South Carolina took some getting used to.

Fans bought a record 62,618 season tickets, though pundits predicted the 2005 Gamecocks would be lucky to win five games. Those pundits royally welcomed the Ball Coach back to Birmingham for SEC Media Days in July.

"I've missed you guys," he said.

Couldn't miss all the photographers shooting his entrance into the Wynfrey Hotel.

"I thought he was the president walking through here," one of his linebackers said.

At the first annual Steve Spurrier Ladies Clinic at the end of July, so many women showed up to hear Spurrier's chalk talk and run onto the field like Gamecock players, the team ran out of artificial smoke.

BELIEVE, the *State* newspaper headlined a 100-page season preview. Sending thousands of believers to Spurrier's first fall practice, discussing the stats and scores of the players he coached—at Florida. Lacking a football identity, willing to take on his, they talked about "ball plays" and "coaching 'em up" on the Proving Ground, watching barnyard birds learn to fly.

———

The Gamecocks opened the 2005 college football season on Thursday night on ESPN, against the University of Central Florida. Driving up to the stadium, Spurrier saw thousands of fans with fingers in the air, trying to buy tickets. Nothing better than a full house and a full collection plate.

"Still the Ball Coach," the announcers said, watching Spurrier motion Blake Mitchell from LaGrange, Georgia, to the sideline to get hollered at. Clutching his unthrown visor, Spurrier turned to Pastor Adrian.

"Did you see that defense was in cover three?"

Pastor Adrian said he saw that. Spurrier turned to his quarterback as the Spurriercam rolled.

"Even the preacher saw it was cover three!"

Mitchell jogged back on the field, saw what his coach and pastor could see, and threw a touchdown pass, then another. The Gamecocks withstood a Golden Knight rally for a 24–15 win, opening the Spurrier era at USC.

Road games at Georgia, Auburn, Tennessee, and Arkansas all sold out, with fans thinking they'd finally see the score run up on Spurrier. In Athens a full house of Dawgs booed his every appearance on the video screen. A South Carolina touchdown got called back, and Mitchell's pass for a game-tying 2-point conversion fell incomplete.

"I'm not going to apologize for it," Georgia coach Mark Richt said after beating Spurrier 17–15.

At Auburn a hobbled Mitchell couldn't play. Backup quarterback Antonio Heffner couldn't keep Tigers and War Eagles from celebrating a 48–7 bashing of the Ball Coach. In Columbia, Alabama embarrassed Spurrier 37–14. He'd never been 0–3 in the SEC. Were the predictions of 5 wins too generous? Mitchell returned to engineer a 44–16 win over Kentucky. Spurrier drew up plays to alternate Mitchell with Syvelle Newton, a speedy receiver who could throw, using formations that put them both on the field to beat Vanderbilt 35–28.

Over 100,000 Volunteer fans filled Neyland Stadium at the end of October to cheer for Peyton Manning as his number was retired and boo the coach in the Gamecock visor, working to flummox Fulmer yet again. At the end USC kicker Josh Brown booted a 49-yard field goal he never could make in practice to upset Tennessee 16–15. USC's first-ever win in Knoxville got "Cock Man" Graham Spurrier even more guff in the Cottage.

"God has smiled on the Gamecocks," Coach Spurrier said, acknowledging to reporters in Tennessee that God once smiled on the Gators.

He took his upstart team into Fayetteville, Arkansas, for a stunning fourth SEC win in a row, outlasting the Razorbacks 14–10. Stirring up deeply divided feelings in Gainesville about the "all-time Gator," and warnings to Urban Meyer from Spurrier's former players.

"Watch out for the Mills Route," they said, fearing the deep post pattern Spurrier named after burner receiver Ernie Mills. "You know it's coming."

On a surreal November afternoon in Columbia, Spurrier saw defensive backs backpedaling and audibled into running plays, pounding away at a Florida coach determined not to get beat by one of Spurrier's bombs—or the Emory and Henry formation, or a fake flea-flicker halfback option pass. Spurrier's 30–22 upset of the No. 12 Gators was the first time USC beat Florida since *Gone with the Wind* was in theaters.

When the winning coach jogged to midfield to shake hands with Coach Meyer, old Gamecocks cried in the stands. Waving at all of them, walking off the field, Spurrier never looked happier, telling a fan in the tunnel, "*They* don't own our asses anymore." Not seeming to mind that *they* was he.

He videotaped a message for fired-up USC fans at "Tiger Burn," the annual pep rally in Columbia—mirrored 131 miles away by "Cocky's Funeral" at Clemson, where a rooster was dishonored with a full military burial in a 55-gallon drum. Delivering last rites for Tommy B. Tiger before his three-story sculpture was torched, the Gamecock preacher prayed, "Lo, though we have walked through Death Valley . . . Lo, you have given us Coach Spurrier . . . We have everything we want."

What did it feel like to be Spurrier for five minutes? The fraternity guy in a black shirt and visor who played the Ball Coach in a skit strutted offstage, fawned on by sorority girls.

And yet the same old doubts filled the campus bookstore and the Piggly Wiggly on Devine Street, after too many losses to an ancient adversary. Spurrier's mastery of SEC foes couldn't get his team more than three field goals against Clemson, keeping the curse alive, 13–9. Tempering the joy over a 7–5 season, an unpredicted second-place finish in the SEC East, and Spurrier's unprecedented 15th consecutive college season with a five-game winning streak. He was SEC Coach of the Year—his eighth time as top coach in the SEC and ACC, going back to the Duke days.

"Didn't think we'd be making this much history this soon," he said. Calling Scotty at Charleston Southern University and telling his son to come home to Columbia, even though he'd have to bust his butt to earn any playing time.

Invited to play in the Independence Bowl in Shreveport, Louisiana, the Gamecocks accepted their 11th bowl invitation in over 100 years of playing football. The alumni association chartered a plane to Shreveport, full of hopeful hollering. "Game!" screamed the left wingers in the plane. "Cock!" responded the right wingers, united by Air Spurrier.

He took a 21–0 lead over Missouri, on the verge of going ahead by four touchdowns when Mitchell threw a pick returned to make the score 21–7. In the second half Tiger quarterback Brad Smith couldn't be contained, downing South Carolina 37–31.

A lame "Game," responded to by a sedate "Cock," petered into the silence of losers flying home. If Spurrier had been madder at Missouri, maybe the trains wouldn't have sounded so mournful all winter clanking through Columbia.

When the York County Gamecock Club met in the spring of 2006 in the banquet hall at Winthrop, the other school Ben Tillman founded, Coach Spurrier obliged every last autograph seeker, finally turning to a woman coming out of the kitchen.

"Do you have any relations in South Carolina?" she asked. "My husband is Wes Spurrier."

Steve Spurrier cupped his chin and looked skyward.

"Well," he said, "we have a punter named *Nate* Spurrier, who's no relation."

The woman smiled like they were related. The coach smiled like he'd made a good call.

Was Spurrier purposely staying mum about his South Carolina relations on Pitchfork's campus—or did he really not know where his forefathers came from? Did Reverend Spurrier not talk with Steve about his great-great-great-grandfather, Thomas Jefferson Spurrier?

The Ball Coach's sermon fired up the York County faithful, and he left in a motorcade for the next Gamecock Club meeting up the road. Happy to speak about the emergence of quarterback Cade Thompson in spring practice, giving Mitchell some competition. In Tampa Spurrier had seen the talent of a big, fast quarterback fixated on Greek warriors, preparing to play his senior season for the Jefferson High School Dragons. South Carolina needed a dual-threat quarterback like Stephen Garcia, who could run and pass and bust through all the old doubts, Spurrier believed.

Defying Lee Corso of ESPN and the Bulldog fans' clanging cowbells, Spurrier beat Mississippi State 15–0 for the 150th victory of his college coaching career. Jetting over to Gainesville, he received a standing ovation in the O'Connell Center at a celebration for the 1996 national championship team.

"I love all you Gators forever," he told them, wiping away a tear. What kind of reception would the Gator Nation give the turncoat introduced with his old team in The Swamp?

"Everyone needs to stand up and love Steve Spurrier for one more day," said his old linebacker James Bates.

More than 90,000 Gators roared as Spurrier walked onto his old field, and Jerri blinked back tears. The crowd roared again a few weeks later as Spurrier returned to the Swamp to be inducted in the Ring of Honor, taking the microphone and thanking Coach Ray Graves, "for bringing this hillbilly from Tennessee to the University of Florida." Adding an 18-foot Spurrier sign topping Florida's stadium to his résumé.

Back in Columbia a provocation in the "entertainment district" called Five Points caused Blake Mitchell to punch out a bouncer, and Spurrier coached up receiver Syvelle Newton to be his starting quarterback. Newton kept defenders on their heels, running and throwing and dodging defenders behind John Hunt's shaky offensive line.

Even when Mitchell returned, Spurrier started Newton for a game promoted on ESPN as the revenge of Kenny Irons. South Carolina's former running back, whom Holtz wouldn't play, had transferred to Auburn and returned to win a game of inches at the goal line. Gamecock fans remembered the blowout they had suffered at Auburn last season and applauded the effort after the 24–17 loss. Spurrier didn't want to hear it.

"Please don't clap when we come close," he told the Gamecock Nation, through the *News at 11* microphones. "I think it sends the wrong message. Our guys thought we'd done something pretty good, when in essence we didn't do anything but let a game get away that we were in a position to win."

Falling to 1–29 against schools ranked in the top 5, losing 20 times in a row to top-5 teams since beating North Carolina in 1981, South Carolina should know close didn't count, the Ball Coach believed.

"I don't know if any coach has ever told our fans, 'Please don't clap after we get beat,'" Spurrier said, willing to be the first—no matter how tough the opponent or how close the score. Gamecock fans outraged to hear there's a reason they have that scoreboard up there said Spurrier's honeymoon in Columbia was over. The fan in the street slammed him for starting Newton over Mitchell, too.

On his weekly radio call-in show at the Wild Wing Cafe, Spurrier said fans wondering whether Newton should be the starter "are either not mentally stable or else they're a Clemson or Georgia fan."

Before the big game against Tennessee, a Spurrier impersonator roamed the roads around the stadium, telling tailgaters in a Tennessee drawl that it would all be okay. Turned out to be another what-if game, with seemingly easy catches and interceptions caroming off Gamecock players' shoulder pads, as the Vols avenged last year's loss.

Newton had the Gamecocks at 5–4 when Spurrier affirmed John Wooden's adage that the bench is a coach's best friend—a fired-up Mitchell would go up against the Gators in Gainesville. Spurrier started Newton at safety, to put him on the field. Hyping Spurrier's return to the Swamp as an opponent, a media frenzy brought out Mitchell's best, in a see-saw game seeing him pass for nearly 200 yards in the second half. For the last three minutes the Gators roared nonstop. Spurrier's offense drove 44 yards in nine plays to set up a field goal attempt for the win. No one who cheered the returning national champion and Ring of Honor inductee wanted to lose to him in the Swamp.

As sure-footed Ryan Succop lined up for a last-second field goal, Spurrier told the cameraman there was no need to focus on him—he'd react the same whether Succop hit the game-winner or missed. Jarvis Moss leaped for Florida's third blocked kick of the game, and a 17–16 win.

"It wasn't our day," Spurrier said. Adding that "When they were singing 'We Are the Boys of Old Florida,' it wasn't as loud as I remembered."

Urban Meyer took a step out of Spurrier's shadow, toward the 2006 national title. Spurrier set his sights on the shadow looming over his team in Death Valley.

Trailing Clemson 28–14 at the half, Spurrier walked to the locker room telling his interviewer, "We're going to keep playing. We're going to keep playing." South Carolina scored 17 unanswered points in the second half to lead 31–28 with time expiring. Clemson fans stared slack-jawed as their kicker hooked a 39-yard field goal try and the Gamecock band trumpeted victory in Death Valley. Spurrier proclaimed that his cursed team had "turned the corner."

He was now surely too good to keep coaching in South Carolina. Alabama offered Spurrier $3 million a year. The University of Miami thought some vast sum would make him the Hurricanes' coach. Vol fans fed up with Fulmer finally revealed their secret love of Spurrier, too.

"I'm tired of talking about all that," Spurrier told his radio crowd. "Let me tell you a good rumor. My high school job is open. Science Hill High School. And if things go real, real bad for me, I might have to consider that as a last alternative job."

"He told me he's going nowhere," said Stephen Garcia, signed by Spurrier after sitting down at the Garcia house in Lutz, Florida, for a family dinner. "He wants to win the first SEC Championship in South Carolina history," Garcia told reporters. "And he wants me to be a part of it."

The long-haired field general who idolized the Greek warrior Achilles finished his high school career as all-time leader in passing yardage and touchdown passes around Tampa Bay, and took off his coat and shirt at a news conference to reveal a Fighting Gamecock T-shirt.

Blake Mitchell followed that strip act by leading South Carolina to a 44–36 shoot-out win over Houston at the Liberty Bowl in Memphis, the team's second consecutive bowl bid and first bowl win under Spurrier. The Gamecocks had earned eight wins for just the ninth time in school history, and Spurrier had matched Joe Morrison's record for the most wins at South Carolina in two seasons.

Making history. Putting together a highly rated recruiting class, topped by the Dragons' star quarterback. Enjoying having Nate and Scotty Spurrier on his team.

"Most people think that I'm not related to the head man, either," Scotty said, after that first official practice with his dad.

"If I drop a couple balls, he'll be like, 'What happened on those? You should have been able to catch those.'"

~

Surely the fortunes of the Gamecocks would rise when Stephen Garcia drove into Columbia in January 2007. Enrolling early, leaving behind his life in Florida and his girlfriend unknowingly pregnant, he drove up Assembly Street in a red pickup truck with cases of beer stacked in the back, hair flapping in the breeze.

Hitting winter workouts and college classes with a new tattoo on his bicep, *Arete*, the Greek word signifying "excellence," Garcia held court on a Saturday night in Five Points at the Knock Knock Club, until he got in a fight out back. Arrested and charged with "failure to stop on police command [and] drunkenness," said the Columbia Police Department incident report.

Jerri Spurrier saw a freshman quarterback needing sistering, maybe mothering.

On a rainy day in early March, a visiting professor zoomed past Garcia to grab the only parking spot in the lot, cursing at the kid behind the wheel. Garcia keyed the professor's car and got arrested again. This time suspended indefinitely from the football team. He got his hair trimmed and apologized to reporters. Developers of more Cockominiums around the stadium still had their money on Spurrier.

"If Steve Spurrier wins an SEC Championship, the prices and demand are going to skyrocket," said Boyce Haigler of Stadium Village Lofts.

Trainers bet on a horse named Spurrier to make a run to the Kentucky Derby. Garcia could only play catch with assistant coach David Reeves, son of John Reeves, after practice.

"Yeah, he looks good," Spurrier said, watching his banished quarterback make all the throws. Maybe the kid had been too privileged, lacking a time in his life when he was "Stevie."

Spurrier reinstated his controversial quarterback in April. Fans around Columbia said the Ball Coach must believe he had a quarterback to back up his brash talk—accepting a citizenship award the night before

South Carolina's most anticipated Spring Game, shocking the state by saying the Confederate flag had no place on the State House grounds.

Spurrier saw a freshman quarterback with unlimited potential missing spring ball, missing his high school prom, missing his pregnant girlfriend back in Tampa. Two more people Stephen Garcia was expected to save. Starting a pretrial intervention program to clear up the charges from two arrests, he had Jerri driving him to most of his 100 community service hours, thinking she knew how to keep high-spirited quarterbacks out of trouble.

Garcia couldn't grasp the offense without practice, and Gamecocks couldn't stand the thought of not seeing him play. Spurrier reassured USC fans, saying Garcia would be the starter next year if he had a good spring. At fall practice the coach was concerned about John Hunt's offensive line, with mobile quarterback Newton graduated and Chris Smelley from Alabama vying with Mitchell for the quarterback job.

A summer embroiled in controversy over the Confederate flag seemingly ended when Spurrier took the Gamecocks into Athens, Georgia, to face the 11th-ranked Bulldogs. Mitchell led only one touchdown drive, but the Cocks outgained the Dawgs on the ground, kept Georgia out of the end zone with a game-saving interception, and shut up the critics for a week with a 16–12 win. Spurrier had lamented not giving Georgia good reason to hate him lately, and he smiled broadly walking off the Dawgs' field as boos poured down from the stands.

Back in Columbia fans who'd professed hatred for their carpetbagger coach gathered at the stadium after midnight to welcome home their heroes. The celebrated victory made South Carolina's all-time record perfectly mediocre: 517 wins, 517 losses, and 44 ties.

Spurrier's cockiness must be back, pundits said when he named Smelley the starting quarterback in Baton Rouge at another stadium called Death Valley. LSU scientists sometimes recorded earthquakes on the seismograph at the stadium after the Tigers scored. The defending National Champs won 28–16, but Smelley played well and rewarded Spurrier's confidence by leading his team to three straight wins. In Tampa

Garcia and his girlfriend, Amanda, celebrated the birth of a son named Memphys, after a penguin in the animated movie *Happy Feet*.

Had Spurrier actually beaten Pitchfork's curse, with the 6–1 Gamecocks ranked sixth in the country? The weekend of the State Fair, he faced the team he belittled at his introductory press conference in Washington. Somehow, after his quarterback threw two picks, his offense could only score two field goals, making Vanderbilt a winner over Spurrier for the first time in 14 tries.

Blake Mitchell rose from the bench to face the other university in Tennessee, in Knoxville, where the Vols built a three-touchdown lead and watched Mitchell's passing tie the game despite the 20th rendition of "Rocky Top." Succop's kick gave the Gamecocks the lead, but he missed the field goal that would have kept the Cocks alive in overtime. Seeing Spurrier walk off that field a loser gave Johnson City great joy.

Garcia played the part of Tim Tebow on the scout team to prepare the Gamecocks for another epic game with Florida. The real Tebow bulled into Carolina's end zone for five rushing touchdowns and a 51–31 Florida win. Leaving USC one chance for redemption: beat Clemson.

A banner flew over Williams-Brice Stadium, proclaiming "Let the Band Play Dixie," emblazoned with a rebel flag. Spurrier kept his gaze on the field, sending out his offense with a 1-point lead and 3:59 left in the game, needing a few first downs for the win. Facing third-and-4, he put the ball in the hands of running back Cory Boyd, trusted more than Mitchell. Boyd couldn't get there. Spurrier watched Clemson drive 61 yards to a dagger-in-the-chicken-heart field goal and a win Pitchfork surely celebrated Tiger cleats digging into Carolina's field.

Worst collapse in South Carolina football history—that was saying something. USC, the nation's sixth-ranked team in October, shrank to 6–6 in 35 days. No bowl game for the Gamecocks. And yet in three seasons Spurrier had set the record for coaching victories at Carolina, with 21 wins.

Be ready for the spring, Garcia's coach told him, sending him into a night of mourning at Five Points. The losing coach would go home and see stars shining in the gator pond out back. Wake up with the Carolina sun. Get his ball, get his sons, and send them both long.

CHAPTER SIXTEEN

At the Gates of the Swamp

IN THE WEST END OF NASHVILLE, WHERE COWBOYS GO TO SING OR DIE, Spurrier buried his face in his hands, sitting beside his wife on the front seat of the bus for quarterbacks, running backs, wide receivers, and tight ends idling in front of Vanderbilt's stadium. Looking up at last to run his fingers through his hair, he could see taunts on the lips of the Vandy players walking past.

"They got a long ride home," said a Commodore in black who knew about losing.

As far as the Ball Coach could see, the 2008 season was over in September. No way to get the Gamecocks to Atlanta after losing to Vanderbilt. Spurrier had just coached a top-rated freshman class through August practice, and it was time to start thinking about next year.

The Commodores blew a foghorn in their stadium when they scored. Blasting out a warning for another rocky season. How could the Ball Coach lose to *this* team again? The loss of star receiver Sydney Rice to the NFL, after the redshirt sophomore told his coach he'd stay another year? The actual existence of a "Chicken Curse," or something worse?

The year started with the worst loss. Marjorie Spurrier would not live to see any real miracles worked by her son at South Carolina.

"She said she missed her husband and she was ready to go to heaven and see him," Scotty told his dad, after his grandmother went to join Reverend Spurrier that winter. The *Gainesville Sun* wrote no obituary. She would beam down from heaven as Scotty got married in February to Jennifer, his sweetheart from Loudon County High School.

"We took the job in Washington to find Scotty a wife," a father toasted his beaming boy.

———— ⌇ ————

Atonement for five straight losses ending last season began on Good Friday 2008, with Spurrier drawing up more plays on the Proving Ground for a quarterback who could run.

"I'm just very thankful he's giving me the opportunity to still be here after all the stuff that happened last year," Garcia said. Realizing now he wasn't ready for college life when he enrolled early. Looking like he had more zip on the ball this spring, and longer hair. Talking to reporters about how fatherhood had changed him.

Saturday afternoon, he had a case of beer delivered to his dorm by his brother Gary, a Harvard man. They sat on the curb in front of the East Quad with their beer, hooting at women until campus police cited Spurrier's quarterback for underage drinking. Followed five hours later by a ticket citing Garcia for the illegal discharge of a dorm fire extinguisher.

"We were cooking, and had a fire," the quarterback told his coach. Wasn't hollering *that* loud on the curb outside the quad, Garcia maintained.

"I am sure that Stephen Garcia has set a record for the most publicity for a South Carolina football player that has never played a down," Spurrier said, suspending his quarterback from all team activities until August, when he had to apply to the university for readmission.

What could redirect the team's focus? Under gunmetal skies, with a tornado bearing down, Spurrier announced he was turning over the headset to his son. Steve Jr. would be calling the plays for Carolina, after his father had called more than 20,000 plays in 24 seasons as a coach.

Reporters surrounded Steve Jr. like he was his father. Jerri Spurrier looked on proudly, seeing her husband give their son a chance to shine.

That year's Spring Game featured no concert, no ESPN coverage, and eight interceptions thrown by Chris Smelley and rising junior Tommy Beecher, with Steve Jr. calling plays for both sides. Scotty scored on the old "off the bench" play, running off the sideline to catch a touchdown pass from Smelley.

"I don't feel like Garcia's a godsend to get that first spot," Beecher told reporters.

The missing quarterback satisfied his reinstatement requirements and walked back onto the Proving Ground in August. Spurrier put his faith in Beecher, the starter for the season opener against North Carolina State.

With Beecher throwing interceptions, rattled by the Wolfpack pass rush, and Carolina clinging to a 9–0 lead at the end of the third quarter, an old Gamecock screamed in the stands, "Jesus Christ Himself couldn't coach this team." Maybe helping the Gamecocks win the closest 34–0 game ever. Prompting Spurrier to ride the Champion bus to Vanderbilt's stadium in Nashville with Smelley as his starter.

After Smelley threw two picks and lost to the Commodores for the second year in a row, caustic commenters piled on USC message boards, saying the game of football had passed Spurrier by.

Then he said the magic words: "There's a good chance Garcia will play this week," against the No. 2 team in the nation, Georgia.

Garcia kept his vow of not speaking to the media until he played in a real game. Spurrier reminded Carolina fans of their own history—USC had never beaten a team ranked No. 1 or No. 2.

Georgia hit Smelley hard. He staggered off the field at Williams-Brice Stadium and Garcia jogged on. From the shotgun formation Spurrier put him in for his first play, he ran for 6 yards on a quarterback draw. Didn't go down easily. The second play he couldn't get off in time. His coach yelled at the refs, saying the clock wasn't working right. The refs agreed. Smelley jogged back onto the field. The crowd booed—either the clock or the coach.

Smelley led the Gamecocks to the Bulldogs' goal line in the fourth quarter and his running back fumbled. Driving Carolina back to the Georgia goal line, Smelley tried to hit tight tend Jarrod Cook and got picked. Another game of inches lost, 14–7.

Spurrier won his 100th SEC game at Kentucky, with Garcia coming off the bench to spark the 24–17 win. Earning his first start against the defending national champs, LSU. He ran and passed his team past the Bayou Bengals for a half, giving Carolina a 17–10 advantage and leading a cheer in front of the student section. Blitz him, Tiger defensive coaches ordered, confounding the freshman quarterback and handing LSU a 24–17 victory.

At least, Spurrier noted, his fans didn't clap for a close loss.

The team rallied around the young quarterback in his second start, beating Tennessee 27–6, with Garcia's three scoring strikes making his coach suddenly sound like his old self.

"The Tennessee band was there last night, weren't they?" Spurrier asked on his Sunday conference call. "I'm used to hearing 'Rocky Top' . . . maybe they only play that when they score."

Two days later Volunteer coach Phil Fulmer resigned, fighting back tears, taking a big buyout from the contract he got after beating Spurrier last year.

Carolina's coach said he'd pick a starter for the Arkansas game after watching his quarterbacks warm up. Garcia warmed up to be the second-down quarterback, as Spurrier rotated his passers in and out like he did at Florida. That strategy seemed to help Smelley more than Garcia in a 34–21 win over Arkansas. They'd be equally challenged in the Swamp, going against a Florida team favored by 22 points. Making Spurrier the biggest underdog of his career, like he said he wanted when he left Florida.

"I just hope we give a good showing," said Jerri Spurrier at the gates of the Swamp. "We know people here." Her hopes were dashed after three interceptions thrown by Smelley and Garcia, leading to a 56–6 romp that was Spurrier's worst loss ever. Reporters who had covered his swagger at Florida reported hearing "un-Spurrier-like phrases," such as, "We were just trying to keep the score respectable" and "We're having a good season . . . 7–4 with a chance to go 8–4."

At the Florida university Spurrier lifted from the swamps of mediocrity, they hadn't heard about Pitchfork's curse in Columbia. Can't help but think about it in Death Valley, where Clemson's interim coach Dabo Swinney beat Spurrier in an interception-grabbing 31–14 Tiger lovefest in the rain. That gave Sweeney a permanent job as head coach of Clemson. Spurrier rode the bus back to Columbia outscored 87–20 in his last two games, fired offensive line coach John Hunt, and told reporters Smelley played all four quarters of that awful game in Clemson because

Garcia had flu symptoms—having to explain why an underperforming quarterback wasn't quickly yanked.

"The Old Ball Coach's act is old," said one message-board poster, speaking for a mob calling for Spurrier to resign.

He immediately named Garcia the starter for the bowl game. Prompting the Outback Bowl to invite a slumping 7–5 Gamecock team to play in Garcia's hometown, against the Iowa Hawkeyes. Carolina practiced on Garcia's old field at Jefferson High School.

"Hopefully someday we're going to have a team that really can compete," Spurrier said. Nostalgia for the Ball Coach and hometown hopes for Garcia couldn't stand up to the Hawkeyes' rushing attack and pass rush. Garcia fumbled and threw away the game on a New Year's Day that felt old.

"Spurrier can't coach quarterbacks," screamed Bart Smelley, father of the benched quarterback, hollering at Spurrier from the stands..

Rushing out of the Buccaneers' stadium after the 31–10 loss, Garcia was the first player on the quarterback bus. Spurrier quickly boarded the bus for the linemen. Slumped over in the front seat, head in his hands. Really ready to quit.

Why did he leave Florida to begin with? He had to wonder, looking out the window of the bus at the palm trees and blue skies on a balmy New Year's Day, if Jesus Himself could beat this curse.

⌐◦⌐

Spurrier didn't quit football in the ninth grade when he seemed small and slow, and he'd keep slogging, signing "Mr. Football" to play for South Carolina.

Rock Hill defensive back Stephon Gilmore, voted best high school footballer in the state, was greeted on his first day at the Proving Ground by Bobby Knight, the Steve Spurrier of college basketball, who knelt with the team in the grass for a pep talk, then grabbed the freshman with Rastafarian hair and put him in a headlock.

"Son," Knight told Gilmore, "if you were on my team, you'd be getting that hair cut."

Spurrier smiled like he'd seen just about everyone's coaching act and got Gilmore ready to be the team's starting cornerback—and the quarterback for the "Wild Cock" formation, a trendy new wrinkle that looked like the old single wing.

A new deputy patrolled the sidelines. G. A. Mangus, Spurrier's former quarterback and assistant coach at Florida, signed on as Carolina's quarterback coach to be a buffer between Spurrier and Garcia—who was actually on the field for the spring.

Scuffles between players that first day of spring ball let out steam building all winter after three blowout losses. Gamecock fans spent the off-season parsing replays, to figure out what coach called which play. Spurrier said the big gainers were his son's calls and the bad plays were his.

After Garcia got his hair cut and actually played in the Spring Game, fans lingered in the stands as a new quarterback walked up to Spurrier on the field. Connor Shaw said that he played for his father, the coach of Flowery Branch High School in Georgia, and Spurrier was the coach he always dreamed of playing for.

He'd enroll at USC the next spring. Wiry, fast, hair soldier short.

In May Steve Spurrier Jr. represented his father at a meeting of the Jacksonville Gamecock Club and told those Florida Gamecocks Stephen Garcia held USC's fate in his hands.

"We'll all have input," was Steve Jr.'s answer to questions about the play calling when fall camp started. He'd continue to sit up in the press box, where he could see everything unfold on the field and talk over the headset with his dad.

"Coach said he's going to come back and start ripping them off," Coach Mangus said of Spurrier's return to play calling on the eve of the Thursday night season kickoff game at NC State, won by Carolina on that crowned field in Raleigh 7–3.

Spurrier traveled to Georgia to find students with their chests painted G-O-B-U-L-L-D-O-G-S; when they turned around, they collectively spelled T-H-R-O-W-T-H-E-V-I-S-O-R. But they didn't get to turn around much, as Garcia led the offense to 37 points. Georgia had 41.

Garcia moved the team down the field on a last-chance drive, running for the first-down marker on fourth down with 22 seconds left and seeing a tight end open for a touchdown. A Georgia linebacker tipped the ball to the turf, for another if-only loss no one back in Columbia applauded. Still, Spurrier's Gamecock visor stayed clean.

A Thursday night ESPN game brought the No. 4 Ole Miss Rebels to Columbia, with a Heisman candidate in quarterback Jevon Snead. Garcia faced a brutal blitz, holding down a 16–10 lead with bruised ribs, hit relentlessly by Rebel defenders, somehow holding onto the ball for the team's biggest win ever at home. At last Spurrier could celebrate a USC victory over a top-5 opponent.

A rejuvenated South Carolina team headed to Alabama two weeks later, where fans of Bear Bryant wore houndstooth everything. Garcia started the game by throwing a pick-6, missing the tackle that would have prevented the runback and giving the Tide 7 points, a play that haunted Spurrier's team the rest of the night. Freshman receiver Alshon Jeffery made a one-handed sideline grab on the final drive to show Spurrier the moves of that go-to receiver he'd been praying for, easing the angst in the plane after a 20–6 loss in Tuscaloosa. Garcia's clutch passing finally gave the team a win over Vanderbilt, 14–10, in the glow of the state fair, with Mangus clandestinely taking over the play calling. Carolina was 6–2 heading into the "Orange Crush" part of the schedule.

Tennessee greeted the Gamecocks at Rocky Top in the rain with orange and black Halloween uniforms, grabbing the slick ball for turnovers that sent Spurrier back to South Carolina a 31–13 loser. Arkansas was a rough place to play, too. Spurrier said he'd be more involved in the play calling after scoring only 49 points in four games.

ESPN called for Spurrier to call the plays, with Florida coming to Columbia. Posters on message boards kept debating whether Spurrier was "washed up" as he drew up ways to attack the team allowing the fewest points in college football, with Tim Tebow back for his senior season.

The Gamecocks hit the field for the CBS game of the day wearing camouflage uniforms with "Honor," "Duty," "Country," and "Service" taking the place of names, to be auctioned off to benefit injured veterans. Florida took a 17–7 lead, and the quarterback wearing No. 5, named "Service," brought his team back to 17–14 at the end of the third quarter. Facing a third-down play to keep a touchdown drive alive, already within range for a tying field goal.

Fans cheering "Thus Spoke Zarathustra" (the theme from *2001: A Space Odyssey*) and "Sandstorm" drowned out "We Are the Boys of Old

Florida." Then Garcia threw a backside slant to Moe Brown. The ball zipped past Brown, bouncing off a Florida defender and into the arms of defensive end Justin Trattou, who rumbled 53 yards to the USC 26.

Spurrier bent over on the sideline, his head in his hands. Tebow scored four plays later to give Florida a 24–14 win, and Spurrier faced another what-if press conference, after a game against the Gators close enough to still not count. Carolina was 6–5, facing Clemson in Columbia's barbecue smoke, down 7 after C. J. Spiller ran back the opening kickoff.

Gilmore took the field as the "Wild Cock" quarterback, eluding Tiger defenders with shifty runs and lofting a 48-yard pass to Jeffery that changed everything. The sideline and the stands erupted as Carolina scored, and scored again, with Gilmore back on defense and Garcia upping his game. Spurrier kept looking up at the scoreboard until the fans applauded a 34–17 win that made a 7–5 season worth celebrating.

A team congratulated all over town felt so good about itself that the running backs coach intentionally gave his players blank tapes to study for the bowl game. None of the running backs noticed or complained.

At the Papa John's Pizza Bowl at Legion Field in Birmingham, Alabama, against the University of Connecticut, the Huskies dedicated the game to a fallen teammate whose image they paraded around the sidelines of the "Ice Bowl." The Gamecocks were just plain cold, suffering through another long winter with one ticked-off coach.

Considering quitting yet again, Spurrier got too mad to quit. The first Gamecock coach to lead his team to four bowl appearances wouldn't let the 20–7 loss in Birmingham be forgotten. No one he knew ever saw him madder. Carrying that anger into every press conference about the intentions of that year's Mr. Football, Marcus Lattimore, the top-rated running back in the nation.

Spurrier told the people who suffered with him in that frigid stadium he had his man. Going to Lattimore's house and dancing the Cha Cha Slide with his mother, Yolanda, would be a formality.

More hope for the running game was found at Appalachian State, where Sean Elliott played, then coached overachieving linemen into shape. He'd watched from the top of Williams-Brice Stadium as his father, a state trooper, directed traffic at Gamecock games. The coach wearing the Buccaneers visor texted Spurrier to hire Sean Elliott.

Bolstering the offense's longstanding weakness led to joy in a packed church in the upstate, where Lattimore stood on the altar with Auburn legend Stephen Davis, Spurrier's disgruntled running back in Washington. Lattimore wore an Auburn ball cap he removed to reveal a Gamecock hat, as "Hallelujahs" and "Sandstorm" resounded.

Why play for Spurrier? reporters asked.

"Because he did the Cha Cha Slide with my momma," Lattimore said.

With little fanfare Connor Shaw walked into his first class at USC carrying Spurrier's playbook. Preparing to challenge Garcia.

At last Carolina's Ball Coach had two quarterbacks who could play, and two Mr. Footballs. He had enough anger built up from the Ice Bowl, the Outback Bowl, and the No Bowl to somehow, someway, make 2010 the Year of the Gamecock.

———

He walked out into the sunlight warming his stadium on Good Friday, the 10th anniversary of his father's death. Was the spirit of Reverend Spurrier furious his son scheduled practice on the day Christ sacrificed Himself for the forgiveness of all sins—or was he sending down plays to get the Gamecocks to Atlanta?

Hearing people in the stands cheering, Spurrier lifted his visor to take in the grass field filled with guys throwing, kicking, and catching footballs. Speedy receivers ran patterns and snagged passes from his oldest son. Scotty stood where the bench would hold players in the fall, waiting to be his dad's graduate assistant.

A father's blessing could be received many ways.

Spurrier's quarterback followed his coach onto the field with his head down.

"Hey, Garcia," called a little boy in Gamecock gear, barely able to see over the wall separating the fans from the players.

"What's going on?" Garcia said, smiling shyly. Eyes locked on the field. Maybe petitioning the Lord for the offense to beat the defense.

Spurrier had to pray for deliverance from the people he'd been fighting for. Telling reporters during a week of trial and redemption that he knew South Carolina's black lawmakers had been calling his black football recruits—asking them to reconsider playing for the Gamecocks because USC's Board of Trustees was losing its only black member.

"We are asking young athletes to be aware," said State Representative David Weeks, chairman of the Legislative Black Caucus, "there are folks in this state who say it's fine to play ball but not be on the governing board." Weeks confirmed recruits and their families were being asked to rethink playing for USC—including Lattimore, who said he stood by his coach and his school.

Spurrier said he didn't worry about what he couldn't control, and still believed the Confederate flag should come down from the State House grounds.

"I would be in favor of minorities in anything," he told reporters for the *State*. The newspaper's sports columnist Ron Morris started a feud with Spurrier anyway, backing the Black Caucus's effort to injure Carolina's football team without mentioning the coach's outspokenness on equality. Morris followed that zinger with a column saying USC should leave the SEC and return to the ACC, the lesser league the school once belonged to—as the SEC Gamecocks marched toward a national championship in baseball.

A parade like Spurrier had been dreaming of filled Gervais Street, with a trophy held aloft at the State House. He could only hope that questioning Garcia's mettle in interviews all spring would really motivate his team's leader.

Jerri Spurrier, the mediator, told Garcia her husband would "push every button you have" to make his quarterback better.

"He already has," Garcia said.

The two met in Spurrier's office overlooking the football field to talk over the criticisms, with Garcia telling his coach he was "on board and ready to get this thing going." Saying that in a crowd of 80,000 fans screaming in the stadium, the only voice he heard was Spurrier's.

Reporters asked the voice of the *College GameDay* show if Spurrier had a shot at winning the SEC East this year. Not a chance, Lee Corso said. Not having seen the freshman running back humbling defenders down at the Proving Ground.

ESPN still believed in Spurrier. For the fifth time in six years, his team kicked off the college football season, with the Thursday evening game pitting South Carolina against Southern Mississippi. Putting Garcia in the national spotlight, after Spurrier's criticisms reverberated through the media all year. Running Spurrier's no-huddle offense, Garcia ran the Golden Eagles off the field.

"Hope I played pretty well," he told reporters. He'd have to watch the film with his coach, to "hear what *he* has to say."

The following Saturday fans had fingers in the air all around Williams-Brice Stadium, trying to score a tough ticket in a pack of Bull-dogs. Cheers rose into the steamy afternoon for a running back who could send those Dawgs home unhappy. Carolina faced a first-and-goal, trying to take a 14–3 lead, and Spurrier headed to the huddle to give Garcia a play that couldn't be stopped—hand the ball to Lattimore.

"It's unusual for me to run the same play over and over again," Spurrier said. "Especially when the other team knows it's coming." But no one in Bulldog red could stop number 21 in garnet, the SEC Freshman and Offensive Player of the Week.

On the sidelines cheering the Gamecocks' 17–6 domination of Georgia was USC's all-time leading receiver Kenny McKinley, on crutches, rehabbing a leg injury to get back to the Denver Broncos, smiling his smile. Nine days later Spurrier had to ask if he could have seen McKinley was in trouble. He'd shot himself in Denver, over gambling debts that made rehabbing his leg take too long. The Gamecocks heard the news at practice the Monday before the Auburn game.

McKinley's No. 11, Spurrier's old number, graced the helmet of every player running onto the "Plains of Auburn" for a battle of unbeaten SEC teams. Reporters alleged that Tim Tebow's former understudy at Florida, Cam Newton, brought a purloined copy of Spurrier's playbook to Auburn. Newton's passing and running were all Newton.

Garcia led Carolina to a 20–7 lead in the Tigers' den, doing all a coach could ask for until the fourth quarter, when he fumbled twice, from indecision and a vicious hit. Agonizing on the sidelines as Spurrier sent Shaw the freshman onto the field to take on the screams and the pressure. Shaw moved the team but threw two picks in the final six minutes. Jeffery had six points in his hands, for a chance to tie, and couldn't hang on. 35–27, Auburn.

Did Spurrier get so mad at his quarterback that he couldn't see Garcia was still the team's best chance? The question lingered over one tough Monday at the Word of Faith Family Worship Cathedral in Austell, Georgia, where more than 1,000 mourners heard Steve Jr. say in his eulogy, "I'm always trying to find another Kenny McKinley." Giving the Gamecocks inspiration to face the other team from Alabama, heading to Columbia, where the *GameDay* show would be broadcast from the Horseshoe.

Spurrier pleaded with USC fans to be civil to Corso. No one waved a rebel flag or heckled the announcer when he put on an elephant head to show the national TV audience he was picking Alabama to win. Just what Spurrier and Garcia needed to play a near-perfect game.

Garcia hit all nine of his passes in the first half, throwing two scoring strikes to Jeffery and another to Lattimore as Carolina took a tantalizing lead. In its history Alabama had never allowed more than three quarterback sacks in one game. 'Bama quarterback Greg McElroy hit the ground seven times, to deafening cheers, as the defending national champs went down 35–21 in Columbia.

Celebrating a win over the No. 1 team in the nation for the first time in the history of South Carolina, the team faced unranked Kentucky.

"Please let Steve Spurrier like my son for one day," Garcia's mother said before the game. "And let today be the day."

Garcia threw an interception on the final play of Kentucky's first-ever win over Spurrier. Prompting South Carolina author Pat Conroy to proclaim at the Miami Book Fair he still believed USC was cursed.

Deliverance could be at hand in Gainesville, where the Gamecocks and Gators would play for the SEC Eastern Division Championship. All South Carolina had to do was win at Florida for the first time in 12 tries.

The Gamecocks' team chaplain stood at the gates of the Swamp, blessing the players as they passed by. Then Pastor Adrian raised his hands to the heavens and prayed.

"If there is any curse affecting this team, Lord, we ask you to take it away."

—◦—

Florida receiver Andre Debose took the opening kickoff down the field for a 7–0 lead—and Carolina wasn't threatened again. Lattimore ran over, around, and through Urban Meyer's defense, outgaining and outscoring the Gators by himself. Garcia ran over Florida safety Will Hill for the door-slammer score, to give his team a 36–14 triumph in the stadium his coach named.

The Ball Coach had to orchestrate his own Gatorade baptism, coaching up players not used to winning trophies. They carried him off his old field on their shoulders, reveling in South Carolina's second league championship in 118 years.

A beaming Danny Wuerffel led a reunion of Gator players hugging their old coach, after he just beat their old team. Florida athletic director Jeremy Foley took Spurrier aside to offer congratulations, too. Garcia and Spurrier shared a vein-popping handshake.

Back at Williams-Brice Stadium after midnight, the team was greeted by thousands of fans, cheering speeches by a coach and players not ready for bed. Would they be ready to play at Clemson, a week before facing Auburn again in Atlanta for the SEC title?

In the visitor's locker room at Death Valley, Spurrier talked to his team about beating the curse that Clemson's founder Pitchfork inflicted on USC, said defensive end Cliff Matthews, who ran through the tunnel onto Clemson's field thinking that curse was the silliest thing he ever heard. He'd just help win the game for his coach.

With the Tigers trying to stop the star running back who grew up near Clemson's campus, Garcia found open receivers. He hit Jeffery for Carolina's second touchdown and pointed at Mangus like a gunslinger. Mangus aimed his gunslinging finger back at Garcia. Spurrier kept talking on the headset with his son, trying to get his team where they aimed to be.

"Something very different is happening in Columbia," the ESPN announcers said; these weren't the same old Gamecocks. Matthews stopped a Clemson drive and got mobbed by teammates, with his head coach piling on.

Garcia stayed in the game, getting knocked around, while Spurrier eyed the scoreboard atop Death Valley until the last tick of the 29–7 win—USC's first repeat victory over Clemson since the Vietnam War. He jogged onto the field, looking for Clemson players to shake hands with, and ran into a crush of Gamecocks storming Pitchfork's field.

Sweeping the Orange Crush opponents, for USC's third nine-win season since 1892, Spurrier would take South Carolina to Atlanta for the first time ever. Named SEC Coach of the Year, even though Coach Gene Chizik had Auburn talking national title.

Reporters covering Spurrier's return to Atlanta after a decade away told him they were sorry they had sided with Corso.

"There were a bunch of us who said, 'South Carolina? Never. I don't care what you do,'" said Fox Sports reporter Charles Davis, joining a host of commentators apologizing for underestimating Spurrier again.

He had newfound fans in Georgia, Alabama, and other unlikely places—rooting for anyone who could beat Auburn, amid allegations Cam Newton cheated at Florida and had his dad ask schools to pay for his son to play. After the NCAA declared Newton eligible for the game, pundits said Spurrier could outscore Cam if anyone could.

"Are you calling the plays?" Cotty Jones asked his old friend on the eve of the biggest game South Carolina had ever played.

"Oh yeah," Spurrier said. "The assistant coaches, they call some, but if I don't like 'em, I don't run 'em."

Inside the frenzied Georgia Dome, the playbook full of long completions belonged to Auburn. Carolina was still in the game, down a touchdown with time for one play before the half—a Hail Mary pass Newton completed for a 28–14 halftime lead Carolina couldn't overcome.

"I apologize to our fans," said Spurrier after the 56–17 devastation was complete. "They were there yelling and screaming, wanting something big to happen, and it didn't happen. . . . We just hope we can get back here someday and win this thing."

He jogged off the field in despair. Summoned right back to Atlanta to play in the Chick-fil-A Bowl on New Year's Eve.

Two nights before kickoff assistant coaches hearing noise after curfew bust into the room of Garcia and backup quarterback Andrew Clifford to find lots of beer cans and two naked ladies in Garcia's bed. Told about the curfew violation, Spurrier went back to sleep. Assistant coaches made Garcia and Clifford sweat out the beer on a treadmill for an hour, then woke them up at 7 a.m. the day before playing Florida State in the Georgia Dome.

On the opening drive Lattimore eluded the Seminole pass defense for long completions down the sideline, then took one loud hit and went to the hospital with his tongue bitten through.

Seminole defensive backs had Carolina's other receivers covered. Garcia almost brought his team back, leading a fourth-quarter drive to get the Gamecocks within 2, but their defense couldn't stop the 'Noles.

While making history Spurrier's team suffered a blowout loss to Auburn and a 26–17 loss to the Seminoles on the same big stage. Giving South Carolina's players and coaches another frosty winter in the weight room. They had to ask, along with a slew of reporters, if Garcia's hotel room antics had dragged down the team in the Georgia Dome.

What kind of punishment, Spurrier had to ask, would get his team back to Atlanta, to be redeemed?

CHAPTER SEVENTEEN

The Fifth Child

EXPECTATIONS SWIRLED AROUND THE GAMECOCKS FOR THE FIFTH spring since Steve Spurrier first saw that big, dark inkblot on his quarterback's arm. At the start of a spring unlike any other at South Carolina, the coach wanted his fifth-year senior to finally measure up to his *Arete* tattoo. Two men with every reason to expect excellence.

The night before the first practice of the 2011 season, Spurrier stood looking at the best bunch of players ever assembled in Carolina's meeting room, around the corner from the trophy they were called to defend. For the first time in school history, the Gamecocks were Southeastern Conference Eastern Division champs. Players in sweat-soaked "Iron Cocks" T-shirts talked all winter in Carolina's weight room about bringing home the big trophy, topped with players in bronze, that Auburn won. Whatever it cost in blood, sweat, and expectations.

What more could a coach ask from his players, in a hushed meeting room? What words would mold veterans and freshmen into champions, that Coach Spurrier never said to a raw spring team before?

"Love your teammates," he told the players looking at each other around the meeting room. "Love your coaches, too," Spurrier felt compelled to add. Maybe wondering what guys marked for excellence really needed to hear, and what ringtone Garcia had for a tough-love call.

⚊

The next afternoon Spurrier sauntered across the Proving Ground adjusting his baseball cap, taking in the team he had warming up on the grass. Seeming not to miss his trademark visor or starting quarterback.

He whistled for the guys to huddle up, under low-hanging clouds, beneath a tower Bear Bryant could look down from and see talent. The rising seniors bowed their heads for a prayer with a hand on each other's shoulders. Praying away the season-ending swoons in '07, '08, and '09 that kept Gamecock fans believing in a "Chicken Curse." Reassuring each other that Garcia had been suspended before, on other spring days when he could throw the ball around only after practice.

The head coach blew his whistle three times, clapped his hands, and walked off with the kickers vying to replace Spencer Lanning, a guy the old punter for the 49ers loved calling "Lanning Spencer." With Lanning graduating, Spurrier's special teams needed fresh legs. Balls sailing through the uprights earned his applause.

Then he hustled off to coach up the three quarterbacks fading back and firing balls across the field. Spurrier waved them in, huddling with Connor Shaw, Dylan Thompson, and Seth Strickland, a walk-on who'd risen to third on last season's depth chart. The Ball Coach is all for the underdog. Strickland wore No. 11, and got a hand on his shoulder along with his instruction.

Spurrier works with who's out there. Showing them all again exactly where to hold the ball, stepping into the throw. Shaw's eyes measured micrometers. His dad didn't raise him to be second string.

In the storied history of Southeastern Conference football, the 2010 Gamecocks were the only team that ever fielded a 1,000-yard rusher and a 1,000-yard receiver in the same season. Spurrier had to teach his young stars how to top themselves. Running back Marcus Lattimore, the 2010 National Freshman of the Year, lined up wide to catch a pass from Shaw, making his coach smile and grab a word with the league's top returning receiver. Alshon Jeffery had a chance to be the best in the country that year. Seeing both Lattimore and Jeffery "in the pattern," Spurrier couldn't hold back a grin.

He'd coached the Gamecocks for six seasons before a fellow SEC coach shook his hand at midfield and said he had a good team. He was ready to see what those coaches would say this year after facing Lattimore and Jeffery for four quarters.

Defensive head coach Ellis Johnson wasn't smiling under his wide-brimmed white hat, watching his safeties and cornerbacks run through interception drills. They needed to get their hands on more passes this year—or shoulder more blame. Spurrier focused on the offense, leaving his defensive guru from Winnsboro, South Carolina, accountable to reporters. Johnson stole a look at the big guys who could make his defensive backs cover better.

Carolina's down linemen looked way too big to hit a red pylon the instant their coach ordered. Defensive line coach Brad Lawing fingered the spot on the grass where those giant hands must "generate the power." Fans 10 feet away couldn't get close enough. Opposing quarterbacks might shut their eyes. Could a team barely .500 in its history actually be favored to win the SEC East *again?* Fans watched Lawing's linemen attack the pylon like their money was on these guys.

"Where's Garcia?" asked a fan behind the rope.

"Maybe doing running drills," another guy in garnet said.

Shaw fired one deep. Cornerback Stephon Gilmore, the serious face of the defense, somehow snared the ball out of the sky. Spurrier grimaced and looked down at his play sheet, always for the offense.

Jerri Spurrier, standing at midfield, folded her arms and smiled. Her husband was a father, a grandfather, and a head coach who still sees a quarterback in the mirror.

The offense moved to the field near the fans for 11-on-11 drills. The trio of quarterbacks rotated in and out, getting spastic signals from Mangus, while Spurrier clutched his play sheet without consulting it. Lattimore was open everywhere a quarterback could want, with Jeffery streaking down the sideline. The other receivers ran, cut, and leaped for overthrown balls, to prove they could play with the best. When the pass wasn't for Jeffery, he had to stop himself from running to the Atlantic.

"Who's going to win the SEC?" Spurrier hollered at his players when they gathered again at midfield.

"Carolina!" they chorused, fists raised as one, loud enough for a missing quarterback to hear.

"Wasn't Garcia on zero tolerance?" a reporter couldn't wait to ask in the press scrum.

"This is something that happened earlier, and we're finally getting around to handling. He's actually been pretty good this semester. He'll be back next week to answer all y'all's questions," Spurrier said, turning and walking away.

"He's as excited as I've seen him," said Jerri, watching her husband pivot and escape. After all, Garcia wouldn't be gone too long. Onlookers cheered as players and coaches strode off the field. Two guys standing in the back of a red Chevy pickup mugged for the Channel 19 camera and shared phone photos of passing heroes.

In a rented house on the other side of the campus, way too close to a Clemson neighbor, a player missing at practice was looking at a new man in the mirror. Sporting a buzz cut. Maybe tuning in the News19 sports report for a message from his coach.

———

Suspended for the first week of spring practice for smuggling girls and beer into his hotel room in Atlanta in December, Garcia heard that morning on a tough-love voice mail. Telling teammates he was "so distraught" he couldn't call Spurrier back. They talked that afternoon in the office overlooking the football field. The view of the goalposts under the student section might remind Garcia what he could still accomplish at South Carolina, if the coach didn't have the words to reach his quarterback.

For a man who quotes John Wooden, Sun Tzu, and the county sheriff, Spurrier leaves some things unspoken. If you're getting coached up, you must be important. If you're getting punished, you must be tougher the next time the enemy wants to sift you like wheat. Spurrier sometimes sent signals only a quarterback could understand.

Did Garcia hate his coach for a moment, behind downcast eyes, as Spurrier handed over a list of 12 ways number 5 could be a better quarterback? What more should Garcia grasp? A coach writes up a list like that for a player he still believes in. Even if it's handed over without a smile.

No missing the line about getting that hair cut. Garcia had heard that one before.

At Stroy's Barber Shop on Assembly Street, he could count on a fist bump from Derrick Bailey, barber to the Gamecock stars—especially the players on the poster hanging by Bailey's barber chair. Garcia looked ready to rumble, posing with eight teammates on the 2010 football schedule poster. A poster of President Obama oversaw the Friday afternoon crowd waiting for a trim. Vintage soul videos played on a screen over the doorway. A Parliament Funkadelic song pulsed through the buzz of clippers and football talk.

But Garcia hadn't been in that week, Bailey said. He cut his own hair this time.

"He hasn't slowed down, either," said his barber and drinking buddy, shaking his head, snipping away. "I can't hang with him all the time. He just wants to chug. And he can get on you pretty good, when you're partying with him. He can be annoying. He gets after you."

The naked girls caught in Garcia and Clifford's hotel room in Atlanta were both with Garcia, he told Bailey. Man, how *do* you tone down a quarterback who can knock down linebackers and brews? Were avoiding threesomes and Dollar Bud Night at the Village Idiot also on his coach's to-do list?

"Spurrier told him to trim his facial hair, too," Bailey said.

Bailey wasn't the only friend of Garcia around town to say that Spurrier's quarterback played hard in every way. A coach can only know . . . what a coach knows. What could anyone say, getting up from that barber chair worried about college students being college students?

"Tell Garcia the people are still with him."

"The people still are," Bailey agreed.

Right down Assembly Street from Stroy's, the stars and stripes and the blue crescent state flag flapped wildly atop the domed roof of the State House. Down on the grounds the Confederate battle flag hung limply, eyed by Governor Ben Tillman's statue. Maybe no wind buffeted the flag because Pitchfork didn't want it to move—just the kind of superstition Garcia had the ability to change. Pitchfork needed to keep an eye on the Proving Ground. Where Spurrier was missing his field general at his team's first workout of the year in full pads. A day Pat Conroy called a "holy day" for a football player.

The head coach stood right over the linemen going at each other. Leaning in to catch the explosive hits, and embarrassing "whiffs" when a defender dodged a blocker, Spurrier exuded pure football joy. Relishing the battle in the trenches. Then he went to work with the guys who waged aerial warfare. They got Garcia's reps but not his passing touch, trying to throw deep into gusts whipping the flags around.

On a clear, breezy Saturday Garcia and Clifford got to rejoin the team in the stadium, wearing shorts, not knee pads. Allowed to throw only during warm-ups. Garcia bounded onto the field, hugged a couple of coaches, and started zipping the ball around the field, working with his receivers in a red-zone drill. Hitting Alshon Jeffery for a score that had defender D. J. Swearinger muttering, "Play ball, boy." Jeffery's hands just conjured the ball out of the air.

Wouldn't you really *want to play quarterback with a receiver like that?* Spurrier sees all, with a blank look, urging on the big linemen hitting the pads. Looking intently at Garcia when the scrimmage started, assessing the quarterback's walk to the sidelines.

"He's my fifth child," said Jerri Spurrier, sitting in the stands watching Garcia watch his teammates play. "I talked to him all day yesterday."

Out of all the players in all the places—she has looked after her husband's football career, and four children, always managing to turn Spurrier teams into a football family—Garcia looked like the freshman most in need of mentoring, as soon as she saw the tattoo.

"He's hurting," she said. "He really wants to be out there. He doesn't want to be separated from the team anymore."

While Jerri talked Garcia through his troubles, her husband huddled with the Gamecocks' PR man. How *do* you explain how a dual-threat SEC quarterback with 28 consecutive starts can have four spring suspensions, going on five? Do you point out that Spurrier's been more patient with Garcia than any other quarterback he has coached, or is that a negative? How much tough love could the rest of the team take? The severest media critics would have to agree the Spurriers had a problem child who could beat Georgia, Alabama, Tennessee, and Florida.

"What he did wasn't really that bad," Jerri said. "When the coaches woke Steve up in Atlanta to tell him what happened, he didn't think it was a big deal. He just went back to bed."

The head coach still facing questions about that December night praised Garcia's leadership in winter workouts.

"I wish Steve would defend him more," Jerri said. "Stephen needs to hear that from him."

Garcia fidgeted while another quarterback made a play, his feet moving toward the field. Then he stopped and clapped, his helmet perched atop his buzz cut like a warrior with an oversize head.

"I told him, 'Stephen, your whole life depends on the next eight months. Don't screw it up,'" Jerri said.

"You've told me that before," Carolina's prodigal son replied.

His most serious challenger was just a rising sophomore—easy to forget if you weren't watching number 14's footwork and decision making through Spurrier's eyes. The quick throws Shaw could make on the practice field were stifled by blitzes in the stadium. On a roll-out he gave those defenders a head fake and raced down the sideline, faster than the starter watching Shaw blaze by.

Would Spurrier be satisfied to win that way, without his trademark passing attack? He smiled at his talented running backs and walked over to Mangus to order more air strikes. After a rainbow from Strickland to speedy Ace Sanders, timed to perfection, the kicking team ended practice with a ball down the middle and a clang off the goalpost.

"Who's going to win the SEC?" Spurrier asked at midfield.

"Carolina!" the team yelled, and headed off to ponder the performance—maybe at a massive St. Patrick's Day celebration in Five Points. Garcia spirited himself past the notepads and cameras, to reflect in the green fountains on Greene Street. As usual, reporters focused too much on the quarterback.

He walked back onto the Proving Ground on Tuesday with a white towel draped over his face mask. Seth Strickland had a towel hanging over his helmet, too, even though he didn't miss a day taking Garcia's reps. Clifford walked back through the gate with an uncovered smile.

Nobody was happier to be back on the field than Brad Lawing, who'd spent the weekend in the hospital facing heart surgery. Heart surgery blinked. Lawing clearly missed working with the monster talents Spurrier had gotten him. At his renewed growl they hit the turf and rolled.

Garcia didn't return to any make-up snaps. Still, during the 11-on-11 drill his passes defied the spring winds, hitting underclassmen with jets for cleats. Mangus signaled in running plays. Garcia's handoffs gained yards. The play caller knows what weaknesses defensive coaches want to work on. Spurrier pointed downfield, jawing at his other quarterbacks, then sent them in. When Garcia got back behind center, he threw a scoring strike down the right sideline, showing he was still master of the March wind.

Spurrier clapped to end practice. Whistled his team over for wind sprints, running ahead, and clapped everyone through that. Guys looking pretty fast. Starting quarterback back. Not to mention one badass D-line coach who didn't need a stent in his heart. It would be another two days before Garcia had to officially explain himself—and those white towels he and Strickland draped over their helmets.

"Really gusty out here," said Garcia, wearing a sweat-soaked "Iron Cocks" T-shirt, carrying his shoulder pads, walking with Strickland. "But that didn't bother me much. It's just good to be back out here."

He looked like a leader in the weight room, hoisting up an unassuming smile. Keeping the pain of being banished behind his eyes.

"Had to cut my hair myself," he said, running his hand through stubble that was fairly even. It was a warrior's atonement, falling on his own clippers. He said he was ready to soldier on.

"Really gusty out here," said Mangus, the quarterback coach a step behind Garcia and Strickland. "It's just good to see all five quarterbacks back out here."

A train horn rose on the wind, warning cars at the crossing between downtown and Five Points.

The Ides of March buffeted South Carolina's basketball team, after a season of high hopes and rim-outs. Two starters left Coach Darrin Horn's program. The team's leading scorer, freshman point guard Bruce Ellington, planned to stay a Gamecock. He just wanted to play ball for Spurrier, too.

Steve Jr.'s cell phone hummed with Ellington's overture. "Bubba," as the receivers coach got called at Carolina, first recruited Ellington, before basketball called louder. The two-sport star was runner-up to tailback Marcus Lattimore, when they were high school seniors, for the "Mr.

Football" title. Bubba had to tell the leading scorer at Colonial Life Arena that he couldn't practice on the Proving Ground until August, according to NCAA scholarship rules. So Ellington showed up in street clothes to watch his new teammates practice, smiling and bouncing a football off the grass.

"I think about it a lot," he told a swarm of reporters. "I can't lie to you. I do think about playing football."

Slot receiver? Punt and kickoff returner? Quarterback in the "Wild Cock" formation?

"Oh yeah, he can help us," Spurrier said, standing on the field, checking out the new kid dribbling the football on the sidelines, wanting to get in the game.

Talent loves talent. Mr. Football 2010, Jadeveon Clowney, the top college prospect in the nation, filled USC's campus with cheers when he put on a Gamecock cap on ESPN on Valentine's Day. Spurrier's squad now sported three consecutive Mr. Footballs, and a runner-up. Not pleasing news at Clemson. Clowney was enjoying a day off from high school, heading down to Columbia to meet friends in Five Points, as practice ended and Spurrier and Garcia spoke to separate press cohorts.

"It was sort of sad watching the offense try to perform," Spurrier unburdened himself to the cameras and microphones, "but tomorrow is another day."

"I have to be smarter," Garcia told his group of reporters. "Bad decision on my part down in Atlanta. Nothing bad is going to happen again. That is a guarantee."

Admitting that "every single thing that I have done has been my fault," Garcia said he and his head coach never stopped talking, and his teammates stayed behind him. "It's a family here," he said.

That white towel he draped over his face, returning to practice? Part of a footwork drill, Garcia deadpanned.

"At least that shows he has a sense of humor," Mangus noted.

Overnight, Garcia's guarantee was yesterday's news. A grainy cell phone photo on the Internet showed Jadeveon Clowney in handcuffs at 1 a.m. in a bar in Five Points, cuffed along with fellow defensive line recruit Gerald G. Dixon, surrounded by outraged onlookers in Gamecock gear.

"They said we fit the description," Clowney said of the Columbia police officers acting on a tip about convenience-store robbers. Gerald Dixon Sr. told reporters not many people look like his beefy son—or the larger-than-life Clowney, who'd "been in the paper for the last year." Dixon Sr. said his son and his famous friend believed someone set them up. Around Columbia the anonymous tipster who claimed he saw the robbers running into a bar on Greene Street was described as a Clemson fan.

In football, as in life, perception can become reality. At the Friday afternoon practice, Columbia police chief Randy Scott huddled with Spurrier. Then the coach faced reporters. At the first question about Clowney, Chief Scott tapped Spurrier on the shoulder, escorted him across the grass, handcuffed him, and frisked him.

"I think this is for show," a reporter said. Lollygagging players laughed. After an exchange between cop and coach, the cuffs came off. Spurrier returned to report that someone held up a convenience store down the road, and a witness said the robber "looked like the Head Ball Coach of South Carolina." After being cleared of wrongdoing, Spurrier said, he was let go. Just like Clowney and Dixon were let go.

"Police have a job to do," Spurrier said. "They don't know who's got a gun and who doesn't. So it's not embarrassing to be handcuffed. That's what I'm trying to say."

When Spurrier asked his star recruit if he was "drinking, being loud, and making a disturbance," Clowney had responded, "Coach, I don't even drink." As for the fans in the bar chanting "Clowney, Clowney," in a video running rampant on YouTube, Spurrier hoped the stadium was the next place he heard them holler.

Chief Scott reiterated that the officers acted appropriately and the players did nothing wrong.

"Like I didn't do anything wrong," Spurrier added.

"Well, maybe you did," a reporter said.

"UGA Slobberknocker" posted on an *Atlanta Journal-Constitution* message board, "Evil Genius is starting to get cocky again. That means he thinks he has a good team." Mainly, Bulldog fans should be alarmed that NFL scouts called Clowney "the LeBron James of high school football."

Somehow, though, breaking a curse still came down to the quarterback. For a week Spurrier said he probably had too many passers at practice. Throwing to receivers who all looked like starters, running crisp routes, beating aggressive defensive backs. Working through the calm before the storm.

On the last day of March, rain pelted the Proving Ground, cancelling practice. State-of-the-art facilities at USC had sprung up under Spurrier—rivaling the athletic palaces at Tennessee, Georgia, and Florida—but a full-team work out at the old indoor practice field was still an elbow-bumper. So the rainstorm changed the spring practice schedule, adding a day of reckoning to the calendar.

❧

Gamecock fans always looked forward to the Spring Game, because "South Carolina always wins." They were ready to fill Williams-Brice Stadium with joy, cheering for the Garnet team and the Black team and celebrating USC's second division title in 117 years at a postgame gathering called "Fan Fest." They'd get to run onto the field to the *2001* theme, jam to the music of Tokyo Joe, and pose with the kids and the SEC East Championship trophy—a new tradition, born of enduring faith.

What could mar the Gamecocks' day? Fans who believed the "next year" they'd waited for could be this year would get a free 2011 schedule poster, without Stephen Garcia on it.

Jeffery, Lattimore, and Spurrier represented the offense, standing by defenders Gilmore, Taylor, Travian Robertson, and the trophy, on posters printed the week before the game. Garcia was front and center on the 2010 schedule poster on display at Stroy's Barber Shop. Since then Garcia had thrown more touchdowns, cut down on his interceptions, and bowled over Florida safety Will Hill for the score that clinched the SEC East Championship.

What signal could Spurrier be sending this time? Maybe there were worse places to turn up missing than on a free poster. Did Mrs. Spurrier, or Coach Mangus, or the PR man ask the head coach not to snub the senior quarterback within reach of all the school's passing records? When Garcia heard about it from his teammates, maybe he shouldn't care what Spurrier thought.

Or was this a call from his coach to rise above his ego? Stay focused on the final battle, and the ultimate prize. Watch out for shadowy forces that supposedly kept USC cursed.

Somehow, Spurrier knew.

The birthday of offensive tackle Kyle Nunn fell on the Tuesday before the Spring Game , when the team should have been on the Proving Ground—but the practice was rescheduled by the March rain. His teammates met up in Five Points to toast the big senior tackle, then headed up the hill to the seminar they had to attend. Sunset lit up the skyline, but it was still sweltering as they filed into the air-conditioning for the "Branded a Leader" seminar—mandated for all SEC athletes since its inception as the "Mentors for Violence Prevention" seminar in 2005.

"The format is like a playbook," according to Jeff O'Brien, director of Mentors in Violence Prevention National, who created the seminars, trained the coleaders, and sometimes ran seminars himself. "The tight ends all run the same pattern, no matter who is on the field," said the former tight end for Canisius College.

The coleaders he chose for the USC seminar were former college football players asked to employ "a Socratic method to engender discussion, asking questions to make student athletes define their values." O'Brien's playbook called for a coleader to give a good and bad example of an athlete with a brand. Spurrier's coaching staff, required to attend a seminar Monday evening, heard professional golfer Tiger Woods derided as the bad example. No one behind the podium or in the audience mentioned Spurrier's quarterback.

Tuesday evening, when the football team trooped through the door, players were divided into three groups and assigned to separate rooms. The players walking in from Nunn's party had trouble settling down, the coleaders couldn't help but notice. Whatever school those former players represented, they did not play ball at South Carolina.

To begin the presentation one of them walked up to the podium and asked, "Who would you rather have as your leader, Tim Tebow or Stephen Garcia?" The question supposed to kick off the discussion was met with stunned silence.

"Tebow is the perfect example of great branding and leadership. Garcia is an example of the opposite." The speaker went on to laud the brand of the Florida Gator quarterback who went on to play for the Denver Broncos. Wouldn't the Gamecock players rather have Tebow as their leader, instead of Garcia?

Some Carolina players responded with sotto voce asides, then protests. Others saw Garcia's agitation. Let it go, his teammates tried to tell him. Then the speaker began to recount Garcia's indiscretions, defining his brand by four bad moments.

"You can be like Tim Tebow or Stephen Garcia," the speaker concluded. "Who would you rather be labeled as?"

What should the leader of the team say to an outsider rehashing all that stuff? Staring up at the speaker from a rival school taunting him behind the podium, Garcia had met the enemy and it was himself. Of course Stephen and Steve expected excellence from big number 5, who could throw on the run. He just had to zing the message bearer, with an F-bomb. Making his teammates groan, seeing a field without Garcia on it.

"What about Cam Newton?" asked a player in the crowd, trying to refocus the discussion on a college quarterback who'd been under NCAA investigation.

"Don't interrupt," the speaker said.

"This is bullshit," Garcia shot back.

The other coleader asked one pissed-off quarterback to leave the room. That coleader smelled beer on Garcia's breath. He didn't have to be told twice to leave the seminar. Nunn walked out, too, hoping to calm down his quarterback.

The fifth bad moment was at hand. Garcia had to find a quiet place to give his coach a call.

Spurrier answers to people, too. He met with athletic director Eric Hyman, and together they met with USC president Harris Pastides. Then Hyman announced that Garcia was "indefinitely suspended" from the team. Garcia heard about his suspension before practice, on News19. Interviewed about the suspension, Hyman said the seminar where Garcia met trouble was called "MVP"—a misnomer repeated by every reporter covering Garcia's fifth suspension in a firestorm of criticism aimed at the quarterback, the university, and the head coach. Seminar founder Jeff O'Brien wasn't giving interviews.

Was USC's quarterback used as the example of bad branding at O'Brien's seminars presented at every school in the SEC? Or was Garcia the subject derided as a bad example only on his own campus, in front of his teammates? USC players sent to the other two seminar rooms told Spurrier the "bad example" cited in their group discussion was not Garcia.

Did he defend himself in a hot-blooded or red-blooded way? Questions flew around the football world, while the players who were actually in the seminar room kept voicing, tweeting, and posting their outrage over the Tebow vs. Garcia comparison and their support for their quarterback, signing online statements "Team Garcia," creating a Facebook page by that name.

Maybe the hoopla about Garcia would lower Carolina's preseason ranking and take pressure off the team, Coach Spurrier could have strategized on the way to the field. After the Wednesday evening practice he spoke to reporters in the glare of the lights.

"Players come and go, as we all know," he said, as whistles tweeted at guys running gassers behind him. "This should never have happened, but it did." Unable to hide his agony but smiling and clapping on cue, he was asked about "the plan for the Spring Game."

"We're not beating each other up," Spurrier said.

Stephen Garcia's Boozing May Help Georgia in SEC East, headlined an *Atlanta Journal-Constitution* sports blog. Posters on message boards in Gator Country proclaimed, "Now we've got a chance." Cyber-prophets from Arkansas to Assembly Street foresaw another USC season cursed.

"Spurrier's problem is, he sees all his quarterbacks as his sons," one USC alum wrote. "Stop Coddling Garcia Once and for All," Internet posters screamed. What did anonymous commentators expect from football coaches, more toughness or more love? At a smaller, more somber gathering, Garcia sat down with his teammates over an ice-cold soda and promised not to drink another beer until they'd caught his last pass.

The day of the Spring Game dawned with mercury rising. Flags of America, South Carolina, and some high-profile fraternities flapped over the tailgaters carrying on. Lattimore, Miles, center T. J. Johnson, and team chaplain Adrian Despres gave talks about their faith to a youthful audience in the south end zone. Then the stadium was overrun by revelers. Talking up the team's progress. Arguing about Garcia. Wondering how the hope of the Gamecocks, Connor Shaw, would play.

Up in the press box, announcers Bill Rosinski and former Miami Hurricanes coach Randy Shannon described the action for ESPN. Shaw was rolling out and finding receivers but couldn't get his team a score. Hitting a 5-yard touchdown pass on the final play of the half, Shaw was overheated, done for the day.

At halftime Spurrier returned his flock to the euphoria of November, unveiling the SEC Eastern Division Championship proclamation on the end zone wall. That 1969 ACC Championship was lonesome no longer. Spurrier looked around at all the Gamecocks applauding and joined in the cheers.

As he basked in the applause, the Gators were unveiling statues of Wuerffel, Tebow, and Spurrier, Florida's Heisman-winning quarterbacks, at halftime of the Orange and Blue Game in Gainesville.

"Welcome home," the announcer said to Tebow, Wuerffel, and Spurrier's daughter Amy, taking her father's place. She took a step back on the grass as the announcer said, "Turn your attention to the GatorVision Board to witness this historic moment. Three, two, one . . ."

Undraped on-screen were the three quarterbacks sculpted in 17,000 pounds of bronze, displayed at the stadium's west entrance. The only Heisman winner ever to coach a Heisman winner stood in the middle, showing the other quarterbacks exactly where to hold the bronze ball. An amazing likeness of that player and coach spoke to Gator fans on the big screen, decked out in Gamecock gear.

"This is one of the best honors I ever had in my life," Spurrier said. "I'm very thankful to my university, the University of Florida." The band broke into the fight song as fans surrounded the statues.

ESPN announcer Shannon predicted another Eastern Division Championship for the Gamecocks, back in the booth in Columbia, with Florida a "close second." The announcers began discussing Garcia's suspension.

"From what we've heard," Rosinski said, "they're concerned about this young man's well-being. He's got to get his life in order before ever coming back on the football field."

"They know what he can do on the football field," Shannon said. "Now get him prepared for life." They showed a clip of Hyman talking about Garcia's future.

"Talk is cheap," Hyman told the viewers. "You've got to back it up."

As the second half clock ticked toward zero, Spurrier finally called the old "off the bench" play, sending walk-on freshman receiver Cody Gilbert running onto the field at the snap count. Gilbert ran a go-route, unguarded, but had to slow down to make the catch and got tackled short of the goal line. In the stands people with schedule posters waiting for autographs were missing the quarterback who could hit a receiver 60 yards downfield in stride.

On the last day of spring ball, Shaw was still awash in adrenaline, somehow overthrowing Jeffery on a go-route. Then Thompson overthrew a screen pass. Spurrier couldn't help turning away. Shaw hit a final throw and Spurrier clapped and called it a spring.

"T. C. Campbell," he said to his senior lineman, "what are we going to win?"

"The SEC!" Campbell said.

"What are we going to win?" Spurrier asked the team.

"SEC!" they chorused with raised fists. Louder than ever, for a man still missing. Mangus collared his charges again, saying, "Do what you're supposed to do this summer."

Spurrier touched his wife on the hand as they passed each other on the field. She was walking toward the quarterbacks who might need more encouragement. He walked toward the cameras and microphones, all grins again.

"Summer is more important than spring," he told the reporters. "We've tried to teach our players, 'Here is what you need to do all summer.' And I mean all summer long. Some guys do it. Some go drink beer all summer."

Spurrier looked into the News19 camera like he could see Garcia.

"Y'all aren't going to use that quote about drinking beer, are you?" he asked the cameraman slyly, revving up the golf cart like he didn't care. Using a misdirection play to get that beer-drinking warning aired for his quarterback.

Then he'd have to wait and see, along with all the Gamecocks, if the marked man got the message.

CHAPTER EIGHTEEN

Home Field

A LETTER FROM A REALTOR UP IN WINNSBORO LANDED ON THE DESK OF the University of South Carolina football coach in late August, with a message from all the Spurriers.

The realtor wrote the Ball Coach hoping he'd be interested in buying a piece of land a few miles north of Columbia, out toward Longtown, where his son could hunt hogs—near the land once owned by Steve Spurrier's great-great-great-grandfather Thomas Jefferson Spurrier, and his sons the stonecutters in Winnsboro, South Carolina, in the years leading up to the Civil War.

Steve called Graham and asked why Mom and Dad never told him where their forefathers were from.

"Mom said you were too busy making history to worry about the past," said his brother, who'd read the family history their mother wrote years ago.

Sitting in his office overlooking South Carolina's football field, Spurrier opened the gift from his mother that he'd been too busy battling a "Chicken Curse" to appreciate.

"When my mother was still alive, I had this book right here," he marveled, turning the pages where she connected his family's roots and branches. "She probably did this around 1990 or so. Got all my children in here. Got the [family] line that I really never paid much attention to."

He had an aching knee, hoping to limp through the season to the operating table. He had a quarterback battle raging on the Proving Ground. And he had the land of his forefathers in his heart, heading to Seawall's Restaurant near the stadium to talk to 400 members of the Columbia Touchdown Club. All psyched about South Carolina's Next Great Season.

Seeing all the Gamecocks in his corner, he began to talk about his family in South Carolina.

Three of his children lived in Columbia, he said, along with 8 of his 11 grandchildren. His forefathers, he was proud to learn, lived up the road in Winnsboro.

Four hundred Gamecocks at the Touchdown Club rose and applauded one of their own.

Time for South Carolina's Ball Coach to know that it was the flag of his forefathers he wanted taken down from the State House grounds.

———

His mother said his father's people first saw the shores of America in the 1640s, sailing up sun-sparkled Chesapeake Bay into Maryland, seeing seagulls sail over lush tidal creeks to an endless forest, greening inland. He had to picture the shoreline before SUVs full of Redskins fans drove over the bay to weekend in Ocean City.

His forebears settled in Anne Arundel County, near the Potomac River, where his great-great-great-grandfather Thomas Jefferson Spurrier was one of six children without an inheritance. The eldest son would own the family land. Thomas was a stablehand who grabbed the horse of a man having his saddle repaired and rode for his cousin's place, between Baltimore and Washington, called Spurrier's Tavern.

George Washington stopped at Spurrier's Tavern for a drink and a rest. Ended up burying his horse there, he wrote in his diary. Maybe not a good place to stop. Thomas got back on the horse and rode west through the Blue Ridge Mountains, 600 miles across Virginia and Ohio to Louisville, Kentucky, where his well-to-do brothers owned farms and businesses on the banks of the Ohio River.

In 1825 the word in Louisville was *gold*, discovered in Kershaw, South Carolina. Inspiring Thomas to saddle up and ride away from his well-to-do brothers, riding 500 miles south through the Appalachians and east through the Carolinas to Winnsboro, where the Camden Trail from

Philadelphia turned westward atop a vein of Winnsboro blue granite. Seeing some of the most lustrous stone a man could work with, he found himself working as a stonecutter by the Anderson Quarry, shaping a granite creation he called "Spurrier's Chair," in a paradise under the palmettos.

Someday his granite would be wheeled south to build a state house in Columbia to make South Carolina shine.

In 1826 he married a Carolina girl from Kershaw named Elizabeth, who blessed him with three children. William Rezin Spurrier, born in 1828, learned from his father to cut and shape the granite people needed in Winnsboro, in the shadow of the mill on Spurrier's Hill.

William married Harriet Hoket, who gave him four sons. His father bought 126 acres fronting a creek running through Longtown, east of Winnsboro, and gave William half the land—giving father and son a chance to cut stone and farm, with a civil war clouding the horizon.

South Carolina mustered up an army to cross the bridges buttressed by Winnsboro blue granite and defend Thomas's right to own slaves. Marching across the granite bridges, General William Tecumseh Sherman torched Winnsboro, impoverishing master and slave.

With their homeland in ruins, William's sons watched him gaze northward. Not afraid to walk out the back door.

Saying good-bye to his father, leaving his land in South Carolina, William moved his family 70 miles north to a town in North Carolina called Paw Creek. Buying land enriched by the Catawba River that his sons Charles, William, and twins John and Edward could help farm. Of course, Edward would fall in love with a North Carolina girl, marrying Margaret Auten in 1875.

He'd want his great-grandson to know that even as Ben Tillman was cursing the University of South Carolina for opposing an agricultural college at Clemson, Ed Spurrier was moving his young family from the farm to the town, going to work at Sam Oglesby's store. Giving Edward's son John Graham Spurrier the business skills that paid off in flour sales.

Warned by the writer and researcher working on a book about the Ball Coach that Thomas Jefferson Spurrier owned slaves in Longtown, which might haunt any public talk about having forefathers in South Carolina, Spurrier had to ponder the evil in his family's past—that most every white Southerner must confront. He just had to believe a Spurrier would take good care of the people who worked to help him.

Praying for the spirits of Thomas's slaves, he could only hope they were still in the camp of the Gamecocks. Who might yet march into battle and win one for the downtrodden people of the state.

Making no more public pronouncements about his ancestry, Spurrier shared his newfound roots with his family and friends in the Palmetto State. Waking up a man who truly belonged in South Carolina, coaching up his 2011 team to win big.

"Oh yeah," he said, looking out over South Carolina's football field, "equal opportunity for everybody. I just think that's common sense. I haven't done anything special."

Of course, he realized, "Some people don't have common sense."

Less sensible, maybe, was leaving South Carolina's fate in Stephen Garcia's hands. Time to fan the flames of that quarterback battle on the Proving Ground.

Garcia graduated from USC in May, with cheers cascading through the Koger Center and a lone heckler hooting as he received his diploma from President Pastides and ascended to cult status—a shadowy figure hovering over USC's football team with a year of eligibility remaining, maybe still a savior.

His quarterback coach, G. A. Mangus, fielded the question everyone wanted to ask Spurrier at the Gamecock Club meeting in Mount Pleasant, South Carolina, which is ten feet above sea level. Was the town's name any easier to justify than a coach's loyalty to one troubled quarterback? How could Coach Mangus explain to a room full of disbelieving Gamecocks what one young man could mean to their university?

"I talk to him about eight times a day, like I have for the past two and a half years," the quarterback coach told the crowd. "If I could legally change his name to Mangus, I would."

"Seems like he's changed his ways," Spurrier wanted those questioners to know at the spring's final Fan Fest in Darlington, South Carolina. "I hope the university lets him back on the team."

As the sun rose on Memorial Day, Garcia walked onto USC's indoor practice field carrying his football shoes. Laced 'em up and started whipping the ball around. Conditionally cleared to participate in summer workouts with his teammates, no coaches allowed.

What could Coach Spurrier do that very day, at the Southeastern Conference Spring Meeting in Destin, Florida, to help his quarterback, and every other college football player in America? He stood before the league's coaches, and reporters, and put forth a modest proposal. Why couldn't he pay each of his players $300 a game, out of his pocket?

"We make too much," he said, eyeing his fellow coaches, saying the players should get a share of "that big pie that's out there." Then he pulled out a document signed by six other SEC coaches who supported his proposal. Naming the coaches, in case recruits were wondering.

The Spurrier Proposal would surely splash across the next day's sports page—leaving less space for reports of his "embattled" quarterback returning to the practice field.

Spurrier stood straight as a lightning rod at the podium in Destin, asking if any coaches or reporters had questions about his plan to pay players. Eyeing all the skeptics who would have been done with Garcia by now.

When a Tigernet.com report castigating Garcia went viral in June, Spurrier turned off the news. Knowing good and well his quarterback was in Tampa celebrating Father's Day with his son—not hospitalized in Columbia from a drug overdose, as the Clemson website claimed.

～

At the final Saturday scrimmage before the 2011 season, Garcia was locked in mortal combat with Connor Shaw. At Fan Appreciation Day on Sunday, the crowd would've voted Garcia mayor of Columbia. Beaming like a loved leader, Garcia posed in a thousand photographs with the sons, daughters, and families of Gamecocks wishing him the best season ever.

Yet he'd been outplayed by Shaw on the Proving Ground, Spurrier announced on his Thursday night radio show. Shaw would start the season opener against East Carolina in Charlotte, breaking Garcia's string of 28 consecutive starts. The senior quarterback would play in the second quarter, Spurrier said.

Senior receiver Jason Barnes couldn't hold onto a ball Shaw put on his fingertips, giving the sophomore quarterback three completions in nine attempts. His team was down 17–0 when Garcia jogged onto the field, nodded at the cheers, and rallied the Gamecocks to a 56–37 comeback over the Pirates. Shaw told reporters Garcia should be Carolina's starting quarterback in the SEC East showdown against the Bulldogs.

Sirens screamed through Athens as police escorted the Champion buses bringing Spurrier's team to town. Bulldog fans partying under red tents and blue skies looked up from their cheers—at another reminder they once gave Spurrier the beating of his life, and hijacked his Gatorade.

"Sometimes," Spurrier told a Thursday night radio audience with Georgia on their mind, "the maddest team that plays under control wins the game."

"Are You Ready for Judgment?" asked a sign held by a preacher with a portable mike and amp, competing for curb space with the ticket scalpers as the Georgia Redcoat Band broke into "Hey Baby" by the Swinging Medallions, followed by "Glory, Glory to Old Georgia." Fans wearing shirts proclaiming "Spurrier Is a Cock" and "Hey Steve, Up Yours" were still singing "Hey Baby," filing into the stadium.

The student section roiled with pom-poms and boos as the Gamecocks took the field for warm-ups. Spurrier got doused with a medium-size boo, swinging his arms, loosening up to give Georgia coach Mark Richt a two-hand shoulder smacker at midfield. When the starting lineup was announced for the No. 12 Gamecocks, the boos for the Ball Coach got super-sized.

Carolina strength coach Craig Fitzgerald ruffled Garcia's hair as the quarterback walked to midfield for the first time as team captain. He'd thrown for more than 300 yards in his last visit to Sanford Stadium but couldn't get the last 7. Those last few yards even his barber said to forget about. Now that east end zone was tough to get out of going the other way. Seemed like even the sun was against him, searing the nosebleed seats, glaring into his eye-black.

His adrenaline put the football where even Alshon Jeffery couldn't reach it. Spurrier gritted his teeth as his quarterback trudged to the sideline. Garcia heard from his coach who'd been open and went over to his receivers to apologize.

The Bulldog offense kept moving the chains, piling up stats and settling for field goals. The Redcoat Band burst into "Paint It Black," by the Rolling Stones—even though Marcus Lattimore gained 186 yards against the Dawgs last year to that satanic soundtrack. With the sun at his back and the tubas playing the Stones, Garcia lofted a 34-yarder to Jeffery for a 1-point lead, earning a Spurrier high five.

When Georgia quarterback Aaron Murray fired a 26-yarder to retake the lead, Spurrier started clapping madly—shaking off his frustrations so his team could see.

With Garcia hit by a safety blitz, the Ball Coach faced fourth-and-7 on his own 32, seeing Georgia line up for a punt return. Why not snap the ball to his blocking back, big ole defensive lineman Melvin Ingram— who ran 68 yards and scored. Carolina players massaged their hands after Spurriers' high fives.

Woofing as the Dawgs retook the field after the half were Frank and Michael, red-and-black-bedecked bankers from New York City. They picked a different SEC game to attend every year, dressed like fans of the home team. No regulation Dawg fans could be more obnoxious.

"Can't find football like this up north," Frank said. "We fly in, hit the bookstore, buy as much team gear as possible, and head to the stadium." Next year, Florida.

They groaned as South Carolina scored twice on Georgia turnovers and cheered when the Dawgs bit back. When Murray hit a pass tying the game, caught in the same spot in the flat East Carolina had attacked, Spurrier looked up from his play sheet and clapped hard. A 15-yard touchdown by freshman speedster Isaiah Crowley put Georgia up 35–31, with 6:23 on the clock.

Dawg fans jacked up on Coca-Cola screamed. Spurrier watched his offense tip back some Gatorade with a crocodile smile. The Redcoat Band played "Paint It Black." Garcia scrambled and hit Ace Sanders 30 yards down the sideline. Lattimore cut left for 36 yards, and two plays later, scored.

"Block that kick," the Coca-Cola guzzlers screamed. The kick split the tuba section. Garcia high-fived every guy on the kicking team. And freshman defensive end Jadeveon Clowney got his second collegiate sack—slinging Murray to the turf, popping the ball to Ingram, who strolled into the end zone. Sealing an unlikely 45–42 win.

Garcia got a handshake from his coach. Banker Frank said his money was on Spurrier all along, despite the investment in Bulldog gear.

"We were extremely fortunate and you were extremely unlucky in this game, and that's why we won it," Spurrier told Coach Richt at midfield, without a back slap.

"Never won a game like this," the coach told reporters. Never been less critical of Garcia, they all noted, seeing Steve and Stephen share a Dawgone smile.

A red and black throng headed for Athens' noted bars, to hear bands with names like the "Dictator Tots" and see the black-and-white pictures of Spurrier the quarterback, pummeled by Bulldogs on that gusty November day.

"I cannot *believe* we lost to South Carolina," wailed a coed in a little red dress, as people chanting "Game" and "Cock" kicked through the crumpled red cups on her lawn. "Get out of our town," she screamed over the moan of a time freight bound for Atlanta.

On the Champion bus screaming through Athens traffic, Spurrier rode with the quarterback who'd enhanced his brand.

⌁

Lattimore carried Carolina to victory over Navy and Vandy—Garcia couldn't hit those passes he used to hit. Honoring his "contract" with the university to steer clear of carousing, he sat at home playing miniature golf on his computer, feeling diminished—the swagger, the deep ball, gone from his game.

"It's a combination of things," he told the press, having to defend a 21–3 win over Vanderbilt in which he threw four interceptions. "Sometimes I underthrow it or overthrow it."

Spurrier defended his struggling quarterback.

"Stephen is actually trying the best he can. That's all you can ask for as a coach."

Uneven play wouldn't do against Auburn, three days after the death of Augie Garcia, number 5's grandfather and biggest fan back in Tampa. When the defending national champs took a 16–13 lead at Williams-Brice Stadium, Garcia walked his wristband full of Spurrier's plays onto the field for one last drive.

"C'mon, Garcia," said the ever-hopeful kid in garnet looking over the concrete wall. "Do something great."

He overthrew Jeffery for what would have been a long gain, then hit a final pass to set up a field goal—as the clock ran out on his time as Spurrier's quarterback.

How could Spurrier and Garcia not avenge themselves against an Auburn team missing Cam Newton, reporters ganged up to ask. Spurrier intimated a change was at hand. Prompting Garcia's teammates to descend on the house he rented near campus for a "throwdown," making everyone feel better for a day.

On Monday Spurrier named Connor Shaw his new starting quarterback, and university officials asked Garcia to pee in a cup for the first time that season, monitoring his partying, as per his agreement. Standing on the home sideline when his team took the field against Kentucky, Garcia congratulated Shaw for a slew of scores, running some of those "fancy plays" in Spurrier's playbook. Arming Shaw with a wild variety of formations and ball plays, Spurrier looked like a new coach, leading the Gamecocks to a 54–3 rout of the Wildcats.

Tuesday, meeting reporters for his weekly press conference, Spurrier told Ron Morris to leave the pressroom, ranting at the *State* columnist for alleging that receiver Bruce Ellington had been "poached" from the basketball team the previous spring. Morris wouldn't budge, so Spurrier took the other reporters back to his office. Marking "black Tuesday" for Gameock fans, when Garcia's dismissal from the team was announced.

Teammates who brought over a few beers to cheer up their quarterback had helped Garcia fail an ill-timed substance abuse test. Ridiculed by commentators across the country for calling out columnist Morris, Spurrier succeeded in deflecting the media glare from the player who'd held Carolina's fate in his hands, and dropped the ball.

Who tipped off the university to test Garcia for alcohol consumption the Monday after the Auburn loss? Speculation on USC message boards ran rampant. The Clemson lady a few doors down hated Garcia, the neighbors agreed. Garcia's pool parties couldn't be missed from her backyard. Packing up his belongings with his father, summoned from Tampa, Garcia couldn't help giving his coach a tough-love call.

Teammates who'd never taken the field without number 5 leading the team had to prepare for Mississippi State, where sophomore Shaw would get his first SEC road start in a stadium clanging with cowbells. Shaw's hit-and-miss day boiled down to a final drive—and a horrifying fall. Lattimore went down, blocking for a teammate, and couldn't get up. His mother rushed down from the stands. Shaw completed the drive with a pass to Jeffery to eke out a 14–12 win that felt like a huge loss.

Spurrier's decimated team can't win now, commentators contended on the TV in the Cottage. A freshman named Brandon Wilds was supposed to take Lattimore's place for the big game at Tennessee.

USC's number 22 took his team 98 yards on a drive taking up most of third quarter in Neyland Stadium, as Vols fans screamed about losing to Spurrier 14–3. No way he's gonna win at Arkansas without Garcia and Lattimore, pundits predicted.

An earthquake in Fayetteville, Arkansas, shook the Gamecocks out of first place in the SEC East, after fired-up Hawgs knocked Shaw out of the game. He needed to get better before the Gators invaded Columbia. Spurrier told his radio audience that beating Florida at Homecoming would be big.

Shaw's running and passing led to louder cheers when the Gamecock baseball team was honored at halftime for winning another national championship in Omaha, against Florida. Spurrier celebrated a 17–12 football win over his old team, making Carolina 5–0 for the first time against the SEC East. Yet Georgia's soft schedule, and the clock that ran out on Garcia, sent the Dawgs to Atlanta despite Spurrier's epic win in Athens.

He could still get 10 wins, matching the best record in USC history, by beating Clemson. Not bringing up any curses in his own locker room. The nation's third-best defense sacked Tiger quarterback Taj Boyd and slowed receiver Sammy Watkins, while Shaw gained over 100 yards on the ground in the first half. His 48-yard rainbow to point guard Ellington for a score nearly brought down the stands in Williams-Brice. In the second half DeVonte Holloman intercepted Boyd, and Shaw hit Jeffery in the back of the end zone for a 34–13 "three-peat" over Clemson that didn't go unnoticed at the State House.

A record-breaking season can take assistant coaches away. Defensive coordinator Ellis Johnson left his home in Winnsboro to be head coach at Southern Mississippi, without taking Spurrier on a tour of Spurrier Lane. Spurrier immediately named assistant defensive coach Lorenzo Ward the defensive coordinator, ensuring his players would play the same defense in the bowl game for "Coach Whammy." A coach who never forgets a whupping couldn't wait to play in the Capital One Bowl against Nebraska. Seeking vengeance for his undefeated '95 Gators. Taking the Gamecocks from the devastation of October to Disneyland.

His team looked serious, lifting weights at Celebration High School as Spurrier tried to convey what the game meant to the state of South Carolina.

On a bright blue New Year's Day, the Big Red team of Nebraska scored two first-quarter touchdowns—and got shut down by Coach Whammy's defense. Alshon Jeffery gave his coach a final highlight at the halftime horn, grabbing a Hail Mary pass going Carolina's way—and got ejected in the third quarter for scuffling with his outmatched defender. Jeffery was still named MVP of the 30–13 bowl victory—South Carolina's historic 11th win.

Weeping for joy at the 50-yard line, Spurrier told his Gamecocks this was the biggest win of his career. Calling fans to come down from the stands and hug the players who'd won 11 games for "all Gamecocks everywhere."

Telling his guys not to get in any trouble, out late in Orlando, his benediction in the locker room included a promise to get them all rings emblazoned with a big silver 11. Mentioning in his exuberant postgame press conference that his quarterback would probably get the ball out of his hands even quicker next season.

"Yes, sir," said Shaw.

Back in Columbia, a packed arena cheered South Carolina's first-ever top-10 finish, No. 9 in the AP Poll, No. 8 in the Coaches Poll, highest final ranking in school history. Cheering loudest when Spurrier said more history could be made, in Atlanta.

"When we hit the land of promise," he told the Gamecocks, "you'll see us hugging and high-fiving."

That promised land no carpetbagger could claim.

———

Over at the State House, behind walls of Winnsboro blue granite cracked by Sherman's cannonballs, Lt. Governor Glenn McConnell gazed out at the Gamecocks celebrating a miracle season at USC.

McConnell was also a man with a cannon, built to the exact specifications of field artillery made in Richmond, Virginia, in 1861. He fired it on weekends in his Confederate Army uniform on Civil War battlefields across the South. Working for the Confederate cause in the 21st century, McConnell brokered the deal that moved the Confederate flag from high atop the capitol dome to the entranceway to the State House grounds, where Pitchfork's statue could keep an eye on it.

How *did* Spurrier manage to win 11 games in 2011—surpassing the legendary "Black Magic" team that won 10 games in 1984, rose to No. 2 in the nation, and lost to Navy?

"I'm amazed at what he's done over there," McConnell said, praising the coach at his alma mater. "Nobody else could do it. Everybody else has tried."

Did Spurrier's historic season worry the Confederate flag's chief advocate at the State House?

Lt. Governor McConnell sat ramrod straight behind his massive desk, saying the Ball Coach surely realized what he was up against, trying to change "the setting that flag is in," which once and for all settled the controversy over the flag, in McConnell's view.

South Carolinians who defended the right to fly that flag were people with "no stake in the outcome," McConnell maintained, "other than a federal army that shelled their town and burned their homes, while they were trying to defend their homeland."

He'd fought the "hardliners" wanting the Confederate flag flying atop the capitol dome, even though "some thought we were traitors." The cohort that moved the flag a few steps from Gervais Street, and fastened it to the flagpole with a bungee cord and a lockbox, had compromised enough, McConnell said.

Spurrier might pull off another miracle and win a trophy for South Carolina in Atlanta, but the Ball Coach had no chance of moving the Confederate flag off the State House grounds, McConnell said—and he believed the man was smart enough to know that.

"Because he's a coach. He respects good opponents. He's a strategist, and knows you have to have a strategy, knows what it is to have a good offense and a good defense. To face a good offense and a good defense." Of course the Ball Coach could see that neither side could "win outright," McConnell said.

"Why continue a fight that's not going to get you anywhere?"

Out front wind gusts whipped at the flag as a rotund black man stood in front of the State House addressing a crowd, flanked by hundreds of shoes on the granite steps. Arranged in pairs, waiting for the next step.

CHAPTER NINETEEN

To the Top

ANOTHER MARCH ON THE PROVING GROUND WHISTLED IN ANOTHER team with the chance to get to Atlanta and win, maybe needing a new rallying cry. Spurrier had to ride across the grass in a golf cart. His new knee had to work its way in, and then the pain should ease. After getting tackled in backyards and stadiums, running endless treadmills, walking those Robert Trent Jones fairways from the blue tees, it was something, what parts of you could be replaced.

Rising out of his golf cart wearing a dark blue Under Armour sweater, wraparound shades, and a white visor with a red Gamecock on it, Spurrier let his team see him standing despite the saw-toothed scar on his knee. Hands in the pockets of his khaki shorts. Eyes behind the shades playing the game.

He could still see Garcia out there, zipping balls across the grass—in the guise of freshman quarterback Brendan Nosovitch, who wore that number in high school in Pennsylvania and didn't fear wearing it here. Bruce Ellington, the basketballer, one shifty receiver, was definitely among the missing, along with most of the sideline faithful on the first day of spring ball.

Spurrier always checks out the crowd, from behind those shades, along with everyone on the field. Players seemingly going about their business had coaches in their "grills," screaming at the first sign of complacency, like the head man said to do.

"That was *last year's team* that won 11," the defensive coordinator yelled. "You haven't won anything yet."

Spurrier had to sit back down in the golf cart, propping up his feet up like the doctor ordered, as his quarterbacks threw strikes and misses.

The first practice of the spring was "different," he told the reporters circling the golf cart.

"Yeah," he said, looking at the empty field and nodding, "it's . . . different."

Different hobbling around the Proving Ground without concerns about Garcia. Different having the fans somewhere else, blithely expecting the Gamecocks to be great again.

After bounding around the field in Orlando, calling for Carolina fans to come down and hug the players who'd finally won 11 games, Spurrier chose the fifth of January to put his worn-out knee under the knife. The surgery "went great," Jerri texted her family, adding that Steve would be out of the hospital Sunday. Giving him time at home before the whistle and the golf clubs called.

Alshon Jeffery, the MVP in Orlando despite getting thrown out of the game, announced he'd be gone in the spring, heading to the NFL after consulting with his coach. Another door opened, admitting USC's fifth Mr. Football in a row. Maybe receiver Shaq Roland would be as good as number 1. For sure he was the face of Spurrier's eighth consecutive top-25 recruiting class.

When the ink dried on those letters of intent, USC gave Spurrier another raise, to $3.3 million a year. He celebrated at center court of the Lady Gamecocks basketball game, rooting for them to win three straight for Coach Dawn Staley. Spurrier watches people who know how to win. Knowing people are always watching him.

"Sometimes crap happens. You just have to deal with it," he said about the NCAA investigation of the Gamecocks.

In February a contingent of Gamecock coaches, university administrators, and USC president Harris Pastides followed Spurrier into a boardroom in Los Angeles, with his legacy on the line. He took a seat before the NCAA Committee on Infractions and officially admitted that some of his players enjoyed a great rate at the Whitney Hotel, and that receiver Damiere Byrd met an overly generous Gamecock booster while being recruited in New Jersey. Spurrier testified he hadn't known about those offenses but would accept the consequences. He'd already taken scholarships away from his own team, and said the NCAA should impose whatever additional sanctions his football program deserved.

The officials at the head of the table promised a final ruling soon and lauded Spurrier for saving his deceptiveness for game day. A Clemson commentator on Tigernet.com, awaiting judgment day for USC, wished that "Sherman would come back through Columbia and burn the town down again."

Spurrier's players sweated out the verdict in winter workouts, bulking up for that challenge in Death Valley against Clemson. For three years strength coach Craig Fitzgerald had worked them out like they were training to box Rocky Balboa, and Carolina had won some big games in the fourth quarter. When "Fitz" left for the NCAA-sanctioned Penn State, Spurrier gave Fitz's assistant, Joe Connolly, a chance to be the head guy. He knew no one spends more time with the team than the strength coach.

"The language in the weight room has cleaned up a lot," Spurrier said about Connolly's capabilities. "Other than that, it's the same program."

———

In the lull before spring ball, reporters rated "Spurrierisms" for quarterbacks goofing off. "Flea-farting" won over "Hee-hawin'" in a landslide. Spurrier revealed in an interview with the *State* newspaper that his wife had attended 415 of the 417 games he'd coached, missing a Tampa Bay Bandits game in Portland, Oregon, in the early '80s, and the Georgia Tech game at Notre Dame in 1979.

"She's seen a lot of ball."

Alpha Tau Omega, Spurrier's fraternity at Florida, tapped Marcus Lattimore to be ATO's first black brother at USC. The soft-spoken Lattimore busted out laughing when he heard he'd have brothers on the coaching staff. Speaking as a coach, Spurrier told Lattimore his membership might benefit the fraternity more than the running back. That was enough for Lattimore, who decided not to pledge.

At the end of another frustrating basketball season, USC fired Darrin Horn and hired motivational scowler Frank Martin to get the men's team playing like Staley's squad. Two weeks after Horn's point guard announced he was sticking to basketball, Martin's point guard returned to the football field.

"That's a decision a young man has to make," Spurrier said. "We all have to make those. Heck, I had to make one when I came out of high school. Basketball was my first love, too." Frank Martin, Spurrier said, could coach any kind of ball.

———

The football coach had to exult, watching number 23 jog back onto the Proving Ground. Ellington rejoined teammates practicing the zone-read offense designed to gain yards on the ground, eat up the clock, and quiet some deafening stadiums.

Those reporters with space to fill on their shows and pages were always asking the inventor of the Fun 'n' Gun offense about his run-first personality change. Had the coach of the "ground and pound" Gamecocks given up on cocking and firing?

Nosovitch, the freshman quarterback Spurrier kept watching, gained more yards at Allentown Central Catholic than any other prep passer in the state of Pennsylvania, where Joe Montana, Johnny Unitas, Dan Marino, and Joe Namath had played high school ball. That new number 5 on the field "is going to help us down the road," Spurrier told the reporters. He could see that from a golf cart.

———

Pro Day at USC, broadcast live on the NFL Network, brought Carolina's top-rated draft talent, and a former quarterback, to their old field under the eyes of their old coach. Balmy breezes and passing clouds welcomed head coaches, general managers, and scouts from all 32 NFL teams. Fifteen Gamecocks were vying to crack NFL lineups that fall, including the quarterback last seen on the sideline congratulating Connor Shaw for scoring on Kentucky.

A Garcia sighting at 10:27 a.m. had GamecockCentral's David Cloninger tweeting. Soon the football world knew Wesley Saunders was there in Steelers sweatpants, alongside Jets coach Rex Ryan, USC athletic director Eric Hyman, Dawn Staley, and the Head Ball Coach. Garcia had slimmed down. Short hair, no beard. Wearing camouflage warm-ups.

He ran the 40-yard dash to cheers from the stands. Jeffery countered questions about his conditioning with a time between 4.51 and 4.55, depending on the stopwatch. At 12:23 p.m. Garcia began throwing for his life.

Four straight out patterns sailed over the sidelines, with the NFL watching. Spurrier could only shake his head. Then Jeffery stepped onto the field, like old times, when he was the only receiver Garcia needed to see. He hit Jeffery for the first time since they connected for 19 yards against Auburn in October, trying for a fourth-quarter miracle. Garcia lofted a deep ball to Jeffery, trying for another.

Jeffery took it to the house, running into the end zone below the coach's office like they were all just getting started—and this time, Garcia would know to stay out of the Knock Knock Club.

"Hard to hug him when he comes back," Spurrier said the next night on the radio, answering a caller like this better be the final Garcia question. For what it took out of Spurrier to keep believing in Garcia, all those seasons, silence was camouflage. Then Spurrier heard that the USC Honors College had been rated No. 1 in the country. He talked up that honor on the air, looking more hopeful about the idea of *arete*.

Carolina's defense talked trash to the offense in the Saturday morning scrimmage, stifling Spurrier's quarterbacks—who have to believe they can beat any defense. Facing reporters, Spurrier aimed his comments at his passers, hoping "we don't have to run the ball every time next year." Then he shot down a proposal by the football coach at Clemson that the schools should play each other in the Spring Game.

"If you want to have a game that doesn't count," Spurrier said to Dabo Swinney through the cameras and microphones, "you do that in baseball and softball and soccer."

Shaw, Thompson, Strickland, and Clifford better be ready for the Spring Game, Spurrier said.

At least the quarterbacks' brand wasn't a worry during game week. Though mandated for all SEC athletes for seven years, Jeff O'Brien's leadership seminar wouldn't be held that spring at South Carolina or any spring thereafter.

Spurrier kept his passers in a Socratic discussion. All virtue is cognition. Read the defense, pull the trigger, and be Branded a Leader.

~~

Connor Shaw cocked his arm and looked downfield, seeing the X receiver open and making that football fly. Zooming across all the grass in the stadium, Damiere Byrd reached up and took it into the end zone.

Gamecocks just sitting down for a football game on an April afternoon, giddy with barbecue and sweet tea, jumped for joy. The Black team led 6–0 after one snap. The rooster crowed for the extra point. Cheers welled up for the pass, the catch, and the promise of more balls in the air.

Spurrier clapped with his play sheet in his hand. He had more pass plays, receivers who could go long, and at least one quarterback who could hit 'em. Shaw got a boisterous fist bump from his quarterback coach. Mangus's silver No. 11 ring flashed like a signal in the sun.

Spurrier called the plays without wearing a headset, hearing the fans cheer all the completions. A father in a black "Beast Mode" T-shirt held up his young son, wearing a No. 1 jersey, for a better look at the ball plays. A dad who brought his twins from Charleston to see some Gamecock football pointed out that the coach had his sons helping him, in matching black shorts, white polo shirts, and shades. Parents who'd competed in the Official USC Tailgating Contest heard their kids recount Marcus Lattimore's talk that morning, about how everyone can be a hero.

They all gazed up at the scaffolding supporting the biggest TV screen in South Carolina, being built over top of the coach's office to replay a big fall. Most everyone had the official 2012 schedule poster, showing Spurrier standing by Shaw.

The coach's gaze settled on his departing seniors, the winningest class in school history, cutting up on the sideline. Not everyone made it, Spurrier pointed out at a banquet the night before, awarding every Gamecock who'd been in uniform in Orlando one of those silver No. 11 rings.

Shaw played so well that Spurrier sent him back in for the old "off the bench" play. Defenders who'd pushed the offense around all spring, until the crowd came out, blasted into the backfield. Shaw spun away from Kelcy Quarles and hit the mystery man running down the seam. The huge defensive tackle looked at his empty hands and shook his head. Shaw jogged to the sideline and took off his helmet as the crowd and the rooster crowed.

Spurrier smiled at his clean-cut quarterback, who'd hit six of seven passes for two touchdowns after being publicly questioned all spring, and said, "If you're going to cut your hair that short, you need a hat out here."

"Yes, sir," Shaw said.

When the last rooster crowed and Fan Fest began, Spurrier's passers had 511 yards and six touchdowns. Man, where *were* those defensive backs? Only one ref saw that receiver run onto the field from the sideline, Spurrier noted in his press conference.

"We might run that 'off the bench' play in a game," he exulted in the hallway.

The quarterback sitting on the floor awaiting his turn to talk to the press looked up and said, "Yes, sir."

At long last, "trickeration" was a luxury Carolina could afford.

～‿⌢

The following Tuesday the venerable Associated Press Stylebook announced that "hopefully," Spurrier's favorite word that wasn't considered a word, now was.

"We now support the modern usage of hopefully," the AP tweeted. "It is hoped, we hope." Just in time for Spurrier to hopefully celebrate his 67th birthday.

Hopefully, he'd get to challenge the national champs in December in Atlanta for the SEC title. Spurrier told reporters that Nick Saban had "a nice little gig going" at Alabama, turning out first-round NFL draft picks every April. "If he wants to be the greatest coach or one of the greatest coaches in college football, to me, he has to go somewhere besides Alabama and win, because they've always won there at Alabama," Spurrier pointed out.

Early on the last Sunday in April, with dogwoods blossoming in the Tennessee hills, the legendary Hilltopper football coach, who'd listened to Chicago Bears quarterback Bill Wade and let that Spurrier kid call the plays, slipped away in his sleep. Coach Kermit Tipton left behind his whistle, for Steve to blow as he saw fit.

———

He chose a Fan Fest in early May in Greenville, deep in Clemson territory, to respond to Coach Swinney's rant back in November. Reporters couldn't forget him saying, "The real USC is in California," and "the real Carolina is in Chapel Hill," in retaliation for something Spurrier didn't actually say. Was Swinney just trying to psych up his team after losing to Spurrier again?

"I don't know, but he won the game," Spurrier told the reporters in Greenville. Recounting his "little blowup last year in the middle of the season, at sort of one sports writer," he noted that Carolina won the next game, and won a bunch more.

"I've been the idiot," Spurrier said of his media image. "So, if you win the game, what you said was OK. If you lose the game, you're a dummy. Simple as that."

Ad writers took note—it's not weird if it works.

Spurrier and Swinney had just played the Chick-fil-A Golf Challenge at Lake Oconee. They talked on the links, Spurrier said, "but not about that." Of course it was Gamecock radio announcer Todd Ellis's on-air outburst, "We sure ain't Clemson, folks," after the Tigers lost in Williams-Brice Stadium, that provoked Swinney's rant—and maybe helped him win that ACC title game.

"We call Todd Ellis his BFF," Spurrier said of the bond between Ellis and Swinney, concluding the seminar on media strategy in Clemson country.

Testing the new knee on the PGA Tournament Players Championship Course in Ponte Vedra, Florida, for Giants coach Tom Coughlin's charity tournament, Spurrier was once again voted the most hated football coach in America on ESPN.

Speaking to Gamecock Clubs around Carolina, still fighting complacency, Spurrier closed each meeting with a call for donations: "Winning costs a little bit, but it's a lot better than losing."

He stopped off in Raleigh to sign star high school quarterback Connor Mitch, telling the mobile passer his coach would be there for his time at USC—and to jump rope.

On Memorial Day in Destin, Florida, SEC football coaches voted in favor of Spurrier's proposal the year before—agreeing to personally pay players up to $300 a week for expenses, around $21,000 a game, about $252,000 a season. They'd pondered the recruiting advantages of giving up that pocket money while Spurrier swept the SEC East. Of course, the athletic directors and school presidents and suits at the NCAA first had to approve Spurrier's plan.

The coaches rejected Spurrier's proposal to count only division games when deciding who went to Atlanta. Spurrier would face LSU in Baton Rouge in October, while Georgia played less imposing Ole Miss.

Was Florida or South Carolina a tougher place to build a team, reporters in Destin wanted to know.

"I didn't build it; it was there," Spurrier said of the place down the coast where '90s SEC teams went to die. "The players were there, at Florida. I mean, they were there. It was just a matter of finding a quarterback, and Shane Matthews was there also."

South Carolina was definitely different, Spurrier said. "If I wanted to be the all-time wins leader in the SEC, I would have stayed at Florida."

Those Florida reporters had to print that. They'd stopped writing about the Decline of Spurrier since he somehow made Carolina a top-10 team, even with backups in the backfield. And his maligned ex-quarterback, whose return from suspension last May was eclipsed by Spurrier's proposal to pay players, was trying out for the Montreal Alouettes in the Canadian Football League

They cheered in the Spurrier house when Garcia was signed by Montreal. Defying a nation of skeptics, Spurrier's old number 5 had a pro football contract.

His current quarterbacks watched game film and threw to their receivers all summer, keeping the faith in their coach's play calling. He knocked in a long putt at the American Century Championship in mid-July and danced a jig on the green that went around the world on the Internet.

For the first time as coach of the Gamecocks, he brought a quarterback to represent South Carolina at SEC Media Days in Birmingham. With Shaw in the wings and fall ball in sight, Spurrier stood at the podium and said what he'd been saying all during "talking season," as he called July: "We've got a good team."

Would that be a passing team or a running team? reporters asked. Spurrier hoped to "keep opponents guessing."

"How much longer are you going to coach?" a reporter asked in the corridor.

Spurrier eyed him for one Mississippi.

"How much longer are you going to write?"

❦

Coach James Franklin at Vanderbilt, Spurrier's first 2012 opponent, planned to be "really, really nice" to the Ball Coach because "you don't want to get on his bad side."

Somehow, another former Gamecock receiver who made it to the NFL no longer wanted to live, despite working relentlessly to rehab a leg injury. O. J. Murdock had been Kenny McKinley's roommate at Carolina until Spurrier kicked Murdock off the team for shoplifting. He still made it to the pros. Spurrier was stunned to learn he'd shot himself in a car parked by his old high school football field.

"Maybe he went over there because he was trying to relive some of his best memories," said his high school coach.

"All of us here are saddened to hear of O. J.'s passing," said Coach Spurrier, trying to figure out how death could tempt any young man with a chance to work himself back into playing shape and be redeemed.

When the blocking was good enough to protect a phantom punter, Spurrier called for a real punt and kicked at the grass in a gust from a lightning storm in the west. August had come again, bringing football back to the Proving Ground. The coach stood in an unpredictable breeze, watching his punt team try to block and cover punts better than last year.

He had maybe a few hundred fans behind the ropes for a mercifully cool opening night. The Gamecocks had a Heisman Trophy candidate, or two, and a top-10 team for the first August since 1892. The thousands of fans who'd cheered Jadeveon Clowney's sweltering debut last year must be at the new Batman movie on a Friday night. Walking away from the punt team to work with the quarterbacks, he broke into a jog.

Could these Top Ten Gamecocks play like underdogs? Was this still a team on the rise, or a pumpkin at midnight?

His star defensive end wore a bigger-than-ever grin. New defensive coordinator "Coach Whammy" roamed the field in a floppy pith helmet hat, talking about shifting Clowney to linebacker on some plays. Knowing the SEC was listening. The whole defense was taking offensive gains personally, stripping the ball and running all the way to the end zone.

Watching the quarterbacks take on those defenders, Spurrier got down into a stance, hands out in front, holding his play sheet with his elbow. Nosovitch threw. Spurrier watched the catch and looked back to catch the follow-through. That kid spent the summer in Famously Hot Columbia preparing to please a famously tough coach. Spurrier would entrust Nosovitch to lead the scout team against the first-team defense, playing the role of the quarterbacks at Georgia, LSU, Florida, and Tennessee.

You know, Spurrier told reporters after practice, that number 5 gets the ball off quick.

What was it the players kept yelling during warm-ups? the reporters asked. Some new rallying cry, that sounded like "Cocks."

"To the top," Spurrier said. No other destination would do.

The hot air returned after Media Day, when Spurrier said SEC coaches spent a lot of time analyzing opponents' preseason remarks—such as his assertion that the Gamecocks would mostly run the ball this fall.

"They are saying, 'Spurrier thinks we believe they are going to be a running team, and they are going to come out and try to throw the first game,'" he said. "So we're probably using reverse psychology, that they think we're thinking that they think that we think they're not going to do that. And then you try to do the opposite, whatever that is."

Then again, Spurrier concluded, "Carolina may be the last running team in college football." Except maybe for Alabama. "They run the ball over there, too."

After a hard-hitting practice, Spurrier couldn't contain a grin. "We're hitting more balls than we've ever hit around here. More balls than we ever hit." In his elation you heard the balls past quarterbacks didn't hit.

He was asked to name the biggest difference between this year and last, sitting in his golf cart with right-hand man Jamie Speronis. Their bemused smiles deepened.

"No Stephen Garcia," Spurrier blurted out. "But I don't want to get into all that."

"To the top," his players hollered the next morning at the snap of every jumping jack.

<hr>

"That number 89 is a good-looking guy," a fan said to his son as their team worked on a red zone passing drill. Freshman tight end Jarrell Adams had a NEXT BIG THING headline in the *State* and two big tight ends ahead of him on the depth chart. Under a floppy brown pith helmet hat, new tight end coach Scott Spurrier stood in the line of fire, taking notes for his dad.

"Who's gonna get better tomorrow?" Spurrier asked the team huddled around him at the end.

"Carolina!" they chorused under raised helmets and gloved fists.

He watched the players walk away, calling over their shoulders, "Did you notice that we're hitting more passes?"

<hr>

Saturday afternoon, friends of Spurrier still in Johnson City saw a college team in orange scrimmaging on Steve Spurrier Field. They called him when the first Tennessee uniform hit the synthetic turf and got a big laugh, and an okay, if that was needed.

The Volunteers were in East Tennessee for a change of preseason scenery, enjoying a rendition of "Rocky Top" on the chapel chimes at Milligan College when a storm swamped the grass practice field. UT coaches knew where firmer footing could be found.

"Glad we could help out the Vols," Spurrier said at the Proving Ground. "Hopefully they'll beat Georgia and a whole bunch of people.

Not us, but a bunch of people." Friends sent pictures of "all those orange helmets . . . on my field up in Johnson City."

One of Tennessee's star receivers stared at the sign reading "Steve Spurrier Field at Kermit Tipton Stadium."

"Is that the same Spurrier at South Carolina?"

"Spurrier Field, baby," his coach yelled, urging the team to do something on it.

At the Cottage, where the regulars liked to say, "We don't like Steve Spurrier and we don't like anybody who likes Steve Spurrier," they could only spin on their stools and hope that taking over Spurrier Field at the high school meant the Vols would take over Spurrier's field in Columbia, at Halloween. Whatever voodoo that might entail.

———

"Big scrimmage Wednesday night," Spurrier announced to the Monday microphones. "Open to the public. We want to turn on the lights and maybe get some fans out."

Because, he said, "Some guys who did well last week . . . didn't do very well today, which is our history."

His patented "Spur Lid" hat showed his hair, while the shades hid his eyes.

Thompson got yanked after throwing two picks under the lights, on a seemingly subpar night for Shaw, and Spurrier assailed too many "loafs" by guys who should know better.

"We don't loaf here at South Carolina. We didn't get to be No. 7 or 9 or whatever in the country in preseason by having a bunch of loafers on our team."

He told his preseason call-in show listeners he had receiver Damiere Byrd running the offense at wildcat quarterback. Receiver Shaq Roland could run it, too, Spurrier said. His quarterbacks better work harder.

On the *Dan Patrick Show*, Nick Saban responded to Spurrier's zinger back in April. "LSU wasn't winning when I went there. Michigan State wasn't winning when I went there. Toledo wasn't winning when I went there. And Alabama really wasn't winning when I came here," Saban said, adding that to satisfy Spurrier, "I guess I gotta go someplace else." But he had to admit, to Dan Patrick and everybody, "I love Steve. I'm always anxious to hear what he has to say. It's always funny."

The Friday before the "Super Bowl," as Coach Franklin called the Carolina game, he appeared on *Fox and Friends*, to showcase the story of his walk-on linebacker getting a Vanderbilt scholarship. Footage of teammates cheering Marc Panu as his highlight video played was already a smash on YouTube.

"They feel good about themselves," Spurrier said, when the buses arrived to take his team to the airport. Not mentioning the scholarship he just gave his walk-on kicker for making one pressure-packed 42-yarder at practice. Spurrier did recall that at Duke he didn't "market" his underdog team the way Coach Franklin promoted Vanderbilt.

"We threw the ball around and scored some points," Spurrier said. "That'll do the marketing for you." Knowing that opposing coach scouted the *News at 11*.

CHAPTER TWENTY

Death Valley

PASSING THROUGH THE GREAT SMOKY MOUNTAINS, PAST THE SHRINES where Davy Crockett and Daniel Boone killed bears, a caravan of cars covered in red roosters rolled down I-40, with signs proclaiming, "On Our Way to See the Gamecocks Play."

The team looked straight ahead, walking off the Champion bus into the stadium, led by Coach Spurrier in a blue business suit. Earphones blasting tunes couldn't drown out the juiced-up fans they had in Nashville on a Thursday night at the end of August.

A sandy-haired man in a rooster-red T-shirt bet everyone in earshot Carolina would wallop the Commodores, holding up the cash he was willing to wager on yardage totals, first down margins, and scoring by quarters.

"My name *is* Cox," he said, challenging a disbelieving Commodore. "Wanna bet?"

The Commodore pulled out $5 and asked to see some ID.

Players warmed up on the special turf in Vandy's spiffed-up stadium in the rain blowing in from Hurricane Isaac. The footing didn't seem to worry Spurrier, jogging a few steps in the end zone as Isaac darkened the western sky. He looked back at the storm clouds and the crowd. Can a coach see too many opening nights in the SEC? He followed his players into the locker room to remind them Vandy didn't have all those "slow dudes" any more.

In a downpour Marcus Lattimore fumbled on his first carry since tearing up his knee in Mississippi—that first hit he was scared of all summer. Senior linebacker Shaq Wilson bailed out everyone with a pick at

Vandy's goal line. Spurrier could see his quarterback struggling to throw through the rain-soaked air. Little green puffballs from the new synthetic turf filled Connor Shaw's face mask. Lattimore got over being nervous and ran the ball into the end zone. Spurrier greeted everyone coming off the field except Shaw and Lattimore.

When the placekicker now on scholarship hit his first college field goal attempt, his head coach raised both arms to signal a score.

Shaw got hit hard by a Vanderbilt helmet and lay on the ground, clutching his shoulder. When he was able to get up, Dylan Thompson came in and skipped a pass off the turf. TV viewers could see the Ball Coach looking disgusted. Still depending on one quarterback almost a year after Garcia had gone.

Shaw could barely lift his arm in the locker room, and asked his coach if he could have a shot of Novocain between the shoulder blades. With the second half underway, Spurrier watched his quarterback walk back onto the field and saw the crowd energize him. He sent Shaw back in.

What could he do, throwing with pain? Vandy led 13–10. On third-and-long he "shot-putted" a pass downfield that senior tight end Justice Cunningham got his hands on, taking a hit that sent his helmet flying. Carolina scored. At the end Mangus had a helmet tap for Shaw as he wobbled off the field a winner. Spurrier had a hug for one gutsy quarter-back, who passed for the fewest yards of Spurrier's coaching career but played through a vicious helmet hit.

What did this game mean, a sideline reporter asked Spurrier while his players sang their alma mater. TV viewers heard it was a good win, even if sportswriters didn't like the 17–13 score. Looking up at the home crowd thinning out because he'd beaten them, Spurrier jogged across the water-resistant turf into the locker room.

"Hope we don't ever have to rely on Thompson," said the fan named Cox, filing out of the stadium looking down like he'd lost something.

Spurrier was still betting on number 17.

The first Friday night in September, Science Hill High School turned on the lights at Steve Spurrier Field, in Kermit Tipton Stadium. Players, coaches, and fans stood in silence to commemorate the late coach, surely looking down on his Hilltoppers. Up on the Jumobotron screen a video of his memorial service that summer showed his son presenting his coaching whistle to his favorite player, who gave a short talk about the inspiration he got from his coach. Everyone at the memorial service and in the stadium waited for Spurrier to blow the whistle, but he never did.

The players knelt in front of the video screen to pray, then went out on the special synthetic turf and whipped Greenville, the defending 5A state champs, 45–21, led by the first player to wear No. 11 at Science Hill since Spurrier wore it.

He told them to bring his retired number back, hearing that quarterback Reid Hayes, formerly the team's go-to receiver, also played basketball and baseball for the Hilltoppers.

The next day East Carolina fans flew purple and gold Pirate flags driving down I-95 to avenge Garcia's comeback last year in Charlotte, coming to see what couldn't be missed in Columbia. South Carolina's money was on Spurrier.

He sat in the front seat of the Champion bus leading the parade down Bluff Road, passing fans waving Gamecock banners in a chaos of cars on the way to the Gamecock Walk down the new Garnet Way. Somehow, in the field back of the train tracks where generations of Gamecocks bought turnip greens at the farmers' market and took their Saturday curse with a side of cinnamon rolls at the Biscuit House, the bricks and gates of the Horseshoe had re-risen around a tailgater's paradise. Since USC's stadium wasn't on campus, the campus had come to the stadium. The spirit had done it all in one off-season.

Kickoff was at high noon. Gamecocks armed with provisions showed up on the hallowed new grounds before 6 a.m., needing just a crack of daylight to see that the South's most revered game-day settings couldn't hold a gas grill to what Spurrier had wrought.

"I've been to the Grove at Ole Miss," said Bruce the Gamecock fan. "This is better."

Beyond the broadcast booths, bounce houses, and palatial restrooms at the Gamecock Village, smoke from centuries of handed-down barbecue recipes filled the sky. Lamppost-lined walkways led to stately white columns upholding dueling bandstands where pickers grinned. Under the enormous "RV Shed" that once housed acres of produce, touring buses surrounded Cocky the personable rooster posing with his young fans. Parents snapped away at the first generation of Gamecocks to inherit a winning tradition.

The buses bearing a top-10 football team shimmered in the heat like a mirage.

Coach Spurrier led the Gamecock Walk through uproarious cheers and what looked to be the ancient gates of USC. Following him was a real step up—more than one quarterback with the arm, the brain, and the will to win.

Trailing the players absorbing the cheers through their headphones, Shaw was a study in gray. Not starting. Scapula still aching from that helmet hit in Nashville. Wanting to be out there but relieved to know Thompson could play in his place. Shaw saw his father waiting by the big brick gate and hugged him as cheerleaders turned flips and the Mighty Sound of the Southeast band played on.

The men who follow the players into the stadium are always talking strategy. "A heavy dose of Lattimore," prescribed a tall, dark-haired man in Gamecock regalia, speaking for the fans hearing a backup quarterback would start. Spurrier's words followed the quarterbacks onto the field for warm-ups.

"We're gonna find a quarterback today," Spurrier must have said a dozen times the previous roasting hot Saturday, at a practice called after the shaky passing in Nashville. "We're not gonna play like that again," he kept saying, making his quarterbacks throw for three hours in heat that left an impression.

"Man, I don't want to go through another one of those Saturday practices," said Thompson as the quarterbacks stretched in the pregame buzz.

"Somebody's got to throw for 500 yards," said Seth Strickland, who realized that somebody might need to be him. For the first time since turning down a scholarship five years ago at Gardner-Webb to walk on at USC, he was the No. 2 quarterback.

Be ready, Spurrier told Strickland all week. Now Shaw stood beside Spurrier, where Strickland usually stood. Could the grass get any hotter?

Fans kept calling for Lattimore when Thompson trotted onto the field for his first college start, magnified on the "Beast Board" atop Spurrier's office. The new $6 million video screen showed number 17 throwing strikes on the first drive and not looking back.

The former backup completed 21 of 37 passes for 330 yards and three touchdowns, in the stats up on the screen. Replays showed a picture-perfect 53-yarder to Damiere Byrd, outrunning a band of Pirates that got no picks or revenge.

Most of the students left at halftime, when a Carolina victory and heatstroke seemed likely. Aluminum slats stared at Strickland from the student section with three minutes left, when Mangus said, "Get out there."

Spurrier called for the tight end to go long. His mantra to "look off" defenders meant eyeing the running back in the flat. The corner was taken in. Strickland looked upfield and fired. The ball hit "Buster" Anderson in stride at the right hash mark, and he sprinted into the end zone. Strickland ran down the field to high-bump with Buster, letting the backup holder handle the extra-point kick, as USC student and sports journalist Avery Wilks triumphantly reported.

Back on the sideline Strickland was congratulated by a fired-up quarterback coach. His head coach just smiled, like he expected to make a produce stand into a parade ground and a walk-on wearing No. 11 into an SEC quarterback.

Sunday dawned with people in the upstate calling the Gamecocks copycats. Clemson commentators on the *State* message board said USC tried and failed to imitate the charms of Death Valley.

At Spurrier's Sunday afternoon teleconference, the play of his backup quarterbacks was all he knew about renewal.

———

At Spurrier's urging, at a Saturday evening home game against the University of Alabama at Birmingham, the Gamecock faithful came early and stayed late, watching in hushed silence as Shaw threw a completion and got upended, landing on the hairline fracture in his shoulder blade. He didn't practice much that week and took a shot of painkiller before the game to get back on the field with the team.

When Spurrier sent in his backup, Thompson was greeted like a different quarterback—a guy who looked downfield first. On third down from his own 6-yard line, he found Byrd for a 94-yard scoring strike. Thompson starting running downfield to celebrate, then ran back to thank tight end Buster for the block that saved the play. To close out UAB, Thompson ran like Shaw for a score.

Reporters wanting to talk about Spurrier's 200 wins didn't write much about Thompson's witness for Christ in the interview room. Were the Bible verses Spurrier gave his quarterback strategically coded? If the Lord was with you, should you fear the blitz? They'd have to ponder that on Sunday.

The South Carolina coach needed divine guidance to serve the players and the fans, the football program and the university, the state and the *State*.

Three days before the Gamecocks played the newly admitted SEC team from Columbia, Missouri, columnist Ron Morris questioned whether Spurrier should play Shaw on Saturday—inviting readers to make that call in a poll. Then Morris spoke on sports talk radio about the dangers of giving a college football coach too much authority. That amounted to the loss of "institutional control" that got Joe Paterno fired at Penn State, Morris said.

Coach Spurrier was still grieving Paterno's death, and the loss of "Joe Pa's" steadfast reputation over an assistant coach's horrific deeds, when Ron Morris spoke from the radio speaker. "This is how things like Penn State happen," Morris said.

Thursday afternoon at practice the Ball Coach welcomed his college coach, mentor, and friend Pepper Rodgers. When Coach Pepper had his first head coaching job at Kansas, those Tigers were the rivals in the "border war." Coach Spurrier reminded his troops of Missouri's comeback win over Carolina in the Independence Bowl in '05. Then Coach Pepper sat in for a segment of Spurrier's radio show at Wild Wing Cafe, where a caller opined, "Coach you should rotate the QBs. I think you might want to look at that for the SEC stretch."

"Well, I appreciate that," Coach Spurrier said, eyeing Coach Pepper. "But I have been coaching quarterbacks for 28 years now. One thing is for sure. I will be calling the shots."

Shaw was fine and would play Saturday, Spurrier told his listeners—even though the hit UAB put on him should have been flagged. Shaw could have finished the game if he had to, Spurrier said. The results of decisions made by coaches around the country flickered on TVs around the bar.

"Our fans know I don't determine if a player can play or not. The trainers and doctors tell us who can or who can't play." The final call was Shaw's, Spurrier added. Not mentioning any columnists or polls.

To the quarterbacks in the meeting room, Spurrier quoted chapter and verse of how writers make a living stirring up stuff to talk about. That was how they did it on sports talk radio in Florida, where daily diatribes about Spurrier made it sound like he quit coaching the Gators last week.

"Always thought the Ball Coach was thin-skinned," said JX Radio personality Frank Frangey, responding to a caller who read Ron Morris religiously.

Should Spurrier start Shaw against the Missouri Tigers? A mishmash of opinions filled the airwaves between Gator and Gamecock Countries.

"Don't listen to it," Spurrier told Shaw. "If Dylan needs to come in and play, he'll do that."

Somewhere the Missouri coaches got the idea to play a "soft" cover two zone against Spurrier's starter. His first pass hit the turf.

"What's he doing in there?" fans hollered at the coach.

Then the completions started adding up. Throwing underneath the coverage, where tight end Cunningham was open, Shaw led a 21-point outburst in the second quarter. He had an 80-yard touchdown run called back for a holding penalty, and kept gashing the Tigers with runs out of the zone-read. When Missouri defensive coaches finally called for cover one, Shaw lit up the Beast Board with a bomb to Ace Sanders for a score. Welcoming Missouri to the SEC.

On third down Shaw saw no one open and outran the Tigers to the first-down marker. Then his coach took him out, after 20 straight completions—one shy of the all-time SEC record set by Tennessee quarterback Tee Martin in 1998. Surely maddening the commentators on sports talk radio. Why wouldn't Spurrier keep playing a record-setting quarterback?

Shaw and Thompson crossed paths jogging in and out, with Spurrier applauding the quarterback who'd bested Wuerffel and Manning. Shaw looked up at his larger-than-life stats and saw a good day passing, even on a Game Boy.

Spurrier praised both his quarterbacks in a statement to the press, with columnist Morris sitting in the interview room. The coach walked out without taking questions. He had a game ball to take to his mentor, who'd watched Shaw pick apart Missouri from Spurrier's office window. And there was a trophy presentation for winning the "Battle of Columbia."

Spurrier signed off his Sunday teleconference without taking questions from a field of reporters that included Morris. Depriving players of publicity, the reporters grumbled.

"No columnist is going to tell me how to play my quarterbacks," was how Spurrier saw it. Choosing the silent treatment over a confrontation with Morris like last year's that had around 400,000 YouTube views.

Morris missed the Tuesday press conference where Spurrier answered questions about the Gamecocks' upcoming trip to Kentucky. Morris wrote in his Wednesday column that his words made Spurrier clam up, and that neither coaching nor writing about football was easy.

Spurrier told his radio listeners that "one of the local writers" had "slandered my name and my integrity. The guy is trying to tarnish and ruin my reputation as a coach." And even though "we all know who the guy is, and that's the kind of person he is," something would be done about it. Spurrier said USC president Harris Pastides and athletic director Ray Tanner were "backing me in this" and that "some good changes" were in the works, according to "the guy that runs the newspaper."

At WOLO, Columbia's ABC TV affiliate, *Mondays with Morris* was off the air. Spurrier's radio diatribe didn't make the *State*. Woe to the next team Spurrier played, history suggested.

Kentucky coach Joker Phillips recalled at his Monday news conference the 54–3 loss last year in Columbia, when Spurrier had said, "Kentucky has a heck of a punter, I know that."

"We got a good punter this year, too," Phillips noted. Diplomatically not mentioning Spurrier's last trip to Lexington, when the 'Cats knocked off the Gamecock team that had just beaten 'Bama—and where Spurrier was greeted by the *Lexington Herald-Leader* headline The Ole' Gall Coach.

Did Phillips put Spurrier's words on the bulletin board for motivation?

"If I put everything that Steve said up there, we wouldn't have any space on our board," Phillips said, being a Joker.

Losing to the Wildcats was no joke, after Spurrier called so many pass plays that Lattimore had only five carries in the first half. Spurrier walked to the locker room telling sideline reporter Jeanine Edwards, "We're going to be in trouble if we don't get smarter." Up in the press box, Morris banged away on his story about 21-point underdogs leading Spurrier's team at the half.

"Clean slate," said the coach in the visitor's locker room. No one could point fingers, he said, because everyone stunk.

After the half he had Lattimore running from the old I formation. Then Byrd caught a 30-yard scoring strike, hushing Kentucky's crowd. Shaw hit 15 of 18 passes, running for first downs with his scapula aching but no one asking whether he should play.

Lattimore ran for Carolina's fourth unanswered score, and Spurrier clapped the heck out of his play sheet. Announcers who'd questioned his first-half moves lauded "one of the few coaches in any sport who was also a brilliant player."

"Loudest Kentucky crowd I've heard . . . well, since two years ago," Spurrier said in the visiting-team interview room, in case room opened up on the home team's bulletin board. Reporters who missed the many Wildcats blocked by number 21 in the first half asked if he'd felt "underutilized."

"I just wait until my number is called," Lattimore said. "I'm coached by Steve Spurrier."

South Carolina had tied the school record with a nine-game winning streak and started off 5–0 for the first time since Spurrier came to Columbia. He expected September to go well.

"We're not bowl eligible yet," he said on the cusp of October, when we'd see which team had the strongest will—or greatest hate.

ESPN announced that *GameDay* would visit the Horseshoe for the Saturday showdown with Georgia, for the first time since Lee Corso donned an elephant head to predict Garcia and the Gamecocks couldn't beat 'Bama. Spurrier heaped praise on Shaw and urged fans to be kind to their telegenic critic, Corso.

"He made a statement eight years ago that we'd never win the SEC, and so far he's right," Spurrier said. "We haven't won it yet." On Wednesday he broadcast to the Georgia defense that "some of these other experts use that pistol formation. Maybe that's what we need to do, also."

Spurrier saw the eyes of his stoic quarterback smoldering. Shaw looked ready for his first start against the hated team from his home state. Ready to run into the guys he'd played with at Flowery Branch High School, coached by his dad—until they took a wrong turn on Hog Mountain Road and ended up blood rivals in Athens.

Spurrier had USC fans on their best behavior, clapping for the host of *GameDay* at the Horseshoe, brokering peace with signs reading, "SC Chicks Love Corso" and "Respect the Visor." Waving no Confederate flags.

Down at the stadium, Dawgs and Cocks held up fingers. Scalpers wanted hundreds for nosebleed tickets. Georgia fans traveled in big packs, said the Columbia police officers who'd run riot drills all week.

What was different about this border war? The invaders no longer shook Columbia's confidence. Those Bulldogs driving in with stars on their "Confederate Army Strong" bumper stickers could see cannons in the yards here, too.

Maybe it was the lights of the carnival setting up across from the stadium, or Corso in a rooster head on national TV. Or maybe the fifth-ranked Bulldogs were beaten before the game began, when the family of US Army Sgt. Scott Faile, of Kershaw, South Carolina, got a rousing introduction at midfield.

Sergeant Faile's image smiled down from the Beast Board with a message for his family and 85,199 fans, from the 36th Signal Battalion at Camp Carroll, Korea. Tammy Faile wiped away tears everyone could see, as her deployed husband talked about the sacrifices she and the children, Ashley, Breanna, and Cameron, made for his military career—and the freedom to cheer at a Gamecock game. He promised to "See you real, real soon," and strode onto the field, into his joyous family's arms.

The most Gamecocks ever to crowd into Williams-Brice Stadium sounded ready to play the game. The visiting team heard it.

Shaw put the ball in the air on the second play, and 42 yards down-field Byrd wrestled it away from Georgia cornerback Bacarri Rambo. Three plays later a pass to Bruce Ellington in the end zone turned up the volume.

Kelcy Quarles charged Georgia quarterback Aaron Murray, tipping his pass to the "Spur" defender. Shaw reminded another defensive coach trying to stymy Spurrier near the goal line to cover the tight end named Buster running a drag route, next time.

Georgia's tandem of running backs nicknamed "Gurshall" couldn't get a first down, as Spurrier watched with folded arms. Sanders juggled Georgia's punt, dodged the defenders rushing upfield, and met the 10 players who'd blocked 11 Dawgs in the end zone. When they jogged to the sideline, Spurrier high-fived them all.

With 5:18 left in the first quarter, the game was over. The Georgia band quit playing "Paint It Black." The $6 million video board even went dark.

As the clock ticked through the second half, Spurrier called no pass plays until he saw Georgia's safety "sitting on one of our routes," leaving the middle of the field open. Shaw "chunked it over the top" for a 62-yard gain. Lattimore got 1 more yard to put the Dawgs down 28–0. Wrestler Ric "Nature Boy" Flair, enjoying Spurrier's takedown on the sidelines, made his exit with a lady in long boots when Georgia mounted a desperate drive to score against Carolina's backups. The Faile family stayed arm in arm for every play.

"How do you score that many points only throwing 10 passes?" Spurrier wondered, after calling 51 running plays and winning 35–7. Counting his wins in the pros, he said, "this was actually my 250th overall win as a head coach, and having it against the Georgia Bulldogs is special, too. That's a team that used to beat my alma mater very well. I've been fortunate as a coach against them, not so much as a player, but as a coach."

Spurrier saw his quarterback standing in the doorway and said, "Alright, Connor," giving him a first bump and a seat before the cameras and lights. Seeing as how he'd led South Carolina to the first win against another top-10 team since that first kickoff in 1892.

"That was the most fun I ever had," Shaw said, getting a hug in the doorway from his high school coach.

Joy filled the streets between the fairgrounds and Five Points. Fans holding a Spurrier for President sign honked and hollered like the SEC East trophy was in their grasp. Georgia fans walked into the Wendy's on Assembly Street with looks the fries with sea salt wouldn't satisfy.

"I miss Stephen Garcia," said a guy in line in a Bulldog shirt.

The Confederate flag looked nervous in front of the State House, falling limp and fluttering as Bulldog fans posed by the pole.

SPURRIERED, read the Sunday headline in the *Atlanta Journal-Constitution*. On the AJC message board, a post read, "Good luck recruiting against Spurrier now. Half his team is already from Georgia."

Other Georgia fans noted that sending Spurrier to Louisiana, while the Dawgs hosted Ole Miss in Athens, might even things out.

"Most of our guys have never been to Death Valley," Spurrier said at his Tuesday press conference. "That is *the* Death Valley, isn't it? Or is there another one around? There's two of 'em? That's right, there's two Death Valleys. I forgot about that. Was LSU the first one or the second one? Who knows?"

"Our guys have never been to USC," Dabo Swinney said the next day, in his office by the basketball court. "California is a long way away from here."

Spurrier's strategy was making Swinney stick to his story—knowing the Tigers at Hampden-Sydney College in Virginia had been playing football in Death Valley almost a hundred years.

"For the record," Clemson's coach told reporters in the upstate, "the original Death Valley is right here, in case anyone has any doubt."

When he was a Gator, Spurrier loved flying into Baton Rouge, seeing palm trees rise up like he was touching down in the Sunshine State. To the coach of the Gamecocks, the land between the Honey Island Swamp and the Mississippi bristled with challenges, landing with a hurt running back and a team with the flu.

He told them the audibles that worked at home against Georgia couldn't be heard in the stadium Louisianans originally called "Deaf Valley," until their Cajun accents had outsiders thinking they heard "death." Foes confusing deaf and death had lost 35 of the last 36 games in there after dark. Tough place to play at night, Spurrier warned.

Unspoken was his belief that a good ball play beats any defense, in any crowd. He just reminded the team they represented a lot of Gamecocks back in Columbia. They ended their Friday night chapel service at the hotel with praise for the Lord—and that bone-crushing ritual Pastor Adrian called "Championship Hugs."

On Saturday sirens screamed down South Stadium Drive, parting a purple and gold throng that didn't want to move for Spurrier's motorcade. In Baton Rouge they believed spells could wound enemies and fans could win football games. That was the strategy of the slaves rattling their chains through those lowlands. Make the master *believe* voodoo could empower the powerless.

Spurrier just smiled when the fans started banging on the side of the bus—knowing no other SEC school tried to rattle opponents like they did at LSU. He could still hear Mike the Tiger, roaring through the speakers they put in the visitor's locker room. It had been almost 50 years since Spurrier went out and quarterbacked the unranked Gators to a 20–6 win over the No. 7 Bayou Bengals. Pastor Adrian raised his hands over the banging fans. The buses kept rolling.

Oddsmakers "are usually pretty smart," Spurrier said, and they had LSU favored by 3 after Gamecocks started sweating and staggering off the Proving Ground. Lee Corso was picking South Carolina to win another SEC showdown—simply not believing a team warding off a century-old "Chicken Curse" could be stricken with the Hoodoo Bayou LSU Flu.

The coach of the Gamecocks didn't need a crystal bus window to see the Tigers were up for the game, wearing purple and gold wigs, waving purple and gold rebel flags, carrying signs downing cocks, chanting incantations against chickens. Pulling up in Van Geaux, a purple and gold "full service voodoo vehicle," a crew sporting "Beat the Cocks" T-shirts called for Spurrier to be tarred and feathered. A banner draped across the Theta Xi fraternity house proclaimed, "Hey receivers, to beat these Cocks you need to hold the balls!"

Backing up that bravado were three gold and purple national championship banners waving above Death Valley, overshadowing the basketball arena known as the House Pete Maravich Built. But the sixth Tiger named Mike to roar for LSU still didn't worry Spurrier.

"The Tiger doesn't play defense or offense for them, not yet, anyway," he said, preparing his game plan. "They keep him caged up, I think."

Spurrier jogged onto the field and the Tiger band blared. LSU players loved to watch opposing teams look around and see what they were up against. They noted Shaw's surprise, running past the empty cage where Mike VI usually growled and glowered. Shaw—a gamer himself—looked wide-eyed when Tiger players introduced on the video screen pixilated into actual tigers.

Chewing grass on the sideline to taste the field, Les "the Mad Hatter" Miles, coach of LSU, did what wasn't expected. Spurrier jogged to midfield and clapped Miles on the back twice as derision poured down from the student section.

The ball soaring through the night sky at kickoff provoked a real Tiger roar. Shaw crouching behind center upped the noise. For the first time since he'd been playing football, he could feel the voice of the crowd rattling his face mask.

After a few plays and a few yards, they could all see the Tigers' D-line digging in. Lattimore's hip injury, which Spurrier had kept secret all week, wouldn't matter if holes didn't open. And those fans would be screaming until tomorrow.

After battling the Tigers to a standstill, Shaw had a man open down the far sideline, if he could find him. Were the receivers wearing special camouflauged Underarmour uniforms colored "South Carolina battleship grey" *too* camouflaged? Shaw threw to a covered receiver on the near sideline, incomplete, and Spurrier's shoulders sagged.

At halftime of this trench war, Carolina somehow led 7–3. Walking off the field, getting interviewed for the world and LSU's coaches to hear, Spurrier asked his quarterback to win the game.

In the third quarter USC safety Brison Williams hit the ground and didn't move. Tiger fans wanting him off their field said, "Get some Viagra, you cock!"

"Throw that damn visor, boy," an old Bayou Bengal yelled at Spurrier after an incompletion, but he just had words with his receivers.

All the shoving, hitting, and hollering came down to Carolina ahead 14–13 with 9:13 to go, facing third down and 6. Shaw rolled out, looking for a receiver to cut back. LSU's cornerback jumped the comeback route. Turning, slipping, his face mask vibrating, Shaw saw Buster the tight end in battleship gray breaking open and tried too hard to get it to him. Spurrier clenched his fists before the ball hit the Tiger's hands.

Announcer Brent Musburger, up in the press box reminding viewers that Spurrier himself was a Tiger slayer as a quarterback, called Shaw's play "a killer of an interception." Mangus patted Shaw on the shoulder. Spurrier bent at the waist to study the ground. LSU defenders jubilated to their sideline and the crowd bowed, acting unworthy of rooting for such a defense.

After an LSU field goal and an LSU touchdown run, Shaw engineered a late-game scoring drive, but the Cocks fell short, beating the spread but losing 23–21. Spurrier walked back across the frenzied field to give Miles a handshake.

Screams, cheers, and chants of "LSU!" nearly drowned out the coach in the visiting-team interview room, saying, "We all got reminded tonight of why LSU was a preseason No. 1."

Asked about Shaw's game-changing interception, Spurrier winced and spoke haltingly.

"We thought we'd get him out of the pocket a little bit . . . Buster was coming by . . . he threw off-balance . . . he didn't plant his feet . . ."

Spurrier said he'd asked Mangus at one point if their quarterback got "hit in the head somewhere . . . 'cause some of his decision making was a little off." Digging into his cheekbone, hair slicked back like he'd played, Spurrier said Shaw had "played beautifully all year [but] wasn't as sharp" against the Tigers.

"Hopefully he can get back to it," Spurrier said through all the screaming and hollering pouring out of the stadium. Generators, spotlights, and country tunes cranked up around the Memorial Tower. The Met Life blimp retreated across the sky as a time freight bound for the Big Easy moaned.

Driving back past the voodoo shops on the neon streets, where they sold hex books and chopped-off chicken feet under signs saying May the Curse Be with You, the Ball Coach could be forgiven for thinking there was only one Death Valley.

Beyond the Perspex window of the quiet plane, next week's flight path clouded down toward Florida.

———◦———

Spurrier kept house in Gainesville under the palms, festooned with a tropical mural, down the street from the stadium with his name on it and his bronze statue throwing the football out front. But with a big red *C* on his visor, he can't go home.

The week he had reservations at the Gainesville Hilton, his quarterback just back from Baton Rouge got the flu, too. Shaw was going to practice anyway, because headlines were flying around the country hyping Spurrier's return to Florida—to face the monster he'd created at the Swamp. The Media Boys didn't dwell on his loss at LSU. In the 24-hour news orbit, Death Valley Days were last week.

While at the University of Florida, the Head Ball Coach revolutionized the game of football and reinvented the SEC, gushed *USA Today* in its preview of the game; *Sports Illustrated*'s cover story claimed he's an even better coach now. "Muschamp has to be up for Coach of the Year," Spurrier countered, praising the Gators' current coach. "Florida was not meant to be 7–0 right now."

Reporters wanted more. You're either a Gator or a Gator Hater—isn't that how Spurrier's saying went? He sighed and smiled.

"Florida is always going to be my school. I love Florida," he said, noting he and his wife and daughters had UF degrees and Steve Jr. got his master's there.

"But I'm a Gamecock now, and this is our team."

He said that when he retired, "in four or five years," he'd be keeping his Cockominium overlooking the Proving Ground. Where players who didn't seem sick last week shivered off the field.

"That little flu bug hit us before we got our flu shots," Spurrier told reporters after Wednesday's practice, listing two receivers, two linemen, and a cornerback among the starters with all the symptoms. Also, Lattimore, Quarles, and Clowney were hurt. No mention of the starting quarterback feeling ill.

In Gainesville they waited for whatever team he brought to town—clearly remembering his last visit.

Entering Gator Country by heading into Sonny's Barbecue in Marianna, Florida (modeled after the one Sonny built in Gainesville in 1968), a South Carolina convert asked, "Do you serve Gamecocks?"

"No," said the hostess, holding onto a menu full of barbecued birds.

"We used to be Gators."

"That's even worse," said the hostess, not smiling at all.

"Should be a great weekend," said the large, jovial manager of Gainesville's Campus Store gas station, watching students race down the sidewalk, rearranging his orange-and-blue hot dog display. "We're up to No. 2."

Yeah, but Coach Spurrier's coming.

Warring feelings crossed his face.

"Well, we'll see," he said, turning back to the hot dog display. "We'll see what ball plays he's got."

At the university bookstore overlooking a fountainous gator pond full of nervous turtles, they had official Spurrier visors marked down to $8. Available only in Gator orange.

At the Gator City Sports Bar, formerly the Purple Porpoise, where Gator fans traditionally downed brews at halftime before Homeland Security forbade re-entering stadiums, students knocked back the Hump Day Special. They heard the name Spurrier and chorused, "Gator Bait."

"Rip the Gamecocks apart feather by feather," advised Carlos W. Clarke. "It's what Spurrier would do."

Most everyone hanging out on University Avenue all week said the Gator traitor must suffer. His photograph hung on the Gators' locker room wall, beside a sign that read, "3:30 P.M. Kickoff. Take Dead Aim at the Cocks."

On a sizzling Saturday morning at the Swamp, framed by the *Game-Day* stage, Corso agreed with the anti-Spurrier crowd, disappearing inside a big green Gator head. The cameras showed Gator fans in a frenzy but not a single "Spurrier is a Cock" T-shirt.

He's heard that one before, in a town he put on the map. Pickers pick against you. Ten-dollar T-shirts talk trash. His brothers at the ATO house could walk Campus Road from their door to the Swamp wondering how many points Brother Spurrier could score on Muschamp's defense. The answer blew through the blue-painted trees, on a day made for Florida football.

"No Lattimore! All the heat's on Shaw," said a Gator girl at a watering hole where signs said not to feed the alligators.

"You think those injuries are for real? Don't trust the Evil Genius," said her friend inhaling from a beer bong.

"Once a Gator, always a Gator," said a passing tuba player, honking out of formation.

Spurrier had seen it all, glancing down Stadium Road and hitchstepping into the visitor's locker room in a gray business suit. Followed by sons with serious faces and Shaw nodding to the beat in his earbuds.

Once again Pastor Adrian prayed over the team entering the Swamp. Nearby a wiry old man in orange Gator kneesocks, blue Gator Keds, and a floppy Gator hat flying Gator flags took in the preacher's prayer and laughed. Then he strolled over to the statues of Florida's Heisman Trophy winners and cackled at Gamecocks posing with the bronze quarterback in the middle. Probably the reason Spurrier told reporters asking if he'd seen his statue, "I drove by it once, I think." Old Man Gator had a sharp laugh.

Surveying his old field, Spurrier took in the "Work 'em Silly, Gators" sign on a bedsheet they hung up at every home game. He clapped his guys into the huddle, heard "To the Top!" and clapped them out. He watched Albert and Alberta, the Gator mascots, holding hands walking past Sir Big Spur, and saw Corso laughing with his brother, Graham, on the Carolina sideline.

UF coach Will Muschamp stood by the Gators warming up, a team that Spurrier hadn't recruited him for as a player, forcing Muschamp to play at Georgia. The Ball Coach could be hard to fathom. But something about his they-think-we-think preseason talk made Muschamp wager the first play call in the Swamp would be a pass.

With 90,000 howling, Spurrier called a swing pass to starting running back Kenny Miles. Muschamp called a corner blitz, sending Loucheiz Purifoy straight at Shaw. Miles lost his footing. The other receivers went long without looking back. Purifoy hit Shaw and the ball. Gator linebacker Lerentee McCray, whose bio said he lived to wipe smiles off quarterbacks' faces, fell on the fumble a yard from USC's goal line.

"Con-nor! Con-nor!" the UF student section jeered.

Spurrier swallowed hard and smiled. Three plays and a yard later, he folded his arms and looked up at the GatorVision scoreboard. Down 7, with the orange and blue nightmare barely begun.

Ace Sanders fumbled a punt the Gators recovered. Byrd caught a deep ball and fumbled. As the half roared to a close, Florida had 20-some yards and led 21–6. Then Spurrier had to walk out and see freshman defender T. J. Gurley curled up on the grass, clutching his knee.

Shaw seemed fine but stood on the sideline in the second half while Thompson played. Didn't matter who stood behind center. Florida's defensive front did what LSU had done. The Gators still had a coach who knew his side of the ball. While the orange and blue multitudes swayed and sang "We Are the Boys of Old Florida," Spurrier covered his mouth with his play sheet, talking to his son inside his headset. Thinking what he thinks when he's definitely getting beat.

At the end he jogged from the 50-yard line to the tunnel without looking up.

"Could have been a heck of a game for everybody," he said in another visiting-team interview room besieged by cheers, sympathizing with CBS. "But we just laid the ball on the ground and said we don't want this thing bad enough."

His guys didn't score one touchdown on that fast grass he had installed.

Coach led them past the taunters on Stadium Road and rode the quarterback bus to the plane at the airport under the palms. Knowing he wouldn't see the alfresco scene above his bed in Florida for a while, or the Georgia Dome.

Who hated losing more, the team or the coach? Spurrier talked to his players about it on his Thursday night radio show—past the time his "24-hour rule" allotted for mourning losses. Some guys acted like they didn't care about getting beat two weeks in a row, which Spurrier called "unacceptable behavior." He vowed to "eliminate the guys that loaf a little bit and the guys that act like they don't give a dang."

All around Wild Wings the TVs flashed sports reports—leading up to another SEC Championship Game that wouldn't feature Spurrier's team.

He told the defensive guys they'd played a great game at the Swamp and could "hold their heads high." Even though they weren't yet bowl eligible.

How many miles had they flown, chasing greatness across the South? How many miles did they all fly home in despair? When they got back to town, the carnival was gone.

⌒

At the Proving Ground Shaw ran his guts out, firing strikes, finally shaking off the flu. His coach could see that he hadn't forgotten the receivers he missed at LSU, or the benching he got in Gainesville.

Spurrier told his team Tennessee had an offense that could score, and a pass defense that could be had.

Let a team leader rise up and say what the players really needed to hear.

Friday night before a home game, they all went to the Radisson Hotel on Bush River Road and out to a movie. Hard to find a good one these days, Spurrier groused. He let his assistant Jamie Speronis pick the best bad film. Back in the meeting room at the hotel, after seeing the good guys noisily win again, Lattimore stood up and spoke.

"I want everybody to play hard. And I want you to play every snap like it's your last," he said, looking at the faces all around.

"Because you never know. It *could* be your last."

His coach nodded sadly. No one had to tell Steve Spurrier they weren't making any more Marcus Lattimores.

⌒

From the air a packed Williams-Brice Stadium appeared on TVs draped with fake cobwebs in the Cottage across from Kiwanis Park. The screens showed Darius Rucker, former lead singer of Hootie and the Blowfish, the chart-topping rock band from Five Points, singing the national anthem. Gamecocks cheered as Spurrier jogged onto the screens. The booths and stools in the Cottage were eerily empty.

The regular Spurrier haters couldn't make a noon kickoff, the morning after the annual Cottage Halloween Party. Could the Vols' underrated offense somehow outpoint the Ball Coach? That hope might get them out of their orange-blanketed beds to root for a 3–4 team before 1 p.m. Skeletons, spiders, bats, chained coffins, and the ghosts of last night joined

Wayne at his stool, in his orange Vols jersey, getting his first beer from his girlfriend behind the bar in an orange nurse outfit.

A portrait of Don, the former owner, who died, had replaced the picture of Spurrier that hung for decades above the beer taps. Sonny, who bought the bar from Don, was in Columbia, on the sidelines with Graham.

"Watch close," said the Volunteer nurse. "We could see him on TV."

Out the back door they had a fine view of the park where Spurrier worked up those ball plays that had Shaw passing and Lattimore running down the field on the opening drive.

"Steve's folks were good people," said Wayne, a veteran with 15 men under him at the VA hospital across the cemetery from the Spurriers' old place. "Steve's arrogant, and always was. He's a jerk."

The Vols could beat him, Wayne said, if they could just get some help rooting. Conjuring up a thin black man in overalls and a black leather ball cap with a big orange T for Tennessee.

"Hey, Farmer Brown, where's your tractor?" Wayne greeted him. An even thinner man with a bushy beard and a red wool cap walked in.

"Did you get wild last night, Cecil? Did it get wild in here?" Wayne asked.

<hr />

The Beast Board in the stadium didn't just look impressive to viewers—it blocked the winds flapping the upper-deck flags from another hurricane off the coast. A light breeze wafted across the sideline. Spurrier realized both teams' quarterbacks could have a field day. He eyed the Vols' defense and switched around his Y and Z receivers, Sanders and Ellington. The orange defenders couldn't cover either.

Tennessee quarterback Tyler Bray kept finding his big burners downfield. The men at the bar cheered, then moaned as Lattimore burst through the Tennessee line, ran 28 yards into the end zone, and flipped the ball to the ref, making his coach smile. Dave Pasch, the play-by-play announcer, and Brian Griese, the color man, said that after a year of rehab

Lattimore looked like his old self. Easily on his way to the twelfth 100-yard-rushing game of his career.

He took the field after another Vols scoring drive and took the hand-off from Shaw. Linebacker Herman Lathers hit Lattimore high, from behind. Defensive back Eric Gordon hit him low, head on—the kind of hit SEC running backs take on October Saturdays on TVs in bars across the land.

Lattimore hit the ground and grabbed the other knee, the one that wasn't hurt last season. His leg stuck out at a terrible angle. The crowd on TV went quiet.

"Looks like Lattimore's leg is broke," Wayne said. "It's twisted like a wet noodle."

"Hope it is," said a big kid drinking beer from a gravy can.

Wayne looked over. "What the hell kind of thing is that to say?"

"I just hope it's broke for the rest of the game," the big kid said. "How about that?"

"That's what I'd like to see," Cecil said, jumping out of his booth. "Then maybe Spurrier'll come running out there and step on him, and that lays *him* out."

"You don't like anybody, do you, Cecil?" Wayne said, turning back to the astounding gathering of players on the field.

Both teams surrounded Lattimore, some on one knee, heads bowed in prayer. Pasch and Griese said in the hushed tones of a golf broadcast that they'd never seen a football player respected like that.

Spurrier gazed across the grass, not planning plays. After 10 minutes Lattimore sat up, holding a Gatorade towel over his face. Touched on the shoulder pads, talked to and prayed over, he was carted across the field to a standing ovation.

Nothing to do but win the game for him, they all said in the locker room at the half. Spurrier huddled with the quarterback bouncing back from a benching to pass his team to a 28–14 lead. That wasn't enough. Keep throwing, Spurrier told Shaw.

With just over a minute left, a 38–35 lead didn't look good for the home team. Bray seemingly couldn't be stopped. He stood 20 yards from Carolina's goal line looking for the win, behind the Big Orange offensive line that had kept Jadeveon Clowney out of the highlights all day. Double-teaming and "chipping" him with backs and tight ends, Tennessee finally did what Spurrier hoped—they made Clowney mad.

Back at the cottage Bray drew cheers, fading back to throw a dagger. He had an extra tight end in the pattern, taking a chance Clowney could be blocked by just one man for just one play.

Clowney ran past that guy and launched himself at the ball in the quarterback's hand. Shaq Wilson dove on the fumble. Game over.

Someone had to win it for Lattimore. Spurrier walked onto the field in his black visor to shake hands with another Tennessee coach whose job he'd cost.

"We snatched defeat from the jaws of victory," Wayne growled, a saying from back when Spurrier was a Gator.

The rest of the bar looked down at their drinks.

"That girl who won the costume contest last night didn't need no costume," Cecil finally said. "She's a natural witch."

In a small white house on a hill overlooking Johnson City's fields and schools, Sid Smallwood sank back in his recliner, exhausted. He'd spent the afternoon cussing Steve Spurrier for not getting heat on Bray sooner. Rooted deep in Tennessee, Smallwood still rooted for the son of Brother Spurrier when he took on the Vols.

"His defense has to hit Bray square in the white meat," Smallwood rasped, talking the best he could. Comforted that father and son "have one thing in common. *Lose* isn't in their vocabulary."

———

Monday was Lattimore's 21st birthday. He'd gotten a game ball at the hospital from Pastor Adrian, and a Sunday morning visit from his coach. Spurrier just wanted to see a smile on the face that had been shrouded by the Gatorade towel, and to say he'd seen Lattimore surrounded by a real caring team. They'd taken another blow when Georgia somehow beat Florida in Jacksonville. The Dawgs they'd routed in Columbia would be playing for the SEC Championship in the Georgia Dome.

Spurrier could only look forward, addressing thousands of Gamecocks gathered on the Horseshoe on Monday wearing Lattimore's jersey.

He was home from the hospital, watching a live stream of his party on his computer with his mom.

"This is not a memorial," said the coach on the porch of the McKissick Museum, framed by Happy Birthday and Get Well signs. "This is a celebration."

Lattimore heard that at his house in the upstate and expected a Clemson joke.

South Carolina senator Lindsey Graham brought a message from Mayor Benjamin that Columbia was officially celebrating Marcus Lattimore Day—along with the state of South Carolina, as proclaimed by Clemson graduate Governor Nikki Haley. Vice President Biden sent word he was a Gamecock fan because of Lattimore.

His teammates spoke, Pastor Adrian prayed, President Pastides led a rousing rendition of "Happy Birthday," and Lattimore texted thanks and blessings to the Gamecock Nation. Standing by the Get Well Marcus poster signed by the team, Spurrier noted that among the tributes to Lattimore was a note "from that upstate school. You know, that school that doesn't beat us much anymore . . ."

When the cheers subsided, he said, "Usually, when that coach up there talks about South Carolina, it's a bunch of garbage, a bunch of BS . . ."

When the laughter died down, he continued, "This time I have to agree with him. Marcus Lattimore stands for all that's right about college football."

With a sweep of his hand, Spurrier imparted his highest praise. "I sort of put he and Danny Wuerffel as the two guys . . . I don't know if they ever do anything wrong or not. Somewhere you gotta do something wrong," he said with a grin, "but I've never seen these guys do anything but what's right."

Spurrier presented the official Marcus Lattimore Day proclamation to Marcus's sister, Ebony. Dylan Thompson led a final prayer, and the Ball Coach bowed his head. Certain that for once the coaches at Carolina and Clemson could agree.

If Spurrier's going to talk like that, he better win.

The following week Mitt Romney and President Obama finally squared off at the polls, after a long preseason. Reporters asked Spurrier if the team had a chance to vote.

"Our guys that are 21 and so forth?" he responded, as reporters smirked. Maybe Spurrier just had 21 on his mind. He put in a vote for Lattimore's backup, Kenny Miles. "His body fat is very low. A lot lower than a lot of you guys."

Even less-fit reporters were needed Thursday to get word to the fans: Show up Saturday and holler! Arkansas had beaten Carolina more times than Georgia, Tennessee, and Clemson combined over the past three years, Spurrier reminded everyone.

Saturday was "a holy day of obligation," Tim Brando said in the broadcast booth, watching the Hawgs and 'Cocks warm up. Spurrier stirred up the crowd before kickoff, gesturing for the noisemakers to make noise and smiling at the rowdiness he saw as his son talked inside his headset.

He was up only 4 on the Razorbacks, 14–10, near the end of the half, facing a crucial third down at midfield. Shaw cocked and misfired.

"Spurrier's coaching him up," Brando exclaimed up in the booth. "Looks like Steve is going to send him back out there."

Shaw took the snap on fourth-and-6 from midfield—where, if Arky could get a stop, they had time to take it the other way. Dodging a linebacker trying to make that happen, Shaw lofted the ball to a wide-open Ellington, who gave the safety a basketball juke and scored.

Shaw gave the coach a high-flying fist bump. The rooster crowed and TV coverage broke for that Bud Light ad saying, "It's only weird if it doesn't work."

———

While the Mighty Sound of the Southeast band marched in a "We (Heart) 21" formation, Spurrier told his guys in the locker room what they needed to do. After beating the Razorbacks 37–20, he walked back onto the field in his black visor to tell their guys, "Good game."

Looking up at the student section, wondering why Homecoming wasn't all about the football game, he sang the alma mater under the fresh paint commemorating the 38 rushing touchdowns Lattimore had scored.

"This crowd really loves its football, and they've never really had this kind of success," Brando summed up the celebration below. "A very unspoiled group, these South Carolina fans."

Spurrier begged to differ, as the Bear Bryant comparisons began. With a win over Wofford, the all-time winningest coach at Florida would be tied for wins at USC—alongside the only other coach to be tops at two SEC schools, the legend in the houndstooth hat.

"Nowhere to go but up," Spurrier said, recalling the day he took the job at USC and promised to persevere to this point. "I like those situations."

Certainly he remembered playing against Bryant's 'Bama team in '64 in Tuscaloosa, diving for a first down and losing two teeth. "Spit it out and kept on playing," he said with a full smile. Why couldn't all the students at USC care about the game like that?

"All these years, we've been hoping to have a winner here at South Carolina," he said to his Thursday radio listeners. "Now we have a team that's winning every home game. So why do they leave?"

"Boo 'em," Spurrier advised the students who stayed. Act like a big-time football school—instead of "how they did it back in 1998 and 1999, when we were 1–21."

Everybody better realize Wofford has a good team, Spurrier said.

His starting quarterback with the hurt foot, trampled by Hawgs, listened to his coach talk about Wofford's toughness and grimly prepared to play. National media boys wanting to talk about the Bear and the Ball Coach poo-pooed his Wofford warnings.

On Military and Senior Appreciation Day in Williams-Brice Stadium, Shaw was introduced as the starting quarterback and Spurrier clapped hard. He sent out his seniors with fist bumps and zipped through the introductory smoke with a smile for the band director.

Wofford ran the triple-option attack to maddening first downs, limiting the time Spurrier had the ball. Shaw threw a pick and his coach threw up his hands. Shaw fumbled and Spurrier threw his hands higher. Shaw came to the sideline after missing an open man and Spurrier and Mangus each took an ear. They all could see Wofford was dropping seven and eight defenders in pass coverage, daring a quarterback with a gimpy foot to run. Spurrier doesn't listen to excuses about what the other guys are doing.

As the flags of the SEC teams swirled around the stadium, Wofford was tied with USC, 7–7.

In four minutes in the fourth quarter, Carolina kicked a field goal, got a fourth-down stop, passed for a touchdown, and ran in a 31-yard fumble recovery. Thompson ran onto the field to congratulate Shaw for hitting Sanders for the touchdown. Spurrier went out and clapped them to the sideline. Shaw waited to walk behind his coach. USC's 24–7 win over Wofford had kept the students in their seats until the end.

Spurrier joined the team and the full student section to sing what he called "my most fun alma mater," propelling his players into the students' outstretched arms. He walked off in his black visor, waving to fans forced to stay for the late-game dramatics.

Did it feel any different to have as many wins at USC as Rex Enright? "Just a tie," Spurrier shrugged. "Ties are, whatever."

Connor just had to let the ball go, Spurrier told him through the microphones. Noting that he "hit the comeback patterns" and "his foot got hurt, but he's okay."

Reporters kept kidding the coach about not knowing the voting age. "When I was 18, I didn't vote," Spurrier said, walking out to let his quarterback in.

Shaw limped to the table bristling with microphones. "I tried to stay in the pocket as long as I could," he said. "But there's always stuff to improve on."

The coach in the visiting-team interview room wasn't happy either. "It's tough," said downcast Terriers' coach Mike Ayers, "to know that we almost beat Goliath."

⁓

The Monday before Thanksgiving, Clemson students gathered for a funeral, asking, "Do you smell dead poultry?" Pallbearers in camouflage carried a black coffin holding Cocky in repose, trailed by two Tigers, one of them the real mascot. The students hooted in the setting sun. Sandy Edge, who advised their careers in the College of Business and Behavioral Science, wiped away tears under his top hat, saying, "I inter these remains so that Saturday these bones will not rise again."

The students swayed arm in arm, singing their alma mater. "Disco Inferno" thumped through the amphitheater as Cocky was cremated in a garbage can. The mourners ate fried chicken sandwiches and reminisced.

Down through the hills to Columbia, 131 miles away, Gamecocks were asked to bow their heads as Reverend Frank Anderson intoned, "We gather this evening to remember and lay to rest a puffed-up, overconfident, and highly overrated pussy cat in an aptly named place . . . Death Valley."

The city dwellers lit their torches. Unlike past years the USC engineering department did not build a three-story-tall tiger with a voice box that could beg for mercy as fireworks exploded over its flaming head.

By Tuesday the Palmetto State was done mourning. Ready for the 110th Game of the Century.

To reporters Spurrier talked up quarterback Tajh Boyd and the Tigers' "high-powered offense," though he'd outscored Clemson 97–37 the past three games. He talked about the loud crowd in Memorial Stadium, where the Tigers hadn't lost since Spurrier's last visit. He had some starters hurting, he said, and wasn't sure who his quarterback would be.

Shaw was sure. The previous week he had gimped into the locker room after surviving Wofford and told Thompson, "Be ready next week. No way I'll be able to play."

Spurrier told the team Monday that Thompson would be their quarterback. He'd let Clemson know about an hour and a half before kickoff.

Clowney, sidelined by a sprained foot for the Wofford game—even though his picture was on the tickets—walked past reporters on Wednesday and guaranteed he'd play Saturday: "Put that in the paper."

Spurrier saw where Clemson was favored by 4, no longer an underdog since their offense had gotten all that publicity.

Spurrier wore a gray business suit and shades, getting off the quarterback bus and stepping into Memorial Stadium like there was no crowd chanting, "Four in a row." His namesake son in shades walked behind him. Up on the terrace by Swinney's office, the USC pep band broke into the fight song. Shaw limped up to his dad and gave him a serious hug. Word of Shaw not starting still wasn't out, but father and son knew.

After the team entered the stadium, Pastor Adrian raised two fists that opened to palms, saying to the Gamecocks holding up four fingers for four wins, "Let us pray."

A Clemson student in corduroy overalls promptly peed in the stadium bushes, under the inscription, "Where the Blue Ridge yawns its greatness, where the Tigers play . . . ," right by the stadium police station.

"Don't you know where you are?" hollered a Clemson police officer hauling the student across the grass, showing him what door he'd chosen to go through.

Going over the pass patterns and protections they'd studied since March, Spurrier reminded his quarterback again of Psalm 100:3: "Know that the Lord Himself is God. It is He who has made us and not we ourselves. We are His people, the sheep of His pasture."

Thompson had his coach's reading assignment on his iPad, along with the plays that could beat Clemson.

Outside the visitor's dressing room, revelers were roaring. A tent full of Clemson fans stomped on rubber chickens under the sign "Eating, drinking, kicking Gamecock butt, ain't life grand?" The Farmhouse Fraternity blasted "Hillbilly Rock Star" under a big green tent by the Agriculture Building, where the future would sprout after the Gamecocks were history.

A truck covered in orange paws towed a bean pot through the crowd. Fingers pointed to a need for tickets. Scalpers from the city traded price tips on cell phones, while students asked $125 for the seats up where the flags flapped. Parking spots downtown went for $100. All around the stadium Tiger statues held fingers in the air.

At the gate to the student section stood tired ROTC students who'd guarded Howard's Rock for a week while beating on oil drums painted in Gamecock colors. A Clemson usher directed Gamecocks up the concrete steps, saying, "Those seats are way up there," though they weren't.

"There's Steve Spurrier, right there on the field," said a Clemson fan amazed the Carolina coach didn't stay away. At their meeting at midfield, he had a big grin for Clemson's Coach Swinney. Booed by the Hater family, a mom, dad, daughter, and boyfriend in orange who could sniff out Gamecocks dressed in black.

"I hate South Carolina," said the daughter, a Clemson student, looking around at the South Carolina sympathizers in her stadium.

"God, I hate you bastards," said her boyfriend, glaring at the Gamecocks in their row.

"We hate you," confirmed Mr. Hater. "Go away."

They booed USC's marching band. Spurrier heard the boos as he jogged all the way across the field. The opening kick boomed through one of those Death Valley roars.

Clemson drew first blood. USC scored a tying touchdown and Spurrier raised a fist that turned into a finger pointing at the ESPN helicopter in the starry sky. The Clemson offense responded with a two-play drive. Somehow, Carolina was down only 14–10 at the half.

Spurrier talked to Thompson's receivers in the visitor's locker room. Telling them to "make a play on the ball, when it comes your way. *Make the play.*"

Carolina took the ball in the second half and marched it out of the bellowing student section. Thompson threw behind a receiver and Spurrier winced. Then Thompson hit Sanders at the 20, and he eluded three defenders and scored. Thompson pointed to the sky with both hands. Spurrier spat and said something into his headset. The Gamecocks were up by 3.

When they got the ball back, Miles took a hard hit and his coach ran out to check on him. Yet another gutsy fourth-down call by Spurrier didn't connect—but Clemson was flagged for pass interference. The students bombarded the field with red plastic cups.

Thompson threw into double coverage in the end zone, and his coach pushed that decision away. Clowney pounced on Boyd and Spurrier squeezed himself, feeling the bones rattle in the other team's quarterback. Another fourth-down try for Carolina had him out on the grass, hollering instructions to his blockers.

"Get off the field, Spurrier," Mr. Hater yelled. He had to be concerned, down 20–17 with the fourth quarter about to unfold. ESPN upped the ante by replaying the coaches' wrangle about the real Death Valley.

"The incorrigible Steve Spurrier," Joe Tessitore said in the broadcast booth overlooking the country's fourth oldest Death Valley, "when it comes to stirring the pot in rivalries."

Spurrier stirred up his offense, keeping the clock ticking, the chains moving, the orange offense on the bench. The student section howled when the Gamecocks moved the ball into the red zone and faced third-and-19. Hold Carolina to a field goal, and a touchdown could win it for Clemson, Thompson knew, looking into the teeth of the howlers on the Hill. Spurrier called a draw play. His supposedly slow quarterback ran for 20 yards, first-and-goal.

Two plays later, third-and-goal from the 6. Back in the shotgun, seeing only four rushers and defensive backs all over, Thompson ran right, looking to the flats, where his tight end slipped and fell. The line kept blocking. Looking back across the end zone, Thompson fired to Ellington, waiting near the goalpost to brag all year to his cousin Andre, Clemson's running back, about the touchdown catch in front of three Tigers.

Spurrier pumped his fist, then extended his fingers toward his backup quarterback. Thompson got a championship hug from Shaw. A Clemson fan flipped the nation the bird on TV.

Clowney took down Boyd one more time, leaving Coach Lawing and Coach Whammy grinning. They'd riled up their star with some inflated stats—thinking he played better when he got mad. In reality he'd broken the single-game sack record in the stadium where acclaimed Clemson defenders played for decades, and he'd played one time.

When the clock ran out, a blonde with roosters on her cheeks yelled "Orange evacuation" at the Haters sprinting up the stadium steps. Spurrier clapped and watched his guys jump up and down, forgetting about the Gatorade. Then he ran onto the field where Tajh Boyd stood with tears in his eyes.

"Don't let them see you like this," a teammate with silver crosses on his cheeks kept saying, as Gamecock players paraded around with the Hardee's Trophy and the invaders chanted, "SEC!"

The coach in the black visor joined in the singing of what had to be his new most favorite alma mater, gritting his teeth to hold back a grin. Holding up the imaginary toast for "Here's a health, Carolina," his hand turned a big thumb up.

"How about those apples!" said a jubilant Coach Mangus, having a better trip to Clemson country than when he got caught peeing on their street.

Shaw strode into the riotous locker room knowing his rival had read the Clemson defense brilliantly and his dad didn't raise him to stand on the sidelines. Thompson took a congratulatory handshake in stride.

Spurrier walked into the visiting-team interview room still playing the game, holding a Sprite getting warm in his hand.

"We were very fortunate, again," he said, sipping his Sprite. "It seems like when we play Clemson, they don't play very well."

Reporters wanted to know if Spurrier thought Clemson thought Thompson couldn't run.

"The quarterback draw just kept coming out, didn't it?" said the all-time winningest coach at South Carolina. "The ball is worth keeping, let's put it that way." He put his chin in his fingers to hold in a smile and ushered in his quarterback.

Thompson quoted chapter and verse of Spurrier's biblical inspiration and said if Shaw started the bowl game, he'd be fine with that.

The coach who promised the Gamecocks he'd stick around to make his mark on their stadium ambled through the underside of Death Valley with his soda. Knowing there was no hurry. Clemson offered the Gamecocks a police escort only for the way in.

After an hour the quarterback bus got rolling. Clemson fans who clamored for Spurrier and got him were back at their computers, posting on message boards, "Dylan F***ing Thompson. Who?"

CHAPTER TWENTY-ONE

What Spurrier Would Do

SPURRIER WATCHED ALABAMA WIN THE SEC CHAMPIONSHIP ON THE TV in the den, after a Georgia receiver caught a ball "he shouldn't have," his dad would say, running out the clock at the goal line. He could only imagine the game *his* team would have given 'Bama, and the feeling of that confetti falling on the Gamecocks.

Then he got cheerier news. Carolina would play the Michigan Wolverines in the Outback Bowl in Tampa—where redemption awaited for "stinking up" the bowl game in '09. They'd practice again at Thomas Jefferson High School, on Stephen Garcia's old field.

The way to win the ball game, Spurrier said, was legendary Wolverine coach Bo Schembechler's way.

"One of his sayings that has followed me is, 'Running teams are tougher teams,'" Spurrier told reporters, beaming about the chance to face Schembechler's old team and Garcia's ghost. "I haven't always lived by it, but I should have. I have reverted back to it recently here at South Carolina."

Let Michigan's pass defense ponder that. Whatever Schembechler-isms made Michigan the all-time winningest team in college football, Spurrier would take.

He took the floor and the mike at Colonial Life Arena to celebrate another state championship. Fans cheered the Hardee's Trophy, the players, and the larger-than-life Clowney.

How did lowly Carolina become such a surefire winner?

"It happened when Marcus Lattimore said, 'I'm coming to the University of South Carolina,'" Spurrier said on the same December day that Lattimore announced he'd go pro.

The all-time winningest coach at South Carolina asked for a contract extension through 2017, saying his recruits should know their coach would be there. He didn't need a raise, he told his AD, because, "I'm already embarrassed by how much I make."

What *was* market value for a football coach who could dispel Pitchfork's curse? South Carolina had clinched an SEC East title and two top-10 seasons since Spurrier and Garcia rode away from the Outback Bowl in separate buses.

"This job is not as stressful as it used to be," Spurrier said, signing his new contract. Sweating with Pastor Adrian, running on the treadmills to the promised land, the coach of the Gamecocks said he appreciated everything that his father did for him, "more and more each day."

Of course Garcia would visit the high school field where he'd passed for over 8,000 yards and hit pay dirt for the Jefferson Dragons, with the blue bleachers and old wooden press box and his coach looking on. Reporters wondered if he'd be welcomed.

"If he comes by that's fine, but we are worried about playing Michigan," Spurrier said. He could understand his old quarterback wanting to hang out with his old teammates, but felt moved to say, "We've learned that winning the game is a lot more important than having fun." They met the belly dancers at Busch Gardens and got back to work.

Reporters from across the state traveled to the Dragons' field to talk about Spurrier's Gator days. Did he realize his Florida players performed impersonations of their old Ball Coach? The best imitation, they said, was Danny Wuerffel's.

"Tell him there are about 80,000 comedians out of work right now," Spurrier said, laughing.

John Reeves and Carl Franks stopped by to tell the Gamecock players how the Tampa Bay Bandits used to do it. They remembered the rain that first spring when the field was underwater and they practiced in the Tampa Stadium parking lot.

"Yes, it brings back a lot of memories," Spurrier said to his old USFL quarterback and running back, whom he'd hired as coaches at Florida. "But we're just trying to beat Michigan."

The Wolverines, like the Gamecocks, lost only to top teams. Their fusion of zone and man coverage made them the nation's second-best pass defense. Plus, they had do-everything back Denard Robinson and were "tired of hearing how great the SEC is," Spurrier contended.

He was getting tired of the Outback commercial with football fans wearing a shrimp tail and a Bloomin' Onion on their heads, offering free coconut shrimp if Michigan prevailed and a free Bloomin' Onion if Carolina won. He knew that people across the country would rather have shrimp than onions.

Looking for an edge, Spurrier had Gamecock Central's David Cloninger ask Michigan's offensive linemen if they thought they could block Clowney one-on-one. Hopefully Cloninger would bring back inflammatory quotations to wave in front of Clowney.

"He plays better when he's mad," Spurrier explained.

He looked jovial during warm-ups, watching his team skip across the grass at Tampa Stadium instead of stretching on the ground, keeping their eyes on the other team—a lesson taught to them by Iowa in the 2009 Outback Bowl. Carolina wore undershirts emblazoned with the Batman logo, issued that morning. Spurrier had both of his quarterbacks watching the Wolverines warm up. Their starting cornerbacks still looked gimpy. Just as Michigan could see that Carolina's running back Miles wasn't himself after that hit at Clemson.

Studio analysts hyped on morning coffee that New Year's Day recalled the last time Spurrier asked his quarterback to win the game. Advantage Michigan?

"No so fast, my friend," countered Corso. "South Carolina, SEC defense, that's all you got to say."

Lattimore stood on the sideline in a black T-shirt and jeans, cheering his team on. Spurrier shielded his eyes with a hand under his visor, looking up to see a parachutist in black drop out of the sky and onto the 50-yard line.

Jon Gruden, who took Tampa Bay to the Super Bowl, was up in the broadcast booth in his Spurrier visor, figuring Spurrier was thinking of some new formation, looking up at that parachutist and asking, "Got any ball plays up there?"

———

Michigan deferred the ball to the second half. On the third play Shaw faced another corner blitz. Miles threw a block that let Shaw hit Byrd for a 56-yard catch and score. Spurrier shook his quarterback's hand and high-fived all his receivers.

When the Wolverines punted to Ace Sanders, he juked, head-faked, ran through the pack, and scored. Spurrier grinned. Michigan returned a score and Spurrier sent Shaw back out.

"We almost got a visor toss from the BC," Gruden said as Shaw got up limping after running for 10 yards. Spurrier expected a pass. He sent Thompson in. Thompson got sacked.

"Spurrier is always criticized for switching quarterbacks," said announcer Mike Trico to Gruden. "And we always have to remind ourselves Steve won the Heisman Trophy in '66. Small things bother him."

"If anybody can handle a two-quarterback system," Gruden said, "it's Stephen Orr Spurrier."

After a word with the coach, Thompson fired one down the seam to Nick Jones for 70 yards, then sprinted right and threw to Sanders to put USC up 21–10. Thompson spread his arms like wings and flew off the field.

"This could be one of those vintage Spurrier games, changing quarterbacks by series or even snaps," Trico said.

Clowney kept struggling against Michigan's big tackle, who popped him in a sensitive area and laughed. Spurrier thought Clowney looked hot and took him out. Which would really piss him off.

"Steve Spurrier always seems like the best quarterback on the field," said Mark May, holding his coffee back at the studio.

In the second half Carolina missed receivers, field goals, chances to score. Spurrier pointed at the players who missed those chances. They knew. Talking over more plays with his son on the headset, he didn't look up as Michigan lined up to punt, on their side of the field.

Out of punt formation Wolverine Floyd Simmons took the snap and dove for the first-down marker—inches short, by the look of the sticks and chains. TV cameras zoomed to the grass between the first-down marker and the ball. First down Wolverines.

"Watch Spurrier come into your picture," said Trico, "and go bananas."

The coach ran across the field, pointing to the space between the marker and the ball. He kept pointing down and hollering. The ref kept signaling first down the other way. Had he gotten turned around, somehow? Spurrier saw he wasn't changing his mind.

"You know the ball did not touch the first-down marker," Spurrier said to another ref nearby.

"I know it didn't," the ref told Spurrier.

"Well, why'd you give it to him?" Spurrier asked.

"I don't know," the referee told the coach.

"We have to take over," Clowney told his teammates. They believed the whole world wanted coconut shrimp.

Coach Whammy called "Cali," a stunt blitz sending Clowney inside. But Michigan's tight end didn't shift. So Clowney lined up at his regular spot, going for the "C gap" when the ball was snapped.

Before the tight end could move, Clowney passed through Michigan's linemen and hit running back Vincent Smith in the chest. The ball and Smith's helmet went flying. Clowney picked up the ball and started upfield, getting yardage before getting tackled.

"What a hit! Ball's free! On the ground! South Carolina deserves to have it and they do," Trico shouted from the top of the stadium, knowing his words would accompany the most-played highlight ever on *SportsCenter*. Teammates chanting "Clowney" showed him the replay on their smartphones on the sideline. A stadium security guard said Clowney would be arrested if that happened downtown.

"They're not going to score a field goal. They're going to score a touchdown," Clowney told his teammates, pointing at Spurrier. "That's how he is."

Shaw threw it 31 yards into the end zone. Sanders dove and tumbled through the grass and into the concrete holding up the stands, ball in hand. A referee flagged his summersault for excessive celebration. A try for 2 points failed. USC led 27–22 with 8:06 to go.

Michigan drove the length of the field against that SEC defense for the go-ahead score. With 3:29 left Spurrier sent out Shaw.

Facing fourth-and-3, he hit Sanders on a slant for a first down. Shaw escaped a blitz and hit Sanders over the middle at the Michigan 43. Shaw took the next snap, spun out of a Wolverine's grasp, and felt his hurt foot tear apart.

Hobbling off mid-drive, he passed Thompson running in. Five plays later, 32 yards from the Michigan goal line, number 17 saw 17 seconds left when he got the call from his coach, "Steamer X."

Maybe Michigan thought Spurrier thought Michigan wouldn't send a stunt blitz at his quarterback. Thompson and Ellington saw the safety edge up. Thompson threw it where Ellington should be open, with his defender hitting the quarterback and smashing Thompson into the turf. The pass floated into Ellington's hands at the 5. He side-stepped two Michigan men and held the ball out to meet the goal line, stunning everyone in maize and blue.

"I can't believe he threw it," said Todd Ellis, voice of the Gamecocks, high above the field to his radio listeners in Columbia.

"Take your steps and throw the ball," Spurrier's quarterbacks heard him say in March. Thompson couldn't see the completion, but he heard it. Shaw pumped his fist into the air and hitch-stepped out to hug Thompson. Their coach extended a calming hand. They had more plays to run.

Gatorade finally cascaded over Spurrier's black visor as the USC band played a Christmas song.

"Here's a health, Carolina," Spurrier sang, as the Gamecocks across the world cheered. Striding off the field, he couldn't help but look up at the Tampa Stadium press box, where much had been written about him in the past. But Ron Morris wasn't up there writing anything.

He gave both quarterbacks a game ball. Reporters noted he was USC's all-time winningest coach in bowl games—after winning three.

He told them Clowney didn't hit that hard in practice because the rule was, "Don't clobber teammates." Then he said what no one ever expected to hear him say after a bad call: "I'm glad that ref did that now."

The team plane was livelier flying home. Spurrier put his feet up and smiled as the clouds rolled by. Back in Columbia he settled in for the evening news. The News19 sports report showed Clowney, Clowney, Clowney.

"There were a whole bunch of big plays, and Clowney's was just one of them," Spurrier said. "I am not trying to downgrade it, but I am upgrading the others." His quarterbacks brought home a January win, he wanted people to see. As for getting the short end of the measuring stick, he'd file no complaint.

"The whole world saw it. It was on television."

Let the world eat onions and see the Gamecocks ranked higher than ever. They'd topped last year's historic final ranking, anyway, Spurrier pointed out, thanks to Clemson beating LSU on New Year's Eve.

More miraculous was the way competitors for that one spot behind center learned to love each other. Shaw had soldiered on, Spurrier knew, until he couldn't take another step—and no one had hugged him harder than Stephen Garcia.

❦

On an uncommonly cool morning in South Carolina at the end of July, Steve Spurrier sat in his office surrounded by the footballs that won him championships, as a coach, ready to give his team another shot at Atlanta. Over the airwaves and all around town, hopes abounded for the 2013 Gamecocks.

Spurrier was still missing the trophy he didn't win playing quarterback. Feeling regrets no story about hijacked Gatorade could excuse.

"Whatever you do in college, you remember the rest of your life," he said, looking out at the field where his players would play.

"We have our reunions, all the players that played with me in the '60s, and we don't have championships to celebrate. And we could have. Looking back, I had fun and all that but didn't achieve as much as I could have."

The bronze Heisman Trophy on the shelf by his first hole-in-one ball didn't say SEC, or offer solace to a quarterback who "didn't prepare as well as I could have.

"I wish I could have done more to get Florida an SEC Championship," Spurrier said. "I could have done more to help our team, and I didn't. When I look back on myself, I didn't do as much as I could have."

Words that sounded like what his father might say could fire up another team with championship potential. His regrets as a quarterback "help me as a coach," Spurrier said. Like the things you did wrong as a kid can help you be a dad.

He looked longingly at his black leather golf bag, emblazoned "Spurrier," ready to be put away. His new knee had worked its way into playing shape during golf season.

Time to get out the football.

How many times did he get tackled in his life, anyway?

"Less than some of them," Spurrier said.

He stared out at the field, working on the words to say to his team through the microphone of the CBS reporter coming in. On the cusp of Carolina's highest preseason ranking ever, No. 7 in the Coaches Poll, No.

6 in the AP Poll, he could still tell that reporter to tell his team, "No one is picking us."

Meaning, once again this year, no one outside of Columbia believed the Gamecocks could win the only trophy that counted—the trophy won in Atlanta, engraved with the name of the SEC Football Champion, with more than one bronze player on top.

If he had to close fall practice to the fans for the first time at South Carolina, to keep out the Jadeveon Clowney media circus from New York and Washington, he'd close fall practice—to keep his team focused on that trophy.

"Just play your best ball, your final season at Carolina," he told his defensive end with the superstar smile and LeBron's and Beyoncé's numbers on his cell phone.

"And you'll always have a home to come home to."

All any player with grits in his belly needed to hear.

"Football," Spurrier told reporters looking for Clowney at the gates of the Proving Ground, "is a team sport."

On a scorching August night in Williams-Brice Stadium, Connor Shaw took the third snap of the 2013 college football season out of the pistol formation, looking at North Carolina's base defense.

Spurrier saw Damiere Byrd run a little square-in, drawing in the safety and the cornerback, and Shaw fading back, firing the ball across the stadium to number 4, Shaq Roland catching it and running it past a lone Tar Heel to all the grass in the house. Almost running down the ref.

Teammates ran to the end zone to hip bump, celebrating with the students in the Cock Pit and the Gamecock Nation. Fireworks boomed. Sir Big Spur crowed.

Spurrier pumped his fist and went back to his play sheet, talking through the headphones with his son up in the press box, oblivious to the pandemonium in the stadium.

They had more ball plays to spur those Heels, and a quarterback who knew what Spurrier would do.

EPILOGUE

The Ladies Clinic

CLICKER IN HAND, SHOWING THE WOMEN AT THE TENTH ANNUAL STEVE Spurrier Ladies Clinic highlights of what those 2013 Gamecocks could do, the season flashes past like a dream. Except after the game at Rocky Top, when Spurrier couldn't sleep.

At a Saturday morning scrimmage in early April 2014, Carolina women in garnet fill the south end zone at Williams-Brice Stadium, cheering for Spurrier's offense. Then he leads them upstairs into "the Zone," to talk football.

Jerri Spurrier introduces quarterback Dylan Thompson and his big friends, who walk out and high-five the garnet women cheering. Then their position coaches start barking orders, putting the ladies at the clinic in football formation.

"Spur left," hollers linebacker and "Spurs" coach Kirk Botkin, until a woman in spur position moves left.

Spurrier gets to sit and smile at the daughters, mothers, and grand-mothers forming a team across the floor. Representing generations of Carolina women longing for the day Carolina football would arise. Recalling Grandma Willie, caring for her family in the duplex in Char-lotte. Mother Marjorie Orr from Billy Graham's backyard, keeping the family going in churches and manses across Tennessee. And Jerri Starr of Fort Lauderdale, moving beautifully in her ball cap, encouraging women in garnet to bond with their Gamecock heroes.

Spurrier can see his littlest granddaughter, Charlotte, studying the football players' moves.

"She's a serious girl," he says, watching Scotty and Jennifer's baby sit up and see all.

A father and grandfather has to smile as his assistant coaches work the room, coaching 'em up like the ladies are players on the field. Coaching the Gamecocks and emceeing the Ladies Clinic isn't nearly as stressful for the Head Ball Coach, while history is still being made.

Time to reflect on the year South Carolina ended up No. 4 in the nation in all the polls, a top-5 team in January, a real miracle, prompting an invitation to the State House for "Steve Spurrier Day."

In March legislators had stood and applauded at the State House as the senate presented a resolution honoring Spurrier's achievements at South Carolina—including five victories in a row over the team from the upstate in orange.

"Whereas, much of their success is due to the celebrated leadership, skill in coaching, personal athletic skill, imagination, and ability to inspire his players that characterize Coach Steve Spurrier, whose arrival in Columbia ushered in the golden age of Carolina football . . ." the resolution read.

Posing alongside AD Ray Tanner and USC president Harris Pastides, Spurrier smiled at the legislators, saying, "It's nice to be recognized for our football program for winning a bunch."

He had no interest in running for office, he told reporters, stepping down from the State House to run the Gamecocks through spring ball.

That had Lt. Gov. Glenn McConnell maintaining on the eve of the Spring Game that if Coach Spurrier won an SEC title for Carolina in Atlanta, he still couldn't get the Confederate flag moved off the State House grounds.

But for the first time McConnell conceded that maybe a national title would get the Ball Coach enough leverage to move that flag to a museum.

"I have learned that in the world of politics, anything is possible," admitted the lieutenant governor, standing on the site of General Sherman's former headquarters in Columbia, now a hotel parking lot.

All the coach can control on a Saturday afternoon at the Ladies Clinic is the clicker, sitting in front of the big screen loaded with highlights of No. 4 South Carolina's season.

Shaw bombing North Carolina, Mike Davis outrunning the Tar Heels, those highlights speed past the delay of the game, the fourth quarter halted for fear of lightning, and the blow-by-blow accounts nationwide of Clowney's opening night, with Spurrier keeping the title of Carolina in Columbia.

Having to live with losing at Georgia the September day when Aaron Murray caught fire and the Dawgs amazingly weren't mad at the Ball Coach. After losing at John C. Calhoun's place the Saturday before, they hated Clemson worse. For once, they didn't boo Spurrier walking onto their field in Athens. He knew right then his Art of War tactics might backfire.

Clicking through a heroic afternoon in Florida, in the University of Central Florida's stadium, Spurrier shows the ladies how UCF star quarterback Blake Bortles scores points, the Golden Knights slam Shaw to the turf, and somehow the Gamecocks still crow in Orlando. He skips the clip of a fourth-and-long play against Kentucky when Clowney was 15 yards downfield in coverage instead of rushing the passer and Spurrier threw his visor for the first time as South Carolina's Ball Coach. With apologies to the preacher and the quarterback in the mirror, he leaves that one off the highlight reel. Showing the ladies Shaw's late-game touchdown pass that got his team past the 'Cats, causing Spurrier to burst into the pressroom saying, "We win again."

The ladies see pigskin poetry in the stadium of the Arkansas Razorbacks, a 45-yard scoring strike to Byrd that got Shaw a helmet pound, a fist bump, a back slap, and a big smile from his coach. When the Gamecocks went up 52–7, Old Man Arkansas stood up in his nosebleed seat by the open window in the press box and hollered, "Spurrier, you'll get yours!"

In Knoxville he had a team full of themselves, after listening all week to the praise of the "newspaper boys" that Spurrier couldn't outshout. Got his team thinking they didn't need to play their best ball to beat Tennessee.

"F*** South Carolina! F*** South Carolina!" the Big Orange student section had chanted all game, hoping to be heard by the man in the visor and headset. The nightmare kicked off at noon and kept Spurrier awake until Sunday, seeing Big Orange players slamming his quarterback to the ground, costing his team a trip to Atlanta.

"Praise hurts," said the coach at his Sunday afternoon teleconference, wishing away the 52–7 win at Arky that weighed down his team at Rocky Top.

Spurrier clicks onward to Columbia, Missouri, on a freezing Saturday night, down 17–0 behind Thompson's quarterbacking, asking his sick, beat-up quarterback if he'd go in.

The ladies see Shaw hit the clutch throws that kept USC fighting until Mizzou missed an overtime kick. The Ball Coach shared a joyous hug with Scotty on the sideline, a whoop over the headset to Steve Jr. up in the press box, and the alma mater, sung as Shaw kissed the silver football trophy won in the Battle of Columbia.

Spurrier clicks with pride through the pass plays by Shaw and runs by banged-up Mike Davis that won the "Orange Crush" games against Florida and Clemson. Looking at Clemson's huge defenders and saying, "If you can't move 'em, let 'em run past you." Leading to the touchdown pass thrown out of the "Wild Cock" formation by number 11 Pharoh Cooper to number 22 Brandon Wilds, sending the Tigers back upstate gnashing their teeth. Giving Carolina the chance to top the Badgers of Wisconsin in the Capital One Bowl and celebrate another 11-win season.

Did God smile on the Gamecocks again? Or was it the lucky black visor Spurrier wore at Missouri for Connor Shaw's miracle comeback? Worn every game since then, every game a win. He put it on the head of USC's President Pastides on the podium in Orlando and hoisted another Florida bowl game trophy, exclaiming, "That state championship trophy ain't bad either."

After leading cheers for "Connor Shaw, the best quarterback in the history of South Carolina," Spurrier had to snatch that lucky black visor right off President Pastides's head—in case, after all those years, luck trumps prayer and fate.

What play would sum up USC's gritty, heavenly season? Spurrier runs it for the ladies to see.

"He had two guys on him and he still got open. That's called a good route, by Nicky Jones," Coach Spurrier says, lauding the littlest Gamecock receiver making a big catch and getting a great Lady Gamecock roar. Still beaming as the women in garnet take the stage with the football and strike Heisman poses.

Walking into the sunlight adjusting his visor, seeing the land cleared for a new indoor practice facility and a new Proving Ground, he kicks at the cement parking lot that will be dug up and carted away. All around his stadium the school will plant grass and maple trees for kids to boot balls through on game day.

At the entrance to the tunnel, he looks out on the rooster-red stadium holding the nation's longest home win streak. He has a new streak started himself, since losing his cool with Clowney in the Kentucky game, vowing once more to keep that lucky visor free of grass stains.

A man of faith has to believe his father and mother see every game he plays.

In the tunnel he asks for silence, then leads the cheers for the *2001* theme. Motioning the women to run through the smoke, out on the grass, in the pattern he showed them, and catch a pass.

ACKNOWLEDGMENTS

I'D LIKE TO GRATEFULLY ACKNOWLEDGE THE EXPERTISE AND FRIENDSHIP of Susan Olsen, director of historical services at the Woodlawn Cemetery, history sleuth and Who fan extraordinaire, presenter of the "Follow That Dream" exhibit documenting Florida's musical pioneers for the Florida State Museum, a woman who walks into the past and sees the Spurriers scouting a path to greatness in Florida and Carolina.

A special thank-you to Steve Spurrier and family: wife Jerri, sons Scotty and Steve Spurrier Jr., late parents Reverend John Graham and Marjorie Spurrier, proud brother Graham Spurrier, and Uncle Bob Spurrier, tennis champ and Ball Coach believer.

Thanks to Cotty Jones of Johnson City, Tennessee, Hilltopper center, quarterback protector through all kinds of weather, benefactor with Spurrier to give Science Hill High School the Kermit Tipton Field, at the end of Cotty Jones Lane. Cotty gave tirelessly to this book, honoring his father, Carl A. Jones, Johnson City's benefactor and publisher of the *Johnson City Press-Chronicle*, the newspaper ably informing this author's account of Steve Spurrier's career as a Hilltopper.

Thanks to the prayerful people in Almost Heaven, West Virginia, at the First Presbyterian Church of St. Albans, heralding, "This is where Steve Spurrier was conceived." "In the church?" Spurrier responded.

Thanks to the late Dr. Willis Garrett and his family, chroniclers of Reverend John Graham Spurrier's time as a preacher in Miami Beach, Florida, birthplace of the Ball Coach.

Thanks to the Maryland State Archives in Annapolis, Maryland, for early Spurrierana.

Thanks to the Presbyterian Historical Society in Decatur, Georgia, and Philadelphia, Pennsylvania.

Thanks to Lee "Doak" and Johnnye Willett, Rusty Shultz, and "Bunny" Duggan in Athens, Tennessee; Tennessee Wesleyan College; and Pastor Leslie Rust and the people of the Mars Hill Presbyterian Church.

Thanks to Pastor Calvin Metcalf and the people of Newport Presbyterian Church, along with Tip Brown, Mike Proffitt, all-American fifth-grade teacher Reba Williams, and basketball coach Jimmy Lindsey. Thanks to Dr. Hobart and Beauanne Ford and their parents, hosts of the best ball games and meanest rooster in town.

Eternal thanks in Johnson City to Coach Kermit Tipton and his family.

God bless Sid Smallwood, a man of faith generous with his time and memories, who helped generations of young people play their best ball.

Thank you, Coach Elvin Little, Science Hill basketball sage and fellow disciple of legendary sportswriter V. L. "Stubby" Currence.

To Hilltopper shooter and pitcher and Johnson City parks director Lonnie Lowe.

To the people of Johnson City—architects, publishers, teachers, coaches, preachers, and steadfast Presbyterians; Grady and Betty Walker, Phyllis Owens, Jimmy Sanders, and his family; Tommy Hager, Joe Biddle, Donna, and Ken Lyon and many more generous souls, thank you for your time and 'Topper tales.

Thanks to Bill Wade, one cool quarterback and man of the Lord in Nashville.

Thanks to Coach Ray Graves, son of a preacher man, and Opal Graves, in Tampa, Florida.

Thanks to Larry Schreiber and Jerry Walker in San Francisco, keepers of the 49er story.

Thank you, athletic director Jeremy Foley at the University of Florida.

Thank you, Chris Doering ("Doering's got a touchdown! Oh my!") in Gainesville, Florida, for your Gator and Redskin insights.

Thank you, Danny Wuerffel, for your Gator memories and inspired play on all fields.

Thank you, George Solomon, sportswriting guru at the University of Maryland.

Thank you, Dan Snyder, owner of the Washington Redskins.

Thank you, Vinny Cerrato, vice president for football operations, Washington Redskins.

Thank you to a great coach, storyteller and host, Pepper Rodgers, vice president for football operations, Washington Redskins, and his convivial wife and artist Livingston Rodgers.

Thank you, Pelham Lyles at the Fairfield County Museum in Winnsboro, historian and South Carolinian.

Thank you, Glenn McConnell, Lieutenant Governor of South Carolina.

Thank you, with prayers for your ministry, USC team chaplain Adrian Despres.

Thank you, USC quarterback coach G. A. Mangus, mentor and friend to Gamecock armchair quarterbacks everywhere.

Thank you to my football writing students at the University of South Carolina Honors College, number one in the country. Spur others onward.

Thank you, USC Honors College football writing student Avery Wilks, a fine young writer who contributed an inspiring moment with USC quarterback Seth Strickland in the "Death Valley" chapter and a quotation from "Old Man Arkansas."

Thank you, Gamecock Nation, for your unwavering faith. Redemption is at hand.

To ministers of the Word, Samaritans in deed, patron saints for a bone-weary writer in Tennessee, Florida, and Carolina, thank you from my heart to all who helped tell this story.

Special thanks to the dedicated researchers of the National Weather Service for making history rain and shine.

To Jim Stiver, essence of the USC Honors College, logician, curmudgeon professor, and friend, and Marta Stiver, a couple extending hospitality to all manner of Gamecock sympathizers, thank you for our time at River's Edge, on Governor's Hill, and at the Parade Ground, helping make this book possible. To the memory of Greg Stiver, Gamecock forever.

To Tom Colley and Richard "Dick" Wesley, heart and soul of the *Bluefield Daily Telegraph*, men of ink and conviction who inform my every word.

To John Dufresne, James W. Hall, Lynne Barrett, Les Standiford, Meri-Jane Rochelson, David Kranes, Rust Hills, Joy Williams, Dan Wakefield, and the writers and mentors of the Florida International

University creative writing program, thank you for your timeless wisdom, generosity, and faith.

To Tom Shroder and Gene Weingarten, my editors at *Tropic*, the Sunday magazine of the *Miami Herald*, thank you for a glorious apprenticeship.

Thank you to my agent, Matthew Carnicelli, for seeing talent in worn-down shoes.

Thank you to my editor and friend Jon Sternfeld, project editor Meredith Dias, editorial director Keith Wallman, and everyone at Lyons Press, believers in Spurrier and Story.

Thank you, cousin and big brother Roland Lazenby and all the Lazenbys, an All-American family..

To T. M. Shine for never answering my calls from the graveyard.

To John Baker, quarterback of the neighborhood, and Robby Brannon, point guard of the town, missed until we meet again. With love for godsons Jon and Sir Jeff Brannon, making music for all our lives. With love and blessings for goddaughter Maranda, keeping Florida's fish in line, and goddaughter Stephanie, scholar of Madison Street.

Thank you, Lord, for the inspiration of Michael and Kris Nevils, loyal Gator Eric Olender, CPA John Coniglio, and the people of St. Johns Catholic Church in St. Petersburg Beach and St. Maurice and Resurrection Catholic Churches in Dania, Florida, blessing us all.

To my wife, Linda, Sugar Best, and our daughters, Sarah and Kristen, believers in Dad's dream of writing a boy's book.

To Mom, feeder of souls, eternally loving and encouraging, a book in your honor for the McGuffey Book Club.

To Dad with love and pride in one tough guy, writing your novel *Jeffersonville* after losing your sight and maximizing your vision, saying I'd never write this book just to spur me on . . . we won.

To all who believe the world can be changed by stories and ball games.

About the Author

RAN HENRY IS AN AUTHOR, PHOTOGRAPHER, AND WRITING PROFESSOR. Henry was a Ralph McGill Scholar at Hampden-Sydney College in Virginia, earned an MFA in creative writing from Florida International University, and wrote for the *Florida Times-Union*, the *St. Petersburg Times*, and *Tropic*, the Sunday magazine of the *Miami Herald*. Teaching writing at FIU, Virginia Commonwealth University, and since 2007 at the University of Virginia, he also teaches football writing for the nation's number one Honors College at the University of South Carolina. He and his wife, Linda, divide their time between Charlottesville, Virginia; Columbia, South Carolina; and a home in the mountains of West Virginia. He first officially interviewed Steve Spurrier in 1986 and began *Spurrier* with an interview with the coach of the national champions in Gainesville, Florida, in 1997.

1-15